Land of Trees

Land of Trees

Scannings From Quinault Country,
the Grays Harbor Region, and Beyond
1774-1997

Text and photographs by Larry J. Workman
Edited with Jacqueline M. Storm

First Edition

Published by
the Quinault Indian Nation
Taholah, Washington
October 24, 1997

Library of Congress Catalog Card Number: 97-92588

ISBN 0-940359-01-4

MCMXCVII

The text of this book is set in Times New Roman. This type was
designed by Stanley Morison based on the old-style Dutch type Plantain
for *The Times* of London. It first appeared in 1932.
This book is printed on 60# Accent Opaque Vellum book, an acid free paper.

Dedicated to all those who wonder

Acknowledgments

As you will quickly see, this is more than just a local history. Regional, national and international events are also included to set the tone of the times. What happens here is also dictated by events in other places, so it is important to set this chronology against the backdrop of this world and others.

This book is meant to be a living journal and tickle your interest in this region's rich history. It is not the intent to record every important historical date, but to give the feeling of the times and perhaps why we have arrived at this place and time the way we are. If you feel there are items which should really be included or others which should be corrected, please let me know, and provide a reference.

I would like to give thanks for the help and assistance I received from the Aberdeen, Montesano, and Hoquiam Timberland Library staffs these last sixteen years. I also received help and assistance from the Washington State Library, Pacific County Historical Society and Museum, Polson Museum, Washington State Historical Society, U.S. Geological Survey, U.S. Forest Service, Department of Interior Reference Library, City of Aberdeen, Bureau of Indian Affairs, Coast Guard Museum (Seattle), Ford Foundation, the Washington Department of Corrections, and the Washington State Department of Natural Resources.

I would like to thank the following people for information or encouragement in the production of this publication: J. B. McCrory, Guy McMinds, Jim Jackson, Delbert Boyer, Jr., Jim Harp, Clifford Bryson, Gene Woodwick, Cara Willis, Sully Pope, Gene Bradford, Charlotte Kalama, Frenchie Mason Chow Chow, Hazel Smith, Crystal Sampson, Joseph DeLaCruz, Richard Sterling, Richard Moulton, Harvey Scott, Lelani Jones, John Larson, and Bette Kobe. I would like to give Herbert K. Beals a note of thanks for his assistance and review of the text between 1774 and 1812 which deals with the history along the Northwest coast. I wish to acknowledge Dora Underwood and Pauline Capoeman for their help and assistance, and to the readers of the *Quinault Natural Resources* magazine for the series *Time Was...* from which much of this material is drawn. I thank them for their continued interest, support, and encouragement over the years. Since my work on this project spanned over sixteen year, many people who helped and encouraged me are no longer with us. I would like to give a sincere note of gratitude to the late Oliver Mason, Charles Clemons, Dan Chenois, Blanch Shale-Mcbride, Bernard "Buzz" Bumgarner, Jim Oliver, Reggie Ward, and Joe Randich.

I also wish to thank the National Federation of Press Women (NFPW) with their support of a mini-grant (1994) which enabled me to do additional research. I want to thank my wife, Janet, and children, Sarah and David, for allowing me all those hours spent buried in library books.

And finally, I would like to give my deepest gratitude to the Quinault Indian Nation and the Business Committee for the support of this project and to Jacqueline M. Storm for her encouragement and assistance in the editing of this work.

Larry J. Workman

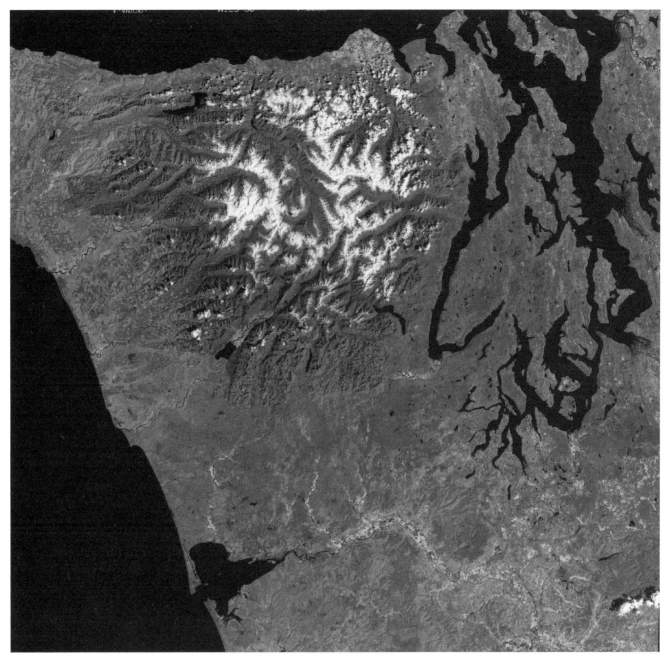

LANDSAT E image taken on April 27, 1983 of a portion of the Olympic Peninsula and Puget Sound. Grays Harbor is at the bottom left corner and Lake Quinault is left of center. Courtesy Department of Commerce.

Contents

Introduction

1997 marks the 75th year since a formal government was established with the passing of the Bylaws (August 24, 1922) for a Federation which became the Quinault Indian Nation. This is a good time to stop and reflect on where we have been and where we are going.

For our ancestors on the southwest corner of the Olympic Peninsula, a great part of the ancient forest was a place of mystery. The thick tangle of underbrush and dark green wetness was forbidding. Anyone who ventured from the beach, streams, river or trails was considered "Ju'ul," a fool.

The first Europeans who saw the land from their ships reported a dense, impenetrable forest. In 1788, John Mears described the land as "... wild to the extreme—immense forest covered the whole of it within our sight, down to the very beach..." Even after the Quinault River Treaty and the arrival of Indian Agents and settlers, *agriculturally minded people*, the forest-covered land was considered an obstacle. They looked for natural openings along the river bottoms and prairies. To them, the land contained poor soils or was too wet and so nearly worthless.

It was not until the 1880's that loggers, speculators, and other exploiters of the land arriving here, revealed the great riches the land held. Our people already knew of these riches, but saw them from a different perspective; one that sustained them materially and spiritually. In many respects, these new comers treated the land, as Daniel Quinn in the book *Ishmael* writes, "as a foe - something to be conquered. But as with conquerors, their foes are left bleeding and dead". Western civilization seems to be slowly arriving at the fact that the land is not a foe, but a living part of ourselves. What we do to the land, we do to ourselves.

This book seeks to capture the essence of the times from a natural resources perspective of a person living and working in the Quinault/Grays Harbor area today. It is not the intent of this book to record every historical event relevant to the growth of this region. The items presented are but a sampling of the natural phenomena, economic, and cultural change in this part of the world. Regional, national, and international events having a bearing on the tone of the times and those ultimately affecting policy, decisions, and "progress" are included, too. This work is a scanning of the time which has passed over these lands.

Quinault Country offers an ideal setting to chart some of the cultural and natural changes that have occurred since the first arrival of Europeans. For our people and other coastal tribes, it uprooted an ancient way of life and changed our people from a self-reliant livelihood to wards of the government and, finally, confident self-determiners.

The photographs included in this book represent some of the natural features of this region and set the stage for the human play. Many of the photographs represent features as they probably appeared in 1774 and did after 1974.

The natural and cultural changes in Quinault Country have been profound. It has evolved from a superb wilderness with rivers and streams serving as roads, to paths cut in the forest, to asphalt thoroughfares and highways in the sky. At the same time, the entire world was undergoing change unlike any other period of time in human history. As a result, this corner of the world is ideal for recording a chronology set against regional, national, and international events. With it we can explore the growth and feelings of time, learn why we are the way we are, see why the land "looks" the way it does, and just possibly see where we are going.

Most of all, this is the story about a land of trees. We hope you enjoy it.

Pearl Capoeman-Baller
President, Quinault Indian Nation

Mount Olympus.

All attempts have been made to keep the wording, phrases, spelling and place names used by the people of those times the same as they were used then. For example the spelling of Quinault may also appear as: Qui-nai-elt, Quinaielt, or Quiniault. Taholah was called Granville in the 1800's and early 1900's (as apposed to Point Grenville). Various Indian agents spelled it Granville, Grandville, and Grenville. Point Grenville, itself, may also be referred to as "The Mountain" and Old Dan's Mountain. Comment or explanation appear as italics enclosed by parentheses.

~ 1774 ~

August 1774

 11 Juan Pérez, Spanish officer and explorer, aboard the Santiago sees a snow covered mountain and names it Cerro de Santa Rosalía. *(Later renamed Mount Olympus, it becomes the first natural feature to be recorded by Europeans of what would become Washington State. There were several Indian names. The Quinaults referred to it as Sunadu and Klauk Manichu, snow or white mountain. See July 4, 1788.)*

September 1774

 5 First Continental Congress meets (September 5 - October 26) in Philadelphia.

~ 1775 ~

March 1775

 16 Second Spanish expedition under Bruno de Hezeta, with Juan Francisco de la Bodega y Quadra second in command, sets sail from Port of San Blas in Mexico to explore coast to the north.

 23 Patrick Henry makes "Give me Liberty or give me death" speech in Virginia.

April 1775

 18 Paul Revere and William Dawes warn of British arrival; American Revolutionary War begins with the battles of Lexington and Concord (18th and 19th).

May 1775

 10 Second Continental Congress meets.

June 1775

 14 U.S. Army founded.

 17 Battle of Bunker Hill.

July 1775

 13 Spanish ships, *Santiago* and *Sonora*, anchor off coast. The crews engage in friendly trade with the Indians. (*The **Santiago** near Point Grenville, the **Sonora** near Cape Elizabeth and the mouth of the Quinault River.*)

 14 Bruno de Hezeta from the ship *Santiago*, goes ashore in a cove (*in the lee of Point Grenville*), plants a cross, and claims the land for Spain.

 14 Crew of the *Sonora*, under Bodega y Quadra, go ashore near the mouth of the Quinault River and are attacked and

killed. Later a canoe of Indians is shot out of the water as they approach the *Sonora*.

14 Hezeta applies the name Bucareli's roadstead (*Grenville Bay*) and Martyrs' Point (*Cape Elizabeth*) to the map he makes of the area.

31 *Santiago* and *Sonora* become separated and the *Sonora* heads northwestward.

August 1775

15 Crew of the *Santiago* attempts to seize two Indians (*near Queets*) they thought they recognize from the massacre of July 14.

16 (or 17) Hezeta maps mouth of a large bay (*mouth of the Columbia River*) and names it Bahía de la Asunción.

23 George III declares the American colonies to be in state of rebellion.

November 1775

28 Continental Congress orders construction of a naval fleet.

~ 1776 ~

January 1776

9 Tom Paine publishes *Common Sense. (The first call for independence.)*

July 1776

2 Congress votes for independence.

4 *Declaration of Independence* approved.

September 1776

6 The first submarine, *The Turtle,* is used to attack the British fleet in New York Harbor.

9 The term "United States" officially replaces "United Colonies".

22 Nathan Hale hanged as a spy by the British.

October 1776

9 A group of Spanish missionaries settle in what would become San Francisco.

December 1776

25 George Washington leads 2,400 of his men across the Delaware River for successful attack on the British-Hessian garrison.

~ 1777 ~

June 1777

14 Congress resolves on a flag of the U.S.

October 1777

17 British forces surrender to American troops in Saratoga, New York. (*Turning point of the Revolutionary War.*)

~ 1778 ~

March 1778

22 Captain James Cook sights and names Cape Flattery. Cook was aboard the *Resolution* and accompanied by Captain Charles Clarke on the *Discovery.*

29 Cook enters "Nootka" and anchors in a place he calls Ship Cove. (*Now called Resolution Cove.*)

April 1778

26 Cook leaves Nootka and sails north.

~ 1779 ~

September 1779

23 John Paul Jones says, "I have not yet begun to fight."

~ 1780 ~

May 1780

10 The Northwest coast was regarded as fully explored and a legitimate possession of Spain. The king ordered that voyages *de altura* should cease.

19 A mysterious darkness envelops much of New England and part of Canada in the early afternoon (*The cause has never been determined, but could have been caused by distant forest fires.*)

~ 1781 ~

October 1781

19 Gen.Cornwallis surrenders at Yorktown. The capitulation yields 8,000 British prisoners, virtually bringing the War to an end.

~ 1782 ~

April 1782

12 Peace talks begin in Paris.

August 1782

7 George Washington creates "Order of the Purple Heart."

September 1782

16 The Great Seal of the United States used for the first time.

~ 1783 ~

February 1783

4 Britain proclaims a cession of hostilities.

November 1783

3 France recognized the independence of the United States.

~ 1784 ~

January 1784

14 U.S. rarified the Peace Treaty with England that ended the Revolutionary War.

September 1774

22 The Russians establish a settlement on Kodiak Island.

~ 1785 ~

May 1785

8 Land Ordinance of 1785 establishes 6-mile square townships subdivided into 36 lots of 640 acres each.

August 1785

9 The British brig, *Sea Otter* (or *Harmon*), under Captain James Hanna arrives at Nootka. (*First European visit to the Northwest coast in over seven years.*)

September 1785
** Hanna leaves Nootka.

~ 1786 ~

June 1786
** The British scow *Captain Cook* under Henry Laurie and the *Experiment* of the East Indian Company arrive at Nootka.

August 1786
** *Astrolabe* and *Boussole* under command of French navigator Jean Francsois Galamp de la Pérouse, map coast from Alaska to California. The Spaniards Martyrs' Point (*Cape Elizabeth. See July 14, 1775*) is noted on his map.

September 1786
17 *King George* under Nathaniel Portlock and the *Queen Charlotte* under George Dixon, both British ships, arrive at Nootka Sound but leave on the 28th to winter in the Sandwich Islands. (*Hawaiian Islands.*)

November 1786
** The ship *Captain Cook* returns to Canton.

~ 1787 ~

May 1787
25 Constitutional Convention. (*May 25 - September 17.*)

June 1787
** Captain Charles Barclay arrives at Nootka on the English ship *Imperial Eagle.*

July 1787
1 Dixon on the English ship *Queen Charlotte* names the Queen Charlotte's Islands.
** Barclay of the *Imperial Eagle* sights a strait (*Juan de Fuca*) but does not enter or name it.
** Five men killed from the *Imperial Eagle* at Destruction Island (*Hoh River*).
** *Princess Royal* and *Prince of Wales* arrive at Nootka.

August 1787
22 John Fitch demonstrates his steam boat on the Delaware River to delegates of the Continental Congress.

October 1787
1 John Kendrick commanding the *Columbia Rediviva* and Robert Gray commanding the *Lady Washington* sail from Boston for the Pacific Northwest.

December 1787
7 Delaware becomes first state to ratify the new Constitution.

~ 1788 ~

April 1788
1 *Columbia* and the *Lady Washington* become separated in a storm while rounding Cape Horn.

May 1788
13 John Mears arrives at Nootka aboard the *Felice Adventurer* (*British*). He buys a small tract of land at the mouth of Nootka Sound, called Friendly Cove, from Chief Maquinna for two pistols.

June 1788
11 Mears sails from Nootka for Clayoquot Sound.
21 New Hampshire's ratification of the Constitution is adopted by the United States.
29 Mears sights and names Juan de Fuca Strait.
29 Mears names Tatoosh Island after Chief Tatoosh.

July 1788
4 Mears names Mount Olympus. (*Previously named Cerro de Santa Rosalía by Pérez in 1774.*)
5 Mears names Shoalwater Bay. (*Willapa Bay.*)
6 Mears sights the great river of the west (*Columbia*) but does not enter because of breakers covering the bar. Names Cape Disappointment and calls the river's estuary Deception Bay, insisting it was no river at all, then turns northward.
11 Mears arrives at Barclay Sound.
13 Mears sends out M. Duffin to explore northern shore of "John de Fuca," later returning to Nootka Sound.

August 1788
14 Gray lands at (*Tillamook*) Bay. Trade with the Indians.
16 Captain's servant killed by Indians.
18 Gray departs Harbor calling it Murderer's Harbor.

September 1788
** *Eleanora*, American brig from New York, off Nootka.
17 Gray on the *Lady Washington* arrives at Nootka Sound. (*Mears makes note of the strange new flag.*)
20 Mears launches the *Northwest America* on Nootka Sound. First European boat built on the Northwest coast.
22 Kendrick arrives at Nootka on the *Columbia.*

October 1788
26 *Northwest America* leaves Nootka to winter in the Sandwich Islands. The Americans winter at Nootka.

~ 1789 ~

January 1789
23 Georgetown University established.

April 1789
24 *Northwest America* returns to Nootka.
29 *Northwest America* sails to Queen Charlotte Islands to trade for furs.
30 George Washington takes oath of office as the first President of the United States.

May 1789
6 Esteban José Martínez, commander of *Princesa,* enters Nootka Sound and finds *Iphigenia Nubiana* (*British*) under Portuguese colors, then sails up to visit Kendrick.
13 López de Haro arrives at Nootka in the *San Carlos.*
14 Martínez seizes the *Iphigenia*, raises the Spanish flag and takes Douglas and Viana prisoners.
26 Martínez releases Douglas and Viana, restores the *Iphigenia* and furnishes her supplies.

June 1789
2 *Iphigenia* sails out of Nootka. Meanwhile Martínez took formal possession of the port and calls it Santa Cruz de Nutka.
9 Martínez takes possession of *Northwest America* on its arrival. Renames it *Santa Gertrudis* after his wife.

** *Fair American,* a small American schooner, arrives at Nootka. Is captured then released by Martinez.

14 *Princess Royal* arrives at Nootka.

14 Gray returns to Nootka in the *Lady Washington* from trade along the north coast.

July 1789

2 *Princess Royal* sails on a trading cruise from Nootka.

3 *Argonaut* (*British*) arrives at Nootka.

4 Martinez seizes the *Argonaut.*

4 Congress passes first Tariff Act to raise revenue.

14 Martinez seizes the *Princess Royal* on its return to Nootka. The *Argonaut* and the *Princess Royal* and their crews are sent to San Blas as a prize. (*Some historians feel that the Americans, especially Kendrick, were instigators of the Spanish actions.*)

** Gray and Kendrick exchange ships. Gray is put in command of the *Columbia* with orders to sail to China. Kendrick said he would do more trade and follow in the *Lady Washington* later.

30 Gray sails *Columbia* out of Nootka, to Hawaii and on to Macao. (*See August 9, 1790.*)

August 1789

7 U.S. War Department established.

September 1789

2 U.S. Treasury Department established.

October 1789

** *Eleanora* off Nootka.

November 1789

26 The first national Thanksgiving Day.

~ 1790 ~

April 1790

7 Spanish Alferez Manuel Quimper in command of *Princessa Real* (the captured *Princess Royal)* arrives at Nootka Sound.

May 1790

31 *Princesa Real* leaves Nootka Sound and begins to explore the northern shores of the Straits of Juan de Fuca.

June 1790

** Quimper sights a high snowy peak which he names La Gran Montaña del Carmelo. (*Later renamed Mt. Baker. See April 30, 1792.*) He also applies the name *Sierras Nevadas de San Antonio* to a range of mountains east of his position in the Strait of Juan de Fuca. (*Cascades. See 1827.*)

July 1790

18 Quimper turns westward and follows the southern shore of the Strait.

August 1790

1 Quimper takes possession of Puerto Nuñez Gaona (*Neah Bay*) to est. a Catholic settlement. (*See May 29, 1792.*)

4 Quimper leaves Puerto Nuñea Gaona.

9 The *Columbia* with Gray in command arrives in Boston, becoming the first American ship to circumnavigate the globe.

October 1790

28 Nootka Sound Convention ends dispute and Spain ends claim to exclusive control of the Northwest coast. (*See May - July 1789, January 1794, & March 23, 1795.*)

December 1790

6 Congress moves from New York to Philadelphia.

Winter 1790-91

** The Spanish ship *Concepción,* commanded by Francisco de Eliza, winters at Nootka.

~ 1791 ~

February 1791

** Released by the Spanish in July 1790, the *Argonaut* arrives at Nootka, collecting furs along the way.

March 1791

** The Spanish *San Carlos* arrives at Nootka.

30 George Washington personally selects the site for the federal district along the Potomac River.

May 1791

5 The *San Carlos* and the *Santa Saturnina* sail from Nootka.

29 *San Carlos* enters Straits of Juan de Fuca and explores the area until August 7th. On this trip Don Francisco de Eliza names a bay he is anchored in, Puerto de Nuestra da Señora de Los Angelos. (*In 1792, Alcala-Galiano shortens the name to Port Angeles.*)

June 1791

** John Kendrick, in the *Lady Washington,* returns from China, arrives at Queen Charlotte Islands. The natives attempt to capture the vessel.

July 1791

12 *Lady Washington* arrives at Nootka Sound.

Summer 1791

** The Spanish *Aranzazu* arrives at Nootka.

August 1791

13 The Spanish corvette *Descubierta* and *Atrevida* arrive at Nootka while on a Pacific-wide exploring expedition.

September 1791

25 *Lady Washington* sails from Clayoquot Sound for China.

December 1791

15 First 10 amendments to U.S. Constitution go into effect.

(Note: *Ships listed along the coast from 1791-1812 were mostly off the Alaskan coast. Some may have ventured along the Washington coast. All are American when listed from an American port city.*)

Others ships along the coast 1791

** *Columbia Rediviva* - Robert Gray - Boston

** *Eleanora* - Simon Metcalfe - New York

** *Fairy* - William Rogers - British

** *Felice Adventurer* - John Mears - British under Portuguese colors

** *Gustavus III* - Thomas Barnett - British under Swedish colors

** *Grace* - William Douglas - British under American colors

** *Hancock* - Samuel Crowell - Boston

** *Hope* - Joseph Ingraham - Boston

** *La Solide* - Etienne Marchand - French
** *Venus* - William Hervey - British

~ 1792 ~

February 1792

20 President Washington signs an Act creating the U.S. Post Office.

April 1792

2 Congress authorizes establishment of U.S. Mint (Coinage Act).

17 The British ships *Discovery* and *Chatham* sight New Albion. (*The Northwest coast as it was known to British sailors.*)

28 George Vancouver aboard the *Discovery* names Point Grenville.

29 Gray aboard the *Columbia* meets Vancouver just below Cape Flattery and tells him of a great river that he was unable to enter.

29 Vancouver enters Strait of Juan de Fuca.

30 Vancouver names "a very high conspicuous craggy mountain" Mount Baker. (*See June 1790.*)

May 1792

7 Gray sails into Harbor (*Grays Harbor*) and trades with the Indians.

7 George Vancouver names a "round snowy mountain" Mount Rainier. He also calls the bay in which they are anchored, Port Townshend.

8 In morning Gray trades with the Indians.

9 Shortly after midnight, Gray's ship loads a nine pounder and "dash'd her [canoe of Indians] to pieces." The next morning they resumed trade with the Indians.

9 Gray sails out of "Bulfinch Harbor". (*Grays Harbor.*)

11 Gray sails in to a great river.

13 Vancouver names *Hood's Channel (Canal)*.

20 Gray sails out of the river, gives to it the name of his ship, *Columbia*, and heads northward.

29 Spanish Lieutenant Salvador Fidalgo anchors at Puerto Nuñez Gaona (*Neah Bay*) and begins construction of the Catholic mission. (*The first European settlement in the future State of Washington, but it would be abandoned in less then a year.*)

29 Vancouver names *Vashon's Island*.

29 To commemorate Puget's exertions in this extensive inlet, Vancouver names the southern extremity *Puget's Sound.*

June 1792

22 Vancouver and his crew in company with the Spanish in north part of Sound. (*June 22 - July 12.*)

24 Built during the winter at Clayoquot Sound, the *Adventure* under Robert Haswell (tender to the *Columbia*) sails with the *Columbia*.

25 *Columbia* strikes a rock opposite Loblip Sound and is damaged.

July 1792

12 British ship, *Florinda,* under William Coles, flying Portuguese colors, arrives at Nootka.

August 1792

28 Vancouver arrives at Nootka Sound and meets the *Daedalus,* the store ship of his expedition.

** *Columbia* is repaired with assistance of the Spanish at Nootka then sails north to meet *Adventure.*

September 1792

20 *Columbia* and the *Adventure* arrive at Nootka and meet Vancouver. Gray tells him of their discoveries since their last meeting.

22 French Republic proclaimed.

26 *Columbia* and *Adventure* arrive at Neah Bay. The *Adventure* is sold to the Spanish for 75 sea otter skins. The *Columbia* crosses to Poverty Cove (*now Port San Juan*) to resupply with water, wood, and mast.

October 1792

3 *Columbia* sails from Nootka for home via Sandwich Islands and Macao.

13 *Discovery, Chatham* and the *Daedalus* sail south from Nootka.

13 Cornerstone of the executive mansion (*White House*) laid.

18 Joseph Whidbey of the Vancouver expedition sails *Daedalus* into Gray's Harbor. He spends several days exploring and mapping the harbor.

20 Lt. Broughton of the *Chatham* enters the Columbia River and begins travels in boats nearly 100 miles upstream.

20 Vancouver names Mount St. Helens.

Other ships along the coast 1792

** *Butterworth* - William Brown - British

** *Prince Lee Boo* - Sharp - *Butterworth's* consort - British

** *Jackal* - Alexander Stewart - *Butterworth's* consort - British

** *Fenis And St. Joseph* - Joseph A. Tobar or John de Barros Andrede - British Brig from Macao under Portuguese colors

** *Felice Adventurer* - Vianna or John Mears(?) - British under Portuguese colors

** *Grace* - R.D. Coolidge - British(?)

** *Gustavus III* - Thomas Barnett - British under Swedish colors

** *Jenny* - James Baker - British

** *Margaret* - James Magee - Boston

** *Phoenix* - Hugh Moore - British

** *Prince William Henry* - Ewen - British

** *Three Brothers* - William Alder - British

** *Venus* - Henry Shepard - British

** *Iphigenia* - Viana od Vicana(?) - British under Portuguese colors

~ 1793 ~

January 1793

9 George Washington witnesses first balloon flight in the U.S. while in Philadelphia.

July 1793

23 Sir Alexander Mackenzie, a British subject, arrives at an inlet of the Pacific. (*Via the Peace and Bella Coola Rivers.*)

August 1793

19 Yellow fever diagnosed in Philadelphia. The nation's first major epidemic, it leads to the creation of public

health departments.

Ships along Northwest coast 1793
- ** *Amelia* - Trotter - Providence, Rhode Island
- ** *L'Emilie* - Owen - French under American colors
- ** *Discovery* - George Vancouver - British
- ** *Chatham* - Puget - British
- ** *Jefferson* - Josiah Roberts - Boston
- ** *San Carlos* - Ramón Saavedra - Spanish
- ** *Princesa* - Salvador Fidalgo - Spanish
- ** *Butterworth* - William Brown - British
- ** *Prince Le Boo* - Sharp - British
- ** *Jackal* - A. Stewart - British
- ** *Flavia* - M. Magon - French
- ** *Margaret* - James Magee - Boston
- ** Tender to the *Margaret*, British built at Friendly Cove on Nootka Sound
- ** *Hancock* - Samuel Crowell - American
- ** *Iphigenia* - Viana or Vicana(?) - British under Portuguese colors
- ** *Jane* - Elias Newberg - Boston
- ** *Prince William Henry* - Ewen - British
- ** *Resolution* - Burling - Boston
- ** *Three Brothers* - William Alder - British
- ** Tender to the *Three Brothers*, built at Friendly Cove
- ** *Lady Washington* - John Kendrick - Boston

Sea otter and pup.

~ 1794 ~

January 1794

11 British and Spanish sign convention at Madrid settling the Nootka controversy. (*See July 1789 & October 28, 1790.*)

March 1794

27 President Washington and Congress authorize the creation of U.S. Navy.

Ships along coast 1794
- ** *Activa* - Francisco de Eliza - Spanish
- ** *Mexicana* - Juan Martínez y Zayas - Spanish
- ** *Aranzazu* - José Tobar - Spanish
- ** *Concepción* - Spanish
- ** *Phoenix* - Hugh Moore - From Bengal, British
- ** *Jefferson* - Josial Roberts - Boston
- ** *Resolution* - Burling - Boston
- ** *Butterworth* - British
- ** *Prince Le Boo* - Captain Gordon - China (British)
- ** *Prince Willam Henry* - Ewen - British
- ** *Jenny* - Captain J. William Adamson - British from Bristol
- ** *Lady Washington* - Captain Kendrick - Boston
  Jackal - A. Stewart - British from China
- ** *Eleanora* - Simon Metcalf - New York

September 1794

2 George Vancouver aboard the *Discovery* along with the *Chatham* anchor at Nootka to prepare for survey to north.

December 1794

3 John Kendrick accidently killed in Hawaii. (*He was sailing to China via Hawaii. While anchored there, he was killed by a shot from the **Jackal**, which at his request was saluting him.*)

~ 1795 ~

March 1795

23 The Spanish ship *Activa* under command of Cosme Bertodano at Nootka; change of flags (*Spanish/British*) made and Spanish formally abandon Nootka and claims in the Northwest.

May 1795

25 *Ruby* a British ship commanded by Charles Bishop arrives at the Columbia River to begin fur trade up the coast.

Other ships along the coast 1795
- ** *Dispatch* - Elias Newbury - Boston
- ** *Jane* - British
- ** *Mercury* - Barnett - Providence, Rhode Island
- ** *Phoenix* - H. Moore - British (winters on Columbia River '94-'95)
- ** *Prince William Henry* - William Wake - British
- ** *Union* - John Boit- Newport, Rhode Island

October 1795

27 U.S./Spain sign Treaty of San Lorenzo which provides free navigation of the Mississippi River.

~ 1796 ~

March 1796

15 Captain Broughton's Sloop, *Discovery*, arrives at Nootka

for repairs, and visits Neah Bay. *Lady Washington* was at Nootka when he arrived.

September 1796

17 President Washington publishes his Farewell Address in Philadelphia's *Daily American Advertiser*.

Other ships along the coast 1796
   ** *Authur* - Henry Barber - British
   ** *Dispatch* - Captain Newbury - Boston
   ** *Fairy* - British
   ** *Sea Otter* - Stephen Hill - Boston
   ** *Phoenix* - Moor - Bengal
   ** *Sutil* - José Tobar - Spanish
   ** *Otter* - Ebenezer Dorr - Boston
   ** *Prince William Henry* - British
   ** *Ruby* - Charley Bishop - British
   ** *Sally*- Joseph Pierpont - Boston

~ 1797 ~

Ships along coast 1797
   ** *Amelia* - Trotter - Providence, Rhode Island
   ** *Sea Otter* - Hill - Boston
   ** *Dispatch* - Jonathan Bower - Boston
   ** *India Packet* - Rogers - Boston
   ** *Hazard* - Benjamin Swift - Boston
   ** *Dragon* - Lay - British from China

~ 1798 ~

July 1798

11 U.S. Marine Corps created by an Act of Congress.

Ships along coast 1798
   ** *Alexander* - Asa Dodge - Boston
   ** *Hazard* - Swift - Boston
   ** *Jenny* - Bowers - Boston
   ** *Alert* - William Bowles - Boston
   ** *Elisa* - James Rowan - Boston
   ** *Dove* - R. Duffin - British
   ** *Dragon* - Lay - British from China

~ 1799 ~

Ships along coast 1799
   ** *Caroline* (formally the *Dragon*) - Richard Cleveland - (American) Salem
   ** *Butterworth* - British
   ** *Ulysses* - David Lamb - Boston
   ** *Elisa* (or *Eliza*)- James Rowan - Boston; In May 1799, she became the first American vessel to anchor at San Francisco.
   ** *Hancock* - Crocker - Boston
   ** *Dispatch* - William Breck - Boston
   ** *Cheerful* - Beck - British
   ** *Dove* - R. Duffin - British from Canton
   ** *Liberty* - British
   ** *Gowland* - Bazilla Worth - Boston

December 1799

14 George Washington, first U.S. President, dies at age 67.

~ 1800 ~

April 1800

24 The Library of Congress is established.

June 1800
   ** The U.S. Federal Government moves from Philadelphia to Washington, the first planned capital city in the world.

Ships along coast 1800
   ** *Alert* - Bowers - Boston
   ** *Jenny* - Bowers - Boston
   ** *Belle Savage* - David Ockington - Boston
   ** *Beaver* - Lewis - Boston
   ** *Rover* - Davidson - Boston
   ** *Alexander* - Dodd - Boston
   ** *Charlotte* -Ingersoll - Boston
   ** *Hazard* - Swift - Boston
   ** *Dove* - R. Duffin - British from Canton
   ** *Betsy* - Captain Charles Winship. First U.S. ship to anchor at San Diego on August 25.

1800
   ** Evidence of large eruption at Mt. St. Helens.

October 1800

1 Spain cedes the Louisiana Territory to France. (*In a secret deal.*)

November 1800

17 Congress convenes for its first session in the new federal capital in Washington.

~ 1801 ~

March 1801

4 Thomas Jefferson inaugurated as third President of the United States.

Ships along coast 1801
   ** *Globe* - Benard Magee - Boston
   ** *Caroline* - Charles Derby - Boston
   ** *Charlotte* - Captain Ingersoll - Boston
   ** *Guatimozin* - Captain Bumstead - Boston
   ** *Catherine* or *Katherine* - Bazilla Worth - Boston
   ** *Betsy* - Cartwright - Boston
   ** *Atahualpa* - Captain Wildes - Boston
   ** *Dispatch* - Dorr - Boston
   ** *Littiler* - John Dorr - Boston
   ** *Lucy* - Pierpont - Boston
   ** *Mary Ann* (Sailed from London for NW coast; no other records.)
   ** *Belle Savage* - Captain Ockington - Boston** *Polly* - Kilby - Boston
   ** *Manchester* - Captain Brice - Philadelphia
   ** *Lavinia* - Captain Hubbard - British from Bristol
   ** *Enterprise* - Ezekiel Hubbell - New York
   ** *Mary* - (Sailed from Boston but no other records.)
   ** *Hazard* - Swift - Boston
   ** *Cheerful* - Barber - British from Macao
   ** *Diana* - Obed Barnard - Boston

** *Guatimozin* - S. Bumstead - Boston
** *Minatinomo* - William Swaine - Norwich, Connecticut
** *Pegasus* - Otis Liscomb - New York
** *Three Sisters* - Peleg Baker - New York

May 1801

14 U.S. and Tripoli go to war. (*Lasts until 1805.*)

~ *1802* ~

July 1802

4 Military Academy at West Point officially opens.

Ships along coast 1802
** *Alert* - John Ebbetts - Boston
** *Amethyst* - Bowers - Boston
** *Belle Salvage* - Boston
** *Caroline* - William Sturgis - Boston
** *Catherine* - Worth - Boston
** *Cheerful* - British
** *Hazard* - Rowan - Providence, Rhode Island (*a different ship from the Boston Hazard*)
** *Jenny* - Crocker - Boston
** *Juno* - Gibbs - Bristol, Rhode Island
** *Lelia Byrd* - William Shaler - Portsmouth, Virginia
** *Louisa* - Robert Haswell - Boston. (*Haswell was on the* **Columbia** *in 1787-90, 1790-93 and in command of* **Adventure** *in '92. He, the* **Louisa,** *and crew were lost at sea sometime after 1802.*)
** *Greenwood* - Rufus Greene - New York
** *Vancouver* - Brown - Boston
** *Hetty* - Jona Briggs - Philadelphia
** *June* - Kendrick - British from Bristol
** *Manchester* - Brice - Philadelphia
** *Atahualpa* - Wildes - Boston
** *Globe* - Magee - Boston
** *Mary*
** 15,000 sea otter skins were collected and carried to Canton this year.
** The custom of wintering in the Hawaiian Islands has now practically ceased.

~ *1803* ~

March 1803

12 *Boston* arrives at Nootka Sound. (*Said to have had the best and most varied assortments of trade goods of any ship going to the Northwest coast.*)

22 Crew of the *Boston* killed by Indians and the ship beached and stripped. John Jewitt, one of two survivors, returned to civilization two years later and published a narrative of "his adventure and sufferings." He was to make knives for the men and bracelets for the women.

26 The *Mary* and *Juno* of Boston arrive at Nootka, but return to sea when the Indians shoot guns while hooting and shouting from the shore.

April 1803

30 U.S. purchases Louisiana Territory from France for $15 million.

Ships along coast 1803
** *Boston* - Salter - Boston
** *Alexander*
** *Hazard* - Boston
** *Hazard* - Providence, Rhode Island
** *Mary*
** *Juno*
** *Lelia Byrd*
** *Vancouver*
** *Guatimozin*
** Alert
** *O'Cain* - Joseph O'Cain - New York
** Russians also send Russian American Company sea otter hunters southward to California.

~ *1804* ~

March 1804

26 Land Act of 1804 lists minimum price at $1.64 per acre and permits sale of Quarter sections.

May 1804

14 Lewis and Clark party embark from the Mississippi-Missouri River for the Pacific coast.

Ships along coast 1804
** *Atahualpa* - American
** *Guatimozin*
** O'Cain
** Caroline
** Hazard
** *Lelia Byrd*
** *Hazard* - Providence

~ *1805* ~

August 1805

16 Lewis and Clark Expedition crosses the Continental Divide.

July 1805

** The *Lydia* arrives at Nootka and takes Chief Maquinna in irons in exchange for the release of John Jewitt and Thompson, the two survivors from the *Boston (See March 22, 1803).* Other ships along the coast in 1805 include: *Atahualpa, Vancouver, Caroline, Catherine, Hope, Mary, Juno*, and the *Pearl.*

October 1805

16 Lewis and Clark arrive at the confluence of the Snake and Columbia Rivers.

18 Lewis and Clark begin descent of Columbia River.

November 1805

2 Lewis and Clark arrive at the bottom of the lower Columbia cascades and land on Strawberry Island.

7 Lewis and Clark sight the Pacific.

14 Lewis and Clark arrive on the Pacific.

17 Lewis survey river and its surroundings from Cape Disappointment.

December 1805

7 Lewis and Clark expedition begin clearing a winter quarters on Meriwether Bay.

20 Construction underway of La Malice Fort. (*First

fort erected by British-American fur traders west of the Rocky Mountains.)

~ 1806 ~

March 1806

23 Lewis and Clark depart for trip back up the Columbia.

26 Congress passes legislation authorizing the construction of the Cumberland Road.

Ships along coast 1806

** *Lida* - Heale - Boston

** *Hamilton* - Porter - Boston

** *Vancouver*

** *Pearl*

** *Hazard*

** *Authur* - Boston?

** *Peacock* - Oliver Kimball - Boston

** *Eclipse* - Joseph O'Cain - Boston

** *Urodel*

** *O'Cain* - Jonathan Winship Jr. - New York

** *??* - Pavl Slobodchikov - Russian

** *Reizo* - Spanish

September 1806

23 Lewis and Clark arrive in St. Louis.

~ 1807 ~

March 1807

3 Congress passes legislation prohibiting importation of more slaves after January 1, 1808.

Ships along coast 1807

** *O'Cain*

** *Amethyst* - Seth Smith Jr. - Boston

** *Aspasia* - Richard Cleveland - New York

** *Atahualpa* - American

** *Augustus* - Hubbell

** *Eclipse* - Joseph O'Cain (chartered by Russians)

** *Derby* - Benjamin Swift - Boston

** *Hamilton* - Boston

** *Guatimozin* - Glanville - Boston

** *Sv. Nikolai*

** *Kad'iak* - Barber - British

** *Hazard* - Boston

** *Mercury*

** *Peacock* - American

August 1807

17 Robert Fulton's steamship *Clermont* from New York to Albany and back inaugurates the era of steamboat transportation (17th - 21st).

December 1807

22 U.S. Embargo Act becomes law. (*Bans all trade with foreign countries and greatly reduces the numbers of ships on the Northwest coast.*)

~ 1808 ~

April 1808

6 John Jacob Astor incorporates the American Fur Company.

June 1808

** Simon Fraser descends a river (*Fraser*). (*There is some question as to whether he traveled all the way to the sea.*)

July 1808

12 Publication of *The Missouri Gazette* in St. Louis makes it the first newspaper west of the Mississippi.

Ships along coast 1808

** *Pearl*

** *Vancouver*

** *Mercury* - (Chartered by Russians)

** *Amethyst*

** *Belle Salvage*

** *Derby*

** *Dromo* - Woodward - Boston

** *Guatimozin*

** *Kad'iak*

** *Otter* - Jobelin - British

September 1808

29 The Russian schooner *Sv. Nikolai (St. Nicholas)* departs New Arkhangel. (*Russian outpost which later would become Sitka, Alaska*), to trade along the coast and then rendezvous with the *Kad'iak* at Grays Harbor.

November 1808

1 *Sv. Nikolai* driven ashore just north of James Island at the mouth of the Quillayute River. The crew is attacked. (*They spend a year and half trying to survive in the wilderness. At first they begin a walk to Grays Harbor where they were to have met the* **Kad'iak**, *but soon give up. Both Indian and Russian accounts remain of this event. See* **The Wreck of the Sv. Nikolai** *by Kenneth Owens and Alton Donnelly.*)

8 Crew of the *Sv. Nikolai* arrive at the (Hoh) River. Indians ferrying them across the river in their canoes, pull plugs and dive into the river half way across. The Russians, by luck of the current, make it back to north shore and avoid capture. Later Timofei Tarakanov would note that even Indians from "Cape Grenville" were present.

~ 1809 ~

February 1809

8 Crew of the wrecked *Sv. Nikolai* abandon their winter camp and travel down river. They capture an Indian woman with whom they hope to attempt to negotiate the release of Mrs. Bulygin, the Russian commanders' wife.

16 The Russian crew learns from Mrs. Bulygin, that she preferred to stay with the toyon (*chief*) by whom she had been held and advised the rest of the Russians to surrender. She also said that Filip Kotel'nikov, a young apprentice, had been taken by the Indians to live at Cape Grenville. (*Thus he is the first known white person to live with the Quinaults. Known as Ku-tin-ove by the Quinaults, he was adopted into the native way of life [Oliver Mason].*) The Russians did surrender and were made slaves until their rescue. (*See May 6, 1810.*)

March 1809

1 President Jefferson signs the Non-Intercourse Act which repeals the Embargo Acts; takes effect on the 15th.

4 James Madison inaugurated as fourth president.

Ships along coast 1809
- ** *Pearl*
- ** *Amethyst*
- ** *Vancouve* **   *Mercury*
- ** *O'Cain*
- ** *Enterprise*
- ** *Dromo* - Boston
- ** *Hamilton* - Boston
- ** *Otter* - Boston
- ** *Otter* - British

~ 1810 ~

1810
- ** Spokane House founded. *(First permanent settlement in what would become Washington State.)*

May 1810
6 Surviving crew of the *Sv. Nikolai* rescued by Brown of the *Lydia*.

26 *Albatross* commanded by Nathan Winship, engaged to hunt otter under Russian contract. They land and establish settlement at Oak Point 40 miles inland from mouth of the Columbia River on the south bank. They abandon site on July 19. *O'Cain, Isabella* (Boston) and the *Mercury* also under Russian contract this year.

Other ships on the coast 1810
- ** *Derby*
- ** *Katherine*
- ** *Enterprise*
- ** *Hamilton*
- ** *Juno*
- ** *Lydia* - T. Brown - Boston
- ** *Otter* - Boston

September 1810
8 Astor's Pacific Fur Company ship *Tonquin,* under Captain Jonathan Thorn, sails from New York to establish fort on Columbia River.

~ 1811 ~

February 1811
2 Russian settlers establish Fort Ross just north of San Francisco as an agricultural colony and trading post for sea otter furs. *(John Sutter would purchase it in 1841.)*

28 *Tonquin* sets sails from the Hawaiian Islands, after a two week supply stop, to the Columbia River. *(They also took 24 native Hawaiians with them.)*

March 1811
22 *Tonquin* arrives at the mouth of the Columbia, but a heavy squall formed high waves on the bar, so the ship could not enter immediately.

24 The *Tonquin* crossed the bar, still covered with high waves.

** Astor sends agent to St. Petersburg to make agreements with Russian American Fur Company on trade on the Northwest coast.

April 1811
12 Crews began the construction of a fort which they called Astoria at Point George.

20 Astor Overland Party under the command Wilson F. Hunt, leaves Missouri River *(near St. Joseph)* for the mouth of the Columbia River. *(See January 18 and February 20, 1812.)*

June 1811
5 After the crew had assisted in the preliminary work of the post, the *Tonquin* sails north to engage in trade for the company. Passing Gray(s) Harbor, an intelligent Chehalis presented himself in a canoe and offered his services as interpreter, stating that he had twice made the voyage northward in that capacity.

** About mid month, the *Tonquin* anchored in Nootka Sound. *(No one has been able to show conclusively where the ship was. Other sources put it at Clayoquot Sound, Kyugout Sound, Newitty, and Nasparti Inlet. About all that can be agreed upon, is that it was somewhere on the west coast of Vancouver Island [Herbert K. Beals].)* For several days there was trade with the Indians. Then there was a confrontation and bloody fighting. Later the ship blew up with 500 Indians on board of whom at least 200 were killed. *(Earlier, the Chehalis chief surrendered himself as a slave. Two years later he was ransomed by his friend on Gray[s] Harbor.)*

July 1811
23 Fleet of canoes and boats head up the Columbia River. Stuart ascends to river called the Okanogan where it joins the Columbia and he builds a fort.

Ships along coast in 1811
- ** *Tonquin*
- ** *Albatross*
- ** *Enterprise*
- ** *Hamilton*
- ** *New Hazard* - David Nye - Boston
- ** *Isabella*
- ** *Juno*
- ** *Mercury*
- ** *O'Cain*
- ** *Lydia*
- ** *Otter*
- ** *??* - Captain Porter
- ** *??* - Captain Blanchard
- ** *Catherine* (Shares with Russians)
- ** *Amethyst* - Captain Meek
- ** *Charon* - Captain Whittemore
- ** *Pedler* (or *Pedlar*) - George Clark - Boston

September 1811
** Indians from Gray(s) Harbor and Juan de Fuca Strait gather in large numbers at Bakers Bay *(north side of Columbia River near its mouth)* to fish for sturgeon. The *Tonquin* massacre was discussed and the rumor reached Fort Astoria where it was taken as a ruse. The Chinooks briefly talked about taking the fort and clearing all the whites out of the country. When McDougall summoned the chiefs to the fort, he told them he was the small-pox chief, they called off their proposed attack. *(Smallpox*

was one of the greatest fears of the tribes in the Northwest as there had been enough of it along the coast, and they abominated it as the double-edged scourge of white men and devil.)

October 1811

2 Schooner *Dolly* launched at Astoria. Her frame was brought from New York. She was used for river navigation.

November 1811

7 Battle of Tippecanoe in Indiana Territory.

20 Construction starts on the Cumberland Road.

~ 1812 ~

January 1812

18 The first group of Astor's Overland Party arrive at Astoria.

February 1812

15 Hunt and the main party arrive at Fort Astoria.

April 1812

20 Louisiana becomes a state.

May 1812

10 The *Beaver,* under command of Captain Cornelius Sowles, brings another detachment of Astor's fur company to the Columbia River.

June 1812

4 Louisiana Territory renamed the Missouri Territory.

19 President Madison officially declares war with Great Britain. War of 1812. *(1812-1814.)*

30 Ten canoes and two barges set out on river from Astoria to begin fur hunting trip.

August 1812

4 The *Beaver* leaves Astoria and sails north along the coast.

** Construction of hospital begins at Fort Astoria.

20 *Albatross* arrives at Astoria from the Hawaiian Islands, bringing news of the war.

Other ships on the coast 1812

** *Isabella*

** *Katherine*

** *Lydia*

** *Mercury*

** *New Hazard*

** *O'Cain*

** *Packet* - Bacon - Salem, Mass.

** *Pedler*

~ 1813 ~

War - 1813

** British blockade keeps most of U.S. Navy bottled up for the duration of the war.

October 1813

16 Pacific Fur Company sells Astoria to Northwest Company.

November 1813

13 Northwest Company takes formal possession of Astoria.

30 The British man-of-war *Raccoon* arrives at Astoria to capture it, but the Pacific Fur Company had already sold

it to the Northwest Company, a British property. (*See December 21, 1821.*)

December 1813

12 England takes formal procession of Astoria and renames it Fort George.

~ 1814 ~

.April 1814

17 *Isaac Todd,* a British ship under Captain Frazer Smith, arrives at Fort George (Astoria) with relief and supplies.

Ships along coast 1814

** *Pedler,* and the Russian *Chirikof* and *Ilemen.*

August 1814

24 British move into Washington D.C. and burn most government buildings including the Library of Congress (24th -25th).

September 1814

11 U.S. boats defeat English troops and prevent the invasion of New York. (*Called Battle of Lake Champlain, the most decisive battle of the war, leads to peace treaty with Great Britain.*)

December 1814

24 Treaty of Peace (*Peace of Ghent*) between U.S. and Great Britain states that all territory taken by either during the war should be restored. (*This included Oregon Territory.*)

~ 1815 ~

January 1815

8 Battle of New Orleans. (*Word had not arrived of the peace treaty, but Americans show great exaltation in winning the war.*)

July 1815

18 James Monroe, secretary of state, states that measures will be taken to reoccupy the post at Astoria.

** The British schooner *Columbia* arrives on the Columbia River.

~ 1816 ~

June 1816

** The British schooner *Columbia* again appears on the Columbia River.

Summer 1816

** The year of no summer; attributed to volcanic eruptions in Indonesia.

** *Sultan,* a Boston fur trader, arrives on the Columbia.

~ 1817 ~

April 1817

** The brig *Alexander* under Henry Bancroft from Charleston, Mass. arrives on the Columbia River and leaves trade goods at Astoria. Loads furs for Canton.

June 1817

12 The British schooner *Columbia* arrives at Fort George (*Astoria*).

September 1817

2 *Le Bordelais*, a French merchantman commanded by Camille de Roquefeuil arrives at Nootka. The first ship to do so since the *Tonquin* in June 1811.

December 1817

10 Mississippi becomes a state.

~ 1818 ~

July 1818

11 MacKenzie and Ross along with thirty men encamp on east bank of the Columbia River. They establish Fort Nez Percé, shortly thereafter called Walla Walla. The Ogden's Party of fur traders had been attacked earlier in the area by Indians.

August 1818

9 U.S. sloop-of-war, *Ontario,* arrives at Astoria and takes formal possession.

October 1818

1 British frigate, *Blossom,* enters Columbia River. 6 *Blossom* surrenders. The British flag is lowered and the U.S. flag raised.

~ 1819 ~

February 1819

22 The Adams-Onis Treaty. Spain cedes Florida to U.S. and establishes the 42nd parallel as the southern boundary of the Oregon Territory.

Ships on coast 1819

** *Brutus* - Boston
** *Eagle* - Boston
** *Ann* - James Hale - Boston
** *Volunteer*
** *Mentor*
** *Hamilton*
** *Thaddeus*

~ 1820 ~

March 1820

15 Maine becomes a state.
30 Missionaries arrive in Hawaiian Islands.

1821

February 1821

24 Mexico declares its independence from Spain.

Ships along coast 1821

** The American brig, *Arab,* lists the following ships on the Northwest coast this year: *Fredie, Pedler, Sultan, Hamilton, Lascar,* and *Mentor.*

August 1821

10 Missouri becomes a state.

September 1821

4 Czar of Russia claims all of the Northwest coast north of the 51st parallel.

December 1821

21 The Northwest Company and Hudson's Bay Company merge. (*See November 30, 1813.*)

~ 1822 ~

May 1822

4 Cumberland Road construction comes to a halt when the government cuts funds as a result of the Panic of 1819.

~ 1823 ~

May 1823

8 *Home Sweet Home* by John Howard Payne sung for the first time.

December 1823

2 Monroe Doctrine. "Americas are no longer open to European colonization and interference."

~ 1824 ~

April 1824

5 (17th?)U.S./Russian Treaty establishes 50° 40' as northern boundary of the Oregon Territory.

June 1824

17 Indian Affairs established as part of the U.S. War Department.

July 1824

26 *William and Ann* leaves London for the Columbia River. Botanist David Douglas aboard.

Ships along coast 1824

** *Herald, Triton, Sultan Rob Roy,* and *Convoy*; all Boston ships.

Fall 1824

** South Pass discovered by William H, Ashley, chief of the Rocky Mountain Fur Company. (*This pass, on today's State highway 28, just south of the Wind River Indian Reservation in Wyoming, would be famous as the National Highway. The Pass governed the movements of the great emigrations of all the overland population to the Pacific Northwest.*)

November 1824

18 A Hudson Bay Company expedition consisting of James McMillan, commander, Thomas McKay, F. N. Annance, and John Work, clerks; and thirty-six French Canadians, Kanakas, and Iroquois leave Astoria to find the mouth of the Fraser River by sea.
20 The expedition arrives at Shoalwater Bay.
25 The expedition arrives on Grays Harbor. They ascend the Chehalis River to a river they call Black River because of the color of the water. The natives encountered thought they had met white men before. The natives put on an attitude of fear and defence; they said, they had been told the fur hunters had come to attack them.

December 1824

5 The expedition arrives on Eld Inlet.
16 The expedition arrives at the mouth of the Fraser River.
26 Returning by their former path, the expedition arrives on the Chehalis River.

27 Work, McMillan, an interpreter, and six men procure horses from the natives and cross over to the Cowliz. McKay, Annance, and the remainder of the men retrace their earlier route down the Chehalis, Grays Harbor, and Shoalwater Bay.

~ 1825 ~

March 1825
3 U.S. Congress authorizes survey of the Santa Fe Trail.

Spring 1825
** Site for Fort Vancouver chosen. During the year, stock and effects were moved from Astoria to the fort.

April 1825
7 David Douglas arrives at the Columbia River aboard *William and Ann.*
8 Douglas learns that Fort George had just been moved to Fort Vancouver.
9 Because of rain and fog, Douglas' ship stays anchored near Cape Disappointment. He goes ashore there and the first plant he takes in hand is salal.

July 1825
4 Construction recommended to extend Cumberland Road westward and calling it the National Road.
** David Douglas travels up coast, to near present day site of Pacific Beach, where he notes pelicans.

October 1825
22 David Douglas meets Tha-a-muxi who lives on Gray's Harbor (*near the current site of Aberdeen*) and begins trip to Gray's Harbor.
26 Erie Canal opens.
28 Douglas arrives on the Harbor.
** Douglas recuperates at Tha-a-muxi's village from an earlier knee injury. (*Near present day site of Aberdeen.*)
** Douglas researched botany near here.

November 1825
7 Douglas starts up the "Cheecheeler" (*Chehalis*).
15 Douglas reaches Fort Vancouver.

~ 1826 ~

October 1826
7 The first American railroad is completed in Massachusetts. (*Three miles long.*)

December 1826
** David Douglas on Grays Harbor.

~ 1827 ~

March 1827
26 Ludwig Van Beethoven dies.

June 1827
27 James McMillan party leaves Fort Vancouver and travels up the Cowlitz River.
28 McMillan arrives at Cowlitz Portage (*Toledo*) and uses native horses to get to Puget Sound.

1827
** David Douglas uses the name *Cascades* for the waterfalls he sees on the lower Columbia. (*In 1841, Charles Wilkes will apply that name to the chain of mountains on his chart.*)

July 1827
3 McMillan to *meet Cadboro* by previous arrangements at Port Orchard, but it did not show up, so the next day they head northward.
10 McMillan arrives at Whidbey Island.
12 McMillan and party leave on the *Cadboro.*
24 After eight days of failure, the *Cadboro* enters the Fraser River.
29 McMillan decides on site to plant Fort Langley.

November 1827
23 Slight shock of earthquake felt at Fort Langley.

~ 1828 ~

April 1828
21 Noah Webster publishes *American Dictionary of the English Language.*

July 1828
4 Construction starts on the Baltimore and Ohio Railroad.

Ships along coast 1828-1830
** *Volunteer, Active, Louise, Owyhee,* and *Convoy* all from Boston. Also the *William and Ann* of Hudson's Bay.

Mount Baker

~ 1829 ~

August 1829
** Salmon trade on the Fraser River at Fort Langley reported as quite brisk. 7,544 salmon were taken in trade for goods. More were offered by the natives than could be received. "What pity that salt and casks should be wanting," says the register.

Summer 1829
** Reports of intermittent fever (malaria like) nearly depopulating the banks of the Columbia River.

~ 1830 ~

May 1830
28 Indian Removal Bill; Congress authorizes removal of all Indians east of the Mississippi to the west, by force if necessary.

August 1830

28 The first steam locomotive, *Tom Thumb*, makes its first run on the Baltimore and Ohio Railroad.

~ 1831 ~

June 1831

30 Black Hawk reluctantly agrees to move to west of the Mississippi.

August 1831

22 Nat Turner leads a slave rebellion. Quickly put down and more laws enacted relating to slaves in the south. (*Since 1790's, when slaves rebelled in Santo Domingo and slaughtered 60,000 people, southerners had been on edge.*)

** An uncommonly dark day. The whole day was as dark as night at Fort Vancouver. Believed to have been caused by an eruption of Mt. St. Helens.

~ 1832 ~

March 1832

3 *Worcester vs Georgia:* Court says Indian Nations can make treaties with the U.S. and that they are the highest law of the land.

May 1832

1 Wagon train leaves Fort Osage on the Missouri River under leadership of Captain Benjamin Louis Eulalie de Bonneville for the Columbia River. (*The Oregon Trail becomes the main route for settlers heading to the Oregon Territory. James Hall's publication* **Legends of the West**, *encourages many to try their luck in the West.*)

14 Black Hawk War: Black Hawk and his group are fired upon for attempting to move back east of the Mississippi River to reoccupy land in Wisconsin.

August 1832

3 Black Hawk's followers are slaughtered. Black Hawk escapes but later surrenders. Indians now know to move east of the Mississippi means extermination.

November 1832

14 First street car goes into operation in New York City.

~ 1833 ~

Throughout 1833

** Intermittent fever (*Influenza*) rampant in Northwest. First reported in 1829 on the Columbia River and growing worse each year.

May 1833

30 Archibald McDonald (Hudson's Bay) arrives and establishes Nisqually House (*Fort Nisqually*); the first non-native settlement on Puget Sound. (*He notes that while a trading expedition "last spring" he and nine other men spent twelve days erecting a 15'x20' store house there and left three hands to care for it; eventually leading to the formation of the Puget Sound Agricultural Company.*)

July 1833

20 Men at Nisqually inform the Indians that they will not trade for skins on Sundays.

September 1833

3 Doctor William Tolmie from Nisqually, first white man to visit to Mt. Rainier.

~ 1834 ~

Spring 1834

** Word reaches Fort Vancouver of a Japanese junk wrecked near Cape Flattery. Thomas McKay and thirty men leave the fort via the Chehalis River to rescue the crew. They arrive at Point Grenville and become disheartened and give up the rescue attempt. In late May or early June the *Llama* rescues two of the crew from the Indians. (*There are other reports of wrecked Japanese Junks along the Northwest coast [1820, 1831 and 1927]. Japanese boats may have drifted across the ocean for centuries before the arrival of the Europeans and provided the coastal people with many non-native items.*)

June 1834

15 Fort Hall established in Idaho by fur trader N. J. Wyeth. Becomes major stop on the Oregon Trail.

30 Congress establishes Department of Indian Affairs to administer Indian Territory west of the Mississippi.

1834

** The Spanish governor in Monterey, California prints the *Alta California,* the first newspaper on the Pacific coast.

~ 1835 ~

March 1835

** Dr. Meredith Gairdner, physician at Fort Vancouver, reports an eruption of Mt. St. Helens.

~ 1836 ~

February 1836

23 Siege of the Alamo begins. 187 men hold off Santa Anna's force of 3,000 for 13 days.

25 Samuel Colt awarded patent for a six shooter.

March 1836

6 Siege of Alamo ends when all defenders are killed.

April 1836

21 Sam Houston captures Santa Anna.

Spring 1836

** *Beaver*, a Hudson's Bay ship, becomes the first steamship on Northwest coast. Steam machinery set in her at Fort Vancouver on the Columbia. (*In the following years she steamed the bays and sounds around Vancouver Island from April to November with the steamer* **Otter** *joining her in 1852 [***Beaver** *ran aground in 1888].*) Other ships along the coast this year include the *Joseph Peabody, Nereid, Europe,* and *La Grange.*

Summer 1836

** Henry Spalding establishes a Presbyterian Mission on the Clearwater among the Nez Percé.

September 1836

1 Marcus Whitman reaches Walla Walla by wagon train through the South Pass (*first with a number of women*). He establishes a Presbyterian Mission among the Cayuses near the junction of the Snake and Columbia Rivers. (*Since these women were able to cross over land through the Rocky Mountains, they became the symbols that families, not only fur hunters, could cross the mountains. This along with a report by John Frémont in 1842 stimulated the Western Movement.*)

~ 1837 ~

May 1837

10 Panic of 1837 begins when New York banks stop making payments. 618 banks fail this year leading to seven years of depression. (*This spurred the westward movement of settlers and helped the Whigs in elections of 1840.*)

Ships along coast 1837

** *Hamilton, Sulphur* and the *Starling*.

December 1837

** W. A. Slacum makes a report to Congress about the lands in Oregon. Spurs "Oregon fever."

~ 1838 ~

January 1838

6 Samuel Morse demonstrates his telegraph for the first time in public.

August 1838

11 Instructions for the United States Exploring Expedition set. Object of the expedition was the examination of islands, reefs, and harbors and the protection of commerce, particularly of the whale-fishing interest in the Pacific.

18 The U.S. Expedition sets sail from Norfolk under the command of Charles Wilkes. The squadrons consist of the sloops-of-war *Vincennes* and the *Peacock*, the brig *Porpoise*, the ship *Relief*, and the tenders *Sea Gull* and *Flying Fish*.

~ 1839 ~

April 1839

10 Rev. David Leslie (*Methodist*) and brother William Willson arrive at Nisqually with intention of establishing an Indian mission.

17 Methodists begin construction of mission building at Nisqually.

21 Roman Catholic priest, Father Demers (*aware of the Methodists at Nisqually*), arrives at Nisqually to "plant the true seed in the hearts of the Indians."

~ 1840 ~

January 1840

19 Wilkes' U.S. Expedition sights Antarctica.

May 1840

21 *Lausanne* (*from New York Harbor*) with a large missionary party (*mostly Methodist*) cross Columbia River bar.

June 1840

13 Assignments made for the missionaries from the *Lausanne*.

August 1840

16 Dr. Richmond, a Methodist minister, marries Miss Chloe Clark to William Willson at Nisqually in the first American marriage in what will become Western Washington Territory.

September 1840

24 *Vincennes* reaches Honolulu after Antarctic and South Pacific cruise. *Sea Gull* lost off Cape Horn. *Relief* was sent home by way of Sydney. *Porpoise* cruised Society Islands, while the *Peacock* and *Flying Fish* cruised south seas to fill time while in Hawaiian Islands.

~ 1841 ~

April 1841

4 After only one month in office, William Henry Harrison dies. John Tyler becomes the first American Vice-President to succeed to the Presidency.

5 The U.S. Exploration Expedition leaves Hawaiian Islands for Columbia River.

10 Horace Greely begins to publish *The New York Times*.

28 Wilkes with the *Vincennes* and *Porpoise* arrive of the mouth of the Columbia River, but due to roughness of the water on the bar, they turn northward.

May 1841

2 *Vincennes* and *Porpoise* enter Strait of Juan de Fuca and anchor in Port Discovery to begin official exploration of Puget Sound and the surrounding country.

8 A mate from the *Beaver* meets Wilkes on the west side of Admiralty Inlet to lead him to Fort Nisqually.

9 Wilkes calls the place Pilot Cove and they sail for the Fort.

11 Wilkes drops anchor at Nisqually. (*For the next several months, the men and ships explored the region of Puget Sound and excursions were made as far as Colville.*)

July 1841

4 While anchored at Nisqually, Wilkes declares a holiday. An ox was barbecued in the first 4th of July celebration on the West coast. He also applies the name of Cascades to his maps for the mountains to the east of Puget Sound.

18 *Peacock* beaten to pieces on the bar of the Columbia.

30 (*Captain Wilkes of the U.S. Expedition ordered Midshipman Eld to take a party across country from Nisqually to Grays Harbor and then to Columbia. W. D. Brackenridge, a botanist with the party kept a journal.*) The party begins descending the Chehalis River and passes the mouth of the Satsop (*spelled "Satchap" by Brackenridge*).

31 The party enters the head of Grays Harbor.

August 1841

1 The party begins survey of Grays "Harbour" in a "Chenook" canoe (1st - 6th).

7 The party shifts camp (*from Charlie's Creek to O'Leary Creek*).

10 The party moves camp to "S. Head or Chehalis Point" (*Westport*).

13 Lt. De Haven & party of men arrive. Had been sent by Wilkes in search of the party and to help them finish survey. They learn of the loss of the *Peacock*. Something that they had feared since a "Chekilis" Indian had told them a large Boston ship had got "brock" on the bar at the entrance to the Columbia.

24 Grays "Harbour" survey complete and the party leaves via coast for Astoria.

** Part of the Wilkes party leaves Astoria overland for California. (*Partly due to the loss of the Peacock.*)

October 1841

** Mid-October the squadron leaves the Columbia to join the *Vincennes* at San Francisco.

November 1841

1 The U.S. Exploring Expedition weighs anchor for Manila.

~ *1842* ~

March 1842

15 Oregon Institute is established near Salem, Oregon by the Methodists.

August 1842

9 Webster-Ashburton Treaty fixes the forty-ninth parallel from Lake of the Woods westward as the dividing line between Canada and the U.S. (*Statesmen of the time thought the line was only to go to the Mississippi, but it was situated 104 miles north of the river. Since it never intersected the Mississippi, the Americans later said it must run west across the whole continent.*)

October 1842

** (*St. Helens enters a violent eruptive phase that will continue intermittently for fifteen years.*)

November 1842

23 Ash from St. Helens falls to ¹/₂ inch deep at the Dalles.

Fall 1842

** English and Russians make agreement to discontinue liquor trade on the Northwest coast for a term of ten years. (*Liquor had caused it to be unsafe for white men to appear at any distance from their forts except in armed bands. Indians at first would not trade their furs once the liquor ban went into effect. Eventually they started trading for ammunition and later blankets. Calm prevailed until in 1849 when gold seekers overran the country.*)

~ *1843* ~

February 1843

2 Willamette Valley settlers meet to decide what to do about wolves and other animals attacking their livestock. (*This became the first of a series of "Wolf Meetings" which led to need for law and order and development of a government in the Oregon Territory.*)

16 Peter H. Burnett (*later governor of California*) reports, "The mountain (St. Helens) burning magnificently."

May 1843

22 1,000 settlers leave Independence, Missouri (for Oregon) in largest wagon train ever.

November 1843

** Largest wagon train reaches the Willamette Valley of Oregon.

~ *1844* ~

January 1844

15 University of Notre Dame receives its charter from the State of Indiana.

May 1844

30 Rev. George Gray in a ship off the Oregon coast writes of St. Helen "throwing up clouds of smoke."

May 1844

24 Samuel B. Morse sends message "What hath God Wrought" by telegraph from Baltimore to Washington, D.C.

~ *1845* ~

January 1845

23 Congress declares all national elections will be held the first Tuesday after the first Monday in November.

March 1845

3 Florida becomes the twenty-seventh state.

April 1845

14 Christopher Columbus Simmons is claimed to be first white child born in what would become Washington State. He is born at Washougal. (*See July 6, 1931.*)

1845

** John C. Frémont publishes *The Report of the Exploring Expedition to the Rocky Mountains in the Year 1842 and to Oregon and Northern California in the Years 1843-44.* (*This became one of the first best selling reports produced by the U.S. and greatly increased interest in the West. See September 1, 1836.*)

October 1845

** Simmons, McAllister, Kindred, Jones, Bush (*a freed slave*), Ferguson, Crowder and Crockett cut a road from Cowlitz Landing (*Toledo*) to near (*Centralia*).

** Michael Simmons, his family, and the others settle in what they call New Market (*Tumwater*). They introduce shingle-making to Puget Sound (*and the Northwest*).

10 Naval Academy opens at Annapolis, Maryland.

December 1845

29 Texas admitted as the twenty-eighth state.

~ *1846* ~

January 1846

5 The House of Representatives passes a resolution to end the Anglo-American joint occupation of the Oregon country. "The right of our manifest destiny to spread over this whole continent." (*The term "manifest destiny" was first used in an article by John L. O'Sullivan in July 1845.*)

May 1846

13 U.S. Congress declares war on Mexico.

1846

** Michael Simmons grist mill begins operation using water power of the Shutes (*Deschuttes,[See October 1845].*)

June 1846

15 Oregon settlement provided that the boundary between U.S. and British territory in Oregon existed at 49th parallel to middle of channel and on a line south and through Juan de Fuca, obligates abandonment of twelve Hudson's Bay trading posts south of that line. (*The U.S. schooner Shark arrived in 1846 and many American settlers on the Willamette [feeling it was now safe] left for lands north of the Columbian River.*)

Summer 1846

** A race course laid out just north of Fort Nisqually by men of the British war vessel *Fisgard*. Indians came from east of the mountains with their race horses.

August 1846

15 The first U.S. newspaper in California, the *Californian*, begins publication in Monterey.

October 1846

** Levi Lathrop Smith builds first structure in Smithfield (*Olympia).*

December 1846

28 Iowa joins the Union.

Winter 1846-47

** Donner Party stranded in the Sierra Nevada Mountains.

~ 1847 ~

March 1847

3 Congress adopts gas lighting fixtures for the Capitol and its grounds.

** Having witnessed several eruptions of St. Helens, Paul Kane paints a picture of it in eruption.

July 1847

1 First adhesive postage stamps go on sale in New York.

24 Mormons, under Brigham Young, arrive in the Great Salt Lake area.

August 1847

20 Simmons and seven others form Puget Sound Milling Company to build a water powered saw-mill at the lower of the falls on the *Deschuttes*; the first of its kind on Puget Sound. (*See October 1845.*)

September 1847

14 Mexico City surrenders to General Winfield Scott, ending war with Mexico.

November 1847

29 Whitman massacre. Indians kill Marcus Whitman, his wife, and party of settlers, followed by the Cayuse War in Eastern Washington which lasts until 1850 .

~ 1848 ~

January 1848

24 Gold discovered at Sutter's mill in Sacramento, California.

February 1848

2 Treaty of Guadalupe-Hidalgo signed and Mexico accepts Rio Grande border and cedes California, Nevada, Utah, New Mexico, Arizona, and most of Colorado.

August 1848

14 Oregon Territory established.

1848

** William O'Leary is "first white settler" on Gray's Harbor. (*See February 16, 1809.*)

December 1848

** President Polk announces discovery of gold in California, setting off gold rush.

~ 1849 ~

February 1849

28 First gold seekers arrive in San Francisco aboard the *California*. Population of California reaches 100,000 by the end of the year.

March 1849

3 Home Department established. (*The forerunner of the Department of the Interior.*)

May 1849

17 Fire destroys more than 400 buildings and 27 steamships in St. Louis, Missouri.

May 1849

** Snoqualmie and Skeywamisk Indians visit Fort Nisqually to see if report of cruel treatment was done to members of their tribe. They attempt to capture the fort, but were unable. An American outside the Fort was killed and another wounded. (*This led to first U.S. soldiers stationed here. They were sent from Fort Vancouver to Steilacoom under the command of Captain B. Hill.*)

August 1849

7 J. Q. Thornton, sub-Indian Agent for Oregon Territory, arrives at Fort Nisqually to investigate facts associated with the killing of the American in May.

October 1849

29 First court convenes (*on Puget Sound*) at Steilacoom. Six Indians indicted and two were executed for the killing of the American at Fort Nisqually in May.

~ 1850 ~

Spring 1850

** Smithfield dedicated as a town and named Olympia by Edmund Sylvester. The name had been suggested by Colonel Isaac N. Edey.

1850

** Eight pairs of English sparrows imported by the Brooklyn Institute to rid shade trees of caterpillars. (*They multiply so successfully that by 1890, New York imports starlings to prey on the sparrows in Central Park.*)

** John Holgate selects a claim on the south side of Elliot Bay.

September 1850

9 California admitted to the United States.

18 Fugitive Slave Act passed.

20 Slave trading abolished in Washington, D.C.

27 Donation Land Claim Act opens up Oregon Territory to homesteading.

~ 1851 ~

June 1851
5 *Uncle Tom's Cabin*, by Harriet Beecher Stowe, begins as a serial in the *National Era*, an anti-slavery paper in Washington D.C.

September 1851
18 First edition of the *New York Daily Times*, becomes the *New York Times* in 1857.

28 Lee Terry and David T. Denny (the Dennys were from Indiana) lay foundation for a cabin on Alki Point. (*Alki, a Chinook word means "by and by" or "after while."*)

October 1851
** Four men decide to create a town site on Port Townsend Bay.

November 1851
13 *Exact* lands party of the Arthur Denny family, John Low family, Boren family, Bell family and Charles Terry *(twenty-four in all)* at Alki Point to join Lee and David. They call it New York. (*The Exact had sailed from Portland on November 5th with passengers for the Sound and gold miners for Queen Charlotte Island.*)

** *Georgiana* wrecked on Queen Charlotte Island and the gold seekers taken as slaves by the Haida Indians. (*They were later ransomed for by white settlers on Puget Sound, and some of them, including the sons of Sidney Ford, first Indian agent of the Chehalis region, settled on the Harbor.*)

December 1851
24 Fire at the Library of Congress destroys 35,000 books, two thirds of the collection.

~ 1852 ~

February 1852
15 A. A. Denny and two others located claims on the east side of Elliot Bay.

March 1852
13 Uncle Sam makes his first appearance in *Diogenes, His Lantern* a publication in New York.

20 *Uncle Tom's Cabin* is published in book form and becomes instant best seller.

31 Dr. D.S. Maynard arrives and locates a claim east of Elliot Bay.

May 1852
** Denny and others lay out a town on the east bank of Elliot Bay they call Seattle after an Indian friend of theirs. (*See May 23, 1853.*)

1852
** U.S. Coastal Survey charts False Dungeness. (*Port Angeles.*)

** Isaiah L. Scammon (*a former California gold seeker*) is the first settler to bring a family to the Chehalis Valley. They settle on the south bank of the river across from the present site of Montesano where the Wynooche River enters the Chehalis.

** Benjamin C. Armstrong builds first saw mill in county on the falls of Cedar Creek below Oakville. Most of the early housing in the Chehalis Valley was built with lumber sawn in this mill.

** Samuel Woodard is first settler to take up donation land claim on Willapa at Wilson Creek.

July 1852
3 Congress acts to establish a mint in San Francisco.

September 1852
11 First issue of the weekly *Columbian* in Olympia. (*The press used to print the first* Columbian *was the same one used in Monterey, California to print the* Alta California *in 1834, San Francisco's first newspaper,* The Star, *in 1836, and later Oregon's first paper* The Old Oregon Spectator, *which later became* The Oregonian.)

Fall 1852
** Nick Delin's mill starts cutting lumber. (*Tacoma.*)

October 1852
24 Daniel Webster dies.

November-December 1852
** Monticello Convention held on the banks of the Cowlitz River to divide up the Oregon Territory.

~ 1853 ~

February 1853
14 Donation Act permits, the purchase of land at $1.25 per acre after occupation of two years.

March 1853
2 Washington Territory formed from the northern half of the Oregon Territory.

17 Isaac Stevens appointed as Territorial Governor of Washington.

19 First theatrical performance in Olympia given by Jack Rag, a celebrated actor and vocalist.

** H. L. Yesler's steam powered sawmill cuts lumber on Puget Sound in Seattle. (*A water powered mill cut lumber in 1847 on the Deschuttes.*)

May 1853
23 Boren and Arthur Denny file the first plat of the town of Seattle.

31 Isaac Stevens' party leaves from near St. Paul to explore for railroad routes from the Mississippi River to Puget Sound.

July 1853
8 Commodore Matthew Perry arrives in Tokyo Bay to secure trade rights and get a treaty dealing with diplomacy and shipwrecked seamen on each others' shores.

August 1853
** Thomas Dryer, first editor of the Portland *Oregonian*, leads initial ascent of Mt. St. Helens to inspect results of the eruptions on the mountain.

Fall 1853
** 171 pioneers, led by James Longmire by wagon train, settle on south side of Commencement Bay.

October 1853
17 Isaac Stevens reaches Spokane House.

November 1853
25 Isaac Stevens arrives in Olympia.

December 1853

13 Hudson's Bay Company's ship *Beaver* lands on San Juan Island with thirteen hundred sheep.

30 U.S. buys 43,000 square miles of land from Mexico in the Galdsden Purchase.

~ 1854 ~

February 1854

24 First Washington Territorial Legislature meet in Olympia.

28 Republican Party forms; ratified on July 6, 1854.

** Mt. St. Helens notably increases its activity.

March 1854

31 Treaty of Kanagawa is signed and opens commercial and diplomatic relations between U.S. and Japan.

April 1854

14 Chehalis County created. *(Renamed Grays Harbor County on March 15, 1915.)*

1854

** George Davidson, a scientist, reports "vast rolling masses of dense smoke," on Mt. Baker.

** Benjamin Silliman, Jr., a Yale chemistry professor, distills oil to produce kerosene. *(For the remainder of the century, refiners consider naphtha [gasoline] a waste by-product, which they either burn off or dump into near-by streams.)*

July 1854

6 Republican Party formally named.

December 1854

4 Second Washington Territorial Legislature meets.

7 Isaac Stevens organized his treaty-making force.

26 First treaty council; Isaac Stevens addresses the Indians during talks at the She-nah-nam or the Medicine Creek Treaty. Leschi tears up official papers the government had given him when Governor Stevens insist that they take high timberland above the creek instead of some of the bottom land. *(See September 27, 1855.)*

~ 1855 ~

February 1855

20 Isaac Stevens meets with tribes on the Chehalis River (February 20 - March 2) in failed treaty attempt.

March 1855

3 Senate of the U.S. ratifies Medicine Creek Treaty.

18 Sheriff of Whatcom County demands taxes for the sheep on San Juan and thirty-four sheep were seized for non-payment of taxes. *(See December 13, 1853.)*

April 1855

10 President signs the Medicine Creek Treaty.

1855

** Having panned for gold in California and the Fraser River, James Karr and his wife Abigail become the first permanent settlers on the west bank of the Hoquiam River (The book, *The River Pioneers,* gives the date as 1863).

** Edward Campbell, also a former gold seeker, settles on the east bank of the Hoquiam River. *(His brother said*

Ed bought his claim from Molasses Doctor, an Indian who lived near the mouth of the Hoquiam River. In 1859 an Indian camp still occupied the site, an important potlatch site.)

** James Pilkington squats near a Chehalis Indian camp *(Cosmopolis).*

July 1855

1 Qui-nai-elt River Treaty.

** Indian Agents Michael Simmons and Benjamin Shaw become first recorded non-Indians to cross the Olympics via the Quinault River.

September 1855

27 Indians attack Porter home on White River in dispute of Medicine Creek Treaty. *(Several bloody skirmishes in following months lead to attack on Seattle in January, 1856. Leschi would become a controversial figure and remain so until the settlers of this era died. See March 17, 1857.)*

Lupin.

~ 1856 ~

January 1856

1 Congress makes use of adhesive postage stamps obligatory.

25 Qui-nai-elt Treaty signed by Governor in Olympia.

26 Indians under Leschi attack Seattle.

March 1856

8 Last battle with the Indians under Leschi where Naches Pass Road crosses the White River.

April 1856

1 Western Union Telegraph Company formed.

21 The first railroad bridge is completed across the Mississippi River.

August 1856

26 U.S. seizes land and begin to erect a military post on Bellingham Bay to protect setters from raids of Indians, Hydahs and Tlinkits, coming down from the north in huge dugout canoes.

November 1856

8 Quiemuth, one of the militant Indians with Leschi *(See*

December 1854 and January-March 1856), wanting to surrender to Governor Stevens is brought into Olympia under cover of darkness by James Longmire and meets Stevens at 2:30 a.m. in his office. Stevens retires about 4:30 leaving Quiemuth and Longmire there to rest. About 5:15 a.m. some men break into the office killing Quiemuth. (*An inquest did not find sufficient evidence to jail the suspect, James Burton.*)

13 Leschi betrayed by his nephew, Sluggia, for a fifty blanket reward.

17 Leschi brought to trial at a courtroom in Steilacoom for the murder of Abraham Moses during the time of the Indian uprising (*See September 1855*). The jurors could not come to an unanimous conclusion to convict him. (*See March 17, 1857.*)

** Following the trial, Yelm Jim, a Nisqually, kills Sluggia for betraying Leschi. He was imprisoned for murder but later released.

~ 1857 ~

March 1857

17 Second trial of Leschi (*See November 1856*) begins in Olympia and he is found guilty. (*In the following months, many fought to save him as there was evidence that he did not commit the killing he was accused of. See February 18, 1858.*)

May 1857

** Major Granville O. Haller arrives at Port Townsend to build fort to protect settlers there against Indian raiders from the north seeking work, or to serve as mistresses to single men.

June 1857

18 U.S. ships allowed to trade in part of Nagasaki, Japan.

30 Sidney Ford (*Ford's Prairie, later called Sharon Prairie, is located across the Chehalis from Porter*) submits a report to Indian affairs about the Indians of coastal Washington Territory. He first became acquainted with them in the spring of 1846. He says that the Quenoith (Quinault) is presently engaged in "petty warfare" with the Indians on the lower Chihlis (Chehalis). He also said that the population had decreased since 1846 as a result of alcohol provided by whites, smallpox, measles, flux (flu), and venereal disease.

Summer 1857

** Thompson B. Speake and his family settle at Point Chehalis (*Westport*).

** A wagon road now existed from Mound Prairie to "Claquamish."

September 1857

14 George Jones completes first cabin on the banks of the Wishkah River. (*West bank near the river's mouth.*)

1857

** Samuel Benn takes up a claim at Melbourne, southwest of Montesano. (*He married the daughter of Reuben Redman, who had a claim on the Wishkah, then traded his claim with his father-in-law and moved his family there in 1868.*)

~ 1858 ~

February 1858

19 Leschi hanged. (*See March 1857.*)

April 1858

5 Patterson Luark and Rev. Charles Byles start work on a trail from Cedarville to the coast near Grayland.

18 Schooner *General Harney* arrives on Grays Harbor with supplies.

May 1858

11 Minnesota admitted to the United States.

20 *Panama* brings five hundred Californians to the Northwest to seek gold in the Fraser Valley. (*By year's end it was estimated that there were nearly 25,000 gold seekers in the Valley.*)

June 1858

18 U.S. and China sign a Treaty of Peace and commerce.

July 1858

** Patterson Luark settles at Chehalis Point (*Westport*) having moved from his failed settlement on Johns River.

27 Luark drives thirty head of cattle and three horses to his new homestead.

Indian Agent report 1858

** Sidney Ford reported that the "Quinaiuts and Queets" could not come see him while he was on Gray's Harbor as they had visitors from Cape Flattery and they were settling some old differences.

August 1858

21 First of seven debates between Lincoln and Douglas.

September 1858

** William Harney promoted to rank of Brigadier-General and arrives at Fort Vancouver Washington Territory.

October 1858

9 The new Overland mail stage completes its first trip between San Francisco and St. Louis in 23 days 10 hours. A stage traveling in the opposite direction arrives in San Francisco on the 10th.

November 1858

2 Body of log cabin raised for a school house at Chehalis Point.

6 Rober Gray Luark is first white child born on the Harbor at Chehalis Point (*Westport*).

Fall 1858

** Gold discovered near Pikes Peak. (*Sets off a new gold rush*).

** James family settled on the north shore of Grays Harbor.

** Post office now established at Fort Willapa.

~ 1859 ~

January 1859

3 School classes begin at Chehalis Point.

February 1859

** Surveyors appear on San Juan Island to lay out plots of land for gold miners who wish to settle there.

14 Oregon joins the Union as a free state.

March 1859

8 Congressional resolution ratifies the Qui-nai-elt River Treaty.

April 1859

4 The song *Dixie* is sung publicly for the first time.

11 President signs Qui-nai-elt River Treaty.

25 Ground breaking for the Suez Canal.

May 1859

** 16 land claims taken by Americans on San Juan. The population balance swings from British to American.

1859

** Mail delivery between Olympia and Chehalis Point begins every other week.

June 1859

15 On San Juan, an American farmer, Lyman Cutter, kills a Hudson's Bay pig for rooting in his potato patch. (*Beginning of "The Pig War" [See July and August 1859].*)

** First major discovery of silver (Comstock Lode) made in Nevada near Virginia City. (*This fuels the gold rush near Pikes Peak and the term "Pikes Peak or Bust" becomes popular.*)

July 1859

16 Captain Wright's 115 foot iron-hull stern wheeler, *Enterprise,* is the first steamer to enter Grays Harbor.

27 By request of Brigadier-General William Harney, Company D, 9th Infantry lands at Griffin Bay on San Juan and Captain George Pickett proclaims it U.S. Territory.

30 The British warships *Satellite* and *Tribune* places Pickett under their guns.

31 *Plumper* joins the two other British warships at San Juan.

August 1859

1 The U.S. *Massachusetts* joins the U.S. Cutter *Shubrick* at San Juan to face the British.

** Ships begin to come and go in San Juan at the prospect of war.

24 The new Washington Territorial Governor, R. D. Gholson, visits Camp Pickett on San Juan. (*See October 1859.*)

27 Oil is found near Titusvill, Pennsylvania.

Indian Agent report 1859

** Sidney Ford reports to Simmons that the country has been settled to the entire exclusion of the Indians. Later in an inspection trip they find that there is no indication of a combination of coastal tribes against the whites. Because of sea otter hunting problems between the Indians and white hunters, Simmons recommends troops be stationed at Chehalis Point. (*See February 9, 1860.*)

October 1859

16 Abolitionist John Brown raids federal arsenal at Harpers Ferry (16-18).

20 General Winfield Scott, sent by President Buchanan, arrives at Fort Vancouver to put a check on General Harney. (*See July 1859.*)

25 General Scott arrives at fort near Port Townsend and begins negotiations with Governor at Victoria to settle San Juan situation.

26 A.H. Fisher takes a claim south of Luark.

28 Thomas James picks a claim near Luark's.

28 Both sides agree to limited military co-occupation of San Juan. (*The boundary dispute lasted for another twelve years as the American Civil War and*

Reconstruction intervened. See May 8, 1871 and November 25, 1871.)

November 1859

24 *On the Origin of Species* published.

December 1859

2 John Brown is hanged in Charleston, Virginia.

~ 1860 ~

January 1860

3 First school house in Grays Harbor area opens at Westport.

February 1860

9 Captain Maloney, his wife, and sixty troops arrive at Chehalis Point (*Westport*) aboard the *Enterprise*.

March 1860

11 *Calamet* enters Grays Harbor with supplies for the fort and other residents on Chehalis Point.

12 Matthew McGee, who has a claim on Point Brown (*Ocean Shores),* is arrested by Captain Maloney for selling whiskey. He is pronounced innocent when jury in Luark's court at Chehalis Point found no evidence of a criminal act.

April 1860

3 Pony Express begins mail service between St. Joseph, Missouri and Sacramento, California.

May 1860

18 *Calamet* arrives with supplies for Chehalis Point.

June 1860

10 *Calamet* arrives to bring supplies to Chehalis Point and to remove machinery from the *Enterprise* which had run aground on Chehalis Point.

July 1860

9 General election held. Seventy-four votes were cast and the Scammon place was selected as the county seat for Chehalis County. (*See 1852. The county seat was moved to Montesano in 1886 and the Scammon place became known as "South Montesano".*)

Indian Agent report 1860

** Indian Agent recommends "land between Point Granville (*Grenville*) and Qui-nai-elt river" be set aside as their reservation. He encourages the Indians to begin trade with their salmon saying that the "salmon that run up the Qui-nai-elt river, in great numbers, are considered the fattest and best flavored of any taken on the coast." (*His use of the name* Granville *instead of* Grenville *was applied to the village at the mouth of the Quinault River which would be renamed Taholah. He may have mistakenly used the name of Major Granville O. Haller who established the fort at Port Townsend in 1857 and was active in the affairs of Western Washington at this time, or just did not know the correct spelling.*)

November 1860

6 Abraham Lincoln is elected president.

17 *Washington Standard* begins publishing in Olympia.

December 1860

20 South Carolina declares Union between it and the United States dissolved.

~ 1861 ~

January 1861

** Mississippi, Florida, Alabama, Georgia, and Louisiana secede from the Union.

29 Kansas admitted to the Union.

February 1861

2 Captain Maloney at Chehalis Point notes that some white men are constantly introducing liquor and selling it to the Indians and that he is endeavoring to put a stop to it.

4 Confederate States of America formed.

9 Jefferson Davis elected president of the Confederate States.

23 Texas secedes from the Union.

March 1861

4 Abraham Lincoln inaugurated President of the United States.

** Sam Williams buys tract of sixteen acres, plats a townsite and names it Montesano in hopes of establishing the county seat there.

14 Town lots in Montesano going for $2.00 each

April 1861

12 American Civil War breaks out with bombardment of Fort Sumter.

15 President Lincoln declares that an "insurrection" exists; The American Civil War 1861-1865.

17 Virginia secedes from the Union.

May 1861

** Arkansas and North Carolina secede from the Union.

20 Kentucky votes to remain neutral. (*Birth place for both Lincoln and Jefferson.*)

June 1861

8 Tennessee secedes from the Union. (*The eleventh and final state to do so.*)

19 Chehalis Point troops moved to Astoria and from there to serve in the Civil War. (*Sam Williams helped himself to the cannon left behind and used it to signal those on Harbor when he had whiskey.*)

25 Town of Cosmopolis plat filed by David Byles and Austin Young.

Summer 1861

** Alleck Smith Survey of the Quinitle (*Quinault*) Indian Reservation complete. He notes in the general description that, "The coast line was to them also a matter of greatest importance on account of the number of Whales that are thrown ashore during the prevalence of the North Westerly Winds, and for the Sea Otter that abound about Point Granville."

July 1861

22 Congress passes resolution stating that the purpose of the war is to preserve the Union, not to abolish slavery.

October 1861

24 Transcontinental telegraph becomes operational. From Justice Field in California to President Abraham Lincoln.

~ 1862 ~

February 1862

1 The Columbia River freezes over.

** *Battle Hymn of the Republic* published.

March 1862

9 First battle in history of fully armored warships: the Federal *Monitor* and the Confederate *Merrimac.* (*Merrimac withdraws after five hour battle.*)

April 1862

6 Battle of Shiloh begins; results in 24,000 casualties.

29 Victor Smith purchases 7/40ths of the beach lands of Port Angeles.

May 1862

20 Homestead Act; allows citizens to acquire up to 160 acres by settling on public land for five years and paying $1.25 per acre.

June 1862

6 The land lying inside Ediz Hook officially designated Port Angeles by the Post Office Department.

19 President Lincoln signs order setting aside 3,500 acres of Port Angeles as a military and lighthouse reservation.

19 Congress forbids slavery in Federal Territories (but not in states).

July 1862

1 Congress passes Pacific Railroad Act which authorizing construction of the first transcontinental railroad.

2 President Lincoln signs the Morrill Land Grant Act; provides 30,000 acres to every loyal State to endow agricultural and engineering colleges. (*Ultimately 69 colleges established under this act.*)

19 The U.S. survey vessel, *Fontleroy*, moves from Shoalwater Bay to Grays Harbor.

Quinault Indian Agent report 1862

** Only one agency building has thus far been erected (*on Bakers Prairie*), and no improvement in the way of farming has yet been done.

August 1862

1 *Fontleroy* having sounded the Grays Harbor bar, reports fourteen feet of water at lowest tide.

September 1862

1 Isaac Stevens is killed as Union Forces fall in the Second Battle of Bull Run.

17 The one day Battle of Antietam leaves 20,000 dead or wounded.

22 President Lincoln issues the preliminary Emancipation Proclamation.

December 1862

13 Fredericksburg leaves 17,000 casualties.

~ 1863 ~

January 1863

1 The Emancipation Proclamation takes effect.

1 The Homestead Act becomes effective throughout the frontier.

March 1863

3 Enrollment Act: first U.S. military draft.

14 Michael Luark moves his family into cabin near current site of Montesano. He soon builds the first grist mill in the county.

June 1863

20 West Virginia admitted to the Union.

1 Battle of Gettysburg; 51,000 killed or wounded. Turning point of the war (1-3).

4 Siege at Vicksburg, Mississippi *(which began on May 22)* comes to an end. Gives control of the Mississippi River to the Union.

26 Sam Williams and his horse team wreck while transporting Territorial Governor William Pickering, C.H. Hale, superintendent of Indian affairs, and Dr. A.G. Henry, surveyor general to Shoalwater Bay, to settle separation between Pacific and Chehalis counties.

Indian Agent report 1863

** Superintendent Hale recommends that the Indian agency be located at the mouth of the "Quinaielt river" instead of on (Bakers) prairie as it is too wet even in the dry season.

October 1863

3 Lincoln proclaims the last Thursday in November a Thanksgiving Day.

3 Schooner *Brant* arrives on Grays Harbor from Puget Sound.

November 1863

19 Lincoln delivers Gettysburg Address commemorating national cemetery at Gettysburg battlefield.

23 Battle of Chattanooga (23-25); Provides jumping-off place for Sherman's March through Georgia.

December 1863

10 *The Seattle Gazette* begins publication.

~ 1864 ~

January 1864

13 Composer Stephen Foster dies.

February 1864

17 The submarine *H. L. Hunley*, torpedoes a federal ship in Charleston Harbor, but she goes down with her crew.

May 1864

7 General Sherman begins his drive through Georgia to Atlanta.

July 1864

2 President Lincoln signs bill creating the Northern Pacific Railway.

Indian Agent report 1864

** At the Qui-nai-elt agency, which has moved to the mouth of the Qui-nai-elt River, new buildings are in process of erection and some land has been fenced and cleared. The loss of a portion of lumber, shipped to that point of June last, will embarrass for a while the progress of that agency.

September 1864

3 Sherman occupies Atlanta and much of the city is burned.

October 1864

26 Western Union complete its first telegraph line to Seattle.

31 Nevada is admitted to the Union.

November 1864

8 Lincoln wins the Presidential contest by a slim margin.

16 Sherman begins his march across Georgia to Savannah and the sea.

December 1864

22 Sherman reaches Savannah, bisecting the South horizontally.

25 Job Carr, Jr., decides on a homestead on the northern side of the Point Defiance Peninsula.

~ 1865 ~

January 1865

16 Sherman begins campaign in Carolinas, which causes even more destruction than in Georgia.

31 Congress passes thirteenth Amendment, barring slavery in the United States.

March 1865

4 Lincoln is inaugurated for second term "With malice toward none; with charity for all..."

April 1865

8 Grant and Lee meet at Appomattox.

12 Army of Northern Virginia formally lay down arms.

14 John Wilkes Booth shoots Abraham Lincoln.

15 Lincoln dies, Johnson becomes president.

26 Booth trapped and killed in barn near Bowling Green, Virginia.

27 Worst ship disaster in U.S. history when the steamship *Sultana* explodes on the Mississippi River. Of the 1,700 killed, most are Union soldiers returning from Southern prisons.

May 1865

10 Jefferson Davis captured and President Johnson declares Civil War at an end.

13 Confederate forces west of the Mississippi River surrender. 360,000 Union men and 135,000 Confederate men were killed during the war.

Special Note:

(The twelve years following the Civil War are some of the most controversial in American history. The theory that American government rested upon states rights gave way to the omnipotent federal government.

The west shared in phenomenal postwar expansion and rapid railroad construction. Immigration from Scandinavian countries soared. The nation focused on the demobilization of the armies in the south and north and got back to the business of making a living with little attention devoted to the reconstruction of the South.

The Civil War led to the collapse of civilization in the south and conditions led to the formation of such organizations as the KKK.)

July 1865

23 Indians, not a part of the treaty, living on Gray's Harbor brought five or six bottles of whiskey from Shoalwater Bay to Quinaielt. Soon after most of the Indians were drunk. They got in a drunken fight resulting in one being killed.

30 *Brother Jonathan* sinks off Crescent City, California carrying 166 passengers, including Port Angeles founder, Victor Smith, to the bottom.

August 1865

5 Joseph Hill, Sub-Indian Agent, Quinaielt Agency

makes his first annual report for the fractional year commencing February 13 and ending June 30, 1865. Most of the Indians live by fishing and hunting. Most of the Indians living on Quinaielt are raising a patch of potatoes on the river bottom, about three miles from the agency, up the river, where there is an abundance of good farm land, after it is once cleared. (*The agent's own potatoes planted at the agency were entirely destroyed by worms.*)

** The Indians here seem disposed to be peaceable, but sometimes rather dissatisfied on the account of the delay in the distribution of their annuities; on the whole, however, there is no room for complaint.

December 1865

17 *Decatur* beaches off-shore, keel-up, three miles south of Point Grenville. Loaded with 300,000 board feet of lumber and 1,000 bundles of lath and shingles.

24 Ku Klux Klan is formed in Tennessee.

25 Union Stock yard open in Chicago. (*Changes the business patterns of the prairies and give rise to Armor and the Swift empires.*)

27 Several men cut hole in the keel of the *Decatur,* but find no sign of the crew.

~ 1866 ~

May 1866

16 Congress authorizes the "nickel."

June 1866

7 Chief Seattle dies.

12 Western Union becomes first U.S. communications monopoly.

July 1866

1 Congress puts tax on State bank notes. (*This leads to an acceptable national currency.*)

Indian Agent report 1866

** Sub-agent Joseph Hill purchased heavy fir for buildings to be built at the Quinaielt agency.

November 1866

** Fifty-foot stern-wheeler, *Satsall,* (Indian name for Black River) launched at Blockhouse. Designed to navigate the shallow waters of the upper Chehalis River.

~ 1867 ~

March 1867

1 Nebraska admitted to the Union.

2 The first Reconstruction Act is passed by Congress over the veto of the president.

30 Secretary of State William H. Stewart arranges for U.S. purchase of Alaska from the Russians for $7,200,000.

June 1867

26 Schooner *A.J. Wester* arrives on Grays Harbor to place five channel buoys.

June 1867

30 Congress ratified the purchase of Alaska.

July 1867

6 *Chehalis* launched at Tumwater.

** Machinery removed from *Satsall (See November 1866)*

and installed in the *Carrie Davis* at Claquato, an important stagecoach community between Olympia and the Columbia River.

Indian Agent report 1867

** "At this time I am having erected at the Quin-ai-elt reservation a good school-house and a house for a teacher, and with the ample accumulated fund will be able to carry on a school without embarrassment."

August 1867

11 *Chehalis* makes first trial run.

25 *Chehalis* enters Grays Harbor (arrived on the 24th but kept at sea because of dense fog).

28 Midway Islands annexed by the U.S.

October 1867

9 General Rousseau of the U.S. Army takes formal possession of the Alaska Territory.

December 1867

21 Sioux in defending their hunting grounds defeat Colonel Fetterman in Montana. Eighty whites are killed and the settlers are furious.

** Ed Campbell gets a permit for a post office in Hoquiam.

~ 1868 ~

January 1868

15 The Columbia River freezes over at Fort Vancouver.

March 1868

16 The Impeachment trial of President Johnson formally begins.

31 Joseph Hill, sub agent at Quinaielt, resigns due to poor health.

May 1868

1 Schooner *Fanny* arrives on Grays Harbor to inspect the buoys placed in the channel in June 1867.

28 Final vote of acquittal formally ends impeachment trial of Johnson.

June 1868

8 Mr. Gordon Henry, son of the late surveyor general of the Territory, and Mrs. Henry, his wife, enter upon duty as teachers of the school at Quinaielt.

8 Congress passes 8-hour day for government employees.

July 1868

9 Weekly mail service begins between Olympia and Chehalis Point.

28 A treaty between China and the U.S. is concluded. Protects the rights for citizens to migrate freely between the two countries.

Indian Agent report 1868

** Wah Kinos, the head Quinaielt chief, refused to let his children be taught, and used his influence to keep others from the school fearing that the children would be taken away and put into slavery. These problems have been overcome by the new sub-agent, Mr. Henry Winsor. (*Wah Kinos, originally lived on Joe Creek [present day site of Pacific Beach] and moved to the mouth of the Quinault with the arrival of the agents.*)

** A decision is made to move the agency from the mouth of the Quinaielt River back to the prairie (*Bakers*). The agent felt that the prairie could be drained to provide good agriculture land and that plants reported to be poisonous do not exist.

August 1868

** E. T. Coleman makes first ascent of Mt. Baker.

13 Morton Matthew McCarver completes survey for a town he plans to call Commencement City (*Tacoma*).

1868

** A. O. Damon arrives between 1868-1870 to establish a post at Oyehut (*the place to cross over*). (*It becomes the favorite freight-handling spot for the North Beach area once the long pier was built to deep water. This was the south end of the wagon route used by Ben Grigsby and David Bileau to ferry passengers and supplies between Taholah and Oyehut. The distance between the bay and the ocean in the 1800's was much shorter than today [1997].*)

Sword fern in a stand of old growth Douglas-fir.

October 1868

** Commencement City changed to Tacoma on McCarver's map, but not filed. (*The name "Tacoma" was inspired by the book* The Canoe and the Saddle *by Theodore Winthrop; the Indian name for Mount Rainier. This book, published shortly after the Civil War is also credited for many moving from the East to the Northwest.*)

November 1868

3 Grant wins in presidential landslide victory.

6 End of first Sioux war. (*Under the treaty, the Sioux think the county is theirs, but the treaty stipulates the Sioux may use it until the U.S. wants it.*)

23 The Seattle *Intelligencer* refers to the new town of Tacoma.

30 Anthony Carr names and files his claim as Tacoma.

December 1868

25 President Johnson gives amnesty to all parties in the Confederate Rebellion as one of his last acts in office.

~ 1869 ~

January 1869

19 The American Equal Rights Association meets in Washington D.C. (*Beginnings of an organized women's movement.*)

March 1869

4 Ulysses Grant inaugurated President of the U.S.

25 Tacoma gets its first post office.

May 1869

10 First transcontinental railroad is completed and ceremony is held at Promontory Point in Utah.

Indian Agent report 1869

** "There is some feeling of jealousy on the Indians' part about the white sea-otter hunters who trespass upon the hunting grounds of the Quinaeilt reservation."

** "The chief source of revenue to these Indians (*Quinault*) is fur and fish. The finest salmon known on this coast are those found in the Quinaielt River; and, with some encouragement, a profitable business could be done in fishing by these Indians."

** "Thomas Hay deems it all important that the (Quinault) children learn and understand and speak 'our language' as soon as possible."

July 1869

13 Riots against the Chinese in San Francisco.

August 1869

26 Thomas H. Hay relieves Henry Winsor as sub-agent of the Quinaielt Indian Agency.

September 1869

24 Price of gold plunges; Black Friday.

1869

** First Olympia city hall and library built.

~ 1870 ~

January 1870

10 Standard Oil Company of Ohio incorporates.

15 The Democratic Party represented for the first time by a donkey in a cartoon by Thomas Nast in *Harper's Weekly*.

February 1870

9 National Weather Bureau is established by Congress.

12 Women in Utah Territory granted the right to vote.

25 Hiram R. Revels, the first black to be elected to the U.S. Senate, takes his seat.

June 1870

22 Congress establishes the Department of Justice.

Indian Agent report 1870

** "Crops planted on the river clearing are excellent while those planted at 'The Anderson house' are tolerable and those planted on the prairie (*Bakers*) were a total failure."

** "The Quinaielt agency is a clearing of 10 acres of land, generally of poor quality. The buildings are a block-house of two stories (the lower used as a jail and store room, the upper as office and quarters of the physician;) houses for the teacher, blacksmith, and a carpenter, agent's office, school-house, sheds, and a building for shops, the latter and the teacher's house being of two-inch fir lumber, the others of logs."

** "The road over Point 'Greenville' has been entirely rebuilt, and is now in good order. A road has been made from the beach to the agency, which saves half a mile of heavy traveling over loose ground and shifting sands."

** "The physician, Dr. Johnson, conducts his affairs with intelligence, skill, and success. The confidence of the Indians in his treatment is increasing daily, and they are gradually abandoning their ta-mah-no-as doctors."

** "The salmon this season are plenty and of superior quality."

July 1870

24 First rail car arrives in New York from the Pacific coast.

August 1870

1 Women vote for the first time in U.S. history in an election in Utah Territory.

** First official climb of Mt. Rainier by Hazard Stevens and Phileman Van Trumps.

October 1870

12 General Robert E. Lee dies at age 63.

~ 1871 ~

March 1871

3 Indian Appropriation Act; tribes no longer regarded as independent entities, but declared wards of the State. Whole reservations are divided among a number of religious groups. (*In two years the religious groups would be ousted and replaced with Indian agencies and a return to the spoils system of government.*)

13 George W. Byrd takes charge of the agency school at Quinaielt.

31 G. A. Henry relieves Thomas Hay as the sub-agent at Quinaielt.

April 1871

10 P.T. Barnum opens a circus in Brooklyn.

May 1871

8 Treaty of Washington. (*One of the six subjects included the settlement of the land dispute at San Juan Island. [See February - October 1859].*)

Indian Agent report, September 1871

** "The road over Point 'Greenville' is impassable during most of the winter for wagons, being washed by the heavy tides and storms where it leaves the beach, so that teams cannot get up or down."

11 "This agency *(Quinault)* is under charge of the Methodist, G. A. Henry sub-agent an earnest, Christian man."

October 1871

8 Great Chicago Fire (8-9).

8 Peshtigo, Wisconsin forest fire. (*An estimated 1,500 people killed and 1.3 million acres of timber land scorched*).

November 1871

24 National Rifle Association (NRA) incorporates.

25 Last British officers and men removed from San Juan Island. (*See May 1871.*)

~ 1872 ~

March 1872

1 Yellowstone is established as first U.S. National Park.

Indian Agent report, Summer 1872

** "Six houses built at the Quinaielt agency by the Indians. It is about a hundred miles to the nearest saw-mill, but fortunately a vessel load of lumber was wrecked on the coast of the reservation a few years ago and blown ashore, and has furnished all the lumber needed."

Summer 1872

** Commercial killing of buffalo begins. (*Nearly 3 million killed each year for their hides only, completely destroying the economic base of the plains Indians. By 1883 only 200 exist in all of west. Many buffalo were killed in the 1840's and 50's along the Oregon Trail.*)

Quinaielt Indian Agency annual report made by G.A. Henry. September 1, 1872

** "They are leaving off many of their savage habits and adopting those of civilization in dress and ways of living."

** "Crops deemed a failure due to extreme drought and early frost."

** "I am convinced, after repeated trials, that the soil of this reservation is of such inferior quality that farming cannot be successfully carried on, and that the Indians must depend chiefly upon the salmon and other fish which they have in great abundance most of the year."

September 1872

** Commissioner of Indian Affairs recommends the enlargement of the Quinaielt Reservation to include the mouth of the Queets River and Quinaielt Lake.

1872

** Northern Pacific establishes a station at Tenino. (*There are many sources which differ on where the name Tenino comes from; the survey stake which had the numbers 10-9-0 marked on it, the number of a locomotive. But, in fact, the railroad used the Chinook word meaning "Junction" in the naming of its station at Tenino.*)

Indian Agent report, Winter 1872

** "Road ascending Point Granville Mountain (*Point Grenville*) entirely washed away by heavy storms and the action of the sea. This is the usual situation and the road cannot be repaid until the storms and high tides of winter are over. This is a constant source of expense which cannot be avoided; for these reasons it is necessary to have supplies for the winter and spring laid up by the last of October."

December 1872

14 Strong earthquake felt on Puget Sound.

~ 1873 ~

August 1873

1 Cable cars first used in San Francisco.

16 First issue of the *Weekly Pacific Tribune* in Tacoma

September 1873

1 G.A. Henry, in his annual Quinaeilt report, describes a trip up the "Quinaielt" River to the Lake, with Lieut. S.R. Jones, United States Army. "The purpose of the trip was to look at the country for enlargement of the reservation. It was felt there was not much farm land and that the Indians should have a larger reservation for a hunting and fishing area. Indians from the Columbia River northward would be included in the enlarged reservation."

** Henry reported that he need the assistance of Lieut. S.R. Jones and a detachment of 23 men to arrest two Indians for disobedience brought on when he took a child out of a head press.

18 Panic of 1873 brought on by failure of Jay Cooke and Company brokerage firm due to over speculating in railroad construction and agricultural over-expansion. (*Brings on five years of depression and leads to failure of many state banks, but ultimately strengthens national banking system.*)

October 1873

19 Clouds of smoke pour from the highest peak of Mount Rainier. (*Last for nearly a week.*)

27 General Canby is killed while negotiating with the Modoc Indians in Oregon setting off an Indian war.

December 1873

16 The last spike driven at 3 p.m. in New Tacoma, connects the railroad to Kalma.

~ 1874 ~

June 1874

22 Congressional Act requires all able-bodied male Indians, between the ages of 18 and 45 to preform services upon the reservation in payment for supplies.

Summer 1874

** School vacation at Quinaielt in July and August allow the children to assist their parents in gathering and drying a supply of berries for winter use.

September 1874

1 G.A Henry in his annual Quinaielt report notes that it is his Christian duty to assist the Indians in every way possible. He said that there are not more than five families of settlers in the country and their letters assure him that the Indians are not troublesome, but in many ways are of assistance to them.

November 1874

7 Republican Party symbolized as an elephant in a cartoon drawn by Thomas Nast in *Harper's Weekly.*

25 Barbed wire patent issued.

~ 1875 ~

January 1875

9 The Columbia River freezes over.

September 1875

1 G.A. Henry in his fourth Quinaielt, reports that "quite a number of Indians can speak the English language, but none can talk it well." He notes that many of the Indians travel to Shoalwater Bay and are employed at oystering making as much as $3 per day.

1876

March 1876

10 Alexander Graham Bell demonstrates telephone (March 7 patent).

April 1876

2 National League Baseball plays its first official game. Boston beats Philadelphia 6 to 5.

May 1876

10 Centennial Exposition opens in Philadelphia.

June 1876

25 Battle of Little Bighorn; "Custer's Last Stand". (*See October 31.*)

August 1876

24 G.A Henry presents a very discouraging account about the agency in his annual Quinaeilt report.

October 1876

6 American Library Association established and Melville Dewey introduces Dewey decimal system for cataloguing library books.

31 Sioux are forced to surrender.

~ 1877 ~

April 1877

7 *The Tacoma Herald* begins publication.

June 1877

** Nez Percé battle the Army in Idaho. Chief Joseph and his people surrender close to the Canadian border on October 5, 1877.

14 First Flag Day; commemorates the 100th anniversary of the flag of the U.S.

July 1877

14 Great strike of 1877 begins as workers walk out on the Baltimore and Ohio Railroad. Strikes, some turning violent, spread during the month.

August 1877

6 G.A. Henry in his annual Quinaelt report says that many of the Indians' living quarters compare favorably with the ordinary class of pioneer farmers. Most of the supplies for the agency come by wagon, canoes, and sail-boats from Portland via Tenino some 259 miles. The average cost of transport is about $45 per ton to Point Brown, where all agency goods are landed.

~ 1878 ~

1878

** Logging begins on the Wishkah, the first valley exploited for its timber resources.

February 1878

19 Thomas Edison receives patent for phonograph.

21 First telephone directory issued in New Haven, Connecticut.

April 1878

1 Oliver Wood takes charge of The Quinaielt Agency.

May 1878

** Yellow fever brought from Havana, sweeping Southeast U.S.

June 1878

3 Timber and Stone Act permits 160 acre purchase of lands "valuable chiefly for timber" for $2.50 an acre. (*Using alien seamen to make dummy purchases, timber barons acquire 3.6 million acres of choice forest lands by 1900.*)

11 District of Columbia government set up by Congress.

July 1878

** First 15 miles of narrow gauge railroad laid down between Olympia and Tenio.

August 1878

1 Free rides on the new train from Olympia to Tenino and back.

October 1878

15 Edison Electric Light Company established in New York City. (*He still had yet to develop the light bulb.*)

~ 1879 ~

May 1879

7 California adds measure of prohibiting employment of Chinese workers.

Exodus 1879

** Mass migration of blacks from the South to Kansas.

August 1879

28 Agent Oliver Wood makes his second annual report on the Quinaielt agency. He notes that the farmer and team are kept busy a large part of the time hauling supplies from Gray's Harbor to the agency and that he does not have much time to work with the Indians or direct them in their work. He states that he requires the Indians to gather up all the lumber that is washed on the beach by the tides and that the Indians have been instructed in making shingles.

** "Crops raised at the Quinaeilt agency: potatoes, rutabaga, turnips, carrots, beets, onions, and peas. Oats do not ripen enough to thrash and are cut and mixed with mill-feed for the team. Grew about 25 tons of hay this year."

December 1879

31 Edison gives public demonstration of incandescent electric bulb.

~ 1880 ~

March 1880

24 First U.S. Salvation Army missions founded.

August 1880

** Oliver Wood, U.S. Indian Agent, in his third annual Quinaielt report writes, "The Methodist Church, to which this agency has been assigned, has never made any effort toward missionary work in any form, and the only contributions made were by the employees for such books as were necessary for Sunday-school purposes."

~ 1881 ~

May 1881

21 American Red Cross is organized by Clara Barton.

July 1881

2 President Garfield is shot. (*Dies on September 19 from blood poisoning.*)

August 1881

22 Oliver Wood reports that agriculture is greater among the Quinaielts than any other tribe belonging to this agency. During the sealing season all the Hoh Indians able to work in a canoe are engaged in sealing and obtain most of their means of living from this source; their sales of seal skins this year amounted to over $1,200.

~ 1882 ~

Spring 1882

** *Orient* arrives with equipment and men for George Emerson's saw mill. (*He was an agent for A.M. Simpson of San Francisco.*)

May 1882

18 The principle business block of Olympia burns.

August 1882

** Oliver Wood submits his fifth annual report for the Quinaielt Agency. It is a very discouraging report and he ends it saying, "I would be happy to make a better showing, but the facts will not allow it, and rose-colored statements are not wanted."

September 1882

4 Edison's steam powered station begins to supply electricity and New York City begins to glimmer with an incandescent glow.

5 New York is site of first Labor Day Parade.

** Emerson's sawmill (*North Western Lumber Company*) begins operation.

October 1882

1 Robert M. Rylatt begins as teacher at the Quinaielt Agency.

** *Orient* loads first lumber cargo from Grays Harbor (*North Western Lumber Company*) to San Francisco.

November 1882

9 *Chehalis (which worked the Chehalis River 1867-69)* is wrecked in stormy conditions near Ten Mile Point on Puget Sound.

December 1882

11 Boston's Bijou Theater is first theater lit with electric lights.

~ 1883 ~

1883

** Hoquiam's North Western Mill has first electric light on the Harbor.

February 1883

1 *The Chehalis County Vidette* debuts in Montesano.

1 Medcalf Brothers to milk 100 cows this summer.

1 New salmon cannery being built on the north side of the Chehalis River near Cosmopolis.

15 Emerson's Mill in Hoquiam is cutting 40,000' of timber per day. Should be up to 80,000' by the spring.

15 If travel increases to any extent this season, the Satsop River will have to be bridged.

22 Boom of logs, containing 20,000' from Cowan's camp, was towed to the Hoquiam mill the other day.

22 The people of Hoquiam are going to organize a Sunday School.

March 1883

1 Mr. Arch Campbell complains about the wretched Postal facilities at Humptulips. He has to employ an Indian to carry the mail from Peterson's Point and that his letters cost him 25 cents each.

8 The Government has placed five buoys at the entrance to Grays Harbor.

9 A subscription to the weekly Olympia newspaper, *Washington Standard,* is $3.00 per annum.

14 Karl Marx dies in London.

22 "We are of the opinion that the Chehalis bottoms near Montesano grow potatoes that beat the world." *The Chehalis County Vidette*

April 1883

12 A large number of passengers came in on the *Miles* last trip. Most were land hunters from the East.

26 *Iowa* a new 60' steamer stern wheeler launched last Tuesday at Montesano. It has a 15' beam and draws 12".

Indian Agent report, 1883

** "The trader, John W. Hume, is greeting suitable buildings for canning the salmon and this will give employment to all adult Indians during the fishing seasons. The Quinaielt River has a greater abundance of salmon, and of better quality than any stream of its size on the coast, and the Indians are highly elated at the prospect of having more constant employment and better pay than ever before."

May 1883

10 "Montesano is booming and don't you forget it."

10 Logs are plenty in Hoquiam and the mill is running on full time.

25 Brooklyn Bridge officially opens.

31 U.S. surveying schooner *Ernest* is now on Grays Harbor engaged in making a government survey of that body of water. "Look out ye falsifiers who burdened the past history of this fine body of water with malicious representations." *The Chehalis County Vidette*

June 1883

7 Six elk were killed by Indians on South Bay last week.

7 Some settlers on Wishkah have started Hop yards.

7 Dr. Price, who has been stationed at the Quiniault Indian Reservation, has resigned and gone to his place on the Quillayute.

14 2,000 acres have been brought in Chehalis Valley in past two weeks. Others waiting until certain lines are established.

19 Woods are full of land hunters now.

28 Mrs. Andrew Smith of the Quiniault Agency at Montesano for a two week visit.

July 1883

5 Barber and bake shops have opened in Montesano.

5 Heavy fire on the road between Olympia and Montesano.

26 North Pacific Railroad Company (N.P.R.R. Co.)

August 1883

2 Its so smoky in Elma, they can taste the smoke. The drought continues.

3 R. M. Rylatt, teacher in charge at the Quinaielt Agency, makes the annual report. There is an average of 25 children at the agency school.

9 An ox was killed at Perkin's camp. The log road is very rough and the animal stumbling, feel and broke its neck.

23 A fine vein of coal has been found near Elma.

30 Two hundred new piles are being driven at Hoquiam for wharf, boom and buoy purposes.

September 1883

3 Railroad to Tacoma completed via Portland as last rail laid at the confluence of Gold Creek and the Clark Fork of the Columbia River in Montana. (*This completes the transcontinental railroad.*)

7 The Government employees now coming down the Chehalis from the big drift near Oakville are making rapid progress and doing very good work in the line of removing snags and small drifts.

21 Fifteen buildings going up in Montesano now and several others will be built when lumber can be obtained.

October 1883

11 The *Miles* carried away 100 cases of salmon from the Aberdeen cannery.

11 The largest shipment of merchandise ever trade to this county was received at the Hoquiam store recently by the schooner *Wing and Wing*. It consisted of over $9,000 worth of goods.

25 Emerson's new steamer *Argo* is in the Harbor and she is said to be a very neat appearing craft.

27 Twelve hundred salmon were canned at Wishkah and the Cosmopolis Cannery also did a rushing business.

November 1883

8 The Cosmopolis Mill is fairly getting down to business.

15 Land is rapidly being taken up on the Wishkah.

18 Standard time zones adopted by U.S. and Canadian railroads (*See March 13, 1884*).

22 The women's suffrage bill has become law in Montesano, having passed the council by vote of 7 to 5.

29 The road between Montesano and Olympia is now in horrible condition.

29 Wishkah Lumbering Company has platted a townsite with 100 lots at the mouth of the Wishkah River.

December 1883

6 Wagons are not running between Hoquiam and Olympia this week.

8 Charles Willoughby, Indian Agent, arrives at "Quinaielt village." Gale inundated village soon after his arrival.

18 Plat for the city of Wishkah filed (Aberdeen).

20 After a considerable delay on account of a broken shaft, the Cosmopolis Mill started up again.

~ 1884 ~

January 1884

10 A great boom at Wishkah now.

17 Report of Chief engineer of the Army seeks $5,000 to clear Chehalis River of snags and drifts.

February 1884

7 Five saw mills at work in Chehalis and Grays Harbor regions. Settlers are taking up agricultural lands and capitalists its timber lands and mill sites.

14 Snow fell to a depth of one foot last week. It reminds one of an old bachelor; sort of cold and crusty.

16 Plat for the town of Aberdeen filed. (*B.A. Seaborg, who ran the Aberdeen fish cannery, suggested the name to Sam Benn as it meant "meeting of two rivers" The name "Aberdeen" was also applied to excellent Scotland salmon and Seaborg expected this to help his sales for the plant he was building.*)

21 "Dinna Ye Hear the Slogan? Aberdeen, the embryo Chicago of the Pacific Northwest". (*First reference to the town of Aberdeen in The Chehalis County Vidette.*)

28 North Western Lumber Company files for incorporation.

March 1884

6 Tools and part of the workmen are now upon the ground selected for the Satsop bridge.

13 Standard Time adopted throughout the U.S. (*See November 18, 1883.*)

20 Indications is that there will be a big boom in Aberdeen this summer.

20 Harry W. Wetheral, the crack shot and chess player of North Beach, has sold his interest in the sea otter business including the famous rock to Mr. Grover and McIntyre.

27 High tide this week and clams are happy.

27 Town plot surveys of Hoquiam are at last complete.

27 Quite an earthquake shock in Hoquiam was noticed about 10:00 p.m. lasting 3 seconds; no damage.

27 First long distance telephone call made; between Boston and New York.

April 1884

4 There are nine rafts tied outside Hoquiam Mill boom in the river and more coming. Lots of logs.

11 Three vessels in Hoquiam at once. This begins to look like a busy seaport.

18 Logging up the Hoquiam River has begun in good earnest. Mack has 25 men and 9 yoke of cattle; Gillis and Murphy each have 10 men and 5 yoke of cattle; and Calder 10 men and 5 yoke of cattle.

May 1884

2 Hoquiam with a population of less then 200, supports 2 saloons.

2 Satsop bridge picnic. 170 foot span (800 feet with approaches) opens.

9 Mr. Campbell has been granted a license to ferry the Hoquiam River.

17 Organic Act organizes Alaska Territory under laws of Oregon.

23 Cosmopolis Mill is averaging 20,000 feet per day.

30 Sometimes there are 5 or 6 steamboats at the Hoquiam wharves everyday.

June 1884

3 Eleven head of cattle arrive at the Quinaielt Agency.

6 Indians are busy engaged catching sturgeon on the Harbor. They get $2.00 apiece.

8 A.J. West arrives aboard the *Groernor Newell* on Grays Harbor with his family. (*He starts third sawmill on the Harbor.*)

20 Eight rafts of logs lying in sight, with more to come to the Hoquiam Mill.

July 1884

13 73,000 feet of lumber cut made at Hoquiam is largest ever made in one day.

24 Montesano money order office is now in operation.

** West cuts his first lumber. (*See June 8, 1884.*)

26 Charles Willoughby, Indian Agent makes his first Quinaielt Agency report. Highlights include:
First mentioning of a "boarding school" at the Quinaielt Agency (L. Lefevre, teacher). He notes that it is difficult to keep the children from the Indian ranches. Five children have died since December 1, all of "inherited and incurable diseases."

The trader has removed his goods, as the store was not profitable.

As a tribe, these Indians are peaceable and easily governed.

31 The Wishkah and E Street wharf is nearing completion in Aberdeen.

August 1884

5 Cornerstone laid for the Statue of Liberty.

14 Weatherwax Bros are doing immense amount of work on their new mill site in Aberdeen. The West Mill whistle will soon be heard in town.

21 The Pioneer Restaurant of Aberdeen is now open serving meals at all hours.

September 1884

18 60 Republican votes in Aberdeen.

25 Fleas are thick in Hoquiam, but candidates for office are thicker.

October 1884

2 Hoquiam Mill is idle, awaiting orders.

9 Lumber selling for $9.00 a thousand in San Francisco.

30 Pile driving has been completed for the Weatherwax Bros Wharf.

November 1884

6 18 ladies vote at Hoquiam on election day.

13 Captain Willoughby and Dr. Price report clearing of ground at Granville for erection of the new school house and agent's quarters upon the new and desirable location, recently chosen for that purpose by the Government.

December 1884

11 Jack Frost is with us again. 20° F. and beautiful 6" snow.

20 The schooner *Webfoot* carries the broom, having made the quickest trip from San Francisco to Grays Harbor. It left morning of December 17 and arrived off the bar on December 20.

25 Sleigh riding, which is suppose to be a decided novelty of this country, has been quite the rage with the young people the past ten days.

31 Owing to vast amount of snow and sleet, it has been slow work loading the vessels at Hoquiam Wharves.

1884

** David Shelton lays out Sheltonville (*Shelton).*

~ 1885 ~

January 1885

5 The recent snow fall which has covered the ground for the past two weeks, disappeared under the Chinook wind and rain. Rivers are higher than ever remembered.

5 Satsop bridge, built last season, was carried away and probably entirely destroyed.

12 Most vigorous freshets known in Chehalis Valley since its settlement by whites. A.J. Smith said is was high in 1868.

17 10,575,511 feet cut in 1884 by the Hoquiam Mill.

February 1885

1 Two rival groups of Chinese get into fight in Eureka, California. When a white councilman is shot in the head, the Chinese declared a menace. (*This leads to anti-Chinese feelings in Puget Sound cities later in the year.*)

6 *Kate and Ann* sailed for Portland with 30 tons of freight and will finish out with a load of Oysters from Shoalwater Bay.

7 The song of frogs and bright sunshine reminds us that spring time has come.

7 Aberdeen favored by having a lady post mistress.

12 We are reminded of the poor mail service on the Olympia-Montesano route.

17 Montesano citizens are taking steps to bring a stream of fine spring water from high ground north of town.

21 Another week of stormy weather

21 Washington Monument dedication.

21 A ten-foot sidewalk is being laid the entire length of Heron Street in Aberdeen. Talk of erecting a church soon.

26 There is every prospect that the coming year will witness a wonderful tide of immigration into the Northwest country.

26 Chas. McIntyre of Copalis Rock, of sea otter fame, says he and his partners have only eleven pelts this season against thirteen of last and that the prospect for the future is not all flattering.

26 J. W. Walsh turns management and control of *The Chehalis County Vidette* over to his successor, A. D. Bowen.

26 Aberdeen now boast a barber shop.

March 1885

12 Three saloons and three hotels in running order in Aberdeen.

19 *The Vidette* will be issued on Friday instead of Thursday in the future.

19 The last issue of *The Grays Harbor News.*

26 Eastman Dry Plate and Film Company produces first commercial motion picture film.

April 1885

1 Coal discovered near Aberdeen.

13 *North Bend* sails for San Francisco and carries first consignment of hops ever shipped from Grays Harbor.

15 Mail was carried on horseback to Montesano today due to obstruction on road.

22 The agitation of telephone lines between Montesano and Olympia continues. "All we need is the wire and we will be all fixed."

22 A. M. Skeen has started a log camp on the Wishkah River and says there is excellent timber on the river.

22 The skating rink in Montesano's Columbia Hall is run every other week. The skates are taken down to Cosmopolis and Hoquiam every other week.

29 Dr. Price, for some time the physician at the Quinault Indian Reservation, has moved to James Point on the harbor to start a chicken ranch.

29 Land is being cleared all along the Chehalis and its tributaries.

May 1885

13 The Satsop bridge only required 48,000 feet of timber. The rest is of iron. Only the elevated road to the river needs be completed.

13 Machinery for Weatherwax's sawmill arrived on the *Lottie Carson* out of New York.

30 Satsop bridge opens to public.

June 1885

10 Three men who robbed the Montesano Stage are now in jail.

10 Heron Street in Aberdeen is being cleared of obstructions in the form of stumps, logs, etc.

24 Various camps on the river and Harbor are putting in large numbers of logs in the water these days.

24 John Eaton started a saloon in Montesano: the town's large majority temperance group have instructed foreman of adjacent logging camps to dispense with the services of any man found hanging around it.

July 1885

2 On Monday night, forest fires were raging in several directions lighting up the horizon and presenting a pretty picture to all who viewed them in Montesano.

6 Orders authorize U.S. expeditions into the Olympic Mountains, issued.

16 Dr. L.C. Toney from Southern Illinois, who received the appointment as physician to the Quinault Indian reservation, is on his way to his post.

16 Lieutenant O'Neil's U.S. Army Expedition of Olympic Mountains leaves Port Townsend to begin trek.

16 Alex Polson has been appointed deputy lumber inspector.

23 A new game called "Wynooche" has been engaging the leisure time of young men. Fred Mathews holds the belt.

30 Mr. Wade says he has several acres of seven-foot timothy.

30 Logging camps are all shut down. Logs have fallen to 50 cents per thousand.

August 1885

4 Montesano elevated road dedication.

5 In his second annual Quinaielt Agency Report, Charles Willoughby says that forest fires have erased some boundary markers and that whites may be encroaching on the southern boundary of the reservation.

6 Forest fires raging on the upper Wynooche.

13 Governor Squires visits Aberdeen on Thursday.

13 Four sea otter skins were brought up for sale. Otter hunting has not been profitable this season.

20 A.J West's mill is kept running full time on local orders.

Looking west over the Chehalis River, Grays Harbor, and the Pacific Ocean.

26 O'Neil's expedition abandoned when O'Neil given new orders.

27 An encampment of the Champions of the Red Cross was organized recently in Hoquiam.

27 A rancher says not to take your fruit or anything else to Aberdeen as they are only paying $2.50 a bushel for plums.

September 1885

7 Anti-Chinese violence begins in King County when several men shoot into the tents of Chinese hop pickers, killing three of them.

10 Fisherman on the Harbor are reporting a great catch. The cannery is running day and night.

17 "It is being demonstrated time and again that no better fruit and vegetable country exists in the world than the Chehalis Valley."

24 The Elma Fair held on the 17th and 18th is pronounced a complete success.

October 1885

2 Aberdeen Cannery has been kept busy and the managers have been obligated to restrict the boats to a certain number, the catch being in excess of their capacity for canning.

3 Chinese ordered out of Tacoma by November 1st.

5 The *Oregon* strikes a whale which becomes lodged in the propeller arch, while off Tillamook.

9 Aberdeen Cannery says that every haul of the net brings large quantities of shad, flounder, trout and sturgeon, but the fisherman have no use for them and they are put back into the water. Here is another source of industry awaiting the hand of enterprise.

9 Earthquake in Olympia.

16 Mark Walker has taken up his abode on the Humptulips, where other families expect to go soon.

16 It is the unanimous decision of the bar captains that the Grays Harbor bar is the best on the Pacific coast.

November 1885

7 The transcontinental Canadian Pacific Railway completed. The last spike driven is at Craigellanhie.

13 Quite an influx of immigrants into Grays Harbor from the East and Texas.

20 The Aberdeen cannery has been shut down for the season after not a very successful season. The run of the first salmon were good, but the silver sides failed to put in an appearance. 8,000 cases was put up and shipped to San Francisco.

20 All the mills are running again.

26 Highest tide of the season last Tuesday overflowed lands here-to-fore considered above the high water mark.

26 Not to be behind the times, Geo. Geissler has put a cover on his stage and his passengers can ride between Olympia and Montesano with a dry skin.

December 1885

1 British shipwreck at Point Grenville. (*See March 9, 1937.*)

24 Mail unusually heavy in Montesano on Monday night, there being over 2,000 papers and 400 letters, all of which Postmaster Bush distributed inside 20 minutes.

~ 1886 ~

January 1886

15 It is reported that the Northern Pacific is making extensive sales of timber on public lands in this territory. Commissioner Sparks recommends a suit to recover four million feet of spruce and fir logs cut in this county.

15 "It is evident that the days of the public land grabber are numbered, as every member of the house of representatives who is identified with the battle to save the public domain finds a place upon the committee of public lands, while not a single name on the list is that of a man known to be controlled by land thieves." *The Chehalis County Vidette*

22 The late 10-12" snowstorm has stopped operations in logging camps for some time. It really looks "old-fashioned" to see sleighs and jumpers flying around.

29 R. M. Rylatt, teacher at the Quiniault Reservation said that three weeks ago a large three masted schooner drifted on the ledge of rocks extending out from the Reservation and stranded. No one was aboard and the crew probably perished. Two weeks ago a smaller vessel also went ashore. The beach from Quinault to Cape Flattery is strewn with lumber and wreckage.

February 1886

5 Capt. Willoughby of the Quiniault says the wreck there is that of the *Lizzie Merrill.*

7 Riots amounting to a small war occur against the Chinese in Seattle. At least 400 are forced from their homes and Federal Troops are required to restore order.

26 There are some signs of activity among loggers in Hoquiam.

March 1886

12 Dr. Tony of the Economic Ornithology Department at Washington, sent a large box from the Quiniault Reservation containing specimen of birds, animals, and fish common to this region.

19 H.G. Blodgett of North Beach, is on his way to Harrisburg, Oregon for the purpose of making several machines for the extraction of gold from the black sand on the coast. He has worked for twelve years on such a machine and only recently arrived at a solution to the problem.

19 Government to be in Montesano. (*Vote was between Montesano, lower Montesano and Cosmopolis.*)

26 County property moved to new quarters on Thursday.

April 1886

9 Lumber is now shipped from California to Chicago. "When this valley *(Chehalis)* secures a railroad to the east, as it will in a comparatively short time, Grays Harbor lumber will become a regular commodity in the eastern market."

30 The crew at the life saving station of Shoalwater Bay were out practicing last week and their boat capsized placing them in imminent peril. Capt. Streams went to their rescue.

May 1886

21 "A good indication that the backbone of hard times is broken is the fact that all laboring men who desire employment are readily obtaining it."

28 Dr, Cotel has gone to the beach to test a new invention for the extraction of gold from black sand.

1886

** CY Blackwell has a dam on the Wishkah.

June 1886

18 A cedar stump was found near Oakville 23' in diameter.

18 The Hoquiam Mill Co. has commenced erection of a four masted schooner.

25 Two years ago there were scarcely fifty stands of bees in the county, there are now over 500.

30 Division of Forestry to be part of the Department of Agriculture; approved by Congress.

July 1886

2 Timberland seems to be in demand. Several parties have been interviewing our real estate agents.

9 The official vote on prohibition in Chehalis County was 417 for and 206 against.

23 The thermometer has taken a stroll up into the nineties.

August 1886

** *Highlights of the Quinaielt Agency report by Charles Willoughby:*

"There is a day school in Queets with an Indian teacher. The Quinaielts are under the immediate eye of the agent and his employees. They still have a strong belief in the medicine-man (Ta-mah-no-as). Many of the Indians on Gray's Harbor labor for the whites. Not a foot of lumber has reached the Quinaielt agency for a number of years. Communication is poor due especially to the dangerous high bluff (Point Grenville) that must be crossed. There has been distemper in the horses. Whites are pressing hard on the reservation boundary to the south. There are seven white and three Indians employed by the agency."

13 The light showers of the past few days have rendered the atmosphere delightfully cool and enjoyable.

13 The *Cruiser,* the new mail boat, has taken her place on the Chehalis River-Grays Harbor route.

20 "The impression which prevails that grain will not ripen on the Harbor; all the region will produce in agriculture is grass and roots. We (*Vidette*) think that is erroneous."

20 Heavy rains Monday-Tuesday.

27 The *Cruiser* met with a mechanical accident last Friday and had to transfer the mail to *Argo.*

September 1886

3 Greatest earthquake to hit the United States centers on Charleston, South Carolina.

10 "Aberdeen has organized a hook and ladder company and will immediately proceed to erect a building and purchase the necessary paraphernalia. Aberdeen can boast four saloons, one little church, and no school house. Only eleven days of school since last March and still people say amen." *Vidette*

10 Alex Polson's new house almost completed; finest residence in the county.

17 Eight cougars have been killed on the Satsop this past two weeks. Cougars are working sad havoc among the sheep.

October 1886

11 The fisherman on the Chehalis are on strike. They have been receiving $50 a month, but now demand 20¢ a fish, with board and rigging furnished.

15 Mr. Parsons, special Indian Agent, has been on a tour of inspection to the Quinaielt Agency.

15 The cannery is getting all the fish that is possible for them to take.

15 The material for the newspaper in Aberdeen has arrived.

22 There were seven vessels at one time on the Harbor last week.

22 The first number of *The Aberdeen Herald* is in hand and it presents a very creditable appearance.

28 Statue of Liberty dedicated.

November 1886

5 Quite a heavy frost.

12 The arrival of the full rigged bark *Will Case,* occurred this Saturday last; is indicative of the importance of Grays Harbor. The *Will Case* is the first deep water vessel that has ever floated on our waters.

19 Montesano Stage gets in late on account of bad roads.

19 "The camps have closed down and the boys are full of life, with plenty of money, and their jokes are as free as of yore, and wonder how they will wear away the winter months." *Vidette*

26 There were 894,000 cases of salmon put up this season.

26 Yesterday's heavy rain will help the loggers get out the products of their season's work.

26 Capt. Willoughby, agent at the Quinaielt Reservation, was in Montesano to purchase several head of horses from George Geissler for the Reservation.

December 1886

3 Washington Territory is herself again and rain once more descends in the most copious manner.

3 Over three million feet of logs have formed a jam at the mouth of the Wynooche River.

10 The weather during the past week has been unusually rough.

24 The Chilean schooner *Nellie Dew,* with a load of lumber and leaking badly, runs up on the beach near Oyehut.

31 Loggers are running large number of logs as river stages are just right. Logs selling for $4 per thousand on Grays Harbor.

~ 1887 ~

1887

First steam donkey in Harbor woods according to the book, *The River Pioneers*.

January 1887

21 The weather has changed from bad to worse this week.

28 12° F. All the mills have shut down on account of the severe weather.

February 1887

8 The Dawes Severalty Act is passed by Congress. The Act was to provide allotment of land to each individual Indian and held in Trust by the federal government for a minimum of 25 years. Indians receiving an allotment also become U.S. citizens and will be assimilated into "American life". (*This lead to further cultural disorganization and the allotment of the Quinault Reservation beginning in 1907.*)

11 Snow, frost and no wood is the general cry in most of the towns on the harbor.

18 Quite a little interest was excited in Montesano last week on the advent of a genuine negro, one of the ante bellum days from way down south. The colored person in point, went by the name of John Thomas, and was on a tour of observation. He claimed to be 65 years old, had been a slave until President Lincoln's proclamation gave him his freedom, and had traveled nearly continuously since. He is not a tramp, but paid for what he received, either in money or labor. He'd traveled in every state and territory in the Union, including Alaska, and is now on his way to his old home in Louisiana to end his days." *Vidette*

March 1887

4 On account of the raise of water, the mail has been delayed.

4 Someone is losing a great many logs for the river (*Chehalis*) was full of them running loose this week.

11 We are informed, that if the rain will stop long enough, a bank, store, three houses, and a Methodist church will be erected in Aberdeen.

18 Robert Smith took a raft of logs down the Satsop River for the first time. It was entirely successful. There is a large amount of good timber along this stream. His success will inspire logging on the Satsop.

April 1887

1 Stages have been unable the past week to accommodate travel into the Harbor and several livery teams have bought down loads of new comers.

15 The stages are coming in each night loaded with passengers and freight.

20 Only four miles remain to complete the Northern Pacific Railroad over the (Cascade) mountains.

22 An earthquake shock, heavy enough in places to shake dishes from shelves, was felt in several towns in this Territory.

30 High tide put 6" of water over the wharf in Aberdeen.

May 1887

6 What is claimed to be the heaviest storm of the season occurred last week.

6 The number of new faces in harbor cities would indicate that quite a respectable immigration is now flowing in.

7 Something like a tidal-wave struck the Quinaielt agency at midnight. Some of the Indian houses were waist deep in water, the inmates yelling in terror as they were submerged during sleep on their low sleeping places. The water receded as rapidly as it came, carrying everything portable in its exit.

10 Fog so heavy it is impossible for steamers to run on the harbor.

13 Charlie Arland's logging team on being yoked up for the first time this season frisked about so lively that one of the most valuable oxen in the team, broke his leg, and had to be killed, which will prove quite a loss, as cattle are valuable this season.

20 Mail now arrives at Montesano (from Olympia) over

the river road.

27 A stage route has been established from Centralia to Oakville to connect with the Montesano Stage at the latter place. It will run on Monday, Wednesday and Fridays.

June 1887

3 The wild strawberries have crimson (on them).

17 At Aberdeen, new faces are seen with each arrival of the steamers. The mills are in full operation, though a little short handed.

24 The Montesano Creamery is shipping large quantities of butter down the harbor.

July 1887

3 The first train from St. Paul to Tacoma over the Cascade division of the Northern Pacific Railroad arrives carrying 600 passengers. "Great is the rejoicing of the Tacomaites over the event." (*Trains had arrived since September 1883, but they were routed via Portland. This was the first time a direct route had permitted trains to come directly over the Cascades using a switchback system which served more as intention than an actual route. A tunnel completed in May 1888 would make this a permanent route.*)

7 A large delegation of Indians, from both the upper valley and Harbor, were camped along the river at Montesano this week and seemed to enjoy the celebration as keenly as their brethren of a lighter complexion. They brought some fast horses.

15 Heavy fires here prevailed in the woods this past week.

29 Blackberry parties have been the order.

August 1887

12 Wm Crist has leased the rink at Hoquiam for the purpose of affording the young people of that burg an opportunity to enjoy themselves on the rollers.

14 Willoughby submits his fourth annual Quinaielt Agency report.

19 The Cosmopolis people are forcing a road into the North River country.

September 1887

23 Travel on the (Chehalis) river is now very heavy, each boat having a fair load each trip.

24 Samuel Sanderson, engaged by parties to blow up the bottom of the wreck of the *Sir Jansetjee Family* lying off the Quinault agency on the point of Elizabeth reef, blew off his right hand while experimenting with dynamite on the river in a canoe with some Indian boys.

30 Charles Clemons who recently had a splinter from an iron wedge lodge in this eye, was obliged to have the eye removed.

30 The Quinault River is full of salmon and the Indians are happy.

October 1887

7 Hop picking is over at Elma and the growers pronounce the crop fair for the year.

7 The recent heavy rains took out part of the Weatherwax' dam on Porter Creek.

7 Cosmopolis streets are being macadamized (*pavement of layers*) with saw dust.

28 Canneries have been reaping a full harvest of fish, but as

the dog fish have put in an appearance, the run will in all probability close soon.

November 1887

4 On its last trip to Astoria, the *Gen Miles* took 2,210 cases of salmon from Grays Harbor.

4 The weather has been unusually fine and everything is fresh and bright.

4 Alex Polson, former county assessor, is building a logging road up the Hoquiam.

11 Evidently the rainy season has set in. The heavy rains makes the loggers hunt their driving crews.

13 The stormiest day in the last four years.

16 Aberdeen nearly deserted as everyone has gone to Hoquiam to see the schooner launched.

18 The heavy rains of the past ten days have carried away large quantities of logs. In many cases the result of a whole season's work.

23 A raft of logs belonging to Chas. Arland, escaped to the sea after the *Rustler* was unable to tow it back.

24 Light fall of "beautiful snow" for Thanksgiving.

25 Whoever saw nicer weather than this past week?

December 1887

2 The large number of rafts coming down the Wishkah is ample evidence that the Wishkah is first class logging country.

6 Storm.

8 Heaviest blow of the season.

9 Heavy rains and rise of streams has caused loss of booms and wharfs. Estimate more than two million feet of logs loose on the harbor.

16 The tug *Ranger* arrives at Montesano — to make runs from here to Portland. She has accommodations for passengers, too.

~ 1888 ~

1888

** The *Beaver* runs aground. *(See Spring 1836.)*

January 1888

** The Quinaielt Agent dies very suddenly.

6 Eggs sell for 40¢ a dozen.

6 One can not go down the streets of Aberdeen without meeting somebody who carries his arm in a sling or walks on crutches; such is the life in a lumbering town.

12 *Abercorn*, full of railroad steel, wrecks on the coast four miles north of Oyehut. *(See August 7, 1891.)*

13 14° F. "Coldest weather in last eleven years. Snow reminds one of his 'back east days'."

16 Chehalis River freezes over.

20 *Cruiser* and *Tillie* unable to make their runs the fore part of the week owing to ice on the river. All mills shut down.

27 Unusually strong wind blowing large quantities of timber down. Everyone has a cold or cough.

29 "Melting snows have sent the rivers to highest mark this season. Very mild weather is prevalent, the frogs are singing and the moss back is happy for he thinks winter is over."

February 1888

12 Wind storm heaviest of the season; A memorable day that will be retold for years to come.

24 Alex Polson is having his house raised, as he does not care about having the high tides enter it.

March 1888

2 The Olympia Montesano Stage run is now daily with the exception of Sunday. Strangers, home seekers, and prospectors are arriving daily.

2 A yoke of oxen just sold for $235.00.

12 Blizzard of 1888 dumps five feet of snow in the Northeast.

16 "We (*The Vidette*) feel that the Sound papers never mention Grays Harbor and they are unitedly opposed to letting Eastern people know there is such a place."

20 Aberdeen incorporated.

23 It is not feasible to get logs out of the Humptulips River yet, as there is a bar one and a half miles long and almost dry at low tide.

30 The event of the season was the moving of the post office in Hoquiam to the right bank or business side of the river.

April 1888

1 Quinaielt, Nisqually, and the Skokomish Indian Agencies consolidated to form the Puyallup Agency. The Agency is in a chaotic state of affairs.

8 "Hoquiam store dudes went to Aberdeen on a sailing expedition and on return, it is rumored, that the boat was tipped over and all took a bath."

13 "People are flocking into Tacoma and Seattle by the thousands, doubtless many would come into this region if the press and people did not so grossly misrepresent it."

20 George Colman, the doctor and teamster of the Quinault Reservation, said he found a sea otter on the beach which had been wounded several years ago by Harry Witheral and survived the effects there until a week or two ago.

20 The Porgies (*silver surf perch*) are now running near Bay City, but the Indians are too tired or too good to fish anymore.

May 1888

4 The logging output is 300,000 feet a day by camps on the Hoquiam River.

4 Indian George has purchased the Blockhouse Ferry on the Chehalis from Wm Brooks and plans to rebuild it.

25 "We always admire flowers in church, but when flowers are placed in a can with a wrapper around it displaying in large type 'Anhaeuser Bush Beer,' there is something about the whole thing that will not harmonize." *Vidette*

27 The Presbyterian church in Aberdeen is dedicated.

June 1888

8 West Reed had a panther (*cougar)* spring at him just below Hoquiam while he was looking after cattle.

15 Business before the U.S. Land Office in Seattle makes travel brisk these days on the Harbor. It is estimated that for the past two months at least $800 per day average has been paid to the office by residents of Chehalis County, principally for timber land.

18 The county auditor issued the first marriage license to Indians during his term in office; Edward Smith of the Chehalis and Miss Rosie Walkeanes of the Quinault.

29 The long looked for water pipe arrived on the *Dolphin.* It will soon be placed in the wire net above the Hoquiam River and the people will have plenty of the pure element in town.

July 1888

4 Weatherwax' new stern wheel river boat, *Capt. Briscoe,* makes initial trip on the Chehalis River.

4 The constant rains of the past few weeks prevent carrying out the (4th of July) program as the streets are in such poor condition.

6 The Seattle census shows a population of 25,000. An increase of 16,000 in the past three years.

13 The Hoquiam water pipe has at last been laid and the people rejoice over the fact that they shall never thirst as they have come pretty near doing at times during the dry months.

20 The drummers and mosquitoes are very plentiful.

August 1888

** "Cosmopolis is now a city in fact."

24 Humptulips settlers send petition to Postmaster General in Washington, praying for establishment of post office in the vicinity known as Axford's Prairie.

31 The Olympia and Grays Harbor telephone line is being rapidly constructed. Poles and insulators are in place between Hoquiam and Aberdeen and the wire will be stretched as soon as it arrives.

September 1888

4 George Eastman receives patent for his roll film camera, and registration for trademark; *Kodak.*

7 Refreshing rains this past week.

7 Railroad rumors from all directions on the Harbor; lots of excitement.

14 The Aberdeen Fir Company is now fully organized.

28 Land seekers and hunters weekly visitors all summer near Humptulips. All surveyed lands taken and there is a general demand for another survey.

October 1888

5 Most log camps on the Hoquiam and Wishkah shut down for the year. A great many booms of logs may now be seen floating upon the bosom of the serene and beautiful Hoquiam.

12 Seventeen miles of the Puget Sound and Grays Harbor Road is now graded and ready for ties.

19 Fish were never more plentiful than at the present time in the rivers and harbor. They are good size, fat, and excellent quality.

21 The *Albatross* has made the examination of the Harbor and made her reports.

November 1888

2 "Someone broke into the *Vidette* office and took the 4-5,000 Republican campaign circularis and put them in the office stove and then the villain seized hold of the galleys containing the type set for the November 2nd issue and threw it onto the floor."

6 "Telephone put into operation in Montesano and election returns its first duty. This places us one step nearer civilization."

16 Beautiful weather after heavy rains.

16 *The Aberdeen Herald* says that Aberdeen cast 45 more votes than Montesano in the late election and that "must be particularly odious" to Montesano.

23 The telephone line is now entirely completed from Olympia to Hoquiam and will be in operation as soon as the instruments arrive.

23 "Hoquiam is the only town of any importance on the Harbor that has no lawyer. But that is not to her credit; she has no newspaper either."

30 "Some boys in Hoquiam indulged too freely in San Pedro wine, that they woke-up the next morning with heads bigger than that of a Montesano lawyer." *Vidette*

December 1888

7 Old ocean has been on a spree this past week.

14 Owing to the many cases of vario loid and small pox on the Sound, the school director had the school vaccinated. The healthfulness of our climate shows there is no danger of epidemic small pox down this way.

28 William's two stages which connect daily with the railroad, come in full nearly every day.

28 "Weather for the last three weeks is the finest anyone could want. It would do honor to Southern California's winter."

~ 1889 ~

January 1889

8 Spring like weather.

14 The trip from Montesano to the railroad was made by the stage in two hours time.

18 "Cosmopolis is lighted by electricity! How is that for enterprise."

25 "Anyone not happy with the weather should not try to live any longer, as they will never find satisfaction with the world."

31 Timber claim fever is not abating.

31 Hoquiam is alive with sanguine people.

February 1889

1 "What does it mean for Cosmopolis when the railroad purchased ¹/₂ section here? No tide mud here."

8 Snow has come at last.

8 Mr. A. M. Simpson procured six bushels of the famous Eastern or Boston clams four years ago and planted them in the waters of Grays Harbor as an experiment. They have multiplied wonderfully and would fill two of the largest vessels entering the harbor.

15 Weather is fine again. The snow has departed.

15 A woman in Montesano heard a noise in one of the rooms of her house and found a railroad surveyor "running a line" through her house.

16 Flag unfurled in Montesano as expression of joy over the passage of the Territorial Admission Bill.

22 President Cleveland signs Omnibus Bill to admit North Dakota, South Dakota, Montana, and Washington to statehood in November.

March 1889

8 Farmers busy with spring work. Land cruisers scouring county in all directions for land.

15 Four-horse coach is now running the Montesano-Centralia route.

15 Logging quiet as lumber market poor. Still immense number of logs cut last year.

April 1889

5 Chas. Arland opens his log camp for the season with two teams of oxen and twenty men.

12 Many strange faces in the county.

13 Clearing starts for Grays Harbor City. Founded by George Washington Hunt with hopes of rail terminus. 6,600 foot wharf built.

19 The machinery is working like a charm on the new steamer *Montesano.*

22 Oklahoma land rush; 2 million acres in the middle of Indian Territory is thrown open to 100,000 whites. (*In next four years 10 million acres pried loose under the Dawes Severalty Act [See February 8, 1887] are opened to similar rushes.*)

26 Surveyors of the Puget Sound and Grays Harbor railroad (P.S. & G.H.) complete the preliminary survey from Summit to Montesano.

26 John Lindbeck put extra heavy charge in canon to fire in honor of George Washington's 100th anniversary inauguration. The canon was blown into a thousand atoms sending parts all over Montesano. It was miraculous that no one was killed or injured.

May 1889

3 Blockhouse Smith Ranch is for sale.

6 One of the most severe wind storms passes over the Northwest coast.

17 The five daily stages coming into Montesano are nearly always loaded.

17 Telephone line now operational between Montesano and Seattle-Tacoma.

17 Five newspapers will soon be published in Chehalis County.

26 90°s.

31 Strawberry crop is immense.

31 The muddy appearance of the Wynooche River was caused by a number of young men taking their first bath of the season.

31 Johnstown flood in Pennsylvania kills between 2,000 and 5,000 when poorly constructed dam fails.

June 1889

7 Keep your cows up past sunset and they will find their way to the pound.

7 There is a fire in Seattle.

14 Chas. Arland has two million feet of timber in the water.

21 The Olympia-Tenino train is the most accommodating train in the West. It stops anywhere to take on passengers who flag it with a red handkerchief.

23 Badly needed rain.

28 The woods are filled with berries this year.

July 1889

2 Blackberry fiends seen every day on the Hoquiam River.

26 The brick and foundation timbers for Montesano's electric light building are on the ground.

31 *The Aberdeen Weekly Bulletin* makes its appearance. It is a very creditable sheet.

Summer 1889

** George Walker tries to locate three men on a swamp and they refused to buy it. The name *Promised Land* is applied to the area when Otto Murhard told Walker, "Well, preacher, you showed them the promised land. If they did not want it, it's not you fault."

August 1889

** Joseph N. Locke is first white to post a claim on land in the valley above Lake Quinault.

9 The new court house foundation is complete.

6 Work on the P.S. & G.H. Railway has bridged the Cloquallum and the bridge is nearly ready for iron.

26 Edwin Ellis in his report on the Quinaielt says they (Quinaults) get most of their living by hunting and fishing. They get their money by picking hops (September) and fishing for the canneries.

"Our Indians seem to us very much like white people. They have not the sterling qualities, however, which will keep them up, but easily slide back to their former condition. Like all lower races, they like their pleasure, and willingly barter substantial benefits for fleeting pleasure." (Most agents were educated in the east and finding themselves in the wilds of the western wilderness had great difficulty relating to another people. In all agent reports since the 1870's we find they set the tone of paternalism and disapproval unto harassment of the old culture, its mores, religion, and language that would persist for scores of years. This ruthless separation from the Quinault past to make the Indians into the white man's image resulted in disorganization, deterioration, and cultural breakdown. This conquest nearly took all the meaning out of their lives and its effects have lasted to this day.)

30 As soon as the hop season is over and the Indians back on the reservation near Oakville, they intend to organize an Indian brass band.

September 1889

11 Did you ever see better weather?

25 The Pacific Bridge Company is building a bridge over the Wynooche River.

27 Severe storm. Heavy rains send logs down stream carrying away the false work for the railroad bridge on the Satsop and the wagon bridge on the Wynooche.

October 1889

17 The electric light plant turned on for the first time in Montesano.

18 The fishing season being at its height, the canneries are running full time and the catch is exceptionally good.

25 Farmers are saying that for the first time on record there are no salmon in the Wynooche. The Satsop, however, is literally alive with them.

25 Large number of people still visiting Montesano's new electric plant. They are no longer anxious to "receive a shock" as they did. Some ladies pronounce it a "horrid thing."

30 Everyone is astonished at the rapid growth of Aberdeen. The impression is that this will be the City of the Harbor.

31 The Satsop River is swollen, but does not appear to

endanger the nearly completed railroad bridge.

November 1889

2 North and South Dakota are admitted to the U.S.

8 Montana is admitted to the Union.

11 Washington admitted as the 42nd state of the Union.

15 The mail stage is arriving late due to rainy weather and it looks like the trouble will infect us for the entire winter. What is the matter with carrying the mail by railroad?

16 Celebration for the completion of the P.S. & G.H. Railroad at Montesano is attended by several thousand people and will not soon be forgotten.

22 30,000 cases of salmon packed on the Harbor this season.

22 The train leaves Montesano at 10 a.m. and returns at 3 p.m. The fare to Kamilchie is $2.25.

28 Thanksgiving is a perfect summer day.

29 The first business to come before the Superior Court of Chehalis County was the application for release of Fred Miller from the jail for the sale of liquor to the Indians. He was released.

December 1889

6 Jefferson Davis, the only president of The Confederate States of America, dies.

6 "Flowers are blooming, grass is green as spring, and many berry bushes are in full bloom. Who wants to trade this for the frozen blizzard-cursed East?"

7 Press Party departs Seattle for Olympic Peninsula.

9 Willapa Methodist church dedicated.

31 Frosty nights and sunny days. Where are the blizzards the Eastern papers say we are subject to?

~ 1890 ~

January 1890

1 New Years Day cold with snow.

17 The marshal has posted notices that all persons throwing snowballs at Chinamen or other persons or teams in the street will be arrested.

24 Influenza "la grippe" striking the just and unjust alike.

24 The heaviest tax payer in the county is John Fleitz of Detroit, Michigan. He just paid $1,051.00 on 9,000 acres of timber land.

31 "It is the same old gag; the worst severe winter ever known here."

February 1890

7 Rain and high water.

14 Logs in the Chehalis River have been coming down lively this past week.

14 The dry kiln in Hoquiam is a huge success and will be an immense benefit to the building trade the coming season.

17 Christopher Latham Sholes, father of the typewriter, dies.

21 Every town around is in belief that it will be the railway center.

March 1890

14 The Chinese residents had another "Celestial" row a few days ago. They are becoming Americanized too fast for the peace of the community.

19 Sam Lee and Sung Lee charged with keeping opium

joints. Each fined $50.00.

28 California quail turned loose in Humptulips Valley in hope they will multiply.

April 1890

25 The new courthouse in Montesano received its first coat of paint this week.

May 1890

6 Cosmopolis votes for incorporation.

11 Press Party arrives at Lake Quinault having crossed the Olympics via Elwa. (*See December 7, 1889.*)

12 Press Party arrives at the mouth of the Quinault River.

23 Elma feels progressive now that it has incorporated.

Old growth Western redcedar and Douglas fir.

June 1890

6 Ben Crane lost part of his finger on a machine he was working on the other day. He sewed it back on.

13 *The Washingtonian* made its appearance this week as a semi-weekly.

13 The Northern Pacific Railway (N.P.) is extending its line from Chehalis to Montesano. Lumber is a scarcity as mills try to meet railway orders.

20 Orders authorize O'Neil to begin second reconnaissance of the Olympics.

30 Showers and cool weather.

July 1890

1 O'Neil leaves Port Townsend to begin U.S. Olympic Exploring Expedition (O.E.E.).

3 The features of the "dago" are becoming quite familiar on the streets of Montesano since railroad building has begun.

3 Idaho enters the Union.

9 Plat for the town of "Quiniault" filed by Chase and Ogden.

10 Wyoming enters the Union.

16 Account of the Press Exploring Expedition across the Olympic Mountains appears in The Seattle *Press.*

August 1890

12 O.E.E. crosses into the headwaters of the Quinault.

** Quinaielt report says that large numbers of white settlers have taken up claims bordering on three sides of the reservation, and that the Indians have been brought into contact with the white man as never before.

15 Hotel Hoquiam formal opening. Manager A. F. Raynor says it is fit for a city of ten thousand population.

22 La Point Bros. have fired their 3rd kiln of bricks. Over 200,000 in present kiln.

22 Quite a lot of travel by stage has taken place lately. It looks like the days of old before Chehalis County had advanced to railroads.

22 Census shows Chehalis County has 9,325 people with the biggest increases this past two years. In 1870 there were 401 and in 1880 there were 921.

September 1890

9 South Bend incorporated.

19 Settlers have squatted on nearly all the unsurveyed land along the coast.

22 Fisher of the O.E.E. starts down the Queets River from its headwaters alone. Others of O.E.E. climb Mount Olympus.

25 Fisher passes Nellis Creek (*Clearwater River*) and said "Ten Boston houses (*ten white families*) were located upon the stream."

25 Fisher spends the night with Queets Indians.

25 Yosemite Park created.

30 Anyone wishing for finer weather than we have been favored with this fall, would not be satisfied with a government office.

October 1890

3 O'Neil gives details of O.E.E. at Hoquiam lecture.

4 O.E.E. given big Hoquiam reception.

9 O'Neil arrives at Vancouver Barracks, officially ending the O.E.E.

11 Feature and color cover illustration about the Quinault Indian fishery appears in *West Shore,* an illustrated journal published every Saturday and published in Portland, Oregon and Spokane Falls, Washington.

15 First frost of the season.

22 O'Neil banquet at the Portland Hotel in Portland.

November 1890

7 "A masked force of Aberdeen men mob John Wing, one of the Chinese Celestials. This cannot be looked upon with any degree of allowance."

14 Six prisoners in the county jail.

14 Olympia got the capital by a rousing majority.

16 O'Neil submits *Report on the Exploration of the Olympic Mountains.* He closed the report writing that the region would "serve admirably for a national park."

21 Some county residents have visited Victoria. What Victoria is to Vancouver Island, Montesano may be to

Chehalis County.

28 The N.P. will not build past Montesano this winter and possibly longer.

December 1890

5 Severe rains this week.

5 The first brick block building in the county nears completion in Montesano.

15 Sioux Indian Chief, Sitting Bull, and eleven others killed at Grand River, South Dakota.

20 Most severe prolonged wind and rain storm. All the logs laying in the sloughs and small streams the last two years are being carried out.

29 U.S. Army slaughterers 200 Sioux men, women and children at Wounded Knee Creek.

~ 1891 ~

January 1891

14 N.P. connection at Elma leads to day of great rejoicing.

16 The weather has been exceptionally fine.

16 Special car (N.P. train) of the T.O. & G.H. line arrives at the depot. Montesano now has trans-continental connection.

23 As yet, not a flake of snow.

February 1891

17 Two hundred fifty attending school in Montesano, 140 in Aberdeen.

17 County Commissioners authorize Sheriff Carter to procure balls, chains, and foot weights necessary to be used with working prisoners.

23 N.P. begins regular passenger train service to Montesano.

24 Those receiving freight since the N.P. connection have noticed a very material reduction in their bills.

March 1891

3 Circuit Court of Appeals established.

3 Forest Reserves or Creative Act. (*The President can close forested areas and establish national preserves on land in the Public Domain.*)

3 Trains come down loaded with home seekers nearly every day.

3 Telegraph wire strung nearly to Elma.

4 International Copyright Act.

10 Glorious spring weather.

24 Names frequently applied by locals:
Montesano - *Key City*
Elma - *Gem City*
Aberdeen - *Local City*
Ocosta - *City by the Sea*

24 Quarter section of school land on the Chehalis River near the boom and known as "Arkansaw" has been purchased for $50.00/acre by the county commissioners for a poor farm.
(*Note: All Vidette issues from January through July 1891 are missing.*)

July 1891

1 *The Vidette* designated as the official County paper.

30 Axford reports a 102° F. reading.

31 The steam shovel's crane caught the telephone and electric lines the other day in Montesano and the shock caused quite a rattling.

August 1891

** *Highlights of E.W. Agar's Quinaielt report:*

"During the past year or so two hundreds of settlers have taken claims along the (Quinault) reservation borders, and it is becoming more and more important that it be surveyed and allotted.

It is very hard for children to become good English speakers when they have so many opportunities of using their own language. The older Indians do not appreciate the work of the school and instead of working with us they are continually trying to keep alive in the minds of the young their old customs.

Fish and game are getting very scarce and the Indians are obliged to find other employment. Fortunately there is plenty of work for them freighting with teams and canoes for the white settlers near the reservation. They make good wages during the hop-picking season in September."

7 A 1,400 foot long wharf from the beach to the wrecked *Abercorn* is practically finished assuring success to salvage 2,500 tons of steel rails. (*See January 12, 1888, June 3, 1892, and September 1894.*)

7 Mail service from Hoquiam to Lake Quinault is two times a week now.

7 Several parties out and others going prospecting in the Olympics.

17 The steamer *City of Aberdeen* makes first run to connect Aberdeen with the train in Montesano.

18 One thousand soldiers and citizens attending Old Soldiers Reunion at Peterson's Point.

21 There are now 2,500 at Old Soldiers Reunion.

24 Thomas Edison patents kinetoscope. (*Motion picture camera.*)

28 Some feel the beach needs a name in the vicinity of Peterson's Point. Chenammas Beach after a chief of a tribe of the Chehalis Indians who lived near here would make a good name.

September 1891

4 Rescuing of remaining rails from the *Abercorn* has been suspended until another season because of increasing risk caused by the surf.

11 Deputy U.S. Surveyor Noel and a party of 20 bound for the Queets country to run lines of the Quinault Indian Reservation and lines of Township 24 Ranges 12-13.

18 Lumber for the new St. Josephs Hospital is being put on the ground in Aberdeen.

18 "Since the railroad has commenced running into Cosmopolis, the citizens of the burg have been annoyed some-what by the noise. One said he was going to move to Aberdeen where it is quite."

22 900,000 acres of Indian land in Oklahoma are opened to settlers.

25 Hoquiam now has a safe which is a genuine curiosity.

25 Indians of the Quinaielt Agency have been searching for the bodies of Tommy Mason and Buker Tuestom whose capsized boat was recently discovered. They feel

foul play as each man had $80-90 when they left Hoquiam.

25 Montesano without electric lights for one week when generator breaks down. The generator is being leveled so the same problem does not happen again.

29 Rain and more rain.

October 1891

9 N.P. track within 5 miles of Ocosta.

12 The Indian Industrial School opens on the Chehalis Reservation.

24 *The Aberdeen Bulletin* has discontinued its semi-weekly edition and is now published on Saturday.

30 Grays Harbor Bar Survey completed.

November 1891

8 The splash dam built by Jas. Gillies on the Hoquiam River gives way and carried with it the county bridge.

27 The work on the piers for the railroad bridge across the Chehalis River has been condemned. They were out of plumb and have to be rebuilt.

30 Earthquake shock slight on Harbor, but heaviest ever experienced in some Sound cities.

December 1891

7 Exceptionally stormy weather.

18 A plank road is to be built from Ocosta to Chenammas Beach.

22 Big blow delays trains and boats.

28 The severest wind in many years does great damage to cities on the Harbor.

~ 1892 ~

January 1892

1 Ellis Island Immigrant Station in New York formally opens.

8 Olympia now has free mail delivery system.

15 *Montesano Vidette* is now printed by steam. *The Oakville Globe* is run by natural gas of the best quality.

15 Rules for basketball published in Springfield, Mass. where it originated.

29 The British vessel *Ferndale,* with a cargo of coal en route from Australia to Portland, went ashore about 15 miles north of Grays Harbor. Seventeen of the crew find a watery grave. (*Coal from this wreck continues to wash up on the beaches as far north as Moclips in the 1990's.*)

February 1892

5 F.E Moore cut a crabapple 22" through at the butt.

12 Lincoln's birthday declared a national holiday.

18 Party of Eastern lumbermen visiting the Harbor area.

March 1892

11 Cosmopolis Mill reports it cut 222,000 feet in ten hours for a special Australia order. It is the biggest one day cut on the coast!

25 *The Hoquiam Tribune* is no more. It gave up the ghost last week.

26 Walt Whitman dies.

April 1892

8 Stormy weather.

14 A breeze played with our primeval forest like summer breezes do with the grain.

14 Regular passenger trains begin running into Cosmopolis.

15 Everyone delights to see the sun once more.

20 The freight train going west from Montesano was wrecked near the poor farm by a cow who claimed the right-of-way.

22 The fine weather is bringing the bicycles out quite numerously in Hoquiam.

May 1892

5 Great Chinese Exclusion Act passes in Congress. Chinese must register within a year or be deported.

6 All the mills on the Harbor have reduced common labor to one dollar per day and board.

7 7th - 9th: The Centennial Celebration of the discovery of Grays Harbor was quite a success in some respects and a failure in others.

15 Storm.

27 The Captain of the steamer *Clan McDonald,* wish to announce that he will give a free excursion to the beach next Tuesday to the ladies of Montesano, if the day is pleasant. (*82 women and some gentlemen and children did take the trip.*)

June 1892

3 The rain of the last few days came just in time for gardening as everything was drying up.

3 A big steam hoisting apparatus came on the *Alliance.* It is to be put to use at the wreck of the *Abercorn* for hoisting the submerged railroad ties (*See August 7, 1891*).

17 A craze for shaving off moustaches in Aberdeen still continues and nearly one half of the male population who formerly wore the whiskers are going around looking ashamed of themselves.

24 Work on the wreck of the *Abercorn* is progressing finely; piling is nearly all driven.

July 1892

20 Blackberrying parties are all the rage now. The launch *Sunbeam* and the steamer *Aberdeen* have made may excursions up the Hoquiam River with the berry pickers and have been crowded each trip.

22 Cedar logs are in demand.

23 Congress bans the sale of alcohol on Indian lands.

29 Handwork of the citizens of Montesano save the town from a disastrous fire.

August 1892

1 Highlights of the Quinaielt Subagency report:

"Fish and game are becoming scarce and the hunting of sea otter, which has been a profitable business for these Indians, can no longer be considered a leading industry with them, there being many more white men hunting now than in the past.

I have surveyed, by running inaccurate lines, 45 claims of 100 acres each along both sides of the Quinaielt and Queets Rivers. These claims have been taken up by the Indians, and each man has a small garden and hay fields. They are slow at making improvements fearing that their claim might be on some other claim than their own after the official survey is complete. I urge that at least the boundary lines and the river bottoms be surveyed as soon as possible."

5 Aberdeen streets through the middle of the day present rather a deserted appearance as everyone that is not at

work is at the sea shore.

19 Fishermen are beginning to reap a harvest now, as fish are becoming plentiful. 2,000 lbs. were shipped on the 16th from Aberdeen to Tacoma.

19 The rain of the last few days has come just in time to insure a large crop of potatoes at Quiniault (Lake). Also a fine crop of mud on the trail for the balance of the year. Antone Kestner has 1,000 tobacco plants on the Quiniault; some four feet high with three feet leaves one foot wide.

26 The lumber market is dull and mills not rushed with orders.

30 Cholera arrives aboard the *Moravia*. First time in the United States.

September 1892

8 Early version of the "Pledge of Allegiance" appears in *The Youth Companion*.

9 "The surveying party that has the contract of surveying the (*Quinault*) reservation, arrived on the lake with their random line of the north side, on August 30th, being 13 days running from the beach to the lake, 24 miles. Having about finished the meander of the lake, they will soon begin the north line."

23 J.T. Harris is superintending the recovery of pig iron and fire brick from a vessel wrecked on the Queets four years ago.

23 The hops in the county are very light this year as in the rest of the state.

October 1892

7 The Slade Mill in Hoquiam is erecting light poles for wires. The company will soon be working overtime.

7 The third annual fair of the Chehalis County Fair Association is now being held in Elma and not as successful this year as the preceding one.

15 1,800,000 acres of land on Indian reservations open to the white settlers in Montana.

28 Edwin Eells, of Tacoma, who is in charge of seven Indian reservation is Western Washington, was down on the Quinault Reservation a few days this week.

28 The *Mary E.* sails for Queets. Capt. Hank will load pig-iron from the wreck there and return at the first opportunity. A most daring sea-going ever done on this western coast in a little smack.

November 1892

18 The *Mary E.* has been unable to enter the Queets River, so wandered to the Sound until calm weather will enable him to return to the Queets bar.

18 The weather has been beastly this week.

18 Mr. Harris of the Queets River country was in Aberdeen (14th-15th) raising money to build a road over several bluffs that run out into the ocean; the balance of the road is along the beach and of a matter of course is a good one.

25 Stormy weather. Over eleven inches of rain fell in Aberdeen between Nov. 13th and 18th.

25 The (Harbor) bay is covered with ducks; more than there have been for years. The local nimrods are having a glorious time bagging Jack Snip which are very plentiful during the wet weather.

December 1892

2 Heavy weather.

16 The steam schooner *Lakme* loaded 719,000 feet last week at the Cosmopolis Mill is largest load ever there.

22 Snow has been falling heavily for the past three days.

25 Two to three feet of snow in Hoquiam. Thermometer went to 18° F.

30 The Hoquiam-Aberdeen Stage has been sporting a double team since the snow.

30 The snow and all its symptoms have disappeared. Will be remembered as the heaviest in history.

~ 1893 ~

January 1893

11 *Mary E.* made it into the Queets, having wandered around Tacoma, where she took on freight for the Queets.

13 The fine weather in Hoquiam has brought out the bicycles like jay birds in corn time.

13 A good many birds have made their appearance that never did before until Spring.

13 A man with Edison's wonderful talking machine was in Hoquiam a few days during this week, making it warble for money.

13 Hoquiam mills are getting out some dressed 2x24x32 spruce to be used in the construction of the World's Fair organ.

16 Hawaiian-born American missionary and sugar interests with the help of the U.S. Marines overthrow native Hawaiian ruler.

19 *Mary E.* arrives in Hoquiam in very dilapidated condition.

20 An unusual number of hobos and vagabonds are infesting the Sound cities and many interior towns. Some on the Harbor, too.

27 Photographer Finch of Aberdeen is putting up a galley on 8th and J in Hoquiam.

31 26" of snow has fallen these last few days of January.

February 1893

3 Severe snow and cold this past week. 10° F. "Cosmopolis doubly quarantined by snow and smallpox. The storm, or rather a series of storms for the past week or two, has been the most severe... reminded us of the Eastern winter weather."

4 85 men on the steamers *Cruiser* and *Edgar* are joined by the *Favorite* from Bay City, sail to Oysterville early in the morning to collect the county records and take them to South Bend.

8 The Wishkah River is blocked with snow and slush. Attempt to get a steamer to break a jam, but none available.

10 "The last snow storm has transformed all us tender feet into pioneers, and we can take great pleasure in the future in narrating to all new comers tales about the winter of '92-'93. In addition to the 26" of snow in the last few days of January, we had 45" in February."

10 There is a redfir in SW section 10 T16N R8W that is 53'

8" in circumference.

14 A burst steam pipe at the Aberdeen light works forced the plant to shut down and left the city in darkness.

24 Twenty-four under quarantine at Hoquiam's Gamboge Hotel.

March 1893

3 Two unknown hunters up on the Humptulips, cornered nine elk in a snow drift during the last heavy snowfall and dealt with them at their pleasure, killing seven and capturing two young ones with ropes.

3 The mail carrier between Hoquiam and Quinault still has to go on snowshoes about half way.

17 The basket factory (*they made fruit crates*) is being covered with shingles this week. The board roofing is being removed.

18 Fifteen ranchers returned to their homes on the North Beach, after spending the winter in various places.

24 The geese have commenced to fly north.

26 Twenty men arrive from Portland to work on harbor improvements. There are presently forty men working for the contractors getting stone across the river from the Slade Mill in Hoquiam.

31 Chehalis County Press Association organized.

31 Rain is finishing up the last of the snow on the Humptulips.

31 *Str. Tillie* towed the first raft of piles out for the jetty in south channel.

April 1893

3 Driving of the piles did not start until today on the south channel due to heavy winds.

6 Dr. Chase and wife went up the beach to take up their new residence.

14 Considerable snow still lies in the gulches and ravines in the timber on the Humptulips.

14 "An editor of a county paper, who is unmarried and dwells in a single selfishness, made a proposition to send his paper free for one year to every maiden who sent him a proposal of marriage and a lock of her hair before Jan. 1, 1893. He now has the largest circulation in his neighborhood and enough hair to stuff a mattress." *Vidette*

15 U.S. gold reserve falls below $100,000,000, setting off panic of 1893.

17 The public school in Quiniault opened for a six months term with Miss Ida Locke as teacher. The school cannot run in winter on account of the children not being able to go through the winter storms.

21 The road from Humptulips to Quinault Lake has been cleared out enough so that pack trains can go over it. A man named Wright will run regular pack trains over it this summer.

21 Dr. Chase and Mr. Roundtree have built beautiful cottages on North Beach this winter.

21 Dept. U.S. Surveyor, I. C. Vickery, says the Quiniault reservation lines not correct on three places in T20N R12W.

May 1893

1 Chicago World's Fair opens.

1 Official weather record keeping begins in Seattle.

3 Will Criss opens a skating ring under a large tent in Hoquiam to a large crowd.

8 Washington's headquarters at the World's Columbian Exposition is at the main entrance to the fair. Washington's flag staff is a single Puget Sound fir 238 feet high from which floats the largest American flag known (60' long) and can be seen from all corners of the fair grounds.

12 Old Neptune is quieting down, a fore runner of good weather.

12 Harry Weatheral has taken up his abode on Copalis Rock, and will spend two or three months shooting sea otter.

17 A 25 ton piece of Washington coal was moved at the World's fair causing a sensation.

19 Hoquiam N.P.R.R. ticket agent has sold 64 tickets to the World's Fair.

26 Eight feet of some animal was seen lying about a foot above the water at Silvia Lake.

June 1893

1 *Mary E.* returned to Hoquiam from Queets with a lot of pig iron from a wreck near the mouth of the Queets River.

16 The vegetable season is late this year.

23 Quiniault lake salmon are now being shipped east from Ocosta.

23 The cigarette law is being strictly observed in Montesano. The little Chinese-made, opium-tainted, health destroyers cannot now be obtained from love or money. "Fiends" can still send to Portland for their cigarettes.

27 Crash of stock market. (*Leads to four years of depression.*)

July 1893

7 The red, white and blue *Westport Daily World* came out on the 4th seemed to have a strain on the resources of that establishment as no other papers came out until today.

14 The Single mills on the Harbor have shut down to curtail the output.

15 Highlight of E. W. Agar report on the Quiniault Reservation:

The reservation is now, and must be for some time to come, quite inaccessible. There is some land on the Queets and Quiniault Rivers and bordering the lake, but most of the remainder is comparatively valueless. Consumption has been destructive and is probably due to the great amount of rainfall and heavy sea fogs which prevail on this agency.

The spring salmon run in this river are among the finest in the world and was more plentiful than in former years. Though the assistance of the physician, the Indians have been able to market a considerable quantity and quite a trade has developed. They are sent to Tacoma and other cities.

Sea otter hunting and freighting for the white settlers have not been so profitable of late as a few years ago. A small sailing vessel was employed by the Indians to bring lumber and general merchandise from Grays Harbor to the reservation. Two Indians have started general stores on a small scale.

16 A mammoth vase six feet high and turned from a single block of red cedar on display at the Washington's building at the Chicago World's fair. Statistics for 1892 showed 246 shingle mills in the state with a yearly capacity of 3,123,000,000 feet.

23 Joseph Locke (*See August 1889*), Robert Locke and Clark Peeler climb to (*what becomes known as Colonel Bob*) the highest peak above Lake Quinault.

28 W. J. McAleer now fills the place of industrial instructor among the Quinault Indians.

August 1893

4 A measuring worm is destroying the great hemlock, fir, and spruce trees along the Hoquiam River. An inspection in section 32 of T19N R9W showed trees dead and it may cover two whole townships.

4 It costs about $75.00 to travel and spend a week at the World's fair.

11 A string showed Lake Quinault 240' deep.

11 Several of our Chinese citizens have indulged in the past time of flying their strange looking kites this week, greatly to the interest of the small boys.

19 Mr. Sparks of Montesano found a tarantula in his bananas.

25 The Yakima hop growers will require about 5,000 pickers to care for the coming crop. We will pay $1.00 per box of 100 pounds each. Board will cost 35¢ per day. White pickers and families will have preference over Indians. We wish the white pickers to supplant the Indians eventually.

31 Hottest day in years.

September 1893

1 The Montesano sewer work is nearing completion.

8 Immense quantity of sardines now on Harbor.

8 Aberdeen Cannery is putting up 300-400 cases of Salmon per day, paying $12\frac{1}{2}$¢ for silver side and 25¢ for blacks.

15 Never since the fire of 1871 have such terrible forest fires burned through northern Wisconsin the past few days.

29 10,000 whites and 2,000 Indians picking hops in the state.

29 Another mile of puncheoning has been done on the Hoquiam-Humptulips road. M.W. Walker has put in sawed plank and the difference in riding over them and the split puncheon or rounded poles is simply immense. They only cost 20% more than the split ones.

October 1893

5 The Aberdeen city council gives fair warning to the hobo element that they not expect to be fed and housed for nothing this winter.

6 The Willapa Harbor Extract Works at South Bend has received a first prize at Chicago for white hemlock tannin extract.

14 Stetson Mill and city light plant burned in greatest disaster ever to visit Montesano.

27 A large sperm whale came ashore at Westport and several people are engaged saving the oil.

27 T20N R12W has been filed, so settlers of that Township may now obtain title to their land.

November 1893

3 Chicago's World Fair closes. 21,458,910 attendance.

10 *The Weekly Vidette* list 130 of the most interesting features at the World's Fair. Included are: a bed worth $950, a 26-ton block of coal, milking by machinery, the *Mayflower's Bible,* chickens hatched by electricity, a chocolate tower worth $40,000, a fountain squirting California wine, a palace built of corn, a 30,000 pound block of salt, a clay pipe smoked by Miles Standish and a gun that could shoot 20 miles.

24 Farmers in our area are beginning to use wider wagon tires; 4" and wider.

24 Strong sou'wester.

December 1893

6 Very high tide.

8 Mail carriers on the Hoquiam/Quinault route are having trouble getting their pay as they are working under a second subcontract. They get a dollar and half a day pay and pay their own expenses.

12 Heavy storms this week.

22 Rain storm.

Key Hole or Arch Rock.

~ 1894 ~

January 1894

12 The heavy rains have swollen the streams.

26 Chehalis County is the banner timber district of the state. There is more timber here than the states of Wisconsin and Minnesota contain.

February 1894

9 The grippe still holds its grip.

9   The mail now leaves Copalis (*Beach*) every Monday, Wednesday, and Friday for Granville. It returns from Granville at 2:00 p.m. on those days for Copalis.

March 1894

2   10" of snow fell at Humptulips last week.

2   The ocean beach from Moclips River to Boone Creek (six miles) has been taken up as placer mines. The gold is there, but the machine to separate it from the sand has not been invented.

23 The boys at the basket factory in Hoquiam went out on strike when they found out their wages were being lowered. They will learn quite a lesson when they find out there are two men for every job nowadays.

30 Some parties are making preparations to catch and ship east this year's run of Quinault salmon.

April 1894

6   The Wishkah River is clear for five miles and every rancher on the river has logs ready to drive.

20 The Simpson Log Camp has offered to ship a car load of fleas if they are scarce in Montesano.

27 General Buell says enough flour gold exists on the surface of the Oregon and Washington beaches to satisfy the national debt.

May 1894

18 The North West Lumber Company struck a cottonwood at a depth of 48 feet while attempting to sink a well in Hoquiam.

25 Canvass awnings are replacing the old wood awnings in front of Aberdeen businesses.

25 Claim jumping seems to be the order of the day at Quiniault lake. Not less than six have been jumped this spring.

25 Quiniault settlers have lived here for four long years without a road. Starting July 9th, each settler is expected to work ten days to build a wagon road to Humptulips.

25 Big Indian Shaker Camp Meeting on the North Beach this past week.

June 1894

1   The problem is solved. Gold can be separated from the beach sand.

15 Strawberry picnics are all the rage at Oakville, regardless of the rain.

20 The *Sea Gull* launched at Hoquiam. The 48' boat is built especially for the coast trade. It will be able to cross the Queets and Hoh bars at anytime.

22 Little work being done on the Quiniault Lake farms. Settlers waiting until survey is made; 30 - 40 settlers in that part of the country.

July 1894

4   Most Quiniault Indians have gone to celebrate the Fourth with their dusky brothers at Chehalis and Black River.

13 94°F.

17 The Quinaielt Agency Report notes that salmon of their rivers has found a market this past season for the first time in Chicago. The floods and strikes stopped the transportation, or more would have been sold.

August 1894

3   Settlers in township 20 are agitating the question of a foot bridge across Joe Creek at its mouth on the beach.

17 An unusually large lot of fine otter have been killed recently by hunters on the North beach.

18 Captain Crosby and three of his crew drowned in the surf south of Joe Creek in dense fog. The men in a whale boat, from the Government vessel *McArthur*, were computing a hydro-graphic signal begun the previous day. The ship has been constantly in sight on North beach for a month, placing beacons along shore.

27 97° F.

31 The late epidemic of la grippe was so severe among the Quiniault Indians, that the physician was worn out and had to call for help.

31 With the heavy fog and smoke, the nights have been exceedingly dark lately.

September 1894

5   Post office established at Menlo.

7   The smoke last week was the densest ever known here, but the rain has cleared it away and probably will put out the fires which caused it.

20 2$^{1}/_{4}$" of rain.

** The people of Aberdeen band together to build railroad into town from rail salvaged from wreck of the *Abercorn. (The line was completed this year and turned over to the Northern Pacific in 1895. See January 12, 1888, and April 1, 1895.)*

October 1894

2   Severe wind-storm.

19 Ducks and Geese are very plentiful on the North beach.

19 The Quiniault Lake Road is progressing finely. All interested settlers having donated ten days of hard work.

November 1894

2   Johnson Waukenas, head man of the Quinaults, writes *The Weekly Vidette* in a letter dated October 29, about attempts to get Quinault Indians to sign a petition to survey and allot the Reservation.

16 For $2.00 per year, *The Vidette* subscriber gets *The Vidette* and their choice of the weekly addition of *The New York Tribune* or the *Chicago Inter Ocean*. For 50¢ more the subscriber also gets the *Seattle Post-Intelligencer*.

30 Heavy rains and high water.

December 1894

6   Snow falls to a depth of 6".

7   The North beach is lined with piling, supposed to be from the raft that went to pieces off the coast of Oregon.

14 Snow gone and rivers in flood.

18 The smoky cap that hangs over Mount Rainier was viewed by the Harbor citizens. It was a beautiful sight.

28 An article in *The Economist* calls the Quiniault Improvement Company "land grabbers." *The Vidette* correspondent says the locals praise the company as it has paid out $3,500 for surveying the lake country, locating a road, and other improvements. It also paid $400 for work on the O'Neal Trail.

~ 1895 ~

January 1895

4   The railroad is rapidly nearing completion in Aberdeen.

11 There is almost a continuous puncheoning between New London and Humptulips City, though rough, yet preferable to mud.

15 The first train arrives in Aberdeen. It was a gravel train (ballast for track). It created as much excitement among small boys as if it had been one of the great lighting express trains.

25 Kirk and the Hanson Bros. turned loose over 100 logs in the recent near record high freshet on the Humptulips.

February 1895

1 Chinese New Year was not so noisy in Hoquiam as their fireworks and candies failed to arrive until the next day. However China gin and China cigars were on tap.

8 Those interested in getting logs down the Hump have gone to work on the jam near the mouth.

15 The filing of plat township 21-9 is the occasion of quite a stampede.

March 1895

8 Indians have returned to the Agency. They were not very successful in trapping this winter.

15 Billy Garfield, an Indian, killed the first sea otter on the 9th.

22 Axford - the clouds broke away at 7:00 o'clock and gave us a fine view of the eclipse.

April 1895

1 The first passenger train arrived in Aberdeen. 700 people gathered at depot to witness the arrival. The Aberdeen band furnished music and the small boys and men added in their voices. (*The rails were pitted by the salt water. As trains came into Aberdeen, the rails created a clacking sound. It became the wake-up call for passengers as they came into Aberdeen. See August 7, 1891, and January 4, January 18, and April 1, 1895.*)

19 North beaches is growing. Another school district is requested for the beaches.

May 1895

24 Earl Pettit in his new light roadster, an *Eclipse*, squared off with Olaf Hanson in an old-style *Victor*. They came together full tilt. The jar of the collision dismounted Hanson.

June 1895

28 Everyone is fishing on the beach.

July 1895

4 Leschi and Quiemuth reburied on the Nisqually Reservation by the Nisqually Tribe. Nearly a thousand people attended the ceremony. *(It is believed that Leschi lead the 1855 Indian uprising and January 1856 attack on Seattle.)*

5 The finest bicycle ground is the hard sand on ocean beach from Oyehut to Copalis River. One can go six miles in 21 minutes.

29 Quiniault surveyors unable to work because of storm.

August 1895

9 Picking blackberries is all the fashion.

13 Correspondent reports 39° F. and frost at Axford.

30 Auditors Annual Exhibit of Chehalis County shows value of personal property in 1894 is $6,249,171.00.

September 1895

7 The first rain of the season worth mentioning.

13 Already the good effects of the opening of the new Queets-Quiniault Trail, which is now passable for footmen, is being noticed. We hope to soon see it passable for ponies.

14 85° F.

14 The three day Montesano Tournament is a wonderful success; Bicycle, buggy, and horse racing events with athletic contest and baseball.

October 1895

11 Proposition for electric light plant at Montesano.

17 A sailor on the Hoquiam tug, *Colman,* was operated on by Dr. Frary for too much blood. The Dr. found it necessary to draw blood from each arm.

18 The North Beach seems deserted since the tourists left.

November 1895

1 We are enjoying the most beautiful autumn at Quiniault lake.

1 Streams are low and salmon have not commenced running much yet.

22 Total rain fall last week was 5", making quite a rise in streams, but not enough to float logs very much.

December 1895

6 Old Neptune has been considerably agitated the last few days.

20 We are having very stormy weather. The river and Lake (*Quinault*) rose very rapidly, claiming several canoes that the owners thought were high and dry.

27 The recent rain brought down large quantities of sawlogs to Hoquiam.

~ 1896 ~

January 1896

3 Accident at the electric plant leaves Hoquiam without incandescent lights for a week. All made a hasty scramble after old coal oil lamps.

4 Utah admitted to the Union.

10 It is reported that in 1895 Washington fisheries yielded $2,858,390, forest yielded $6,500,000 and that there were 3,213 miles of rail.

17 Quite a calm after the storm.

24 The late freshet in the Humptulips River was the highest in ten years.

February 1896

7 If the rate of decrease of Indians is maintained at the level of the past quarter century, there will be no Indians in 100 years.

27 Boom at the mouth of the Humptulips broke and many logs escaped into the harbor.

28 The Indians at Quiniault have begun canoe making much earlier this year than in previous years, probably because so many canoes have been wrecked during the numerous storms.

March 1896

1 The Ethiopians defeat Italian troops at the Battle of Adwa. (*The first time an African army defeats one from Europe.*)

4 Snow falls six inches deep on the beach.

6 The Cemetery Association accepted the proposition

from J. R. Karr and secured land from him for the cemetery in Hoquiam.

13 The Quiniault salmon are beginning to run and the Indians will soon be "at home" at the lake.

20 The testive bicycle is getting rather numerous in Hoquiam and Aberdeen. When you hear the whistle or bell, get out of the way.

April 1896

6 The first modern Olympic Games begin in Athens, Greece.

17 Nearly every store on 8th street in Hoquiam has a bicycle exposed for raffle. Everyone will be riding a wheel soon.

17 A list of tax delinquent lands and lots in Chehalis County since 1892 fill 17 pages in *The Weekly Vidette*.

May 1896

8 5,426 cars of shingles and 28 cars of lumber were sent out from Aberdeen in April.

June 1896

12 The Indians are catching a great number of the famous Quiniault salmon at present. An Aberdeen firm is handling them this summer.

12 The bodies of Capt. Crosby and the sailors who drowned while attempting to land at Joe Creek on August 18, 1894 and which were buried near Wreck Creek, were washed out by the high tides last winter.

15 Northwest Lumber Company's big mill at Hoquiam burns. Loss estimated at $70,000 with no insurance.

1896

** "*The Yellow Kid*" becomes first comic strip and appears in *The New York World*. (*Leads to the term yellow journalism for sensationalistic articles.*)

July 1896

17 A good many Indians are at the lake fishing.

19 95° F.

August 1896

1 A fine rain, catching some hay out, however.

12 Gold discovered on Klondike Creek near Alaska. (*News of the discovery will not reach San Francisco and the south until July 14, 1897. Seattle would then become a major staging area for this gold rush.*)

14 Quite a lot of hay spoiled last week by rain at Quiniault.

September 1896

25 A small work force is at work on the Humptulips Road. At one place where they were splitting puncheon they had to burn out some hornets nests. When they came back the next evening they found their tools and sixty feet of puncheon burned.

October 1896

16 The beach was lined for miles one day last week with a row of smelt about four feet wide and three to four inches deep that had been driven in by the storm.

30 The Indians have posted notices forbidding the white trappers from trapping on the Quiniault Reservation.

November 1896

6 It appears Mckinley has been elected as our next president.

6 The rains of the past few days have raised the level of the rivers and the loggers, who can, are making a drive of logs. Those in Big Creek did not start and most on the

Humptulips are hung up on the bars.

12 Rain and wind storm lasting three days. Quiniault River three feet higher than ever known. The house of Swedes which just moved in was washed away by the Quiniault and they had to abandon it in the night.

December 1896

5 The steamer *Thistle* was unable to get to within a mile of the wharf at Oyehut owing to the ice.

11 All the rivers on another tear. Owing to the very bad weather, there is but little work in the camps.

25 Work on breaking the log jam at the mouth of the Humptulips is progressing fairly well and the river will soon be clear again. Once it is clear the logs at the mouth of Big Creek will be turned into the river.

~ 1897 ~

January 1897

8 Logging camps start-up after the holidays.

8 Plank road between Aberdeen and Hoquiam is in need of repairs.

8 Quite an exodus from this vicinity to Rossland and Colville for gold digging.

15 The incandescent dynamo at the Hoquiam electric light plant met with an accident a few nights ago and the people have had to depend on kerosene for indoor lighting.

15 Heron Street in Aberdeen has received a new dressing of saw dust and the improvement is great.

15 The black sand on the beaches of Grays Harbor will prove valuable for the iron that is in it.

25 The Northwestern Lumber Company which burned this last June 15th, reopens bringing universal joy and gladness to Hoquiam.

26 Charles N. Byles, the founder of Montesano, dies.

February 1897

19 Rain, wind, snow, sleet, with burst of sunshine is the distinguishing features of the weather this week.

22 The Olympic Forest Reserve with 2,188,800 acres created by President Grover Cleveland.

26 Someone is sawing off the ends of logs and has been stamping them with another stamp at the mouth of the Humptulips River.

26 Mail route from Quinault to Queets had 4$^{1}/_{2}$ miles cut off and Bruce only has to go to Evergreen now.

March 1897

10 The train run between Aberdeen and Montesano hit a tree across the track. It was rotten and the train is ok, but the fireman, thinking the worse, jumped before it hit and was knocked unconscious.

19 Hoquiam Shipyard now an assured fact.

27 H. M. Sutton in Humptulips is taking the filings of settlers in 21-10.

April 1897

9 The trouble at the boom at the mouth of the Humptulips River is the main conversation. Unless some more trustworthy management takes charge, there will be but little logging done there this season.

19 First Boston Marathon.
23 A poor fishing season closed on the Harbor this last Saturday.

May 1897

14 Spruce logs on Grays Harbor are scarce and the demand greater for than output; worth about $5.00 per 1,000, cedar is $4.50 per 1,000, and most loggers will not sell fir at the current $3.50 per 1,000.

June 1897

4 The Organic Administration Act is established to manage lands set aside as Forest Reserves.

18 24-11 has now been filed.

18 Indians at Kettle Falls claim the white man's fish wheels are robbing them of their rights as no salmon have found their way up the river for three years; the Indians are suffering from want of food.

July 1897

9 Quinault Indians are not making a very good catch of salmon.

14 News of gold strike in Yukon in August 1896 reaches San Francisco aboard the *Excelsior,* setting off gold rush.. (*The Excelsior was carrying a half ton of Yukon gold. Seattle became a major staging area for this gold rush and the gold discoveries at Nome in 1898 and Fairbanks in 1902. See July 17.*)

16 Bids opened last Friday for Gray Harbor improvements; five years to complete them. A Chicago firm, Helmire and New, put in a low bid that struck coast contractors dumb.

16 24-11 thrown open for entry.

17 The *Portland* arrives in Seattle with a ton of gold from the Yukon. (*See July 14.*)

23 Foundation for Government Lighthouse at Westport about complete.

30 Party of prospectors, including Hon. C. E. Cline (speaker of the last state legislature) left for Olympic Mountains.

August 1897

13 Clondyke (*Klondike*) fever is running high on Harbor.

23 Cornerstone laid for Westport lighthouse.

September 1897

10 Travel to the beach has practically ceased.

10 Aberdeen ice factory is running night and day.

24 Fine weather.

24 The state has selected 18,758 acres in 24-11 for charitable education, penal, and reform schools.

27 The Commissioner of Indian Affairs is in receipt of communication from chief Mason, head of the Quinault Indians. Mason wants to know laws of the reservation, "since Mr. Edwin Eells was agent, we never know anything."

October 1897

22 *The Vidette* prints its first in a series of stories about Chehalis County resources.

November 1887

26 *The Vidette* prints its last in a series of stories about Chehalis County resources.

26 Storms of the last week have been very severe.

December 1897

10 More storms and high water.

January 1898

31 The winter freshets left the ford across the Humptulips impassable and another one has been found and a road needs to be built to it. $3^1/_2$" of snow.

February 1898

4 Work to commence on the Government Jetty on the Harbor by Hale and Kern of Portland, the second low bid. No explanation given why the Chicago firm with low bid was not selected.

11 A cruiser from Kent is in the county cruising school lands. The easy work is being given to cruisers who cannot tackle the work in the mountains where a man must camp where night finds him.

15 An explosion destroys the battleship *Maine* in Havana Harbor.

March 1898

11 Farmers making good use of the fine weather.

18 Quite a crowd of amateur Kodak fiends were in Aberdeen this week, taking free pictures of course.

April 1898

15 Salmon fishing season draws to a close on the Harbor and several of the fisherman and dealers have left for the Columbia.

22 Voluntary Army Act passed by Congress. Rough Riders become first Volunteer Cavalry.

25 The U.S. declares that a state of war has existed with Spain since the 21st.

May 1898

13 The Quinault Indians are not catching many salmon at the lake this spring.

13 It is reported that the surveying (Quinault Lake area) is at last accepted. It is almost three years since the survey was made. Settlers feel quite happy.

13 Certain parties are doing much bogus cruising between Oyehut and Quinault.

20 A cable ferry will soon be completed across the Humptulips.

20 There is a revival of the otter industry; the Indians have shot eight fine ones recently.

June 1898

3 Passengers made a complaint against the Postmaster at Granville. They vowed the mail wagon was kept two hours while the Postmaster wrote his private letters and until the tide rose so high as to put their lives in peril on the way down the beach.

3 The forest reserve will have to be modified if Quinault Lake, one of the prettiest places in the world and the fertile valley around it, is to be developed.

10 U.S. invades Cuba at Guantanamo Bay.

17 Professor Kampmeir, teacher at the Quinault Agency (and native born German), resign temporarily, to join the army to take a hand in thrashing Spain.

24 Theodore Roosevelt with 1,000 regular troops and the "Rough Riders" are victorious in the first land battle in Cuba.

30 The Westport Lighthouse is lit up.

July 1898

7   President McKinley signs Bill annexing Hawaii.

8   Fine weather at the beach.

15   U.S. Government Assay Office opens in Seattle.

26   The Spanish-American War comes to an end when Spain requests peace terms.

29   *The Weekly Vidette* prints "The Hermit of Point Grenville, *Clatawa Jim*" and his story.

August 1898

5   Dwellers in the North Beach are now entering upon their annual delightful feast of wild huckleberries.

12   Hostilities between Spain and the U.S. halted.

September 1898

23   The question of what to do with our stump lands is fast assuming importance in Western Washington.

October 1898

1   Peace negotiations begin in Paris between Spain and U.S.

25   *The Weekly Vidette* features work on the Grays Harbor Jetty.

November 1898

18   The mail route has been discontinued to Granville. It is expensive and perilous route and wholly for the accommodation of a few Indians.

December 1898

9   Frank Lamb recommends "Systematic reforestation for preservation of our timber lands."

10   The Treaty of Paris is signed formally ending the Spanish-American war. Spain cedes the Philippines, Guam, Puerto Rico and Cuba to the U.S.

~ 1899 ~

January 1899

10   Hoquiam hit a building record in 1898.

13   Gravel trains have been busy in Hoquiam and work on rail beds is nearly complete.

20   Plan for the proposed road between Aberdeen and Montesano have been filed.

February 1899

3   *The Weekly Vidette* features the proposed Grays Harbor Canal.

10   The Polson Bros. are going to get the advantage of the telephone, having run a line to their camps.

14   Congress approves the use of voting machines for federal elections.

14   The "horseless carriage"... will never, of course, come into as common use as the bicycle - *The Literary Digest.*

March 1899

2   Congress establishes Mount Rainier National Park, the nation's fifth.

3   Settlers in Queets Valley discouraged with growth caused by lack of roads and the Forest Reserve. The valley is capable of sustaining a thousand people.

10   Hoquiam is the hotel town of Grays Harbor.

31   New state bicycle law regulates license and riding of bicycles.

April 1899

7   All logging camps running.

May 1899

5   Hemlock is coming to be recognized more and more as a staple lumber product.

19   Over production threatens as there are more logs than the mills can handle on the Harbor.

19   Dr. Clase, retiring forest superintendent, believes much of the Olympic Reserve should be thrown open for settlement.

June 1899

28   30 of the 33 head of cattle purchased from F.F. Williams of Humptulips, drown when a scow in tow of the tug *Thistle*, capsizes on the Chehalis River.

July 1899

21   Salmon run light until this last week.

28   Chief Gifford Pinchot has been in the state of Washington this week, talking about starting forestry schools and planting trees.

August 1899

1   The most important government work in the state of Washington is the improvement to the entrance of Grays Harbor.

18   Dr. Chase reports the largest lot of campers this year ever on the North Beach.

September 1899

1   It is hard to get a supply of fresh eggs in Cosmopolis. "Why don't somebody go into the poultry business in a large scale?"

15   The Olympic Preserve should be maintained for timber and elk.

22   N.P. Railway depot in Hoquiam under construction.

October 1899

6   As the big Hoquiam Hotel structure is being painted, it is taking on a handsome appearance.

14   President McKinley becomes first president to ride in an automobile (Stanley Steamer).

20   Five logging engines in the Humptulips country make it the foremost logging section in the country.

November 1899

3   Silverside salmon began running freely... and they are fine ones.

10   Forest supervisor Shellar surprised by the large amount of agriculture land on his survey to the Queets Country.

17   Seiners and gillnetters have profited on Harbor, the trap men less. The U.S. engineer declared the presence of traps in most localities to be a menace to shipping.

24   Frederick Weyerhaeuser and other millionaire lumbermen from the Midwest are purchasing Northern Pacific lands. They are on a tour of Washington to inspect these lands and were in the Harbor on the 20th and 21st.

29   Heavy winds build seas to highest ever seen.

December 1899

1   Storm last week did considerable damage.

8   5,000,000 feet of logs put in Humptulips River started for the Harbor on big freshet. 2 million make it to boom and 3 million form a jam about 12 miles above boom (*See March 30, 1900*).

8   Most logging camps have closed until after the first of the year.

22   44 lumber laden vessels cleared the Harbor for foreign

ports this year. Of these, 24 cleared for Honolulu.

22 Stormy weather.

28 Contract signed to build bridge across the Hoquiam River.

~ 1900 ~

January 1900

2 Weyerhaeuser Syndicate pays $6,500,000 for one million acres of Northern Pacific timber lands. (*169,560 acres in Chehalis [Grays Harbor] County.*)

** *Plank Island* is the seaman's name for Aberdeen.

26 Captain Hank's little schooner has been wrecked and badly damaged again trying to enter the mouth of the Hoh River.

26 A new dynamo has just been placed in the Aberdeen Lumber and Shingle Company's mill and their yards and mill will here after be lighted with electricity.

29 American Baseball League forming.

February 1900

9 North Western Lumber Co. in Hoquiam is getting out some big sticks that are beauties; some measure 36" x 36" and 75 feet long.

16 Polson Bros. opened their big logging camps this week.

March 1900

2 First Quinault Salmon of the season arrived in Hoquiam last week. This is a month earlier than normal and the Indians say that this means an early spring.

14 U.S. adapts gold standard for all currency.

18 Rainfall heavy all week.

30 With the fish season closed on the Harbor and a big landslide near Point Granville (*Grenville*), the markets have experienced considerable trouble supplying the trade.

30 Humptulips loggers wear broad smiles as the last big freshet nearly cleared them the entire river of logs and set into the boom (*See December 8, 1899*).

30 T21N-R9W sold a few weeks ago to eastern parties.

April 1900

3 Barge *Washtucna*, carrying over one million feet of timber for San Francisco. Largest cargo load ever to go out of Grays Harbor.

6 The new long wharf at the end of eighth Street in Hoquiam is now in use and has become a dumping place for garbage; that is not what it was intended for.

13 A second camp of gypsies arrived in Montesano. They seem a prosperous bunch. They plan to work the hitherto un-cultivated fields.

20 "The gypsies in Aberdeen attracted the attention of the Marshal's weather eye beaming over the fence and have left for greener scenes and landed in Hoquiam."

20 Carl Dick and Tom Williams, two Indians arrived in Hoquiam. They have asked for transportation to Victoria from the British vice consul. Claim they have been lost in a canoe from the British sealing schooner *Viva*... They landed near the Quinault Indian Reservation in good condition.

27 The western hemlock will be the subject of special investigation this summer by the division of forestry.

30 Casey Jones dies while trying to save passengers on a runaway train.

May 1900

4 All shake mills have been shut down for a short time to strengthen the prices somewhat.

22 Associated Press incorporated in N. Y. as a non-profit news cooperative.

25 It has been dangerous for women and children crossing Heron Street in Aberdeen as they have to be on the lookout for stray balls from all the baseball practices.

31 Boxer Rebellion breaks out in China.

June 1900

8 *The Weekly Vidette* goes from 23 x 15 inch to 25 x 17 inch format.

9 Snags have been cleared out of the Chehalis River from Montesano to the Harbor. The annual clearing this year took about one month and removed 400 snags and stumps.

15 Nine head of cattle, averaging 1400 pounds each, have been driven from Lake Quinault to Montesano in four days.

15 Chas. Clemons's new mammoth logging engine is ready to go just west of Montesano. It will be able to yank the monarchs of the forest into the water from a distance of a mile and quarter. (*See Sept. 7, 1900*).

22 There are about 22 settlers at Lake Quinault or there abouts. They are anxious to have a road from Humptulips to the Lake.

July 1900

6 The Indians who freight up the river to Lake Quinault, came up with one ton of goods for the store at the Lake.

6 Several hundred new phones have been placed in the county this spring.

13 The annual driving of pilings, to be used as fish traps, at the mouth of the Humptulips River by the Grays Harbor Packing Company. Other fisherman say that they are obstructions to navigation and they are prevented from using the best fishing spot on the Harbor and want the pilings removed.

20 Zeppelin airship makes first flight in Germany.

27 A few Indians are at Lake Quinault from Granville on the reservation for summer vacations. The settlers are busy, so little news.

27 The Italians are greatly improving the railroad near Porter.

August 1900

8 6,000 die as hurricane strikes Galveston, Texas.

10 The people near Lake Quinault have commenced to dig their potatoes.

15 Highlights of Quinaielt subagency report by Frank Terry:

"The opening of the forest reserve and the contemplated allotment of the Quinaielt Reservation is even now bringing hundreds of adventurers thought the reservation. Friction between them and the Indians is inevitable

I have promoted the industry of basket making."

17 A geographic survey party is now in Queets Valley.

18 A Frenchman named Perskyi puts Latin and Greek words together to come up with "Television".

24 Small boys in Montesano are causing considerable annoyance at the rail depot when the train comes in. Parents should keep their boys home.
31 J. Pluvious (*heavy rainfall*) drives Westport visitors away.

Coastal storm.

September 1900
1 Epidemic of the grippe is raging among the Eskimos of Alaska and has killed half the population in some places.
7 Chas. Clemon's camp shutdown because of broken drum on the big engine (*See June 15, 1900*). This is the third accident of its kind to the big engine.
7 Weyerhauser Timber Company has established minimum price of 40¢ per thousand feet for all merchantable timber they buy in western Washington.
18 A 70 foot whale was sighted in Grays Harbor near Humptulips sand spit. The captain of the steamer *Ranger,* slowed and several shots were fired into the monster. It rapidly dove and did not appear again.
21 Thomas Thompson, forest reserve superintendent of the Olympic Reserve, has made a complete circuit of the reserve. The trip was a hard one. At one time he was without food for 50 hours, having become separated from his pack horses.

October 1900
12 The Indians who have been working at the hops fields are returning to their homes and numerous boat loads of them go down the (*Chehalis*) river every day.
26 The stormy weather has helped the fishermen and the canneries are cramped for room.

November 1900
2 It is estimated there are a hundred new buildings going up in Aberdeen.
6 All logging camps were closed for election day. McKinley win carries the Republican party across U.S.
9 Deep sea fishing will be an important industry on the Harbor someday.
19 Cold snap and six inches of snow. The earliest seen in 30 years.

December 1900
10 A railway tunnel opens in the Cascades.
14 A new telephone directory has been published for Aberdeen. There are now 185 telephones in use with an all-day and all-night system in effect.
14 Total salmon pack in Aberdeen was 34,000 cases.
21 Fiercest storm off old Ocean for several years.
28 The bad weather has made some of the eastern people sick of Washington and they are awaiting a chance to escape.

~ 1901 ~

January 1901
4 Fish Commissioner, A. C. Little, opposed to logging dams. Says that they injure the fish industry.
10 Automobile Club of America (New York) to install signs on major highways.
11 Large pack train of 27 ponies arrives in Montesano. It is a Northern Pacific survey party on route to the North Beach area.
11 Word is that the (Lake) Quinault mail cannot get through, as trail is blockaded (by fallen trees).
21 The two-mast schooner, *Swan*, has gone aground on North Beach.
22 Queen Victoria dies.
25 Oil search in county has grown to epidemic proportions.

February 1901
1 Several transcontinental lines to put *Homeseekers' Excursion Tickets* on sale again. Cost is $30 from Chicago to west coast.
8 Northern Pacific Railway survey crew is camped at Boon Creek.
15 Miss C. E. Drummond has secured the last foot of public land open in T19 R12.

March 1901
1 David Bilyeu, the Quinault Agent mail carrier, says that numerous slides of blue oily clay has obstructed the road north of Granville Mountain (*Point Grenville*) to such an extent that teams cannot pass except at very low tide. It is further reported, the same strata of oily clay has been discovered at various points cropping out along the Quinault River. It would appear that the Quinault Indian Reservation is nearly the center of the oil belt. (*Note: As we see in the next item and will see in future dates, there was much speculation on the open of the Reservation to non-Indian settlement. Items about the great oil wealth [such as here], the great timber wealth, and rich*

agricultural lands along the river had settlers' eyes hungry for the great wealth they imagined on the Indian Reservation.)

1 M. Chas. McTntyre says that there are 65 families on the Quiniault Indian Reservation. That means that each Indian would get 3,500 acres of land if the land is allotted to them.

11 Polson Bros. received a huge locomotive. It's a ten-wheeler weighing 35 tons.

12 Polson's new locomotive loaded onto big scows and taken up river to their camp on the Humptulips River.

29 Twelve million feet of logs jammed on the Wishkah River. Plans are to build dams to improve the river for lumbermen.

April 1901

12 Dr. Chase has erected a fine new addition to the *Pioneer* at Iron Springs.

25 New York becomes first state to require auto license plate.

26 Track laying has commenced on the Northern Pacific Road to North Beach.

26 There is so much teaming between Humptulips and Hoquiam, that the county should repair the road, as it is in need of it.

May 1901

9 Largest single-day break on Wall Street since 1803.

10 A Polson dam on the Humptulips washed out one day last week.

24 Mr. Oliver and wife of Hoquiam will soon take the place of Mr. and Mrs. Ruder as Indian trader on the Quinault Reservation.

29 First oil strike in the state made at Tenio.

June 1901

12 Becquerel presents his work on radium discoveries.

14 A gang of ten men is at work on the Quiniault trail from Humptulips. It will be in pretty decent shape for visitors to Lake Quinault this summer.

21 The railroad surveyors are near the Quiniault River.

21 Many logging camps have shut down as there is a surplus of logs on hand and prices have fallen.

21 Twelve years ago it was just a sea otter hunting ground, but soon with completion of the Northern Pacific Railway, a large country will be open to the city (Hoquiam).

July 1901

5 Six rangers have been assigned to the Olympic Reserve.

12 The Congressional Committee on rivers and harbors is making a tour of the county.

12 As a result of special agent Armstrong's report to the Indian Dept., a survey of the Quiniault Indian Reservation will at once be ordered. Land will be allotted to the Indians for their needs and throwing the balance, about 200,000 acres, open to sell and settlement.

15 The Olympic Forest Reserve reduced by 456,900 acres. (*It had also been reduced 264,960 acres in 1900.*)

17 The liner *Deutschland*, crosses Atlantic, east to west, in 5 days, 11 hours and 5 minutes.

22 The *Thistle* made a special trip to Oyehut with a full load of land seekers in advance of the president's proclamation to open some of the (*Olympic*) forest reserve.

26 300 men are working on the Northern Pacific extension.

August 1901

2 Commissioner Hermann of the General Land Office in Washington has ordered Surveyor General Kingsbury to survey the Quiniault Indian Reservation preparatory to throwing it open to settlement.

2 The wood near Humptulips are over run with cruisers and land seekers since the opening of the Forest Reserve.

3 The huge automobile which runs between Aberdeen and Hoquiam, jumped from the plank road, fell onto its side in the mud flats. It is said that the auto which can carry 35 passengers, is altogether too heavy for the road.

9 Exquisite summer weather with lots of campers at Lake Quinault.

9 Settlers given vast Indian lands in the Oklahoma Territory.

16 Forest fire in the Black Hills.

16 The automobile has made its last trip between Aberdeen and Hoquiam. The road is too hard on it. Most recently a valve between the engine and the boiler broke. Will be sent to California.

21 Fifty Chinamen arrive in Aberdeen to go to work for the Grays Harbor Packing Company.

30 The presence of a large herd of sea otter near Copalis Rock is carrying great excitement among Indians and sea otter hunters on North Beach. Not since 1891 have these animals visited the coast in large numbers. Two Indians, Harria Shields and Cultus Jim, killed two from their frail canoe. May sale for $600 each.

September 1901

6 Penalties fixed by law for setting forest fires that destroy property.

7 Peking treaty ends the Boxer Rebellion.

14 President McKinley dies of assassin's bullet on September 6th. Theodore Roosevelt becomes 24th president.

20 Mrs. Oliver intends closing her hotel at the Quiniault Agency. Land seekers will regret this.

20 The new school house at Humptulips is ready.

20 Steel has been laid as far west as Grays Harbor City.

29 The *New London Road* between Hoquiam and Humptulips is now open for all kinds of traffic.

October 1901

11 The Quinault Indian Reservation will not be thrown open soon. The dear public will be in luck in 1905.

14 Steamer *Hating*, wrecked off coast of Vancouver Island. 200 persons and $250,000 in gold rescued.

24 Eastman firm will manufacture Kodak camera.

24 Anna Edson Taylor is first person to go over Niagara Falls in a barrel and live to tell about it.

** October was free of rain and most pleasant in past ten years.

November 1901

8 Recent rains and labor shortage have retarded the Quinault extension of Northern Pacific Railway. Grade work is to Humptulips River.

13 After seven years of darkness, electric lights shone in Montesano.

15 North Pacific survey party is now camped on the big burn about six miles from Quinault Lake.

15 Big storm.

26 The Hope diamond is brought to New York.

29 Word was brought to town that Polson's large bunkhouse at Camp #4 burned down with all the boys bedding and clothing.

December 1901

2 Gillette to market a replaceable razor.

6 George Campbell has secured a $10,000 contract for surveying the Quinault Indian Reservation to begin next summer.

6 The Indians killed six sea otters this year.

8 The British bark, *Pinmore*, lost in surf off North Beach. Six of crew drown. On the 9th, the tug *Tyee*, pulled her off beach and towed her to Port Angels.

10 Sweden awards first Nobel Prizes.

12 Marconi sends wireless message over the Atlantic Ocean.

13 The French bark, *Ernest Reyer*, was driven ashore at the mouth of the Quinault River in last week's fierce wind storm.

13 There are a dozen holes on Hoquiam's end of the Aberdeen-Hoquiam plank road. A horse has to be an artful dodger to make the trip without breaking a leg.

27 The new Wishkah dam, a few miles north of Aberdeen is a failure. The big dam does not provide a large enough splash.

27 The tides have run so high for a week, that David Bilyu carried the mail on horseback and part way on foot to Granville (Taholah). He is also the road watcher and has patched several holes.

~ 1902 ~

January 1902

1 First Rose Bowl Game: Michigan 49, Stanford 0.

10 Freshets free log jams on Harbor rivers.

11 Two cases of smallpox in Aberdeen.

11 Quinaielt Reservation is a long way from opening.

25 12°F.

February 1902

4 Indian war imminent; argument between a store keeper and a Quinault.

19 Big freshet moves many logs down stream to tide water.

22 Report states that Yellow Fever is carried by mosquito.

March 1902

1 Plenty of rain.

4 American Automobile Association formed. There are 23,000 automobile owners in the U.S.

19 Oil has been struck on the Hoh.

27 People want land out of the Reserve on upper Quinault above the lake.

April 1902

29 Chinese Exclusion Act passes Senate. "The livelihood of American workers would be threatened by cheap Asian labor."

May 1902

22 A. H. Baldwin and I.B. Glidden report discovery of a natural free flowing oil well in the Clearwater area.

22 Crater Lake National Park established.

June 1902

19 Our lumber supply is not inexhaustible

21 Weyco directors visit the Harbor; to build at once.

28 Bill authorizes President to pay $40 million for the rights to build canal across Panama.

July 1902

** Many articles in local newspapers about the killer Tracy.

23 Men's bib blue overalls sell for 50¢.

August 1902

2 Polson Bros. to buy out Weyco.

7 Story of Tracy's last stand.

30 Quinaielt Agency report notes that the Northern Pacific Railway Company has been surveying a route for a branch line across the reservation. Mr. George Campbell in now engaged in running the interior lands of the reservation, dividing same into proper township, sections, and quarter sections.

September 1902

9 Dark as midnight at noon in Shelton because of smoke from forest fires.

10 Salmon run light; Cannery people using "Army of Chinamen to fish."

12 Huge fires burn all about county.

12 In the Yacolt area east of Vancouver more than 200,000 acres of virgin timber burn and thirty-five people perish.

13 New London destroyed.

13 Smoke making day into night.

October 1902

7 John Shale held in Tacoma jail after confrontation with Indian Agent Cox at Grandville. *(Later named Taholah.)*

14 *Review Club* gives account of Chehalis County Indian War of 1856.

17 First Cadillac sold.

24 The passenger train (from Aberdeen) was delayed thirty minutes this morning, caused by the loading of fish.

25 Aberdeen Cannery is having a hard time to can the supply of fish. Salmon is piled several feet high on every available foot of dock and scows tied to the pilings are loaded to waters edge.

November 1902

4 *The Daily Bulletin* has feature on railway building through the forest. It deals with the N.P. Hoquiam extension.

14 The passage of the 15-ton American Mill engine over some Aberdeen streets left nearly every plank cracked or broken.

18 Hunting sea otter profitable but lonesome sport on the North Beach.

23 Eight businesses burn in Elma.

28 Train from Aberdeen to Seattle takes six hours and ten minutes (132 miles). Locals wanted it speeded up.

December 1902

1 Heavy windstorm.

10 North Shore Electric Company now has 150 hp dynamo. "Hoquiam now has best electric light system on coast."

10 Mile long Aswan Dam on the Nile River declared complete.

~ 1903 ~

January 1903

2 Harry Bail, one of the oldest rangers on the Olympic forest reserve, says the winter in the Olympic Mountains is proving the hardest in recent years.

2 Charles Gant issued the first number of his weekly paper last Saturday. "It is well gotten up."

2 Indians from all around the northwest are spending the holiday season at Granville.

2 *"Thirty feet of water from Aberdeen to the Pacific Ocean"* is to be slogan of the members of the Merchants and Business Men's Association from now on.

9 The rain storm last week was one of the worst that has been experienced in many years.

9 Sailors from the schooner *Solana* have gone on strike. It is loaded with a million feet of lumber for Sidney, Australia.

16 Aberdeen has 325 telephones now.

30 Grays Harbor Power and Light forming.

30 The beach is hard to travel now. The Indians have stopped hauling salmon.

February 1903

6 The mail carrier is obligated to pack the mail to Quiniault on his back due to snow conditions.

6 An exciter burned out in Wilson's Mill in Aberdeen. Good thing they had another or sections of the city would have been deprived of electric light.

13 Contract for the building of a plank road on the east side of the Hoquiam River goes for 95 cents a lineal foot. That's nearly a $5,000 dollar contract.

13 The first brick burned in a temporary kiln was taken out last Friday. It is on exhibition at the Crescent Hotel; a fine red color.

27 There is more than 16 feet of water over the bars on the Chehalis River, so no trouble hauling lumber from Montesano.

March 1903

9 The past two days have been the coldest, most disagreeable days so far this year on the North Beach.

13 In spite of storms, almost every team on the beach is hauling freight up the beach.

13 Granville will remain the base for distributing the mail to the Queets and Clearwater countries.

20 Eleven canoe loads of Indians were on the ocean hunting sea otter of Grays Harbor. The ocean is as quiet as it has ever been.

20 Nearly all this season's crop of fish, 6,000,000 Black salmon, were turned out of the Chehalis River Hatchery.

27 Forest ranger B. J. Northup's report dated Quinault Indian Reservation, says John Oleson sold five tame elk for $475 to Los Angles park. Also he reported that timber wolves are slaughtering baby elks. The severe winter in the hills has driven the wolves down.

27 A new 6-ton fire engine was delivered to Aberdeen last Tuesday.

April 1903

3 Hoquiam ordinance passed to let Grays Harbor Power and Light Co. to construct and operate a railroad over and upon its streets, alleys, or highways.

10 Reports are that the Quinault salmon runs are very light, but should improve as the days become warm.

17 A team of Quinault Indian ball players has arrived to play Hoquiam on May 2 and 3.

24 The Quinault salmon are running. Teams are hauling them to Oyehut then shipping them to Hoquiam on the *Ranger*.

24 The New York Stock Exchange's new building dedicated.

May 1903

1 N. P. Railroad received a permit to cross the Quiniault Indian Reservation.

1 "Bad blood" developing between oil men and settlers on the Queets River.

8 Polson Logging Company has incorporated with a capital of $800,000.

8 N.P has built a puncheon road from Humptulips to Joe Creek.

15 It will be at least two years before the Quiniault Reservation is thrown open for settlement.

22 N.P. says they will finish line as far as the southern boundary of the Quiniault Indian Reservation this summer.

29 The Raft River Indians are having a great time with the carcass of a whale thrown up there last week.

29 Harry Sole lost his wagon and five boxes of salmon trying to round the point north of the mountain (*Point Grenville*).

June 1903

5 Dave Kurtz, trader, told the Indians he would pay only 10¢ per fish. The Indians held a mass meeting and decided not to fish. "This is rather a hardship on the Indians, coming as it does right in the midst of the principle 'run' of the year, on which they depend to make enough money to carry them through the winter. However the Indian is peculiar and thinking he is wronged, he will starve before he will fish."

8 Aberdeen's Grays Harbor Packing Company's Cannery with 15,000 cans of salmon destroyed by fire.

12 Three canoe loads of Quillayute Indians came down to visit friends at Granville.

15 Fifteen sacks of eastern oysters provided by the state, planted at Westport.

16 Henry Ford forms an automobile company.

19 The ocean seems to be alive with smelt.

19 4,000 given vacation as Puget Sound logging camps shut down to improve logging market.

26 People traveling up the beach had better travel on the tides as the trails are simply awful.

26 After the 4th the (*Quinault*) Indian ball team will start a grand tour of the Sound cities.

July 1903

10 Bears are carrying off Mrs. Stancliff's chickens on the North Beach.

17 N.S. Richards, the instructor of the Indians located at the Quiniault Agency, says, "I look for the country (*Quinault Reservation*) to support a large population in time, for when the timber is gone one of the richest

agriculture sections in the state will be left." He thinks the land will be open to settlers soon.

22 Aberdeen's big Wilson Mill burns.

23 The Ford Motor Company sells its first automobile, a Model A, in Detroit.

24 Weyerhauser buys 11,271 acres from N.P.R.R. Company in county.

31 Daily round trip on the *Ranger* is $1.50 between Aberdeen\Hoquiam and Oyehut. Sunday excursions are half fair.

August 1903

1 "Calamity Jane" dies.

7 Mr. Easteel and three Indians have been working on the rocks around Point Elizabeth, endeavoring to make a trail, so one can pass at almost high tide.

7 Johnny Shale killed a sea-otter last week.

7 Grays Harbor Iron Works just contracted with Polson to build a mammoth logging engine.

17 At 7:00 AM two war ships were in sight of Point Elizabeth. They were under full steam headed for the south. It was a wonderful sight. Their hulls and rigging snow white and black smoke curling in great volumes skyward. The effect was greatly heightened by the sun of a perfect day.

21 Most of the Indian Tillacums (Chinook jargon for friend; people) will start for the hop fields soon, some will go to Oakville and some to Olegua on the Cowlitz.

21 A Model F Packard is driven from San Francisco to New York in 51 days.

22 Special excursion rates ($1.70) on all lines of rail travel from the Harbor to Centralia to see Ringling Brothers World's Greatest Shows.

23 The dry spell that served to yellow gardens has broken by one of those gentile Washington rains.

September 1903

7 Reservation school opens with Mr. N. S. Richards in charge.

11 Most of the Indians (Quinaults) are off hop picking.

11 Tourist have deserted the beach and travel to Queets country is rapidly falling off.

18 U. S. Board of Engineers investigate resources on the Harbor.

25 The Indians are catching and hauling fish and picking cranberries at Chabot's.

October 1903

2 Aberdeen police records show the last two weeks is about the worst the city has been struck for long time by drunkenness and crime.

2 County and Hoquiam officials find it their duty to clean out and the dance halls must go for good.

5 Gifford Pinchot, chief of the Bureau of Forestry in the Department of Agriculture, met representatives of nearly all the counties of western Washington at Tacoma to discuss the forest reserve question. Chehalis county Reps. requested the elimination of agricultural lands in the Quiniault valley from the reserve.

9 Most Indians back from hop picking. They are now on their Kilapie (*kel'-a-pi*) for their Illahees (*Il'-la-hie*). (*Chinook jargon for return and ground.*)

9 The new store at Granville will be occupied by Jack Morris. Its the largest and nicest building in the village.

13 First World Series ends in Boston. Boston, of the American League, wins over Pittsburgh, of the National League, in five games to three.

16 The long-expected fire arrived and wiped out the business section of Aberdeen.

23 The railroad is now finished to within four miles of the beach.

28 The fourth large fire within the year destroyed the commercial block on Market Street in Aberdeen.

30 The mammoth log, which is to be featured at the Washington exhibit at the St. Louis Fair is on exhibit in Seattle now. The toothpick is 36 feet long and 9 feet 11 inches in diameter. In one end is an office and the other is a cage to be occupied by a bear, a cougar and a squirrel.

30 The new railroad station at Joe Creek where P. H. Roundtree is laying off a townsite, is to be called "Pacific Beach." Other names considered were Bluffton, Roundtree, Illihee Beach, and Ocean View.

30 E. L. Follett, a noted timber cruiser and locator, is interested in the opening of the Quiniault Indian Reservation and says it will open one of the finest bodies of farming land in the state. He thinks there is little good timber there, but nearly all will be valuable for farming.

November 1903

6 This has been a beautiful fall.

6 S. R. Castile has been engaged in completing the trail along the beach from Granville to Queets. The new trail over the Point (*Cape Elizabeth*) will be of great assistance to those who travel the beach.

6 Quite a bit of sickness now prevails among the Indians; a sort of grip. Old Chief Mason has been very sick.

13 The heavy rains have kept the rivers full for nearly two weeks.

20 The Humptulips River is very treacherous now since they splash (*release the water from behind the dams to float logs down river*) so often on the upper river, as we never know when it is safe to ford.

27 The Aberdeen Electric Light Company is securing a list of persons who burn lights in their houses all night long and other places when unnecessary.

30 *Acme* carries cargo of 500,000 feet of lumber from Montesano. Draws nearly 15 feet and has no difficulty in going down the Chehalis River.

December 1903

11 It has been nearly impossible to ford the Humptulips with teams since they began splashing at the upper camps.

11 Heavy rains which swelled the Quiniault are over and we are enjoying clear frosty nights.

11 Polson purchased the entire outfit of the Washington Logging Company.

17 Wrights fly heavier-than-air plane at Kitty Hawk, South Carolina.

18 The long disputed question of the boundary line between Jefferson and Chehalis Counties is apt to be settled soon.

25 The Quiniault Indians are busy now freighting and fishing, as this is one of their heaviest months.

25 The Indians during the past week have picked-up on the beach quite a bit of new lumber. We presume some schooner has been wrecked.

~ 1904 ~

January 1904
8 The water main which crosses the Chehalis River to Aberdeen is broken again.

8 *Clallam* flounders in Juan de Fuca with the loss of fifty-one lives.

30 Linemen who have been working for the electric company in Aberdeen were discharged because they refused to work on Sunday.

February 1904
5 Oil all around us; gushers will soon be flowing the real thing.

6 Snow fell to a depth of six inches.

10 Japan and Russia declare war.

19 Weyerhaeuser Timber Company will try forestry.

19 The first scouts of the Bluebacks are now coming into the Quiniault River.

19 The windstorm of last Thursday was considered the hardest in years.

23 Raymond post office opens with Leslie Raymond postmaster.

March 1904
4 Aberdeen Electric Light Company will put in new electric street lights and put meter in all residences.

11 Cleveland Jackson and N. S. Richards of Granville are visiting Hoquiam. Say, "the Indians are coming out with a crack-a-jack team next season and will scoop the county. We want revenge from last year and we will get it."

18 Hoquiam-Aberdeen Electric Road nears completion.

18 The constant snow falls of January became very tiresome, but now the incessant downpour of rain have been actually annoying.

25 All the big loggers of Chehalis County except for Chas. Clemons have incorporated as the Grays Harbor Loggers Association. The object is to keep up the price of logs and to secure a good scale from the mill men.

25 Contractors are beginning work again and will close that gap on the railroad near Joe Creek. With the plat made for Pacific Beach, we feel we will grow.

April 1904
1 The road around the bluff (*Point Grenville*) has been impassable for three weeks.

1 The Indians have had a hard time this winter. As soon as the weather clears, we will begin to clear away the wreckage and build four new houses and put the village (*Granville*) in good shape once again.

8 Mrs. Ocelia Gracie gave birth to twin boys. They are the first twins ever born on the Reservation within recollection of the oldest Indians.

11 First car to pass over the streets of Hoquiam crossed the bridge making the run to the end of 8th Street.

15 Story about Quiniault land slide grows in size as story spreads.

15 Plat is filed of new townsite on North Beach; Pacific Beach.

22 The road around the bluffs (*Point Grenville*) is still impassable, but a good northwester should put it in good shape.

29 The Blueback run has at last commenced. It has been latest in coming in for many years.

29 Quite a lot of freight has accumulated at the mountain (*Point Grenville*), as the beach road is still impassable.

30 The St. Louis Worlds Fair, known as the Louisiana Purchase Exposition opens. Introduction of the ice-cream cone.

May 1904
5 Cy Young, of Boston Americans, pitches major league's first perfect game.

13 Travel has become heavy on the beach.

13 The Indians are catching about 300 Blueback a day.

13 Report of a cold spring which oozes forth a mixture of mud and water across the river from Granville. (*Garfield Gas Mound*.)

June 1904
17 Blueback run proving to be one of poorest in years.

15 1,000 people, many of them children, may have died when the *General Slocum* caught fire and sank in New York Harbor.

July 1904
15 A large number of squatters are reported above Lake Quinault along the river.

31 Trans-Siberian Railway completed.

August 1904
1 In its most recent folder, the Northern Pacific Railway calls attention to the Grays Harbor area's natural resources and opportunities.

4 Quinault survey completed and sent in. To be used in allotting Reservation lands.

10 A Grays Harbor spruce at the St. Louis exposition, measures only 38 feet in length and 9 feet in diameter, because larger logs won't go through rail tunnels. It has been "excavated" to make rooms as in a house. It was sent to prove that big trees exist in the Pacific Northwest.

September 1904
20 Wright Brothers make public flight with *Flyer II* at Huffman Prairie, Ohio.

October 1904
4 Plat of Raymond filed.

7 N. P. running a night and day force with their steam shovel. A construction trail will run to Pacific Beach in a few weeks.

21 Tons of salmon are being shipped on ice from Aberdeen to Tacoma by N. P. Express Company to Tacoma.

27 New York City opens underground railway.

28 51,000 acres in Olympic Reserve open for settlement; fine chance to get farm cheap.

28 Eleven vessels cross Harbor bar in one day; six of which were four masters.

November 1904
4 The surveyor general has received notice of acceptance of the survey of the Quiniault Indian Reservation.

11 President Roosevelt and Republicans take everything in

sight in county's elections.

11 10,000,000 feet of logs lying in mud of Big Creek, a branch of the Humptulips, as a result of the going out (*burst*) of the big dam of the Humptulips Driving Company.

18 Joe Bilyeu, while driving the mail stage up the beach (11th), was nearly caught by a huge breaker. Then near Joe Creek, he was caught by surf and his wagon thrown against the cliff, while the sea broke over his horses and wagon.

25 The inclement weather is taking its toll.

December 1904

2 Harbor businesses complain about slow, nearly all day's journey by rail to Sound cities.

2 Quite a number are finding it more convenient to use coal for donkey engines, instead of wood, as herefore. Local dealers are well satisfied with the change.

3 The small vessel *Albatross* runs ashore at the mouth of the Quiniault River in heavy seas.

9 Montesano electric light plant runs only till midnight. In winter it is turned on at 5:00 AM.

9 The N. P. construction train is at work on the beach at Moclips.

16 Reports are that offices in Washington D. C. are endeavoring to have Quiniault Indian Reservation thrown into the forest reserve.

23 The Joe Creek Bridge is good scenery, but the road leading to it from the beach is completely filled with logs.

23 Mr. Bilyeu, the mail carrier, reports a bad landslide on the south side of Dan' Mountain and blocks the road so he cannot pass with a wagon.

24 A white Christmas at Lake Quinault.

~ 1905 ~

January 1905

1 Rev. W. E. Cox preaches first Methodist sermon in school house in Raymond.

12 Ice thick enough on tidelands to support a good sized boy.

13 Heavy snowfall; all electric cars stopped in Aberdeen.

13 Sixty men working for Northern Pacific on terminus grounds at Moclips.

14 Prior to the recent snowfall, the Indians had been hunting sea lions.

17 Live wire kills a team of horses in Aberdeen.

20 Its now possible to get through with a wagon over the road constructed by the Indians on the bluffs back of Point Gra(*e*)nville and they are busy corduroying it with cedar puncheon.

February 1905

1 The Transfer Act transfers Forest Reserves from the Department of the Interior to the Department of Agriculture and establishes the U.S. Forest Service.

7 Storm ruins the wire.

10 The approaches to the Joe Creek bridge are now completely blocked with logs and the banks on both sides are washing out.

13 Cold weather brings an epidemic of "La Grippe" to Harbor.

14 Russia has lost 50,000 sons in war with Japan to date.

26 The sand has washed off the rocks at Copalis Point and it is almost impassible. "Old Dan" of Dan's Mountain (*Point Grenville*) stripped one of the wheels, of his buggy, of every spoke on Tuesday. It will be a blessing when the new road is finished.

March 1905

3 J. Brown, of Kalalock, passed through the Agency on his way home with a band of fourteen Angora goats.

3 Delightfully clear, sun shinny, dry weather on North Beach for the last ten days.

4 Theodore Roosevelt inaugurated.

8 Street demonstrations call for overthrow of Russian monarch and end of war with Japan.

13 200,000 killed as Russians leave Mukden.

17 Another week of fine dry weather on the North Beach.

24 Jules Verne dies.

24 Schooner *Albatross* is anchored in the Quiniault River.

25 Evangelist Mrs. Spohn "To chase after Sin in Aberdeen."

31 Allotment must be made first to the Indians on the Quiniault Reserve. May not open for two years to the settlers.

April 1905

21 There is talk of opening the Quiniault Reservation for settlement.

28 38,000 acres north of the Quinault Indian Reservation will be opened to settlement by Government on July 13.

May 1905

5 An unauthentic source says Mr. Roundtree has sold his Pacific Beach property to Joe Stearns of Hoquiam.

19 Montesano and Northern Railway Company formed to build railroad northward into Mason County from Montesano.

June 1905

1 Lewis and Clark Centennial Exposition opens in Portland

2 N.P.R.R. will no longer carry passengers to North Beach. Work train riding is dangerous and the company does not want the liability.

16 The steam shovel has been put to use in Roundtree Cut and a work train is hauling gravel now. The N.P. depot at Moclips is assuming shape rapidly.

16 There is quite a crew clearing the Humptulips of snags and other obstructions with a donkey engine.

21 Railway to Moclips completed. First train to be July 1.

30 Riots break out all over Russia.

July 1905

6 Jack Donnelly charged with manslaughter after Fred Ross dies of injuries from their July 4th Boxing match in Aberdeen. He is exonerated on the 7th. Largest headlines to ever appear in *The Aberdeen Daily Bulletin*.

11 Russia and Japan accept President Roosevelt's proposal for a peace parley at Portsmouth, N.H.

20 Strike hits Grays Harbor mills.

August 1905

1 Lizzie Harris and Dora Mann get into slashing affray on Hume Street.

21 Twenty-five lumber ships in bay. Grays Harbor currently recognized as the largest lumber shipping port in the world.

September 1905

2 6000 HP turbine installed by Electric Company in Aberdeen

5 Russia and Japan sign Peace Treaty. Roosevelt hailed as hero of the hour.

October 1905

2 Thriving Little Village reported growing at Moclips.

November 1905

6 Moclips Beach Hotel burned to ground.

December 1905

6 Norwegian explorer, Roald Amundsen, has discovered that the north magnetic pole on King William Island has moved somewhat since John Ross, a British explorer, discovered it 60 years ago.

Marine clouds

~ 1906 ~

January 1906

9 Road to Montesano from Aberdeen now assured.

17 Train service to and from Aberdeen must change; Aberdeen no longer a little town.

23 Storm stirs up lots of trouble.

February 1906

1 *The Raymond Herald* begins publication.

3 Three story brick skyscraper to loom up grandly on Heron Street in Aberdeen.

19 Storm causes hold-up in shipping traffic.

26 Lizzie Morgan's opium joint unearthed in Aberdeen.

28 Indians ready to go on warpath-dispute about sheep grazing at Point Grenville and dogs.

March 1906

1 Cold snap a surprise to Harbor.

13 Susan B. Anthony, American suffragist, dies.

April 1906

7 174-foot steamer *Quinault* launched at Aberdeen.

18 Bay City (San Francisco) ravaged by earthquake at 5:10 a.m. and the fires that followed (*the rebuilding of the city greatly stimulated logging on Grays Harbor*).

May 1906

7 Steamer *Norwood* collides with Chehalis River Bridge, some of which collapses on the 8th.

19 The 12 mile long Simplon Tunnel, world's longest, opens between Italy and Switzerland.

28 Ad in *The Aberdeen Daily Bulletin* for Pacific Beach homes with ocean view selling from $75.00 to $100.00.

June 1906

16 Aberdeen mills suspend operations in wake of seamen strike.

30 Pure Food and Drug Act becomes law.

July 1906

16 Aberdeen population grows to 10,173 from 3,000 in 1900.

23 60,000 troops in St. Petersburg.

August 1906

2 James Standfield awarded contract to build new Hoquiam school house for $1,457.40. He was the only bidder.

16 Move afoot to move county seat from Montesano to Aberdeen.

September 1906

13 Congressmen pledge support for a deep water port at Grays Harbor.

22 Ad appears in *The Aberdeen Daily Bulletin* for free mill sites in Raymond.

October 1906

6 First American troops arrive in Cuba.

21 2,000 watch launching of the 185 foot steamer *Hornet* in Aberdeen.

November 1906

1 *The Aberdeen Daily Bulletin* favors move of county seat from Montesano to Aberdeen.

13 Contract quickly awarded to build new court house in Montesano.

13 Raft of cedar log breaks free in Hoquiam and heads to sea.

15 Violent storm falls tree across flume which supplies Hoquiam water supply. Mills use up water over night for their boilers and city is left without water. Greatest storm in city's history.

15 The mud lark, a 3" lizard like microbe, came out of water pipe at *Bulletin's* office.

16 Schooner *Emma Claudina* lost off Harbor. Genuine Chinook prevails.

18 42 lost when steamer *Jeannie* rams steamer *Dix* near Seattle.

December 1906

1 Grandma Mason, mother of Chief Mason, dies at 120.

1 Hoquiam water infected with bacteria.

3 Steamer *Quinault* sets new record for round trip between San Francisco and Aberdeen in just under seven days.

7 Much havoc from storm.

7 Northern Pacific to build second line. This one along the north bank of the Chehalis River.

11 Hoquiam flume again broken by windfall.

21 168 foot steam schooner *Berkely* launched from Lindstrom's shipyard.

~ 1907 ~

January 1907

14 Glass (*thermometer*) drops to 18° F. (14° F. on the 17th) and mills suspend operations due to frozen water.

18 Three inches of snow.

February 1907

15 Senate and House favor Bill to create Grays Harbor County.

16 The people of Hoquiam think they should get their own county if Aberdeen gets one.

March 1907

8 Rumor that angry Queets settlers hanged a cruiser. (*They were upset, but did not hang him*).

19 Steelhead sells for up to 7$\frac{1}{2}$¢/lb as poor season closes.

** 745,500,000 feet in 75 cargoes break all records this month.

April 1907

15 Quinaults leave to visit President about forest reserve.

15 Three day Shaker revival meeting at Chenoise Creek.

May 1907

4 State road from Aberdeen to Montesano opens; Mr. Rutherford first to drive it.

6 "Floater" pulled from Harbor; makes 9th in last 60 days.

7 County Commissioners fight division of Chehalis (G.H.) County.

12 First Mother's Day in Philadelphia.

15 Seymour Simmons and his Quinault performers leave for Coney Island, New York to present water events and canoe demonstrations. Several in group had saved ship wrecked Marines and were decorated for bravery in rescues.

June 1907

3 Train collides with automobile on Summit Street in Aberdeen.

11 Post Office name changed from Granville to Taholah.

17 Twenty-one graduate from Aberdeen High School.

29 Dr. Lycan's 270 room Moclips Beach Hotel opens.

July 1907

3 Heavy thunderstorm.

13 Grand opening of Moclips Hotel.

18 John Copalis made comment on Dahj Brothers trial for digging up Indian graves.

19 385' steamer *Bessie Dollar* of Mexico, largest vessel ever to visit Harbor, taking on lumber for China.

23 Theodore Roosevelt establishes the Copalis National Wildlife Refuge by Executive Order. (*Extends from Copalis Rock north to Kalaloch.*)

24 Iron Springs is a popular resort.

27 Police and Customs Officers raid Hoquiam opium joints.

28 Great Coney Island fire.

August 1907

2 Tales of bad conditions on Reservations; Smallpox at Chehalis.

5 Raymond incorporated.

13 The west peak of Mount Olympus reached "offically" for the first time by a group of eleven members of the Mountaineers of Seattle.

17 Pike Place Market opens in Seattle.

18 1,000 on beaches from Pacific Beach to Point Grenville; 550 on one train to new Moclips Hotel alone.

24 Steamer *Grays Harbor* launched at Lindstrom's Shipyard.

September 1907

5 Eleven die in Webb Hotel fire in Shelton.

11 Secretary of War Taft delivers speech to immense crowd at Aberdeen.

20 Six inch coal vein discovered on High School Hill in Aberdeen.

21 Steamer *Tellus*, runs aground on North sand spit at entrance of Harbor; is total loss.

28 Polson caricature in *The Aberdeen Daily Bulletin*.

October 1907

3 Fourteen Windjammers now loading on the Harbor; most ever.

28 U.S. allotting agent F.R. Archer will complete his field work tomorrow on the Quinault Reservation. Over 500 allotments have been made. "The natives were simply allowed agricultural land, the timber being held for the government."

November 1907

3 Loggers break big log jam (12 million feet) on Wishkah River. The logs, which belong to several companies, make it to salt water.

11 Wood mills pay workers with clearing house certificates.

December 1907

21 Steamer *Capistrano* launched from Lindstrom's shipyard.

23 Strong southwesterly.

~ 1908 ~

January 1908

5 High wind causes highest flood tide in years.

6 Three year old girl falls from sidewalk in front of her home in Aberdeen tide flats and drowns.

7 *San Jacinto* launched from Matthew shipyard in Hoquiam.

February 1908

11 Work on Brown's Point Jetty well underway.

11 Steamers *Olsen* and *Mahoney* leave with Grays Harbor lumber for the Panama Canal.

27 Engineer's report on tide flat filling completed.

March 1908

3 Moclips citizens convince County Commissioners to allow all Moclips saloon licenses to expire on September 1.

6 Seattle people to erect brick building on Heron Street this season.

13 Heaviest rain storm of season welcomed by lumbermen, but impeded railway traffic.

16 The 400 foot British *Indravelli*, largest ship to visit Harbor, arrives.

16 Schooner *Mildred* wrecked on Grays Harbor Jetty.

21 Boom breaks in Moclips River and lets logs (*mostly cedar*) go to sea. Most collect on beach for mile or two north.

21 Governor Albert Mead addresses Newsboys and others at Aberdeen's Baptist Church.

25 J.R. Converse, Seattle hardware salesman, will start using auto to cover his territory, which includes Grays Harbor. He thinks he can best railway schedule and that the auto is the way of the future.

April 1908

27 Summer Olympics begin in London.

28 Fresh Quinault Blueback salmon will be shipped east to large U.S. cities.

May 1908

3 Aberdeen Presbyterian Church dedicated.

3 A number of autos use Aberdeen-Montesano road. Not only passable, but in good condition. The road to the beach should be in good condition by summer.

5 Coast Saloon closed, when dredging in river by Northern Pacific Railway weakens foundation. Billy (*the notorious*) Gohl, secretary of the Sailors Union, whose office was in the same building, said "[The] building cracked and groaned until I thought it was going down."

20 Aberdeen Mayor Frances has his picture taken.

20 Sixteen battleships pass Harbor; imposing scene.

20 Flying squirrel shot at Polson's Camp. To be exhibited at Log Cabin Bar.

22 A party of 3 autos left this morning for Tacoma. Trains are filled to capacity with excursioners. Many going to tour battleships now at Seattle.

28 Two [train] carloads of seed oysters for planting reach Harbor.

June 1908

1 *The Aberdeen Daily Bulletin* renamed *The Aberdeen World*. Now under ownership of noted cartoonist John Gilbert.

6 Frank Cline finds gold just north of Queets.

8 Washington Forest Fire Association formed.

12 Chief Mason and a number of Quinaults went by train from Moclips to see the circus. Say these are busy times at the agency fishing and that they are paying considerable attention to agriculture and lots of potatoes have been planted.

20 Northrop Brothers say they found huge chunk of ambergris on Tribal beach. (*Ambergris is a waxy substance from the intestines of sperm whales and used as a fixative in perfumes.*)

23 Wireless now working between Aberdeen and Westport.

30 John Lindstrom, former Aberdeen Mayor and wealthy ship-builder, falls four stories to his death in Salem, Oregon.

30 Huge explosion over Tunguska in Siberia flattens 850 square miles of forest. (*It would take 88 years before evidence was found pointing to a meteorite which fragmented four miles above the ground, releasing 10 to 20 megatons of TNT [1,000 Hiroshima bombs].*)

July 1908

2 Paving of Aberdeen streets to begin. The Mayor is opposed to planked streets.

7 Copalis-Hoquiam road nears completion. It is the last link in coast to coast highway.

8 75,000 Quinault salmon caught this season; worth $35,000 to the tribesmen.

9 Chehalis Indians claim entire county.

18 Forest fire raging near Aberdeen.

20 Sotomish, 100 year old Quinault leader, dies.

29 Fire wipes out many buildings in Aberdeen: four saloons, two blacksmiths, one hotel, two storage buildings, a trestle, and a dock.

August 1908

4 Fires burn 45 square miles along Wishkah and East Fork Hoquiam rivers.

8 No smoking to be allowed in new Aberdeen Library.

12 Rain is death to big forest fires.

14 Congressman Cushman wants unallotted lands on the Quinault Reservation opened up.

September 1908

16 Businessmen interested in plan for a national park of several hundred acres on shores of Lake Quinault.

18 Orville Wright injured in airplane accident. His passenger, Lt. Thomas Selfridge becomes first person killed in an airplane accident.

28 Indian Jack Oyo's forested property on the north side of Hoquiam to be sold.

October 1908

1 Model T introduced.

26 Nome, Alaska and Seattle communicate by wireless, a new long distance record.

29 Union Pacific Railroad buys land in Hoquiam.

November 1908

3 William Taft defeats William Jennings Bryan for presidency.

24 At thirty cents per Pound, a shortage of turkey for Thanksgiving.

26 Moclips raises $400.00 to save Indian land to build seawall in front of Moclips Hotel.

29 First Catholic Mass in Raymond.

December 1908

12 Severe gale rages on Harbor; steamers are bar-bound.

17 Harbor is Mecca for railway crews as they gear up for U.P. work.

23 Chehalis only county not cruised.

26 Moclips threatened with destruction if violent gale does not let up soon. Seawall washed away.

~ 1909 ~

January 1909

1 *The Aberdeen World* prints its first edition "Along Big City Lines" on Duplex Press.

8 Cold and snow force Harbor loggers to quit.

11 Grays Harbor Earthquake, 4:03 p.m.

17 First edition of *The Sunday World*.

19 Gale sweeps all of G.H. District.

22 President wants nation to preserve natural resources.

February 1909

13 Canoe accident on the Quinault River leaves baby dead.

17 Geronimo, Apache leader, dies.

25 Crew begins work at Rochester on Union Pacific grade to Grays Harbor District.

26 Work now underway on *Finch Building* in Aberdeen; will "equal any building on Pacific coast."

March 1909

2 President Roosevelt establishes the 610,560 acre Mount Olympus National Monument.

4 *The Aberdeen World* becomes *The Aberdeen Daily World.*

17 Indians at Taholah hold Pow-wow to regulate upcoming Blueback season.

18 Quarantine placed on Elma; 18 cases of smallpox.

18 Worst log jam in years has formed on Deep Creek, which empties into the Humptulips. Contains more than 10,000,000 feet of logs. Another mammoth jam forming near Berg Ranch.

20 Swing bridge opens to traffic across Wishkah River.

29 Gov. Cosgrove dies. He took office on Jan. 27. Marion Hays new Governor.

April 1909

6 Robert Peary at North Pole

11 First photos of wrecked schooner *Charles Falk* at Copalis Rock.

23 F.R. Archer, government agent, responds to rumor saying he will not allot land to any white children adopted by Quinault Indian families. *(No such ado>òhÚn f´d–contemplated by the Indians.)*

May 1909

4 Federal Judge rules no Japanese may become U.S. citizen even if in armed forces.

10 Street car hits horse and buggy at Broadway and First in Aberdeen. Kills horse.

26 Aberdeen files report on water and suggest Humptulips or Wynooche for city water supply.

June 1909

1 President Taft opens Seattle's Alaska-Yukon-Pacific Exposition with gold key.

4 Sec. of Interior rules that Quinaults must fish rivers or lose them to Government.

6 47 tons of explosives hurl mile long hill into Satsop River to make way for railroad bed.

17 Grocery and meat markets closed on Harbor so merchants could go to Moclips by train for picnic.

22 30 Quinault families take in 120,000 salmon in 90 days for new record.

24 Special Agent Downs praises Quinault District and says Quinaults rich.

28 Newlun's Restaurant in Moclips will be destroyed as source of diphtheria.

July 1909

2 E. White, a well known logger, was arrested for failure to provide fish ladders in his log dam; will test the law.

4 Had the wind not shifted, a major port of Olympia would have burned.

5 Advertisement for Moclips.

7 John D. Rockerfeller, 70, richest man with $700,000,000.

10 Anti-cigarette Act voided by Superior Court.

14 Ed Payson ends 105 day transcontinental walk to San Francisco.

20 Orville Wright stays in air 1:20:25.

25 Louis Bleriot crosses the channel in Aeroplane.

26 Ad: City of Florence makes a good Harbor investment.

28 U. P. railroad construction underway between Aberdeen-Hoquiam.

August 1909

10 Chief forester, Pinchot, affirms allegiance to Roosevelt.

11 The American ship, *Arapahoe,* while off the coast of Cape Hattereras, North Carolina, becomes the first to use SOS.

12 Big War game near Boston, uses Aeroplane.

16 99,807 make application for land on Spokane Reservation for 41 claims.

29 California flood takes over 1,200 lives in Monterey.

31 Hawaii takes much lumber from Harbor.

September 1909

25 First aeronautic show; in New York.

30 Major controversy erupts over who was first to North Pole. Peary or Cook?

October 1909

2 Orville Wright soars to 1,600 feet.

13 Salmon catch sets high record.

16 Alaska-Yukon-Pacific Exposition ends today in Seattle.

29 Aberdeen population is, 22,000.

November 1909

3 Loggers suffer heavy losses in freshet; rivers choked with drifting sticks. Three mile jam on the Chehalis River at Cosmopolis.

11 Work begins on U.S. naval base at Pearl Harbor.

18 Storm isolates Harbor from the world and effects heavy damage.

23 Ten thousand logs float out to sea in Harbor freshet.

29 Storm sets records; maroons Harbor.

December 1909

7 Snow covers Harbor with 8" white blanket.

11 Southwest gale again sweeps Harbor.

14 Gifford Pinchot, chief forester, urges railroads to buy forest lands for ties and post and to reforest.

27 In a test case, Court upholds authority of Aberdeen to make tide flat fill. *(West of Broadway and east of Division.)*

~ 1910 ~

January 1910

8 Monoplane flies to 3,300 feet in France.

13 Thirty die when *Czarina* strikes Coos Bay Spit.

February 1910

3 William Gohl is accused of Murder. May clear up some mysteries of "Floater Fleet."

8 Boy Scouts of America incorporated.

7 Anonymous writer threatens to burn *The Aberdeen Daily World,* for it's reports on the arrest of Billy Gohl. Says he speaks for the Sailors Union, of which Gohl is president.

23 Washington State Good Roads Convention held in Aberdeen.

28 Storm covers Harbor area.

March 1910

3 Harbor District is isolated by washouts from storm.

April 1910

1 Finch Building opens in Aberdeen.

2 Artificial synthesis of rubber perfected in Berlin.

11 *The Aberdeen Daily World* buys *The Tribune*.
16 Halley's Comet visible to the naked eye.
21 Mark Twain (Samuel Clemens) dies.
23 Union Pacific begins work on Chehalis River Bridge.
25 Place corner stone of new court house in Montesano.

May 1910
2 Billy Gohl murder trial opens in Montesano.
23 Those who climbed out of Harbor fog onto surrounding hills or traveled to Elma, witnessed a total Lunar eclipse and Halley's Comet shinning in wondrous glory.
24 Court sends Gohl to prison for life with no appeal.

June 1910
2 Summer homes made available at Lake Quinault. Government opens 1,240 acres on south shore of Lake for residence.
13 Gohl taken to Walla Walla today.
14 *Quinault Salmon* run increases greatly in last three days; 5,000 fish per day.
15 New transcontinental line, Union Pacific (Grays Harbor and Puget Sound Railroad), reaches Harbor.
15 Congressman wants to start mail service by aeroplane.
16 Aeroplane to become useful medium in war.
22 Regular passenger airship service inaugurated in Germany.
24 Grays Harbor channel 22 feet at low water.

July 1910
2 100 Seattle cars arrive in Aberdeen on journey to Moclips.
4 Race riots erupt nation-wide when Jack Johnson knocked Jim Jeffries out in the 15th.
11 Quinault Indians save white rivals in surf riding contest at Moclips.
16 Forest fires on the Wishkah.
20 Forest fires rage on logged-over lands.
26 Speed law opposed by auto owners.
28 Tide flat fill ordered as Aberdeen's biggest project is launched.

August 1910
8 Broadway Hill on fire.
15 Two railways begin Harbor passenger and freight service.
25 Fires burn logged-off lands; Polson's Landing goes up.
26 259 die in Idaho fires.
27 Talking pictures is Edison's latest invention.
30 Dog, rat, and fleas to come under new Aberdeen ban. (27,000 dogs in city).

September 1910
6 Stop waste, says former president Roosevelt. Conservation to put stop to private use.
8 Rain breaks drought and stops fires.
27 Seattle businessmen astonished at Harbor progress.

October 1910
3 Heavy Storm along coast.
4 Lake Quinault pioneer, A.V. Highley, is moved out by government; will fight for rights.
9 Forest fires sweep Minnesota killing 300 and leave 3,000 homeless.
10 Canadian forest fires take awful toll of life.
10 Record salmon catch keeps Harbor cannery busy.

11 Roosevelt takes his first air flight.
14 Airplane flies over White House.
22 Accomplice of Gohl is denied another trial.
24 Salmon run breaks all records on the Harbor.
26 Want to merge three Harbor cities in four years in time for canal completion.

November 1910
2 Aberdeen Plant breaks salmon packing record - 100,000 pounds of fish in 24 hours.
5 Milwaukee [railway] opens line and trade territory to Grays Harbor mills.
8 Aberdeen will grant women the right to vote.
9 Democratic tidal wave sweeps country.
10 Gale sweeps Harbor.
17 Bar now stands 27 feet at low water.
20 Russian writer, Leo Tolstoy, dies.
22 Storm puts new Chehalis bridge out. Line to Moclips closed by slide.
29 Work begins on telephone line to Westport.

December 1910
15 Aberdeen to build highway around bluff.
21 Many loggers now on Harbor for holidays.
23 Corn feed North Dakota turkeys reach Harbor.
29 Whole Aberdeen police force dismissed; Archer is new Chief.

~ 1911 ~

January 1911
2 Polson trains barred to use in other camps.
3 Mrs Hilda Willponene is first woman to register in Aberdeen as voter.
13 Grays Harbor shivers in blast from Boreas' ice cold dominions.
18 Eugene Ely lands a plane on cruiser and proves worth of aeroplane in naval war fare.
19 Heavy rain over, but flood damage feared.
25 Snow compels logging camps to shut down.
26 Harbor electric companies merge.

February 1911
1 Billions of feet of Harbor timber will be needed for San Francisco fair.
1 Colville Indians face starvation as Government red tape unwinds.
10 Court says no to daily train service to Ocosta. Twice-a-week is plenty.
13 Moclips Beach Hotel partially destroyed by huge waves. Fierce storm threatens entire town; relief train on its way.
25 Tide flat filling west of Broadway St. underway.
27 West Lumber plant at Junction City totally destroyed by fire.

March 1911
16 Logging concerns must quit if Hay approves fire law, avers Polson.
23 Heavy rain and wind storm sweeps Harbor.

April 1911
1 Wishkah Valley farmers defend logged-off land as productive.
3 County to plank road from Humptulips to Quinault Lake.

10 Snow comes to whole of Harbor country.

11 80 cruisers at work in timber lands of county.

15 American troops cross Rio Grande to aid Mexican rebels.

May 1911

1 Union Station opens in Tacoma.

4 Rain is worth $1,000,000 in extinguishing small brush fires and in floating of logs on rivers.

19 50 mph late season storm.

24 *The Aberdeen Daily World* progress edition.

30 The first Indianapolis 500.

June 1911

9 New Washington (State) labor law says women not to work more then eight hours/day.

13 Rock for Grays Harbor jetty reaches Harbor.

17 Quinault Indians to put on big show at Aberdeen Fourth program.

26 First two whales brought in yesterday to new American Pacific Whaling Plant at Stanford Point.

July 1911

1 Self-starter developed for the automobile.

1 The word "vitamin" used for the first time.

13 500 lives lost in forest fires in Canadian woods.

13 Heat wave sets records on the Harbor; more to come.

15 Fear of fire in Harbor woods begins to haunt loggers.

21 Single mills operating at minimum levels due to poor market conditions.

24 Another warm wave finds way to Harbor; 94°F.

24 Two humpback whales stranded on beach at Moclips. Indians cut them up.

August 1911

1 Bids for new Moclips school. Old one swept away in storm last winter.

17 Chinook salmon retails for 15¢ per lb.

19 Wampum found 4¹/₂ miles south of Taholah by John Morgan.

25 Hoquiam Library dedicated; opens on the 26th.

September 1911

1 Tribes hold big three day Potlatch at Moclips.

15 Gold wealth to be gleaned from the foothills from Quinault to Flattery.

15 Rain fall records broken; 2.42" to date.

18 Rain prevents heavy timber loss. Orders to burn forest slashings given by Esses.

22 Tribe members feast on whale that washed ashore at Wreck Creek.

23 Harbor welcomes two railroads. (*Full front page of the Aberdeen Daily World.*)

25 Railroad Day Celebration (*on the 23rd*) in Aberdeen proves success.

26 Big salmon run on the Harbor keeps canneries busy.

28 Copalis cannery destroyed by fire.

October 1911

2 First Annual Puyallup Fair.

10 First Chehalis (*later Grays Harbor*) County Fair opens.

11 Earthquake in Southern California kills 700.

19 Good roads for Quinault is idea of Congressman Warburton.

21 Three million acres of logged off land in Western Washington wait development.

29 Joseph Pulitzer dies.

November 1911

1 Chevrolet Motor Company incorporated.

1 Tug *Phoenix* is a total wreck in Queets River. Used between Aberdeen and Queets two times a week to carry supplies.

8 Heavy salmon runs in Quinault and Queets Rivers. Coming so fast that the canneries can't keep up.

9 Three inch snow.

13 Snow vanishes under mild but heavy rainfall.

20 Rainfall sets record; 11" in eight days, 4" in last 24 hours.

25 Seawall swept away last winter, is replaced in front of Moclips Hotel.

28 Dressed turkeys sell for 26¢ - 30¢.

December 1911

2 Grays Harbor now terminal point.

11 Port District will put Harbor strictly on map.

12 Port passes in election and three commissioners elected.

14 Roald Amundsen reaches the South Pole.

22 Jetty deepens water on bar to thirty feet.

22 Old beach hotel at Moclips may fall under sea's high tides.

23 Harbor salmon pack to exceed 120,000 cases (5,813,808 cans).

~ 1912 ~

January 1912

1 Chinese regime becomes a republic.

2 Gasoline car to be operated on Harbor.

3 Lumber out of Harbor is big in 1911; 600,000,000 feet.

8 24° F.

12 County cruiser says elk are being killed for their teeth.

18 Tide flats may be turned into beauty spot.

19 John Shale has smallpox; Taholah quarantined.

22 Smallpox under control on the Reservation, but diphtheria has appeared.

23 Heavy rain.

February 1912

2 Applications begin for lots on Lake Quinault from Forest Reserve.

3 Football field reduced from 110 to 100 yards long.

8 Heavy storm.

12 Fear that smallpox will spread on the Reservation.

12 Motor Service for Moclips is railroad plan.

12 F. R. Archer and others upset in Quinault River and nearly drown in canoe accident.

26 Elma picked as permanent headquarters for county fair site.

March 1912

1 First in-flight parachute jump made in St. Louis.

4 Moclips business district suffers heavy loss by fire.

April 1912

4 27,000 dogs in Aberdeen.

3 Quinaults to vote on adopting new members.

15 Iceberg sinks *Titanic*.

View of Mount Ranier from the Black Hills.

May 1912

14 May forest fires in county and the Quinault valley.

20 Aloha Road may be stopped by court order.

23 First auto arrives at Lake Quinault.

June 1912

6 Harbor roasts under heat wave; 91° F.

10 Cuban rebels attack U.S. Marines; Battleship and Cruiser sent to Havana.

11 Mount Katmai eruption is largest in Alaska history.

25 Indians leave Taholah in three canoes on Sunday to hunt whale for the 4th of July.

26 Large electrical storm.

July 1912

17 95° F.

August 1912

15 The Raymond Land Improvement Company donates ground for the East Raymond Methodist Church.

16 Heavy rain.

20 Three drown at Point Grenville. Later report said they clung to rocks and survived.

21 86°F.

September 1912

7 Heavy rain.

October 1912

1 Efforts to combine Quiniaults and Quiliutes Agency have failed according to Allotting Agent F. R. Archer.

19 Storm cripples phone service on Grays Harbor.

27 Tuberculosis Day. (*TB kills 200,000 in U.S. each year.*)

November 1912

6 Democrat is elected President; Woodrow Wilson.

6 *Harbor Belle* gets plank stuck in its wheel; drifts into a snag and sinks on river near Montesano.

12 Worst storm of the year visits Harbor.

23 Polson denies private sale of Quinault Indian Reservation timber.

December 1912

3 The great new steel passenger and lumber carrier *Columbia* arrives in Aberdeen.

16 Heavy wind and rain hits the Harbor sections.

17 Jetty has made clear channel over the Harbor Bar.

17 Milwaukee rail plan causes a boom in Port Angeles.

20 Log scarcity is cause of short holiday season this year.

28 Terrific storm drives British Bark *Torrisdale* onto jetty and is now on beach.

30 Tons of dirt slide on east side Aberdeen property.

31 600 telephone lines out due to storm.

~ 1913 ~

January 1913

11 Lull in storm is welcomed by all on the Harbor.

11 North Pacific to build line from Cosmopolis to Kelso.

14 More snow hits camps; outlook bad for mills.

24 Melting snow and heavy rain cause trouble.

25 Early Spring? Pussy Willows out.

27 Jim Thorp stripped of Olympic honors.

29 First big cargo of lumber for the Panama Pacific Exposition at San Francisco leaves Harbor.

31 Olympia-Harbor Canal proposed.

February 1913

1 Aberdeen Electric Block opens; brilliant illumination inside and out.

10 Its learned that Captain Robert Scott and his Polar party

perished on their return from the South Pole in 1912.

14 "More liquor sold outside the saloon in South Aberdeen than in it."

18 Benn offers 600 acres of logged-over land to actual settlers in Chehalis County at $5.00/acre.

25 The 16th Amendment to the U.S. Constitution giving Congress the power to levy and collect income taxes, declared in effect.

March 1913

4 Wilson becomes first Democratic president in 16 years.

3 *Weir* opens with all-star Vaudeville Bill.

7 Oil discovered in the Hoh River district of Olympics.

19 Rare March snow covers Harbor Country.

22 Cowlitz Tribe wants cash settlement, not land on the Quinault Reservation.

26 Dayton, Ohio on fire.

April 1913

11 Indians confer over claims for Federal lands on the Quinault Indian Reservation.

12 Grays Harbor will be Milwaukee Terminal.

18 Outlaw and murderer, John Tornow, is dead.

22 Aberdeen's wholesale block burns.

May 1913

3 Lts. Kelly and Macready of the United States Army completed the first non-stop trans-continental flight in a *T-2* monoplane in 27 hours.

5 Timber cruisers say there is enough timber in the county to pave a 30' wide street around the world in wood.

8 Oregon-Washington Railroad and Navigation Company announces that beginning on the 10th, the Night Owl will leave Aberdeen at 11:15 p.m. for Centralia. There, the sleepers will be connected to either the Seattle train or Portland train; arriving in Seattle at 6:15 a.m. and in Portland at 6:45 a.m.

20 Cranberries to be raised near beach in swamps.

21 U.S. Navy testing flying boats.

30 N.P. to operate Moclips Hotel during the summer.

31 Sixty children spend night marooned on the *Kennewick* on Vincent sandspit, opposite Grays Harbor City.

June 1913

10 The proposed Hanson Road would shorten distance from New London to Humptulips and give outlet for 600 loggers in camps.

16 Loggers demand Hanson Road be built.

24 East side farmers say they have no market on the Harbor.

30 Veterans pour into Gettysburg for big battle-field reunion.

July 1913

4 All Harbor celebrates 4th in Hoquiam; 8,000 today.

18 Spell of summer strikes Harbor; 90° F. today.

21 Rabies infected dog bites two others before he is killed in Aberdeen.

24 Aberdeen/Hoquiam butcher's and grocer's picnic at Moclips draws 2,300.

August 1913

9 Potato blight is menacing Chehalis County crops.

21 85° F.

24 5,000 picnic at Moclips; Auto parties are many.

28 Smoke hangs thick over Grays Harbor, but no reported

forest fires in county. The east winds may be bring the smoke from the interior.

30 New fish law says that men may catch salmon for own use at any time, any place and in any manner except by dynamiting.

September 1913

5 The Indian Oil Company of Tacoma, to begin oil drilling across the river from Taholah.

5 Loggers reap benefit of rain.

9 Joseph Capoeman, a rich Granville Indian, can't get money to send his wife Lucy, who is suffering from tuberculosis, to a sanitarium.

12 16,000 acres of Quiniault land leased for oil drilling rights.

12 First concrete road in Chehalis County to be laid near Montesano.

13 All the splash dams on the Humptulips were opened and 13,000,000 feet of logs liberated to Harbor booms; usually can only be done in winter.

27 Government opens Quiniault Indian Reservation to oil prospectors.

30 Indian Oil Company of Tacoma starts drilling just north of Taholah. Sinks drill 8 feet first day.

October 1913

3 North Beach to be a Coney Island by next summer.

10 Harbor rejoices over "last blast for Panama Canal" in fine celebration at Hoquiam.

12 Storm King pays visit to Harbor, worst blow in years; gale reaches near 90 mile velocity.

16 Rumor spreads of oil strike near Taholah. Absurd, says Craey, the well is only down 73 feet.

28 Montesano Judge Irwin, rules Quiniault Indians must get a license to fish.

November 1913

24 Drilling at Taholah near Garfield gas mound hits some oil and gas. Drill down 347 feet.

29 Winter's worst storm brings floods; Moclips Pavilion in ruins.

December 1913

2 Moclips Pavilion is left in ruin by storm.

17 Indian oil well may come in soon.

20 Taholah well is reported as rich.

23 Federal Reserve System created.

~ 1914 ~

January 1914

2 "A city is appearing in the wilderness" as the construction of Carlisle progresses rapidly.

7 Winds and rain ravage county. Moclips Hotel almost destroyed by high tides and waves.

19 Japan's Sakurjina volcano in the news.

25 60 mph winds.

February 1914

26 Russian aviator, Igor Sikorsky, carries 17 passengers in a twin-engine plane.

March 1914

3 Story in *The Aberdeen Daily World* "Federal Care for Indians in Shame. Quinaults in Poverty despite land

holdings."

9 Railroad offers help for Moclips seawall.

April 1914

1 Road contract let on Quinault Road.

7 Quinaults opposed to Federal Fish Hatchery on Lake Quinault "too much missionary work in fish industry."

7 Indians denied credit, government will not stand behind debits.

10 Sullivan John drowned while hunting sea otters.

27 Quinault timber offers problems as allotments made on timber land.

May 1914

4 Quinault Simon Charlie hired by Fish Commission to rid Grays Harbor of Dog seals, which are eating fish.

22 Many forest fires in Western Washington.

28 Best Quinault salmon run in years. Quinaults get 25¢ per salmon from Moclips packing plant.

** Driest May in 22 years; 2.15" of rain.

June 1914

* Mount Lassen in California erupts on May 30; has 14 eruptions in June.

** Poncho Villa/Mexico fill the news.

28 Ferdinand's assassination in Sarajevo ignites War. *(World War I. See September 11, 1939.)*

July 1914

4 Smith Tower opens in Seattle.

16 Hoquiam to switch from horse drawn fire equipment to "fire autos" by September 1st.

23 Over 4,000 merchants from Aberdeen, Hoquiam, and Cosmopolis at Moclips for their second annual picnic. Most came by train to sunny and warm weather.

29 Fire danger acute; many small slashings ablaze along Humptulips River.

August 1914

1 Germany declares war on Russia as the European war grows and spreads.

5 First traffic lights ever installed. *(Cleveland, Ohio.)*

15 Panama Canal opens with the passage of the U.S. War Department liner *Ancon*. The official opening will be next spring.

27 Downtown Shelton destroyed by fire.

29 There has been unusually dense fog off the coast for several days.

September 1914

5 Earthquake in Olympia felt over 1,000 sq. miles

12 Grays Harbor Country Club opens.

16 Eight buildings in the Moclips business district destroyed by a fire begun in Hintons pool hall. Only a sudden wind shift saved the rest of the village.

October 1914

10 Antwerp falls to the Germans.

22 Quinaults meet Congressmen Albert Johnson to discuss needs of Indian sick.

November 1914

4 County goes dry; State in doubt on liquor issue

6 Dr. Eliot, special Indian commissioner, and other federal officers visiting the Quiniault Indian Reservation.

7 Dr. Eliot promises Indians a hospital.

12 Winter gale of great severity sweeps Harbor.

25 Ad for Queniult Oil appears.

28 Quiniault road work to the lake suspended for the winter. Road should open by July 1. The trip from Aberdeen to the lake will take not more than two hours.

December 1914

8 Mrs. D. L. Emerson donates a block of land at K and Emerson in Hoquiam on the condition it is used for a park. It would be Hoquiam's first public park.

11 First breath of winter touches Harbor; 24° F.

21 Harbor records of 14 years broken by cold; 14° F. Longest cold/dry December ever.

24 Lone German Aeroplane drops bomb on Dover.

~ 1915 ~

January 1915

7 Quinaults report best run of Steelhead in years.

13 50,000 die in Italian earthquake.

26 21° F.

** World war news.

February 1915

12 Cornerstone for Lincoln Memorial laid.

20 Panama-Pacific International Exposition opens in San Francisco.

22 Taholah road urged.

26 Quinault salmon run setting records. Steelhead selling at 6.5¢-7¢ per pound.

March 1915

2 President Wilson declares U.S. will remain neutral as war grows in Europe.

10 A Seattle grain ship sunk by Germans.

15 Chehalis County renamed Grays Harbor.

16 The giant Dreadnaught *Pennsylvania*, the largest battleship ever built, is launched.

24 President Wilson dedicates World Fair.

April 1915

1 Wynooche may be Aberdeen's water supply.

6 Graveling of Quinault road to start.

10 New Aberdeen Post Office opens; built in 79 days.

20 President Wilson says war in Europe drawing to end.

22 Quinault run to set record.

22 Tacoma rocked by an earthquake.

30 German shell 64" long by 16-1/6" wide is terror of war.

May 1915

7 *Lusitania* sunk by German submarine; shocks world.

15 President Woodrow Wilson reduces the Mount Olympus National Monument by almost one half.

18 Quinault salmon widely distributed. Claimed to be the best fish in the world.

21 Big eruption at Lassen Peak pours mud over valley.

24 Italy declares war on Austria.

June 1915

17 Marines sent to Mexico.

19 Battleship *Arizona* launched.

29 Schooner *Annie Larsen* is found loaded with rifles and ammunition on the Harbor, but with no manifests or customs papers.

July 1915

19 88° F.

29 Allotted Indians are working three days each on the road from Pt. Grenville to Taholah. Other Indians work one day.

August 1915

5 Warsaw in German hands after Russians abandoned it.

18 Moclips swept by fire; second in less than a year.

25 Firebug burns Moclips. Two fires today lead to almost total ruin of town.

28 90°F.

30 Quinault Indian land sale flayed.

September 1915

1 Germans torpedo ships by submarine. Back off after U.S. demands. (*The design for the German submarine was bought from an American after the U.S. Navy refused to buy it.*)

9 German Zeppelins bomb London for the first time.

October 1915

21 First transatlantic radio telephone communication.

26 Pacific Fisheries Company (*at foot of "G" street in Aberdeen*) took in 10,000 salmon today.

November 1915

23 Biggest storm of the year.

25 "Cute little" 70-mile blow sweeps Harbor.

December 1915

8 Harbor lashed by fierce storm.

9 80' high log Dam gives way on Big Creek, a branch of the Wishkah.

10 One millionth Ford.

18 President Wilson weds Edith Galt.

~ 1916 ~

January 1916

1 First permanent Rose Bowl.

3 5" of the beautiful (*snow*) cover the ground in Aberdeen.

11 14°F coldest since January 1909.

26 Snow deepest in 23 years. All logging camps closed.

29 Continued cold today (13° F. today).

30 Air battle above Paris is fierce.

February 1916

3 29" snow in Seattle; winter ties up whole Northwest.

7 Floods follow Chinook.

March 1916

1 Germans renew submarine war.

6 Fifth Moclips blaze in a year wipes out the Moclips Hotel.

9 Poncho Villa razes American town of Columbus, N.M.

15 American troops enter Mexico. Expedition to track down Villa.

April 1916

** Daily headlines on Villa campaign and Mexican relations. Reports of Villa death are hoax.

10 First professional golf tournament in Bronxville, N.Y.

May 1916

21 "Photo play" *Birth of a Nation* opens at Grand Theater in Aberdeen; 30 in orchestra.

27 Thousand here see *Birth of a Nation*.

30 John Rambo and W.M. Hutton open first sawmill on shores of Lake Quinault with 10,000 bd. ft./day

capacity.

31 James Hill funeral in St. Paul. He was the Northwest Railway Empire Builder.

31 Whaling season opens.

June 1916

2 German and British Fleets fight one of world's greatest Naval battles in North Sea.

July 1916

7 Building boom at Pacific Beach.

26 In annual report, Olympic Ranger shoots seven black bears and two cougars to "save" elk. One man is treed by wolf.

30 Ammunition blown-up on the dock near Jersey City, New Jersey, is believed the work of German sabotage.

31 *Oregon* launched. First vessel built at Aberdeen in eight years.

August 1916

9 Lassen National Park established by Congress.

16 U.S.-Canada sign migratory bird treaty; will protect insect destroying birds in North America.

24 90° F.

25 National Park Services established as part of Department of Labor.

September 1916

** Europe war news.

30 Chinook run is early and heavy.

October 1916

2 Engineers plan deep sea port (30') for Grays Harbor.

19 Quinault Forest cruisers map 89,000 acres of Reservation forest over last six months; will complete survey next season.

28 Long delayed fall gales arrive.

29 Oliver Mason, 10 year old son of Chief Billy Mason, dies of diphtheria.

30 New German submarine crisis springs up.

November 1916

1 Logged Land Bill.

7 Republican Jeannette Rankin of Montana becomes first woman elected to Congress. Women cast 4 million votes in national election.

10 Woodrow Wilson wins by women's vote.

20 Aloha Camp suspends operation till after first of the year.

20 Fifty gallons of whisky and beer recovered during a raid on the steamer *Quinault*.

20 Recruiting stations here enlist large number.

21 Joe Creek Shingle Mill Company begins operation.

26 4-5,000 watch launching of schooner *Santino* from the Grays Harbor Shipyard. It will carry two million feet of lumber.

27 Southwester lashes Harbor.

29 225' steamer *Idaho* launched at Aberdeen Shipyard. It nosed into the Wishkah River bank but suffered no damage. Seventh launching on Harbor this year and five others now being built.

December 1916

4 Two die as fierce gale ravages Harbor.

8 U-boat at crisis stage again.

17 Two killed when the 465 Northern Pacific Passenger Train hits a giant cedar snag which had fallen across

tracks two miles west of Copalis Crossing.

~ 1917 ~

January 1917

1 4,842,139 motor vehicles in U.S.; 719,2446 in rest of world. Fords sell for $415.70.

10 Buffalo Bill dies.

23 Prohibition "Dry" raids on Harbor cities.

27 Snowing.

29 10° F.

February 1917

3 WAR LOOMS; U.S. relations with Germany broken.

7 American ships cancel bookings.

19 *The Aberdeen Daily World* begins Associated Press Wire Service on an experimental basis.

22 Carlisle Hotel razed by fire.

23 Heavy snow closes logging camps.

March 1917

2 Texas company to reopen Taholah oil well.

9 President will arm merchant ships.

14 Fifteen new ships to take to water on the Harbor this year.

15 Czar is ousted in Russian Revolt.

23 Raging storm.

28 Whole of nation being mobilized.

April 1917

2 President Wilson asks for war on Germany.

6 U.S. enters war with Germany.

10 Russian munitions plant blows up in Pennsylvania.

17 German submarine ("*diver*") attacks *U.S.S. Smith* 100 miles from New York.

19 American steamship *Mongolia* sinks German diver.

27 First catches of Quinault salmon good; 37¢ at Taholah and 40¢ at Moclips.

May 1917

2 "Diver war" menaces Nation.

11 Block of Moclips destroyed in fire.

25 Government awards seven ship contracts to yards on Harbor.

June 1917

4 Queets Indian says he was attacked by road supervisor.

9 Latest X-ray equipment installed at Aberdeen General Hospital.

July 1917

4 Celebration for the completion of the Lake Washington Ship Canal in Seattle.

19 Troops ordered to Harbor in wake of sawmill strike.

21 Grays Harbor County sends 339 men in first Army draft call.

August 1917

1 All shipyards idle because of strike in Harbor mills.

11 Victory in [World] War, depends on Grays Harbor Spruce, says Allied aviator.

19 Whaling crew witnesses a battle to the death between a Sperm Whale and a Thresher of Cape Flattery.

27 Harbor shipyards reopen.

September 1917

14 Spruce output on Harbor commandeered by govern-

ment for the war.

25 Fifteen vessels built on Harbor in past 12 months.

October 1917

3 Indian "Billie" Charley murdered.

12 Raymond has six sawmills, two veneer plants, a shipyard, five single mills, a box factory, one wood working plant, two machine shops, one foundry, two railroads, and a street car line for a total monthly payroll of $250,000.

19 Russia plans to move capital from Petrograd to Moscow due to German threat.

27 Americans enter trenches with French. "Tipperary" is march tune.

November 1917

5 Americans battle Germans; produce first U.S. war casualties.

7 Bolshevik Revolution begins.

9 Vice-President Thomas Marshall speaks in Aberdeen.

December 1917

1 First Federal wooden ship *Abrigada* launched before crowd of 2,500 on Harbor. Sets world record for construction of wood ship.

7 U.S. declares war on Austria.

8 *Jacob Jones*, U.S. Destroyer, sunk by German U-boat.

8 Storm sweeps Washington; Railroads suffer.

~ 1918 ~

January 1918

2 Over 1,600 Harbor sons in service.

3 Spruce of Harbor County mapped by H.S. Shorey for airplane stock.

4 Indian affairs puts Georgetown Indian Reservation spruce on the market).

22 Spruce logging puts a big burden on roads, notably those from the Quinault Region.

22 *Marie DeRonde* is the 22nd ship launched since ship building was revived on Harbor in February, 1915.

28 500,000 Americans at war front; 1.5 million more ready to go.

February 1918

5 War costs U.S. $24 million each day, and growing.

7 Trucks with soldiers begin to arrive with legend, Aviation and Signal Corps, U.S. Army. They are the first of the soldier/loggers of the Aircraft Spruce and Lumber Company.

8 First issue of Army's *Stars and Stripes*.

March 1918

1 Mills and camps switch from a 10 to an 8-hour work day.

6 Petrograd evacuated, Moscow to be new Russian capital.

6 Aberdeen census shows population of 20,802.

11 Half of all Sitka spruce used in war effort comes from G.H. County.

23 British line broken. Paris shelled by giant German gun 80 miles away.

April 1918

2 Mysterious disease grips Ford workers in Detroit.

14 First American air ace, Lt. Douglas Campbell, shoots

down his fifth German aircraft.

May 1918
1 Peninsula spruce to be cruised.
7 First German war prisoners to arrive in U.S.
7 First American tank is a 45-ton steam powered monster called *The America.*
15 First airmail route open between New York and Washington, D.C.
22 Hoquiam Spruce Mill burns.

June 1918
3 Germans ("Huns") bring war to U.S.; sink five American ships off New Jersey Coast.
5 Two rafts of spruce arrive on Grays Harbor from Queets and Hoh.
7 The *Fonduco,* built for the U.S. shipping board, is launched on Willapa Harbor as 7,000 watch.
8 Total eclipse of sun. Overcast sky deprives view to most of Harbor. (*It was visible at Taholah.*)
14 Fishing locations distributed at mouth of Queets River.
22 Whale catch to date of 54 for Harbor is considerably below normal, but two months remain in season.
24 Charles Gelden of Hoquiam is first Harbor man to die in the war (May 29th).
28 First U.S. unit lands in Italy.

July 1918
3 U.S. Army totals two millions; 900 men from Harbor in service.
16 Bolsheviks execute Czar and family.
18 Allies halt the German's four-month drive in fight known as the Second Battle of Marne. (*250,000 Americans and French mark turning point of war with the Germans.*)
26 Sugar ration reduced to two pounds per month.

August 1918
10 America joins with Japan in occupying Vladivostok and drags America into the internal affairs of Russia.
22 Aloha mill plant swept by flames. Bomb likely caused fire.

September 1918
3 The *Myrtle May* tows 20,000 feet of airplane Spruce from Hoh River; makes record run to Hoquiam.
11 *Petrograd* (old Russian capital) put to torch.
12 All men 18-45 must sign up for U.S. draft today.
12 New gas device is used by Germans.
12 Drug habit is growing. Congress urged to act.
21 Heavy shore fog over Harbor.
** Twenty-eight days had no rain this month.

October 1918
5 Seattle closes public places in influenza battle.
5 The speedship *Aberdeen,* built in 17½ days, sets world construction record for a wooden ship.
7 All public places closed on Harbor in wake of Spanish influenza.
14 1,000 die in Minnesota forest fire.

November 1918
4 Austria surrenders.
11 Germany surrenders.
13 Spruce work on Harbor is halted. Loggers had cut 132 million for airplane stock.

23 Airplane Spruce soldiers begin to depart Harbor.

December 1918
6 Rainfall heavy first five days of this month.
23 Eggs 80¢ a dozen.
28 Harbor swept by heavy gale.

~ 1919 ~

January 1919
6 Ex-President Theodore Roosevelt dies.
10 Northwest still suffers from *the* flu.
13 Washington state legislature approves "dry" national amendment.
16 Fierce gale sweeps harbor.
23 State approves $65,995 for Olympic Highway.
25 League of Nations gets its start.
29 Last state needed, ratifies prohibition.

February 1919
6 First general strike in Nation's history begins in Seattle.
14 UPS incorporated.
25 Oregon puts first tax on gasoline; for road construction.

March 1919
1 10 million died in the *Great War.* Germany first with 1,808,000, then Russia. The U.S. has the lowest with 115,000. The Spanish influenza killed an additional 20 million.
3 Boeing flies first U.S. international airmail from Vancouver B.C. to Seattle.
11 Radio phone of 150 miles sets record mark.
11 First "Hoquiam column" appears in *The Aberdeen Daily World.*
15 American Legion formed.
29 Gas boat *Phoenix* runs aground at mouth of the Queets.

April 1919
** Bolshevik fears fill newspapers.
3 Five die in Clemons Logging Company railroad train wreck.
4 Pacific Beach cannery destroyed by fire.
8 *Myrtle May* goes on bar at mouth of Queets.
8 Geneva named as League of Nations headquarters.
17 Hoquiam Rod and Gun Club discusses opening streams now cut off by unused logging dams.
24 Aberdeen and Hoquiam give fine welcome to returned "warriors."
30 Daily train to Moclips planned.

May 1919
12 Moclips "Oil lands" brings $125 per acre: Investors get busy.
22 U.S. occupation Army marches into Germany.
27 U.S. Navy seaplane, *NC-4,* completes first transatlantic air flight.

June 1919
12 The motorboat *Olympic* makes record Queets/Hoquiam run, 8 1/2 hours. It's been hauling oil drilling supplies for King Oil.
28 Greatest World War brought to formal close with peace treaty signing at Versailles.

July 1919
1 Officer is bitten by a cannibal who was appearing in Hoquiam carnival.

8 *The Aberdeen Daily World* special section on Timber, shipyards, oil, and other Harbor natural resources.

14 92° F.

16 Washington announces plans for National Guard.

28 Twenty women from Oberline College in Ohio at Moclips studying geology. The trip from Ohio took five passenger autos accompanied by a truck, and three weeks.

August 1919

4 Surveys for Milwaukee Line made; railroad would circuit peninsula if oil found.

11 Cars and trains carry 7,500 to Pacific Beach Picnic; thousands left behind.

September 1919

9 Salmon trollers get big Blue Shark off Harbor.

13 Harbor may get *wireless* government station.

October 1919

8 Coast to Coast air race is on with 47 planes.

17 Radio Corporation of America (RCA) created.

21 Sugar supply to Harbor improves; $.12/lb, but may be rationing.

November 1919

3 Loggers return to work as rain has returned water to streams. However, still not enough water to drive logs.

10 Harbor Chum run sets record.

11 Industrial Workers of the World (I.W.W.) members accused of murdering three and injure several in Centralia Armistice Day Parade. (*I.W.W. members often referred to as Reds or Wobblies. See January 1920.*)

12 I.W.W. rooms raided on Harbor.

27 23° F. on Thanksgiving Day.

Trumpeter swans.

December 1919

11 Harbor salmon pack valued at half million. Fishing too intensive for good of business. Six canneries operating in Aberdeen.

12 6° F. continues the cold spell which began before Thanksgiving.

16 I.W.W. membership made a federal crime.

~ 1920 ~

January 1920

16 Prohibition goes into effect.

23 9° F.

26 Trial starts in Montesano for eleven I.W.W. members charged with Armistice Day murders in Centralia.

February 1920

** Daily accounts of I.W.W Trial in Montesano.

12 Work has started on bridge over the Quinault River at lower end of Lake. Will be important link in Olympic Highway.

23 So far, no rain this month on the Harbor.

24 Flu among Jurors postpones I.W.W. trial.

25 80 soldiers from Camp Lewis to do guard duty at I.W.W. Trial.

28 President returns railroads to private control.

March 1920

1 The Queets Trading Company acquires cannery, hotel, and other plants. To open soon. Say they will install modern Delco lighting.

6 Spruce program called a big farce. No real serviceable planes sent to France during War.

13 Montesano Court finds seven I.W.W. members guilty.

April 1920

2 Two 108" diameter circular saws weighing 896 lbs. each, the largest in the world, recently installed at Coats Shingle Company in Hoquiam.

3 Powerboat *Phoenix* fails to cross harbor bar for the 5th time. Crew blames cross-eyed black cat and two caskets destined for Queets for tabooing the attempts.

5 Centralia I.W.W. slayers get 25-40 years for murder.

7 Queets Trading Company discourages group of Japanese from settling in Queets Country.

20 Copalis Bridge broken by a heavy truck.

May 1920

1 Fire at gas plant disrupts gas supply to Aberdeen and Hoquiam, upsets daily life.

8 Hoquiam City Hall burns, but records saved.

8 Slashings set afire by sparks from a locomotive. Section and half allowed to burn while a 50-60 man crew stand-by. Will save timber from fire in the dry season.

10 Penny's opens in Hoquiam.

27 Aberdeen Weatherwax School closed for ten days as precaution in smallpox epidemic.

27 Log drives and river splashing held a public function by Montesano Court in Humptulips case. Settlers and others along the river banks cannot get a court injunction to stop work.

29 Big barge on beach at Moclips.

June 1920

1 Chief Mason's Will and some of his history.

5 Harbor residents must run their cars on 75% gasoline and 25% kerosene until shortage is relieved. Gas stations may serve their regular customers first before they sell any to strangers.

22 *Myrtle May* tows first log raft from Hoh River and arrives in Hoquiam today. Fine timber opens a new epoch.

30 Small catch of Quinault Salmon this season.

July 1920

14 Whale season best in years on Harbor.

19 Swanson plans to build berry cannery 3 miles above Lake Quinault fish hatchery.

17 *Curtis* plane lands at Pacific Beach and is slightly damaged when it flips upon landing in soft sand.

21 Reports from Taholah: Jim Cole, Simon Charley and Ham Ron, returning from a seal hunt Sunday, were rescued by powerboat *Smith* when their canoe overturned in surf at mouth of the Quinault River; Progress is being made on road from Queets to Taholah; Berries plentiful.

22 Concrete paving of Simpson Ave. begins in Hoquiam.

25 3,500 throng Pacific Beach for Loyal Legion of Lumbermen and Loggers Picnic; 1,142 went by train, others by car. A novelty of the day was a race between a 85 mph motorcycle and an airplane.

28 Poncho Villa surrenders to Mexican Government.

29 First mail to cross U.S. by airplane begins.

August 1920

3 Powerboat *Blazer* of the Queets Trading Company, off on Maiden voyage to Queets.

8 4,000 at American Legion Picnic at Pacific Beach. Airplane rides, dancing, boxing and wrestling.

8 Queets section of the Olympic Loop Highway finished to Quinault River.

11 *Blazer* sets new Queets-Hoquiam record: 7 hours.

16 Queets section of Olympic Highway now finished between Hoquiam and Quinault River.

17 Fire spreading on Powder River Company land west of Copalis Crossing.

17 Boeing Sea plane plans flight to Queets River.

23 Quinaults opposed to big shingle mill at Lake Quinault. Claim sawdust from the mill deadly to young fish.

26 American women win right to vote.

26 Disabled fishing sloop on beach at Moclips.

September 1920

3 Powerboat *Defender* goes aground just north of Queets.

15 Seaplane at Hoquiam. It plans to take air-photos of Harbor mills.

17 Simpson Ave. paving near completion. Has been delayed due to wet September weather.

23 Sea otters, the enemies of salmon, have reappeared along the beaches and lower Harbor. Last seen in 1900. Numbers should not increase.

October 1920

4 6 inches of rain in 3 days at Aberdeen.

7 Work resumes on Moclips oil well.

9 Queets gasboat brings fish pack to Harbor.

9 All of Simpson Ave. is now paved; opens today.

13 Little Hoquiam dams blown up to allow salmon passage.

15 First International airmail contract: Seattle to Victoria, B.C.

27 The Grays Harbor Mill cuts 317,000 feet of lumber to establish new one day record for any Northwest mill.

28 Hair seals prey on coast salmon is claim.

November 1920

2 KDKA in Pittsburgh makes first radio broadcast. Announces the Presidential election returns.

3 Harding sweeps country.

5 Chehalis Highway opens; new entry way on the east side of Aberdeen.

15 League of Nations sessions open.

17 Oil situation is serious, must look abroad for supply.

19 Logged lands of county labeled as big asset.

27 Gale tossed barge, *Pirrie,* is missing along coast.

December 1920

3 Twenty bodies found in wreck of barge *Pirrie.*

4 The new Duthis shingle mill at Lake Quinault to open soon. Quinault tribesmen fight the mill as there is a plan to float cedar on the lake.

13 Harbor shaken by severe storm.

13 Taholah residents ask for funds to complete third segment of Moclips/Taholah Road. First two segments were completed this past fall.

24 A small tidal wave sweeps beaches, washes 12 Sunset Beach cottages from their foundations.

~ 1921 ~

January 1921

3 Heavy rain floods roads.

27 State legislators prepare Bill to bar Japanese from land possession.

27 Quinault timber sale to proceed despite protest over unit plan.

28 Hoquiam Rod and Gun Club to release a dozen wild turkeys in Quinault River bottoms.

29 Harbor gale toll is great. Arrives at 4 p.m. (*This became one of the greatest storms ever to strike the west side of the Olympic Peninsula.*)

February 1921

2 Airmail service begins between New York and San Francisco.

2 Quinault-Queets Road is indorsed.

5 The plank road from Copalis Crossing to Aloha being replaced by gravel.

7 Millions of feet of hemlock were blown down in the heavy storm of January 29.

9 The new Moclips-Taholah Road awaits bridge over the Moclips River.

11 Clearwater-Queets damage mounts in wake of the January 29 Hurricane.

16 Urge extension of the N.P. into storm-swept district.

17 Nine stores burn in Elma.

18 The January 29th Olympic storm worst on record, is forestry report.

March 1921

12 Quail to be planted at Lake Quinault.

25 Forks oil well down 2,333 feet. No oil.

26 Timber damage from January hurricane is almost too vast to be estimated.

April 1921

1 Steamer *Grovernor* rammed by freighter near Point Townsend.

9 Aloha plant is prey to flames; whole town is menaced.

11 Boxing match broadcast in U. S. marks first sports radio coverage.

15 Moclips oil well down 3,805', but casing is frozen in place.

22 Allies give Germans $33 billion bill for war reparations.

29 Salmon count on Quinault River dwindles to 10,000 yearly and U.S. Government hopes to bring it back.

May 1921

5 Queets settlers to receive mail.

11 50 men at work on the Quinault-Queets Road.

24 Ten huge freighters to load cargoes on the Harbor in next twenty days.

27 More then 3,000 Quinault salmon pass by new weir at the outlet to Quinault Lake.

June 1921

1 Quinault ranchers have telephones and Queets and Clearwater phones to be connected today.

2 Run of Quinault Blueback salmon gaining larger by third than last season.

13 Crab catch for season is 150,000.

July 1921

7 Queets Highway progress is good.

15 Quinault Chief Mason to take air voyage.

19 W. B. Sams assumes duties as new Taholah head (superintendent of Reservation). He succeeds Dr. Eugene W. Hill.

29 Fishing on Quinault River poor; only 22,000 Blueback caught at season's close on the 1st. Average weight of 3.5 pounds and sold for 22¢ per pound.

August 1921

18 Queets store sold by Queets Trading Company to Charles O. Swanson.

23 Shingle Mill at Aloha to rebuild; will replace mill destroyed by fire on April 9th.

September 1921

5 New Indian agent cleans up Taholah. New paint on Government buildings, and building seawall. Road to connect with county is half done. (*The seawall was not much more than a superficial effort.*)

14 A 1,000' long suspension foot bridge was completed on river above Lake Quinault.

October 1921

5 The World Series broadcast on radio for the first time.

10 White pine raft coming to Harbor.

15 Electric storm damages plants. Largest in two years.

26 Hard southwester; Wynooche Bridge destroyed.

29 Beach track washed out.

November 1921

7 Mussolini makes himself Duce "leader" of Italian-based Fascist Party.

11 Americans unknown soldier comes home three years after the end of the war.

19 Harbor isolated by "snow" storm.

21 Severe storm grips Harbor.

22 County faces flood menace.

25 Hirohito becomes regent ruler of Japan.

December 1921

1 Many washouts; rivers high.

8 Billy Mason's great-great-aunt, Patty George, over 100 years old dies.

12 Log train on Clemons line wrecks.

12 Harbor isolated by floods.

~ 1922 ~

January 1922

3 British Liquor ship runs aground at Westport.

4 Timber wolf taken near Satsop.

5 Quinault power survey finished.

10 Log railroad to tap rich timber; Aloha constructing 13 miles of rail with 150 men to log red cedar.

17 Submarine beached at Point Grenville at low tide; "tall tale?" Booze laden sub.

19 Cold wave hits.

February 1922

5 First edition of *The Reader's Digest*.

24 Aloha working to connect its logging road with N.P. Its own lines now run 13 miles north of Aloha.

March 1922

25 Olympic Highway gets dollars for Quinault to Queets section.

27 Chief Billy Garfield predicts great Blueback run.

April 1922

21 Gasboat *Wipple* grounds on spit at Queets with 15 tons of cargo aboard.

22 Aloha railroad nearly complete into SW corner of Reservation.

May 1922

8 Fred Hulbert saves two men on Lake Quinault.

30 Lincoln Memorial dedicated.

31 Forest fires menace Copalis.

June 1922

1 Carlisle suffers worst in forest fires; damage heavy in Grays Harbor County.

5 Big Quinault salmon haul nets more dollars than 1915 run.

14 President Harding first president head on radio; WEAR of Baltimore.

15 Forest fires at Humptulips and Carlisle.

20 Forest blazes under control with light rain; first since May 25.

20 Indians protest fish trap at Lake Quinault.

29 Bay City Plant nets 33 whales this season.

July 1922

1 Ford sedan sells for $645.00.

6 Hobi Company high bidder on Cook Creek Logging Unit on the Reservation. Third unit sold this year; the first was to Aloha and the second to M.R. Smith.

8 Plans to move Indian office from Taholah to Aberdeen.

27 Whale season may set record.

August 1922

2 Quinault tribal members meet with Sen. Miles Poindexter to object to federal fish program at the Lake which is trying to control the salmon run on the lower Quinault River.

3 Joe Creek blaze whipped to fury.

8 Harbor drought worst since 1910; ½" in 76 days.

24 Quinaults plan Tribe Federation. Establish By-laws.

25 Big sharks stop Harbor bathing. May be following whale carcasses in from the ocean to the whaling station at Bay City.

27 People should refrain from trespassing on the filled area in Raymond owing to dangerous mud holes, some nearly 18 feet deep.

30 Electric storm a Harbor novelty.

** Aloha starts logging timber on the Quinault Indian Reservation.

September 1922

13 Quinault River trips lure many.

21 Lake weir must go to save fish industry claim.

26 New port on Grays Harbor dedicated.

27 Quiniault weir stories arouse fishermen's ire.

October 1922

3 Mrs. W.H. Felton first woman named to U.S. Senate seat.

5 J. P. Kenney, Indian Agent Forester from Washington D.C. and here on a weeks visit, announces that the Quinault Indian Agent to be moved from Taholah to Hoquiam in near future.

6 Hoquiam to get Indian payroll.

8 Lillian Gatin becomes first woman to cross the U. S. by airplane.

9 Canning season looks bad in Hoquiam.

11 John Wakatup, 100 year old Quinault, dies. The well liked and respected Indian had been employed by the Indian Department as police Judge of the Quinaults at Taholah.

12 Redskins protest office transfer from Taholah to Hoquiam.

19 Falls Creek Campground at Lake Quinault to be enlarged.

24 Indian office transfer from Taholah to Hoquiam's Masonic Building has begun.

25 The New Indian Office opens in Hoquiam.

25 Bids opened for Lake Quinault Logging Unit on the Reservation.

28 Whaling season ends with a take of 163 for the Harbor.

30 Harbor fisherman take in over 100 tons of salmon over the weekend.

30 Mussolini's Fascists march into Rome.

November 1922

1 Great Quinault tract is sold. Polson concern buys timber in Lake Unit; the largest timber deal ever made in the Northwest.

3 Indians to get monthly checks.

14 BBC begins first daily radio broadcast

15 Antofagasta, Chile is big lumber customer of the Harbor over the last 20 years; much of the lumber is destined for mining operations.

17 Winter closes ocean log rafting.

21 Harbor fish season ends. Pack light despite late run.

26 King Tut's tomb is found.

December 1922

6 Snow storm cripples Harbor.

4 *United States vs Payne;* The Federal District Court rules that the government must issue Tommy Payne an

allotment on the Quinault Indian Reservation.

8 Great fire sweeps Astoria. More then 30 blocks wiped out in blaze.

16 Mercury drops to 12° F.

18 Snow is traitor to moonshiners.

25 Harbor rivers full from heavy downpour.

26 New submarine cable under Wishkah River will soon supply power to Montesano and other east county towns (Grays Harbor Railway and Light Company).

26 Log crisis ends as log camps closed due to several snowstorms resume operations.

27 New gale and rain whip Harbor.

30 Vladimir Lenin proclaims the establishment of the Union of Soviet Socialist Republics (USSR).

~ 1923 ~

January 1923

1 Gale, high tide, and rain beat Harbor region.

9 County floods rage unabated.

11 M. R. Smith Lumber and Shingle Company logging begins in Indian area north of Moclips yesterday.

24 Russia seeks airplane spruce from Harbor mills. Plants flatly reject proposal; will close first says one.

30 14° F.

February 1923

1 The *Cub*, a 65' launch, made first trip of the season to pick up supplies for the Grindle Canning Co. on the Queets River.

3 Photos of an auto trip to visit Gray's Monument published in *The Aberdeen Daily World.*

7 The 15 passenger stage nearly destroyed by fire on the Beach road west of Hoquiam.

12 Carlisle Mill electrified.

13 Blizzard makes the Harbor shiver.

14 Heaviest snowfall since 1893.

15 Coastal gale takes big ship toll; four reported lost.

26 Harbor loggers given 50¢ pay boost. Minimum wage is now $4.50/day.

28 Special Commercial edition of *The Aberdeen Daily World* is the largest ever. Covers the port, timber, salmon, tourism, farming, and more.

March 1923

1 Mounts Logging Unit now up for sale; last timber sale south of the Quinault River on the Reservation.

6 Logging starts on the Quinault Reservation timber tracts. First logs taken out by Aloha last August, then M. R. Smith in January and Hobi should begin early next month.

10 Telephone service should be completed to Kalaloch in the next few days.

10 Queets postal service scored.

23 UW begins Harbor razor clam study.

29 The new Pacific Sea Foods Company Cannery to open on the Little Hoquiam River on April 1. Principle pack will be the Quinault Salmon.

April 1923

3 Quinault fish season starts; 45¢/fish.

9 Now 50¢/fish; about 75 fisherman on the Quinault River.

21 Harbor beaches called hot-beds of petty crime.

27 Harbor lumber ship, *Brush,* breaks in two off Oregon coast.

May 1923

1 Harding rules American ships to stay dry.

7 I.W.W., strike called off; Logging camps to resume.

8 Northwest Mill in Hoquiam has fierce morning blaze.

11 Salmon run on Quinault begins; Indians get $500 for first day; catch is early.

23 Aberdeen in midst of great building boom.

26 Cold puts back season on Quinault River.

June 1923

1 Harold Lloyd in *Safety at Last* appearing at Bijou in Aberdeen.

6 Aloha Company successful bidder for fifth and last timber tract south of the Quinault River on the Quinault Indian Reservation.

8 Small Quinault salmon pack; less then half last year's and snow water has not reached the sea yet.

15 Season ends; Quinault catch at 150,000 fish. In 1922 it was 266,000 fish. 65 Indians fishing river this year.

23 $8,000 to be spent on Moclips-Taholah Road and Queets Trail.

26 Logging camps ban cigarettes to reduce fire hazard.

27 YMCA to have summer camps at Point Grenville.

30 Quinault Lake-Queets highway work to start soon.

July 1923

2 Whalers ahead of 1922 catch.

11 Mile long train stalls in Hoquiam blocking automobile traffic.

12 Taholah almost deserted as Indians go on vacation and seek summer off-reservation jobs.

15 Thousands watch automobile races at Copalis Beach.

20 Poncho Villa killed.

30 Big Carlisle Mill Burns; whole plant menaced.

August 1923

2 President Harding dies.

11 Whale record to be set.

11 30 register for YMCA camp at Point Grenville.

15 90° F; new record.

21 Albino salmon caught on the Humptulips River.

24 26 hours to fly Continent with mail.

25 Advertisement: Last opportunity to secure Oklahoma Indian Lands.

30 Nation to see Curtis photos; talks of Elephant Rock.

September 1923

3 Japanese earthquake kills 90,000.

12 Proposal for Wynooche dam.

12 Forest to last 85 years; reforestation urged.

13 Alex Polson says woods will last 1,000 years; must eliminate fires.

18 Clearwater best route for road.

October 1923

2 Taholah road to open this winter. The new Moclips bridge opened last summer (Moclips to Pt. Grenville section, on beach).

24 Clams survive heavy seas.

November 1923

7 Famous Elm tree in Cambridge, Mass. under which Washington assumed command of the Continental Army, reportedly crashed to earth recently. (*This had an aftermath pertinent to Seattle. Years before the old elm died, a University of Washington botanist took scion from the tree and brought it to the Seattle campus to grow. He was successful, and a beautiful off-spring of the original elm stands on the campus. After the Boston tree died, the UW tree provided scion to Boston, and growing there now, in the very place of the original, is a tree from the UW's Washington Elm.*)

20 Pacific Beach sewer job let; to be completed by June 1924.

December 1923

5 Heavy rain, high tides with gale; suspension bridge one mile above Lake Quinault destroyed.

24 Christmas Eve gale of 80 mph with heavy rain.

~ 1924 ~

January 1924

1 1,128,750,000 board feet of lumber cut in 1923 on the Harbor; a new record set.

21 Vladimir Lenin dies.

28 Large Steelhead run reported.

February 1924

2 Forest Station for Northwest supported by Hoquiam.

3 Woodrow Wilson, the "War Time President," dies.

11 Heavy rains.

23 Phone line connects Copalis Beach to Hoquiam.

March 1924

6 Grays Harbor Rail and Light Company seeking power rights on Quinault River.

** Teapot Dome.

19 *The Aberdeen Daily World* publishes a seven section annual special about the County. Covers the Quinault Indians, Whaling, Lumber, Port, Forest, Logging, Fur Trade, Olympic Road, Dairy Industry, Fisheries, Beauty Spots, and Construction.

April 1924

19 Morck Hotel formally opens in Aberdeen.

23 Indian estates to be awarded on the Quinault Reservation.

26 Eleven large forest fires burning in Western Washington and Oregon.

May 1924

8 D&R Theater opens with *Scaramouche,* a film on the French Revolution and Vaudeville acts

8 A round trip by train from Aberdeen to Washington, D.C. cost, $141.56.

16 Moclips-Taholah road dried out from winter and is passable.

20 Indians win claim to allotments on the Quinault Reservation; Tommy Payne Case.

28 Small Blueback return as little snow in the mountains.

June 1924

2 Congress passes Snyder Act; gives citizenship to all Indians born within the borders of the United States.

7 The Clarke-McNary Act directs the Sec. of Agriculture to cooperate with states in promoting fire prevention,

conservation, reforestation, and forestry education.

9 88° F.

15 Blueback catch half as large as last year. Only 75,000 caught. Season closes today.

16 Annual Quinault Council discusses timber land holdings.

July 1924

3 Miss Marie Lohre, who won first place in a contest for all west coast Indians last month and posed for a bronze statue to be put up in Seattle to represent Indians of the west, was crowned queen for the 1924 Harbor Splash.

15 Standard Oil opens gas station in Moclips.

26 Morton destroyed by forest fire.

28 Forest fires, burning in Harbor forest and Western Washington since the 24th, were quelled last night by rain.

August 1924

4 The Government's dredge barge *Culebra,* working on the Grays Harbor Bar since May 15, has deepened the channel to 28^1/$_2$ feet and 300 feet wide.

9 E.R. Merritt, Assistant Commissioner of Indian Affairs, and W.B. Sams, local Indian agent, inspect roads on the Reservation leading to Taholah.

13 Robert Sampson, who filed a suit against Baker and Warford of the Moclips Fish Company for non-payment, settled for the balance of $1,393.89. He had sold them 7,070 Blueback caught between April and June at 60¢ each.

28 Lake Quinault Hotel destroyed by fire early this morning.

September 1924

3 The right-of-way clearing between Lake Quinault and the outlet of the Queets River has been completed except for a three mile stretch near Harlow Creek. The slashings are being burned and the timber saved.

5 Tribal Chief Riddel (*Albert Kayloupich*) who went east in April to try out for the Olympic swim trials, has returned. He drove and the entire trip cost about $500.00.

13 Aloha has a wildfire near Moclips. A fire is also burning near Salmon River caused by slash burnings on the road clearing project.

24 176 whales have been brought into Bay City since the season started in May. The whalers believe the whale population is increasing.

October 1924

3 Agahel Curtis, sponsored by Aberdeen Chamber of Commerce, shows 157 colored slides with lantern projection of Olympic Peninsula wonders. Sets off a three months series of articles in *The Aberdeen Daily World* and prompts promotion for development of the Peninsula.

11 The death of the photographer Jeffers on Mount Olympus' University Glacier in August of this year inspires admirers to recommend the glacier be renamed "Jeffers Glacier."

13 Whale season ends with 181 whales captured.

23 Great gale hits Harbor.

27 Freshet hinders Quinault fishery.

31 Severe series of storms appear to be over.

November 1924

4 Coolidge wins presidency in sweeping victory.

12 Weyerhaeuser logged-off land company formed to solve reforestation problems.

19 Eddie Black, 17, drowns while dip netting at mouth of Quinault River.

** November rainfall below normal.

December 1924

20 On display at the Hoquiam Chamber of Commerce is a Red cedar log that had been cut by the Quinaults 250 years previously at Lake Quinault. The log had a 175 year old hemlock growing from it.

21 The Billionth Foot Celebration on the Harbor results in joyous civic celebration.

24 Two week cold spell continues in teens and 20s.

~ 1925 ~

January 1925

6 President Coolidge signs and sends a certificate to Quinaults to thank them for war service.

10 The State of Washington receives land in the Clearwater drainage eliminated from the Olympic National Forest. (*By Executive Proclamation, the State could carve out of national forest blocks of land, known as "lieu" lands, as grant to the state. This was because there was little Bureau of Land Management land in Washington which could be used as 'school lands'. Eventually some 375,000 acres of the total three million acres of state-wide owned uplands were established on the north and west portions of the Olympic Peninsula.*)

10 First full electric house in Aberdeen.

13 Pathe News releases Billionth Foot Celebration film.

February 1925

1 60 miles per hour gale sweeps Harbor.

** Stories appear about the trapped cave explorer, Floyd Collins. Fills the news from 3rd - 18th.

March 1925

3 Dense fog.

25 Aberdeen has Wynooche water plans.

31 Quinaults gather at river at midnight for early opening of Blueback season.

April 1925

9 *Mason vs Sams*; Court rules that the treaty has reserved the fishing rights on the Quinault Reservation exclusively to the Indians.

10 Salmon run on the Quinault is heavy.

15 The Norwegian ship *Dagfred* carries first Harbor cargo direct to Europe.

17 Federal Judge Edward Cushman says Quinaults exempt from ruling by Secretary of Interior that they have to pay royalties to fish caught over a certain limit.

24 First U.S. aircraft carrier, *USS Saratoga*.

25 Polson Logging.
American Forestry Week, April 27 - May 3.

27 Heavy runs on Queets and Quinault rivers.

May 1925

8 Herbert 'Iron Man' Frank, well known Quinault

pugilist, drowns in surf while clam digging.
8 George Hyasman's body found. His wife and baby were also lost when their canoe overturned in the Quinault River on March 10.
15 86° F. Fire season underway.
29 Allotments to Indians proceed; most in Queets District.

June 1925
15 "Dinosaur" skull dredged up in Hoquiam River.
24 87° F.
26 Mammal bones found here may change history.
30 Moclips forest blaze believed under control. Began on 27th.

July 1925
2 Flames sweep 10 sections of the Reservation near Moclips.
10 Scopes evolution tribal begins.
11 Stevens Pass Road opens.
26 William J. Bryan dies.

August 1925
3 Over 1,000 attend *Dokkies* (Dramatic Order of the Knights of Khorassan) Beach Fete at Pacific Beach with Quinault Indian entertainment.
15 Word is that the road from Point Grenville to Moclips will not be built until 1927 at earliest.
21 Government declares war on bootleggers.

September 1925
4 Survey of Reservation begins anew for allotment.
5 Quinault to get new hotel.
12 First step taken in scenic Chalet project.
23 32 oz. tooth of monster found in Humptulips River.

October 1925
31 Northwest Congress of Indians opens in Spokane.

November 1925
7 Elks Building in Aberdeen under construction and Saint Mary's School nears completion.
18 Eastbound Harbor train wrecked just west of Olympia.
28 Pack horse mail express to Queets Valley difficult.

December 1925
23 Two bills filed in Congress: one for water works and the other for Moclips-Taholah road.
30 The new State Game Laws worried Quinaults, but are told the Reservation not affected.

~ 1926 ~

January 1926
1 Woman trapped on new Wishkah Bridge. She hung on until it lowered.
2 Clear dry weather marked 1925; 137 clear days.
14 Quinaults plan suit over treaty violations.
16 Harbor lashed by severe gale, 90 mph on coast.
27 In London, John Bairdgines makes first public demonstration of the transmission of a moving image.
27 U.S. resolution to join World Court.

February 1926
4 Carter Expedition to uncover Tutankhamen's tomb is winding up.
6 New plane promises 18 hour U.S. service to London.
6 Barge may haul Queets freight.

14 42" steelhead caught in Chehalis River.
19 Olympic resources await road.
22 Tenn. and North Carolina seek $1,000,000 to purchase Smokies to give to the U.S. as a park.

March 1926
4 Government engineers surveying for the new road between Moclips and Taholah.
5 Japanese freighter *Horaisan Maru*, rolls over inside Grays Harbor, but does not block channel.
10 Special edition of *The Aberdeen Daily World* on Harbor resources.
12 U.S. now landing airplanes by catapult from ships.
20 New tourist mecca at Lake Quinault since completion of Loop Road.
31 Fifty Quinault maples planted in Roosevelt Park in honor of the 45 Grays Harbor County soldiers who died in the World War.

Black bear.

April 1926
2 Electricity to replace oil at Westport Lighthouse.
6 400 pounds of mail sent by air from Northwest (Pasco) for first time. The plane was lost between Boise, Idaho and Elko, Nevada on 7th.
10 First west bound air mail letters arrive in Hoquiam.
20 Sea hunt fails to tempt Quinaults as other occupations more profitable and safer.
** Book-of-the-Month Club begins.

May 1926
1 First photographs sent by radio over Atlantic.
1 N.A. Jones of Neilton buys 10 acres at outlet of Lake Quinault and plans development. Would become Amanda Park.
9 Admiral Richard Byrd and Floyd Bennett fly over the North Pole, winning the race to be the first.
16 New Methodist brick sanctuary dedicated.
18 Revivalist Aimee Mac Pherson kidnaped. Some claim it was a hoax.
21 Big seas batter coast. The *Cub* and the *Olympic* power boats take 10 hours from Queets to Hoquiam; 8 hours normal.

June 1926

6 84° F. Auto race on beach at Copalis.

16 Cedar trees fall for Chalet at Low Divide.

24 Thousands of Jewish immigrants troop monthly into Palestine, their new homeland.

July 1926

6 Quinaults returning to Taholah; most had left to attend horse races in Shelton.

10 Pacific Beach growing into tourist center of importance.

13 Bid 3-story hotel burns at Carlisle.

17 The *Cub* and *Olympic* powerboats convey cargo to Queets on the new Grindle Cannery Company barge.

18 6,000 attend third annual barbecue at Lake Quinault.

21 Forest fire danger still high.

August 1926

2 Fires line Harbor highways.

5 First talking movie, *Don Juan*, shown in N.Y. (*Phonograph sound.*)

6 Miss Gertrude Ederle, 19 and from New York, is first girl to swim English Channel (14 hours 31 minutes). Betters the best of the five men who swam it by more than two hours.

6 Raft River Bridge (Olympic Highway) ready for cars.

9 Polson firm buys big Carlisle stand.

16 Tribesmen get Indian Agency to ban powerboats on Lake Quinault.

18 Quinault Hotel open. Built in 10 weeks for $75,000.00.

26 Lake residents protest powerboat ruling on Lake Quinault.

28 Raymond's new golf links open.

September 1926

7 George Neil, 75, lost 9 days in Raft River wilderness, found by four Quinaults near Wolf Creek, who took him to mouth of Raft River where a group from the Olympians Hiking Club were camped. They helped him.

7 30 students at Taholah School. After the 8th grade, the students are sent to Tulalip or Chemawa.

17 Raymond's Quinault Lumber Company burns.

24 Superintendent Sams tells Hoquiam Chamber of Commerce that Quinault Indians can regulate powerboat use on Lake Quinault by their treaty rights.

29 Washington State Sportsman Association tries to make steelhead a game fish.

October 1926

15 Autumn leaves clogging fish nets at Taholah.

15 Southwester with strong winds and heavy rain.

20 Big Silver salmon catch begins following heavy rains. Averages 10 fish per fisherman per day at Taholah.

22 Ocean City gets its own post office.

24 Second Annual Quinault Valley Produce Fair.

28 Low Divide Chalet completed.

31 Ole Strom, 17 year old Taholah resident, dies from football injuries while at school in Chemawa.

November 1926

12 Heavy rains.

25 Difficult to reach Taholah during high tides and storms. Everyone will be glad when the Moclips to Taholah road is finished.

26 Indian Lake plans regret of white man.

30 Indians resent hatchery on Lake; feel it damages natural runs.

December 1926

1 Quinault River raging torrent following heavy rains.

2 Slide cuts off Aberdeen's water supply.

4 Quake shakes Northwest.

12 Quinaults may allow angling on the Lake.

15 Snow covers whole state.

22 Dense fog halts Harbor traffic. 26° F.

29 Harbor lashed by severe gale.

~ 1927 ~

January 1927

3 Unusually intense electrical storm with 1¼" hailstones just south of Lake Quinault.

4 Lake lease holders say they are reluctant to build summer homes because of Quinault restrictions on the Lake.

7 Radio-telephone inaugurated between New York and London.

21 Quinault River level lower than ever in summer because of cold snap; 16° F.

February 1927

7 Southwest Washington's largest bank, Hayes & Hayes, suspends operation.

12 Hoquiam Indian Agency says that Indian Tribes under them are healthy.

14 KXRO takes to the air waves at 7:30 p.m. with a speech by Frank Lamb.

18 60 mph winds lash Harbor.

March 1927

5 Taholah Indian deliver two tons of clams to Aberdeen canneries.

7 New $6.5 million State Capital Building occupied in Olympia.

10 W. E. Boeing predicts that the age of the passenger plane is approaching.

17 Polson reports on 14 year old experimental planting; "Redwood fastest grower here."

21 U.S. Marines in Shanghai.

31 Taholah-Moclips road work progress well.

April 1927

4 Graveling starts on Moclips-Taholah road. Gravel coming from mouth of Wreck Creek.

15 Blueback season opens; they shy from Indian nets.

19 New homes rise at Lake Quinault.

25 Canners agree to pay 60¢/Blueback at Taholah dock.

May 1927

3 Tourist booklet to boost Harbor throughout U.S.

4 Great amounts of "moss" clogging Blueback nets brings fishing to halt.

21 Lindbergh completes first solo non-stop flight to Paris.

June 1927

6 Grindle Cannery at Queets, destroyed by fire in April, rebuilt and operating for two weeks.

10 Upper Quinault snow melting, Blueback start into freshet.

16 Quinault ban non-Indian fishermen on Lake Quinault and on the river below the Lake.

27 Blueback run near end; peaked two weeks ago with 2,000 fish caught/day.

29 First San Francisco-Honolulu Flight.

July 1927

8 Webster Hudson, President of Tribal Council, talks to Hoquiam Chamber of Commerce about Indians desire for fish and possible white fishing at Lake.

15 Low Divide Chalet opens.

17 1,200 attend annual Lake Quinault Barbecue.

18 Quinault tribesmen scatter over state's berry and fruit fields.

20 First shipment of fresh fish from Queets by truck over new road; 2 tons/day.

20 Surveyors find fine route for Copalis Beach-Pacific Beach road.

21 Phone lines currently being extended from Humptulips to Quinault.

30 Bids called for mail delivery to Queets County; will begin on August 30th.

August 1927

3 Proposal that timber strips be left along both banks of lower Quinault River to protect scenic beauty.

5 Olympic timber survey underway.

17 Fire rages on upper Quinault; delays timber survey; 96° F.

19 Taholah water system plans approved.

20 Moclips-Taholah Road nears completion.

22 Peninsula Indians meet with congressmen at Lake Quinault.

26 Phone lines completed to Lake Quinault.

September 1927

9 Start of school at Taholah is delayed till mid-month when one of two teachers falls ill.

10 Taholah nearly deserted as tribe members are in hop fields.

14 Lindbergh circles Harbor several times in the *Spirit of St. Louis* in honor of the spruce struts on his plane which came from the Harbor (Quinault).

October 1927

5 The Olympic Monument of 615,000 acres is closed to hunting.

8 Queets salmon catch is currently larger than that on the Quinault.

10 Supreme Court rules that Teapot Dome leases void.

31 Lumber shipments for Harbor exceed all other coastal ports.

November 1927

1 An 85' Japanese fishing schooner appears off coast with lifeless crew. Had drifted here from Japan.

1 Queets daily mail begins today from Quinault.

7 First snow on hills around Lake Quinault.

12 There is now a motor lodge in Queets.

15 Olympic Highway finished to Queets River.

16 Still seized in Copalis Beach.

19 Terrific gale rakes Harbor with 65 mph wind.

23 Survey for new village site at Queets done; allotment plans for Washington Coast Indians.

24 Japanese steamer *Tenpaisan Maru* goes ashore at Copalis during gale.

30 Queets ferry proves no toy.

December 1927

3 New road to Taholah featured in *The Aberdeen Daily World*.

31 50-60 suing for membership in Quinault Tribe. Trial in Tacoma Federal Court delayed.

~ 1928 ~

January 1928

9 Quinault Tribal actions delay 60 from getting on tribal rolls for land grant.

10 Bids close today on large timber sale (10,440 acres) on the Quinault Reservation.

21 Large Steelhead runs on Queets and Quinault Rivers.

21 First trip of "war" canoe equipped with an outboard motor on the Queets River.

23 Thirty Taholah Tribesmen work to clear big slide blocking the recently completed Moclips-Taholah Road.

26 Fred Halbert building 10 summer cottages on east end of Lake Quinault. Many other structures being built along the lake shore as well.

February 1928

10 Sites in new Queets village to be allotted.

17 State to rush Queets Bridge construction.

18 *The Aberdeen Daily World* features "The Peninsula; its highways and scenery."

21 The 6,791 ton, 561 foot long freighter *Robert Dollar* berths in Aberdeen; largest ever to visit Harbor.

28 Taholah police route three inebriated whitemen running amok in village.

March 1928

1 Blueline Bus Company extends its lines to Queets.

12 Queets school classes start with 10 pupils and an Indian Service teacher from Arizona.

25 Olympian's hiking club conduct its 100th hike to Point (*Cape*) Elizabeth; were ferried across the Quinault River in canoes by tribal members.

26 Storm fells timber, blocking roads to Quinault region.

28 State occupies new capitol building. It's the seventh [and current] home since territorial organization.

April 1928

10 First bridge on Queets River opens. It is a 356 foot cable span foot bridge near Harlow Creek.

11 Queets Bridge bids called for.

15 Quinault Blueback season opens.

17 Six buyers in Taholah pay 75¢/Blueback; highest price ever.

23 Large road construction tractors move supplies across Queets River and up and down beach.

24 Most Harbor mills signify intent to merge.

27 Blueback prices leap to 85¢/fish at dock in Taholah. Run light so far.

May 1928

6 Harbor has airfield hanger raising.

8 Highway committee adopts big road oiling program.

11 7,000 in Hoquiam watch opening of the "Great Simpson Avenue Bridge". Governor Hatley cuts ribbon. Quinault Chief Billy Mason part of ceremony. Hoquiam Policemen

wear new uniforms, adding metropolitan touch.

11 WGY of Schenectady, New York begins first scheduled television broadcast.

18 Neff Mill in East Hoquiam destroyed by fire.

24 Hobi Brothers to inaugurate air school here.

25 Blueback run still small.

26 Central Park, a new suburban beauty spot.

29 "Juice" turned on at 8:10 p.m. to Pacific Beach over new 28 mile line from Hoquiam.

30 Quinault question "right" of whitemen to operate boats for hire on Queets River.

June 1928

8 Grays Harbor oiling program launched.

16 Harry Shale elected president of Quinault Tribal Council, William Garfield as Vice-President, Mrs. Cleveland Jackson, Secretary. William Toby Sox, Tommy Payne, Cleveland Jackson, Mrs. Rosie Garfield, and Max Hudson appointed to business committee.

19 Bivalve hunters get big catches.

28 Rain delays Hoquiam-Quinault Lake road oiling. All but six miles now oiled.

29 Pacific Beach to Copalis road oiling completed.

July 1928

5 McCamman Hotel leveled by fire in Moclips.

6 Henry Steer says land ownership on the Quinault Indian Reservation is a big problem to forest management.

10 Hoquiam's 7th Street Theater opens.

16 Forest blazes cover wide area in Quinault timber. Sunday visitors to Lake Quinault were prevented return as flames cross road.

16 Giant meteor lights up night sky and Harborites hear rumble.

21 First sound film, *The Lights of New York.*

23 Forest fire licks up camp and bridge near Moclips.

24 94° F.

30 First color motion picture exhibited by George Eastman.

August 1928

2 A new ruling, limits the operation of "for hire" boats and canoes on the Quinault Indian Reservation rivers to members of the Quinault Tribe.

20 A giant Ford Tri-motor Monoplane visits Harbor.

22 Part of a huge tusk from a mammoth found near Polson Camp 7 on the Quinault River.

23 U.S. Fisheries to build fish trap on Big Creek.

26 Oakridge golf course opens.

September 1928

3 The Quinault Hotel Company, which had just put a Hydro-electric system in Gatton Creek, had to close it as it took most of water supply to operate.

7 Harbor becomes Convention Mecca Center: 4,000 here this season.

October 1928

2 Workmen now pouring cement for new Queets River Bridge.

2 William (Billy) Gohl, the notorious Grays Harbor Mass Murderer from 18 years ago, dies at Medical Lake Asylum.

November 1928

6 The Quinaults are making large catches of Silver and

Chum salmon on lower Quinault River.

7 Herbert Hoover defeats Al Smith for President.

27 Albut Pruce, 76, Quinault Valley Settler in the 1880's, drowns in the Quinault River.

December 1928

12 Lake Quinault Hotel will use hydro-electric to heat part of the hotel.

23 Quinault and Quillayute tribes have a 3-day fete in Taholah.

25 65 mph sou'wester rakes the coast.

27 Quinaults hold a "Tribal Palaver".

28 Fishing now poor with cold and snow on the upper Quinault.

29 Big gale and heavy rain.

29 Judge Campbell gives interpretation of early pioneers as to the meaning of Indian Treaties.

31 One million dollar fire destroys McCleary Mill.

~ 1929 ~

January 1929

11 Cosmopolis train crash kills two.

12 First train passes through the longest railway tunnel in North America. The eight mile long Chumstick Valley Tunnel in the Washington Cascades is part of the Great Northern line.

15 W.B. Sams, Taholah Indian Agent, travels to Olympia to clarify state laws with Indian treaty fishing claims.

17 Mammoth fossil find $3^1/_2$ miles below the lake on the Quinault River. *(See August 22, 1928.)*

30 16° F. Logging camps closed.

February 1929

1 Harbor in the grip of a silver thaw.

8 Northwest Indian tribes seek legislation to clarify fish rules.

12 Wyatt Earp dies.

14 St. Valentine's Day Massacre in Chicago gang wars .

22 Committee of unbiased persons from the Harbor formed to explore conditions on the Quinault Reservation, in wake of nation wide exam of the Indian Department.

29 More on Quinault Mammoths.

March 1929

1 Bivalve diggers throng beaches on opening day.

2 Fire sweeps Hume Street block.

4 Frank Law of Taholah, to enlarge the Big L Garage and add service station.

7 Quinault timberland north of the Quinault River will be on block as soon as maps can be drawn.

9 O'Neil, first surveyor, lauds Olympic Mountains.

12 Forest Service urged to allocate big timber stands for Harbor mills.

12 Brilliant light flashes in the sky.

12 Coco-Cola founder, Asa Candler. dies.

14 Moclips people form its Chamber of Commerce.

16 Quinault Indians hold tribal "palaver" about timber sales north of the Quinault River. They demand shift in burden of timber fires to buyers.

20 3,500 trees planted on tribal tract under direction of Henry Steer.

21 Chalet to rise in scenic (*Enchanted*) valley.

27 Moclips-Queets highway proposed. Federal aid sought.

30 Anglers must get permit from Indian Service before fishing in the Lake or on any Reservation rivers or streams.

April 1929

22 Early Blueback run good.

May 1929

4 Report of vast earth upheaval on the Queets near M.M. Kelly Ranch.

14 Pacific Beach citizens hope to get permanent road to beach. Joe Creek washes out road with winter storms.

15 200 boats on Harbor fishing for salmon.

16 First Academy Awards.

June 1929

11 Fire destroys two blocks of Montesano business district.

17 Clearwater people marooned when ferry on Queets breaks moorings.

18 Four timber firms bid on four large timber units on the Quinault Reservation. No competition offered.

18 Rain laden gale smites Harbor.

27 Queets Indian war canoes become auto ferry for Clearwater people.

July 1929

4 Hardwood on way to Harbor from Japan for door manufacture.

6 Queets and Hoh may get great power system.

7 TAT is first passenger air service coast to coast. One way fair is $351.94.

16 Fire demon lays waste to large area in Black Hills near Olympia.

18 Pontoon bridge spans the Queets at Harlow Crossing.

19 Hammer Mill Paper starts production of first white paper in Hoquiam.

22 Record breaking tourist traffic on coast and Lake Quinault. Vacation traffic taxes Horse Packing Service from Quinault to Low Divide.

23 Quinaults restrict boats on Lake.

26 Large gravel removal from mouth of Queets River. "Enough to surface the entire Olympic Loop Highway."

29 84° F.

30 Flames lick up 18 buildings in downtown Cosmopolis.

31 Quinaults protest state role to prevent them from fishing at Peacock Spit on the Columbia.

August 1929

2 Aberdeen-Raymond Highway to be done soon.

5 Indian Bureau rejects timber bids on the Quinault Reservation. Some see it as a hold-up to boost railroads.

24 Harbor's 38% divorce rate leads state's 23%.

29 *Graf Zeppelin* completes round the world flight. New York to New York in 21 days.

29 Indian Affairs Administration code proposed.

September 1929

3 New plan proposed for Federal Government to buy Quinault Reservation and Lake and open it to Public.

3 Scientists inspect fossil beds at the Bluebanks on the Quinault River..

16 Smoky gloom enshrouds Harbor from forest fires.

17 Gravel laid on Queets Highway.

23 Fishing lean for Quinault tribesmen.

October 1929

3 *The Aberdeen Daily World* runs a series of articles about management of Quinault Forest.

7 Harbor 31st Port in Nation.

21 Billions lost in stock crash.

24 Black Thursday: Stock Market Crash.

November 1929

2 Harbor built on Fir; rests future on Hemlock.

5 26.6 miles of Quinault Road to be resurfaced with crushed rock to Harlow Creek.

16 Tribe may stop white men from fishing Quinault waters as a violation of privileges they have had.

18 Indian Service (*Quinault*) to reforest with Redwood, and White Pine as well as native wood.

21 Grays Harbor Mill completing experimental cut of hemlock.

30 Byrd flies over South Pole.

December 1929

3 Hoquiam Chamber of Commerce feels that the U.S. Government should buy the (Quinault) Reservation from the Indians.

6 $10,000 appropriated for Taholah light and water project.

12 Aberdeen population is 26,073 and Hoquiam is 16,763.

13 Rain laden gale lashes coast. The freshet writes finis on Queets pontoon bridge (*See July 18, 1929*).

21 Shipment of Steelhead from Quinault Reservation seized by state.

24 Tacoma Court opens hearings on Indian battle for fishing rights at Peacock Spit at the mouth of the Columbia River.

25 Christmas gale hits Northwest.

~ 1930 ~

January 1930

1 Harbor leaders predict a big year.

3 Steelhead battle opens in Montesano Court.

8 Packers win Steelhead battle; Shipments from Quinault Reservation not in violation of State Law.

15 Snow and cold cover Harbor.

16 Prohibition law battles 10 years after its enactment. Frequent accounts appear in *The Aberdeen Daily World* about police seizing a distillery somewhere in the County.

24 Three buildings burn on First Street in Raymond.

February 1930

7 600 foot bridge now open on the Queets River at Queets, but five miles of road just south of it are not yet ready.

13 Hoquiam Elks aid forest men in planting seedling trees on Indian land.

18 (Quinault) Indian Service spurs reforestation.

24 More bones unearthed in ancient Mammoth wallow on the lower Quinault River.

March 1930

13 Ninth planet discovered.

17 First full page of comics begin in *The Aberdeen Daily World*.

17 White men may fish Quinault waters with a permit, tribesmen say.

23 Corpse of Humpback whale on beach attracts 5,000 to Westport.

29 Dedication of bridge over Columbia River at Longview.

April 1930

9 Blueback sell for 65¢ per fish.

15 Henry Steer, head forester for Quinault Indian Agency, to leave May 15 after 10 years. Feels reforestation and establishment of the Quinault Experimental Forest have been his most notable efforts.

26 Quinault Salmon (*Blueback)* runs begin to pick up despite high water.

28 Gale swamps three Harbor fishing boats.

May 1930

1 Federal inspector says radio reception on Harbor the worst in Northwest.

2 Quinaults make big salmon catches; 65-100 fish per day per fisherman.

5 45,000 trees planted in Quinault Experimental Forest this Spring at a cost about $10.50 per acre.

16 Hoquiam takes over water system.

16 Highland Golf Course opens; marks 5th golf course in this county.

17 Fox D & R Theater inaugurates Saturday Mickey Mouse Club.

27 Record Quinault salmon run underway. Fishermen get 55¢ per fish.

28 Graveling work on Loop Highway sets fast pace.

June 1930

3 Road between Copalis and Pacific Beach nears completion.

6 Frozen food enters commercial market for the first time.

7 Sticky blue clay slows Olympic Loop Road work.

12 Hoquiam spruce wood bathing suits in demand for Massachusetts bathing suit fashion show.

16 Indians spurn Northup plan and Lake sale at the annual Council meeting.

17 Work starts on Queets River Bridge near Clearwater.

18 No more angling on the Quinault River by non-Indians after this year.

20 W.B. Sams, Indian Agent, thinks the Quinaults are the most progressive Indian Tribe and will govern themselves in 25 years.

24 Pacific Beach Commercial Club marking out boundaries for airfield just south of Joe Creek on beach.

30 Harbor gasoline prices drop to 11¢ from 21¢.

30 Quinaults net more then 310,000 Quinault Salmon this season.

July 1930

2 Indian Forest Service reviews progressive year: 145,000,000 feet cut; they have 1 superintendent, 1 timber clerk, 2 senior rangers, 4 rangers, 4 patrolman, 2 lookouts and 13 scalars. N. O. Nicholson replaced Henry Steer in May.

8 Royal Hawaiian family visits Lake Quinault.

11 Indian Service building fire road from Pt. Grenville to lookout.

18 W. B. Sams to retire as Tribe agent. Quinaults want him

to stay on for another two years.

21 U. S. Family of four can eat well for $13.72 per week in summer.

25 Pontoon bridge now crosses Quinault River half mile below forks.

August 1930

1 W.B. Sam steps aside as Tribe Agent and N. O. Nicholson takes over.

2 Tribes hold big beach rally at Copalis Beach.

5 Forest fire situation grows serious.

6 First auto draws up at Kelly's Queets Ranch.

13 Fred Morell, assistant U. S. forester, and other noted foresters visit Quinault Experimental Forest.

14 Hemlock easily produced assert experts.

18 Leo, the famous M-G-M lion, is on the Harbor to "roar" in the "Greater Talkie Season" for the 1930 Harbor season.

18 60' fin-back whale stranded on the beach between Raft River and Queets.

21 Aberdeen host to 4,000 here for state American Legion Convention.

27 Moth pest hits Olympic trees.

September 1930

1 10,000 acres of logged-over land ablaze on upper Wynooche.

8 Port plans huge tidelands fill.

16 Olympic Railway Permit issued; grants rights for railway from Moclips to Hoh River. (*Never built.*)

October 1930

1 Aurora Borealis is at its best - radios sputter.

2 Hailie Selassie crowned Emperor of Ethiopia. (*Will become color feature of a National Geographic Magazine.*)

4 Forest Service insist that salmon barrier on West Fork of the Humptulips River must be removed.

8 Dreams realized, as highway that joins Grays Harbor and Willapa Harbor opens today; 1,000 cars make the trip.

17 John Clipp, a nearly 100 year old Quinault Indian at Taholah, regains his eye sight lost three years ago. He is once again wandering the streets of the village. The miracle has all amazed.

20 Moclips hit by big blaze; Theater block leveled.

23 Prohibition education program launched.

November 1930

1 Queets Bridge opens today.

7 A new type of beetle discovered in the Queets Valley has interest of a zoologist.

15 Winter storm attacks Harbor.

22 Inter-harbor bus service starts.

December 1930

1 Feds descend on Harbor in mammoth prohibition raid.

2 72 arrested in Harbor raid.

2 Six mile extension of North Shore Road to be started soon.

29 *Pioneer Packing vs Winslow;* The Washington State Supreme Court rules that Quinault Steelhead belong to the Indians, not to the State and that the Indians have the right to sell them in interstate commerce.

31 The Blueline Bus Company now has daily service

between the Harbor and Kalaloch.

~ 1931 ~

January 1931

2 Storm lashed tide sweeps into Taholah.
5 Five mills resume work from mid-winter shut down.
7 U.S. sets aside big Olympic area as perpetual wild.
7 Taholah water hazard passes.
8 Port to dredge Chehalis River.
10 Big slide on highway isolates Taholah.
14 Road open to Taholah again. Also, Indians guilty of minor offenses are building levee at Taholah.
22 Rain-laden gale smites Harbor.
28 Sea may force Indian town of Taholah to move itself inland.
28 Harbor to start Oyster industry.
31 Nature fast repairing damage done by Great 1921 Peninsula Storm.

February 1931

3 A 240 foot suspension bridge opens on the upper Hoh. Could support a 4 ton truck if there was a road to it.
6 Steelhead Bill to be discussed.
17 12 year rainfall record set for one day.
21 Fire razes Pacific Beach business district.

March 1931

3 *The Star Spangled Banner* becomes official U.S. national anthem.
12 Quinault allotment policy rapped by court.
14 New Taholah gymnasium dedicated.
15 South beaches to get electric power.
15 B.B. Jones in Taholah to get publicity photos.
19 Nevada legalizes gambling.
31 Knute Rockne killed in plane crash.

April 1931

4 Potential Quinault River electric power resources are big.
7 Spruce is being stripped out of the Queets Country by A.A. Fletcher and Nansen Anderson. (*See May 4.*)
8 Eight Harbor cargoes bound for the Orient.
13 Work on the new East Entry Project for Aberdeen began last week.
22 County fire situation serious.
27 Work on the Taholah road entrance has started. Work on the streets to begin soon.

May 1931

1 May Day brings rain.
1 Empire State Building formally opens today as world's tallest building.
4 Queets floats first raft of spruce. (*See April 7.*)
11 In the 80's this week.
16 George Hubble opens new ten room hotel at Queets.
20 Oiling of road to Lake Quinault starts.
** Weyerhaeuser purchases three sawmills and a shingle mill on Willapa Harbor.

June 1931

1 *Halbert vs United States;* The Supreme Court says Indians did not need to live on the Quinault Reservation to get an allotment.

3 A.A. Grorud of the Federal Indian Dept. continues his inspection of the Quinault Indian Reservation.
4 Forks, once outpost, now thriving center; gains population fast.
5 Hoh River Bridge, final Loop Road span, is finished. 87° F.
6 Gasoline cost 15¢/gallon.
16 Quinaults vote to open lake to white fisherman for a $2.00 fee.
25 June rainfall on Harbor nears record.
26 Blueback catch poor this year.

July 1931

2 Harbor spruce in Global plane which Wiley Post and Harold Gatty used to circle the world in less than nine days.
6 Christopher Columbus Simmons, the first white man born in the state (*April 14, 1845 at Washougal*) dies.
7 Cedar mills organize a firm.
13 Jams block the lower Quinault.
16 Scientific poison, calcium arsenate, killing the hemlock loopers near Raymond; is life saver for the timber.
18 First car to circle the Olympic Peninsula in one day is an *Essex Super Six* driven by Warren Smith.
20 Big Baker Prairie Fire burning through Aloha's slashings.
22 Loggers recall big hemlock looper infestation on the Wishkah in 1891-1892.
22 Aloha forest fire eclipses sun on the Harbor.
23 Baker Prairie Fire burns more then three full sections.
28 New Jefferson County span on Matheny Creek opens Queets Valley Road.

August 1931

3 Timber surveying on the Reservation.
4 Indians pose for newsreel man.
6 New school for Queets advised.
12 Enchanted Valley Chalet to open.
14 Road to Taholah being graveled.
17 Railroad men visit area.
17 Neah Bay road opens.
24 Quinault seedling nursery.
24 Cook Creek Forest Fire.
25 Olympic Loop Highway Celebration program 25th -27th.
25 Skyline Trail dedicated.
25 *Aberdeen Daily World* devotes entire section to Loop Highway resources. Also entire issue on 26th.
26 Formal dedication of the Olympic Highway at Kalaloch.

September 1931

9 200 Indians celebrate at big Queets Water Carnival.
12 Story of Hoquiam wood cutter's battle with eleven foot snake on driftwood flats has city agog. (*From description of the snake's behavior, it sounds like a cobra. Such a snake could have arrived on a visiting ship.*)
23 O'Neil talks about Olympics 42 years ago at the Chamber of Commerce.
23 Taholah's new one mile high land entrance road avoids river flooding.
28 State cuts big Harbor contract for Montesano-Aberdeen Highline road.
29 Rains increase run of salmon at Taholah.

October 1931

27 Aloha buys 1,000 salmon from the Quinaults to feed their unemployed.

30 J. P. Kinney of Washington D.C., arrives for short visit to make survey of Indian forest.

Roosevelt elk.

November 1931

6 Rain laden gale assails Harbor.

6 Record salmon rush continues. Largest in history of the oldest Indians.

14 Gale and rain sweep whole of Pacific coast.

16 New fish trap at Lake Quinault helps hatchery.

19 Oil discovered on the Hoh at 805 feet.

20 Hoh oil prospects stir state.

23 Frost blankets state; 24° F. here.

27 Record cold weather continues.

30 Fight for coast road from Moclips to Queets.

December 1931

3 Free samples of Sim's Hoh oil at the *World's* office.

5 Salmon run big, but prices poor.

17 Gale wreaks havoc on Harbor with 70 mph wind.

18 Wind and water do much damage on the Harbor.

18 Oil companies invade Harbor.

24 *Aberdeen Daily World* photo of the 385' suspension bridge on Hoh.

31 Tremor shakes up Puget Sound and Hood Canal.

~ 1932 ~

January 1932

6 Land allotting agent, Charles Robin, returns after four year absence to spend several months allotting lands on the Quinault Reservation.

8 Olympic Loop to lure 100,000 cars in '32.

8 Harbor oil prospects rosy.

11 75 mph winds lash Harbor.

21 Nurse for Queets Indian children sought.

22 Poachers slay scores of elk; halt requested.

26 Queets Indians invite Harbor leaders.

February 1932

4 Queets village unique to U.S.

5 New road helps Taholah people.

6 Beach picked clean of driftwood because of depression.

24 38,142 acres in county set aside for forest.

25 Rain and winds.

27 Melting snow and rain floods close roads and high damage.

March 1932

2 Oil sand is reported at Leslie well.

5 John Philip Sousa dies.

4 Downpour sets 30 year record; 4½" in 24 hours.

* Daily news on Lindbergh baby kidnaping first half of month.

7 Fuel (gasoline) drops from 19¢ to 12¢.

9 The 3 story Higley log house at Lake Quinault burns.

April 1932

5 Light Blueback catch so far even though season opened early because of depression.

May 1932

5 Hemlock loopers in area.

9 Story of Gray and his Harbor discovery.

12 Lindbergh baby found dead. (*See February 1932.*)

17 Gas at Quillayute.

17 Salmon catch is big at Quinault.

18 Looper warfare rouses interest.

24 *Akron* airship over Grays Harbor.

June 1932

2 Indian crew building road to Queets mouth.

3 Raymond's paper "Oyster money" is in full circulation.

10 91° F.

22 Run of Blueback slackens.

25 Indian Services Inspector here.

July 1932

1 Big slash fire started near Cook Creek from five arson fires.

2 Wintery storm hits Harbor.

4 Despite 2" rain, Cook Creek Fires still burning.

7 Cook Creek fire still menacing; has burned 4 mile long

and half mile wide strip.

8 Tribe closes fish season. Fair season (far below normal) and poor prices.

11 Despite weekend rains, Cook Creek Fire still a menace.

13 Rain putting damper on Cook Creek Fire.

18 Indian Institute pastor is here.

20 Hitler taking over in Germany.

** Rainy wet month.

August 1932

2 Indians removing log jam on the Quinault River.

5 90° F.

20 Tribesmen open two day Powwow at Lake.

29 Taholah Agency ready to move; setting up office on second floor of Hoquiam Post Office Building.

September 1932

12 Dr. Ray Lyman Wilbur, Secretary of the Interior, to visit the Quinault Tribe.

October 1932

7 Flames rage on Olympic Loop. Fire burns on 10 mile front along highway near Quilcene.

7 Edict outlaws axe at Quinault. 1,400 acres of Timber to be protected forever; will be known as the Quinault Natural Area.

9 Soviets open world's largest hydroelectric plant on Dnieper River.

12 Quinault Indians report that the recent rain has speeded up the salmon run.

18 Brown's cannery at the mouth of the Queets River is now operating full time.

November 1932

1 Southerly gale lashes Harbor.

1 It's reported that the colonization at Carlisle by Hungarian and Russian families will be completed by spring.

5 Storm ravages coast.

8 Tribesman are catching 2,500 to 3,500 salmon/day at Taholah.

9 Roosevelt wins by landslide.

16 Rain pours down on North Coast.

December 1932

1 Heavy sea up at Taholah base. Pile driver from M. R. Smith, Moclips, moved to Taholah to drive some protective pilings.

2 Vast downpour deluges Harbor.

5 New Federal Building opens in Hoquiam. New Post Office on the first floor, and Taholah Indian Agency on the second floor.

7 Open house at the new Federal Building.

8 Survey for new north side (of Grays Harbor) road to beach starts.

8 Road to reopen soon to Pacific Beach once graveling is complete.

12 Harbor shivers at 16 above zero.

15 Four schools to be combined into one near Queets.

17 Aloha is hauling piling for emergency work on seawall at Taholah. Indians, under Cleve Jackson, are floating cedar down the river as part of the work, too.

22 Most severe gale of the winter.

22 Two questioned in Quinault Indian Dewey Wain's

death. He had been run over by a M. R. Smith train on the 20th.

23 Telephone service inaugurated between U. S. and Hawaii.

~ 1933 ~

January 1933

5 Jupiter Pluvius has started a concerted washing attack on Grays Harbor.

11 'Old Betsy' pioneer of logging locomotives, being brought down by Polson barge today for shipment to Chicago World's Fair.

14 Auguste Piccard, explorer of the stratosphere, sees stratosphere as world's future superhighway. He recently ascended to 53,152 feet in an airtight gondola attached to a hydrogen filled balloon.

14 N. O. Nicholson, Indian agent, says the depression is hitting the Quinault tribesmen hard.

18 6" white blanket falls here.

18 Thousands of feet of Queets spruce, now being cut, is allowed to rot because of the lack of cheap transport. (Only the best logs were taken out.)

23 Harbor shares richly in Washington number of February issue of National Geographic.

30 Adolph Hitler assumes helm in Reich.

February 1933

13 Work begins on the Taholah water system.

15 Assassination attempt on president-elect Roosevelt.

18 "Buy American" week in Grays Harbor climaxed by fine parade in Aberdeen.

23 "Quinault Hatchery greets millions of infant salmon."

March 1933

1 Robert Pope, 90, dies at his home.

4 Roosevelt becomes president. "The only thing we have to fear is fear itself."

6 Roosevelt declares a Bank Holiday.

9 Shaker rituals crowd Taholah.

10 Indians resent state ban on early Blueback.

12 Roosevelt's first Fireside Chat.

21 Roosevelt proposes Work Army.

30 Congress authorizes Work Army. The Reforestation Relief Act establishes the Civilian Conservation Corps, CCC. (Participates would be paid $30.00 per month, part of which went to any dependents. By the time the CCC ceased in 1941, about two million young men had worked in its projects.)

April 1933

4 73 lives lost in Akron crash; may mark the end for the big dirigibles.

6 Grays Harbor hit by worst disaster in Ports history. Sudden gale trap trollermen, over 200 boats imperilled; 19 fishermen feared lost.

7 Beer flows again after 13 years of probation. Beer supply on Harbor vanishes in short order; 15c/bottle.

8 Queets school site is selected along Olympic highway.

14 1,000 Harbor men to be put to work in the federal reforestation project.

19 Roosevelt takes U.S. off the gold standard.

May 1933

10 Geodetic Survey is setting up at Lake Quinault.

10 Nazis burn banned books in Germany.

13 *King Kong* opens at Warner Bros.'s Aberdeen Theater.

13 Blueback catch still below normal.

16 The *Constitution, "Old Ironsides"*, arrives in Aberdeen for visit.

17 Aloha Weaver's strike shuts down mill.

18 *"Old Betsy"* leaves for Chicago Fair. Renamed *Minnetonka*.

19 Entire issue of *The Aberdeen Daily World* devoted to *Old Ironsides*.

19 Moss handicaps Tribe fishermen.

25 Storm keeps *Old Ironsides* here another day.

26 *Old Ironsides* leaves for Port Angeles; 60,051 visited ship while it was on the Harbor.

27 Chicago Fair opens.

31 Harbor clam pack is 35,000 cases.

June 1933

2 Gold strike reported by a Queets miner.

2 100 tribesmen, 10 years or older, are being enrolled in reforestation camps on the Quinault Indian Reservation.

6 Commission favors Harbor Canal.

6 First drive-in movie theater opens. (*Camden, N.J.*)

8 Wintry shower deluges Harbor.

8 The big tower water tank for Taholah arrived yesterday.

9 Two camps to be established on the QIR in connection with the Federal relief program.

10 Mount Olympus National Monument transferred from the Department of Agriculture to the Department of Interior.

16 President Roosevelt signed into law the National Industrial Recovery Act (NIRA); gives control of industry to the government. (*The New Deal, is a phrase used by FDR in his acceptance of the Democratic presidential nomination in 1932.*

In his first hundred days, never had Congress passed so many important laws so quickly. One of the most important was the NIRA. This Act created the National Recovery Administration, NRA, and more than 25 New Deal agencies such as the Works Progress Administration (WPA), CCC, and the FHA. While the New Deal did not end the depression, it gave Americans faith in the system and relieved some of the economic hardships.

A result of the New Deal was the establishment of the Democratic party as the largest political party.)

19 Oiling of Hoquiam-Lake Quinault Highway underway.

22 Draught beer is legalized for Aberdeen.

27 A beetle to fight the hemlock looper will be loosed in North River region of Grays Harbor next week.

29 Work on four trails started by the CCC boys.

30 Indian Welfare camps to open next week.

30 The Quinault Blueback season closed with poor season.

July 1933

1 Established in 1862, the Makah Indian Agency in Neah Bay is abolished and will move to Taholah Agency.

3 Northwest Indian Federation conclave opens in Hoquiam. Chief William Penn is chairman. Discuss Northwest Indian Protection Association, sale of fish. Also parade and ball games.

6 Quinault urges road construction to Enchanted Valley.

6 First forest camp at Queets opens; first of three on the Reservation. 25 men working on road construction. Other camps to be at Taholah and Aloha. 100 men total on road work.

11 Contract for construction of Grand Coulee Dam signed.

12 Queets School job is started. Contract awarded to Frank Northup and Charles Mason to clear land on U.S. 101. Building to be started in winter.

13 A big, three-year old bull elk entered the ocean near Point Grenville and swam several miles south along the coast. It may have taken refuge in the water to escape dogs. It headed for shore several times, but was frightened by people watching it and returned seaward, up to a mile off shore. Finally it came ashore at Joe Creek, where two men shot it. Angry spectators nearly mobbed the men who were later arrested.

14 84° F.

17 NRA goes into effect .

27 Fire danger great in woods.

31 Gandhi begins new campaign.

August 1933

1 NRA's "Blue Eagle" makes its first public appearance.

3 Horse racing begins at Longacres.

7 18 tribe members move into forest camp at Clearwater; only two from west part of state.

9 New Colonel Bob Lookout station.

13 Violent revolt ousts Machado in Cuba.

14 84° F. highest of the year.

14 Taholah busy installing pipes; $20,000 water system recently completed.

22 91° F.

24 Fire explodes in Oregon's Tillamook country.

25 Signs being put up on the Olympic Loop Highway.

25 About Lake Quinault Hatchery.

26 Flames rage in Harbor forest.

28 Many Braves at Quinault CCC camp.

September 1933

8 Cook Creek blaze under control.

15 Oil found in Hoh River drilling.

15 Quinault CCC sets fine mark in August work.

22 Indians predict mild winter; heavy rains in early fall after a dry summer usually brings a mild winter.

27 Robert Marshall, new forest for the Indian Department director, and assistant director, Lee Muck, visit Taholah from Washington, D.C..

October 1933

4 Tribe to widen Moclips-Taholah Road.

11 Olympic oil quest to get state aid.

23 Quinaults lose contest to fish at mouth of Columbia.

30 Indians granted big work funds to continue CCC work through winter.

31 Hundreds of little flying spiders float down the Quinault Valley as cool dry weather follows rainy spell.

November 1933

17 Clearwater CCC Camp officially dedicated; will build Clearwater Road to connect with the Hoh River Road.

17 U.S. recognizes U.S.S.R.

18 2,000 jobs allotted to Harbor area under Public Work Administration.

December 1933

5   Prohibition ends.

11 Winds and 7 inches of rain in three days.

18 Flood ravages Harbor; 90 mph gale and six inches of rain in 24 hours. 15' 8" tide.

21 More rain and wind; Lake Quinault at highest level in 10 years.

~ 1934 ~

January 1934

9   312,000 men in CCC camps.

12 Civil Works Administration (CWA) funds used to build seawall in Taholah, construction of which is underway. Emergency Conservation Works (ECW) funds to be used to plant 1,000 acres on Reservation.

13 74 mph gale and heavy rain.

17 At 9:00 a.m., clear skies provide background for a spectacular meteor fireball, "the size of the moon," which sped over Lake Quinault, creating a flash of light and thunderous roar.

February 1934

12 State engineers on Reservation since January 12, surveying a new right-of-way from Moclips to Taholah and a site on the Quinault River for a bridge crossing to extend the Roosevelt Highway.

28 The Queets Olympic Indian Club hold meeting about the timber policies on the Reservation.

March 1934

10 Braves oppose new Indian Bill (Wheeler-Howard or Indian Reorganization Act).

29 Queets Community Hall nears completion.

30 Foundation poured for Queets-Clearwater school.

April 1934

3   800,000 trees planted on the Reservation by ECW, mostly tribal members.

10 Blueback arrive in large numbers with recent rain.

11 Ninety recruits from Grays Harbor County join 86 new crew members at the Clearwater CCC camp; former crew sent to Cle Elum.

23 Strange fossil found on Hoh River.

30 Driest April on record; only 2.28" of rain in Aberdeen.

May 1934

1   State cannot tax fish sold off-reservation.

7   Indian timber bill approved giving Secretary of Interior right to modify existing contracts and to make Polson Railroad a common rail carrier.

8   ECW Reservation program continues with construction of truck roads, trails to lookout, and log jam clearing on the Quinault River.

14 88° F.

29 Polson Railroad now stretches three miles north of the Quinault River.

June 1934

1   Sustained yield logging begins in Federal Forest today. A "New Deal" for trees.

5   Reservation lookouts ready early this year because of dry spring.

9   James Howorth, former head of Quinault Forestry,

returns today to replace F.R. Moffatt; vows to continue ECW program.

16 Humptulips gets CCC camp, the 936th.

18 Indian Reorganization Act. (*See March 10, 1934 and December 10, 1934.*)

19 Communications Act establishes the Federal Communications Commission, FCC.

26 Big tuna landed in blueback net.

27 At annual Quinault Council meeting, Harry Shale elected President; Ben Charlie, Vice-President; Anna Jackson, Secretary; and Frank Law, Treasurer. New committee includes: Cleve Jackson, O.V. McCloud, James Bryson, Herb Capoeman, and John Shale. Meeting favored extension of road from Moclips to Queets; to charge $1.00 for whites to leave boats on Lake; set canoe fees for trips; and discussed fisheries.

28 National Housing Act establishes the Federal Housing Administration, FHA.

30 Blueback season fair; starts briskly and ends slowly.

July 1934

3   The Federal Hatchery at Quinault has received 200,000 Black spotted trout eggs from the Rocky Mountains.

7   Large school of herring come ashore at North Cove when chased by a whale. A similar phenomenon happened seven years ago on same beach.

7   A sea serpent, washed ashore at Ocean City and widely reported by the press, turns out to be a badly decomposed whale.

9   Quinault Council grants three years extension to M.R. Smith (Pt. Grenville Unit) and five years to Aloha (Mounts Creek Unit). Both logging contracts were to have ended March 31, 1935. Recommends reforesting 5,000 - 10,000 acres of allotted land.

12 Queets Post Office to close for good on the 31st.

15 Freak summer storm with heavy rains and 60 mph winds in evening.

22 John Dillinger killed.

August 1934

4   President Roosevelt visits Grand Coulee Dam construction site.

10 Movement started to get Indian Hospital on the Peninsula.

15 Grays Harbor County has 269 taverns.

22 Governor orders a halt to logging in Western Washington because of dry weather.

29 Quinault Tribe members consent to reduction from $5 to $3 per thousand for cedar, spruce, and fir and $1 for hemlock and all other trees in the Lake Quinault Unit.

29 Olympic timber survey begins.

September 1934

11 Lightning and heavy rain in the evening.

17 Indians ratify reductions in timber prices on Polson Contract.

17 Quinaults removed a large log jam and several small ones on the Quinault River this summer, making it navigable.

24 Construction begins on the Queets-Clearwater School.

Fall 1934

** Development of a State nursery begins (*Mike Webster*).

October 1934

7 Southerly gale sweeps Harbor.

10 Salmon run heavy on the Harbor following freshets.

21 Harbor ravaged by 90 mph winds and flood. The *Lone Tree* at Harbor mouth destroyed.

25 Floods menace State's west side.

31 Rioting merry makers wreck the closing of the Chicago World's Fair.

November 1934

10 Clearwater CCC Camp quarantined for suspected diphtheria.

28 Tribe reviews Wheeler-Howard Act (Indian Reorganization Act [IRA]) in Taholah.

29 Three big slides on upper Quinault have reduced salmon egg survival.

30 50 mph gale.

December 1934

10 John Collier, Commissioner of Indian Affairs, discusses Wheeler-Howard Act (IRA) in Taholah and declares a "New Era" for Indians.

14 New super-plywood that can be used outside is invented at Harbor Plywood.

25 Christmas Day gale sweeps harbor with 65 mph winds. Store in Kalalock dedicated.

27 Snow blankets Harbor for first time in two years.

~ 1935 ~

January 1935

17 Four inch snowfall; two feet in the hills.

21 Gale melts snow; 12" of rain in 24 hours at Lake Quinault. Gigantic landslide near Lake Quinault. (*An interesting eyewitness account appears in the book* **Rain Forest**, *by Elizabeth Marston published in 1969 and new edition in 1974.*)

22 Flood waters isolate Harbor area and flood Taholah.

25 Record high flood waters begin to drop.

28 ECW workmen open detour around big landslide at Point Grenville.

31 Photos of giant landslide five miles west of Lake Quinault appear in *The Aberdeen Daily World.*

February 1935

13 Quinaults to curb illegal fishing on Lake Quinault with more patrols.

13 Bruno Hauptmann found guilty of kidnapping and killing Lindbergh's baby in March 1932.

20 Federal Government to improve Lake Quinault Hatchery.

March 1935

10 100 pound rocket soars from Pacific Beach ½ mile into the sky.

12 Chinook storm deluges Harbor.

14 Taholah to have "Hall of History".

23 Great fur seal herd of three million moves north along coast. Coast Guard monitors the migration.

25 Cold winter gale sweeps Harbor leaving 2" of snow at the Lake.

27 Quinault Tribe presses for a coastal road from Taholah to Queets.

April 1935

1 Blueback season opens 15 days early.

8 Bill for an Olympic National Park opposed by the Grays Harbor Chamber of Commerce.

15 Bureau favors an Indian hospital on the Peninsula.

16 Voting on the IRA takes place.

18 Dust clouds and storms worsen in the "Dust Bowl".

24 Tribal timber confab called.

27 Fire hazard in woods is serious.

27 Soil Conservation Service established.

May 1935

6 Several forest blazes north and west of Hoquiam.

6 Works Progress Administration, WPA begins. (*Name changed to Works Project Administration in 1939.*)

7 Lumber industry goes on strike in Grays Harbor.

13 Quinaults analyze timber changes in Lake Quinault Unit.

15 Indian Timber Service adopts sustained yield policy.

25 George Weyerhaeuser, age 9, kidnapped for $200,000 ransom.

27 NIRA and NRA declared unconstitutional.

31 Indian Agency to seek right-of-way for Taholah-Queets road.

June 1935

1 Weyerhaeuser's kidnapped son set free. Believed to have been held in Grays Harbor area. (*See May 25.*)

6 Blueback catch remains slim.

17 Harry Shale elected General Council President. Most of General Council meeting devoted to Queets water system.

20 Tribe pushes for Taholah-Queets road.

24 The huge Howeattle log jam several miles above Taholah removed with 1½ tons of blasting powder by IECW crew.

July 1935

6 Emperor Haile Selassie appeals to the U.S. and the League of Nations over the next three months to prevent Italy's invasion of Ethiopia. The Emperor forecast "the danger of a world war again". (*The failure of the League to stop Italy would lead to its eventual demise and Italy's invasion of Ethiopia on October 2.*)

10 Blueback season closes today. Nearly 4,000 fish caught daily in mid-June.

11 Quinaults create a scenic Point Grenville Park called *Indian Dan's Mountain.* Dan was captured in war with the Bay Center Tribe and made a slave. After he won his freedom he decided to live here. A one mile road was built to the park by the IECW (Emergency Conservation Work).

13 103° F. in Queets.

22 Harbor lumber strike nears end.

August 1935

1 Tribesmen hold 12 as poachers of clams and crabs.

2 New steel lookout tower near Queets and a lookout tree on Lone Mountain supplement the tower near Point Grenville and the Cook Creek Lookout.

4 Eleven man Queets canoe at Lake Quinault thrills crowd.

6 CCC loop trail through Big Firs at Lake Quinault open.

12 Tribesmen conquer dangerous fire one mile east of

Taholah.

14 President Roosevelt signs Social Security Act.

15 Will Rogers and Wiley Post killed in Arctic plane crash.

16 100 men fight slashing fire one mile south of Polson Camp #14.

September 1935

3 The car *Bluebird* goes 301 mph at Bonneville.

17 Samuel Benn, founder of Aberdeen, dies at age 103 last night.

20 Tribesmen voice opposition for timber contract revisions.

28 85° F.

October 1935

2 Italian troops invade Ethiopia under cover of air raids. This war would be the headline news for the remainder of the month and into November.

9 Queets fishermen make largest haul in memory of blacks (kings) and silvers this week.

9 Quinaults to press for big damage suit (fish claims and North Boundary).

11 Whalers back from Aleutians with good catch. Had to go for North because of lack of whale here.

16 Harry Lynch to head IECW work on Reservation.

19 92-pound black (king) caught at Taholah.

28 Work started on Queets to Moses Prairie Road and around big slide near Point Grenville.

31 19° F. and continuation of summer's fair weather.

November 1935

2 Third day of 19° F. weather.

11 Manned balloon sets record of 74,000 feet over South Dakota. Report of intense cold and "Black Void."

22 *China-Clipper* begins Maiden Flight.

22 Hoh-Clearwater road completed.

23 Taholah Street job completed.

25 State says Indians own shellfish within boundies of the Quinault Reservation.

December 1935

6 Governor Martin pours first concrete for Grand Coulee Dam.

9 Indians ask for free hand in sale of steelhead.

20 Indian Agency now stamping furs from the Quinaults before they can be sold.

21 Heaviest surf in years batters beaches.

24 George Charley, 83 years old, was swept to his death at the mouth of the Quinault River by the surf, while dipnetting.

~ 1936 ~

January 1936

1 Storm rings in 1936.

2 President Roosevelt signs Soil Conservation Act.

3 Body of George Charley found. (*See December 24, 1935.*)

4 Alfred James, 21, drowned at same place as George Charley and in same manner.

7 Horton Capoeman fined for trapping coon at inlet to Lake Quinault; claimed he was on Tribal land.

16 Quinault Tribe hopes to plant 10,000 acres of slash under IECW.

20 Columbia River smelt milling around in mouth of Quinault River. Three tons dipnetted yesterday and today.

21 $17,000 application by WPA for Taholah-Queets Road.

February 1936

2 23° F.

2 Tribesmen find U.S. responsive to Lake Quinault Unit Plan.

18 All business and commercial activity ceases at Pacific Beach near sunset, so everyone could watch the most gorgeous sunset display that has been occurring for a fortnight.

18 Robert Polson dies. He started in logging in 1892-93, the year of the Big Snow.

22 50 mph Chinook ends long cold spell.

26 Gale, freshet beset Harbor.

29 Wet leap-year day.

March 1936

25 Indians bank on Treaty to solve fishing dispute.

27 Winter takes belated rap at Harbor with rain, then wet snow.

30 Third snow in three days.

April 1936

1 25° F.

1 Federal Government measures Lake Quinault.

2 Large number of whales sighted along coast and many glass floats washing ashore.

6 Olympic Park Bill hearings in Washington, D.C. all this month and May. Little or no local support for Park.

6 Aloha adds new logging site.

20 Tribe accepts price revision on Polson's Lake Quinault Logging Unit.

May 1936

2 Tribe may build own fish plant.

4 Emperor Haile Selassie flees Ethiopia.

5 Mussolini's troops enter the Ethiopian capital, Addis Ababa (*New Flower*).

8 Weyerhaeuser kidnapper captured. (*See May 25, and June 1, 1935.*)

9 Mussolini annexes Ethiopia.

15 Oliver Morris recalls days of Copalis otter hunting in *The Aberdeen Daily World.*

June 1936

* *Gone With the Wind* by Margaret Mitchell published.

16 Quinaults elect new tribal officers.

16 Television years away; to be costly.

17 Grays Harbor welcomes the West Coast Plywood Company.

28 Charlotte Marie Cultee, Princess of Ma-Tuse Celebration in Queets. Speakers urge Indian Resort at Lake.

30 Taholah-Queets Road authorized.

July 1936

1 Small nations walk out of League of Nations over Italian-Ethiopian conflict. Spain soon at war.

15 Construction of IECW camp near Queets begins.

17 Over 4,000 perish in "Dust Bowl" heat wave.

17 Lewellyn Logging Company bridges Upper Quinault River for the first time with a 120' stringer bridge.

27 IECW Indians now busy on new Queets-Taholah Road.

August 1936

2 Olympic Games open in Berlin.

5 Polson signs new big stand contract on Quinault.

13 Fire threatens harbor forest.

September 1936

2 Five foot long snake captured at Oakville. May have escaped from carnival.

3 Queets students striking to protest Jefferson County's prohibiting Indians from voting in the primary.

3 Washington sportsmen say the proposed Olympia National Park would allow the cougar population to build which in turn would destroy the elk.

11 Four Olympia men arrested by Quinault police for fishing on Reservation.

25 State "fires" 58,000 acres of slashing in last 10 days to save forest by preventing wild fires.

25 Allottees signing with Polson on revised timber deal in Lake Quinault Unit.

25 Queets-Raft River Road construction has been slow going for the IECW.

October 1936

7 70 year old woman survives six days in Olympic wilderness. Walks out at Kalalock.

9 Fire hazard in forest acute; 82° F.

12 Schooner *Santian* destroyed by spectacular fire while in port at Aberdeen.

19 Quinault tribesmen fight timber decision that says timber will be left along Olympic loop highway where it crosses Reservation.

Foggy forest.

November 1936

2 23° F; sudden frost chills Harbor.

4 F. D. Roosevelt carries 46 states.

9 Great Social Security Census starts.

3 New survey underway for gravity flow water system in Taholah.

11 Cook Creek to get 150,000 trees from Wind River Nursery for CCC planting.

12 World's largest, 8½ mile long, San Francisco-Oakland Bay Bridge opens.

17 Five houses leveled in Pacific Beach fire.

18 Five accused of illegally cutting timber on the Quinault Reservation's Polson Lake Unit.

24 Turkeys 25¢ per pound.

26 Quinault River exceptionally low and wells going dry.

28 Fog halts all coast traffic.

December 1936

6 Drought broken when wind and rain buffet Harbor in season's first storm.

7 Big salmon runs follow rain; 1,000 caught at Taholah in one day.

14 Harbor rivers crowd banks following storm.

18 Good, old-fashioned Chinook sweeps Harbor.

31 Taholah agency says past year the most beneficial and active in decade.

~ 1937 ~

January 1937

19 18° F.

22 County encased in ice following heavy snow, heavy rain, then deep freeze.

26 Quinault Tribe resists State's Blueback Laws which prevent the sale of salmon in March and April.

29 Snow plows finally open road between Lake Quinault and Kalaloch.

February 1937

1 Heavy snow falls on Harbor.

5 60 mph gale rakes Harbor; snow melting.

March 1937

9 Ancient dead-eye, part of a ship's rigging, found on Taholah beach. Recalls when a British ship was wrecked on the Point Grenville rocks on December 1, 1885. The sailors fought off the help of the Quinaults, as they believed that natives along the Northwest coast were cannibals.

20 Taholah water system contract awarded to Cast Iron Pipe Company of Seattle. Work to start in May.

31 Some believe that hemlock may be a Cinderella tree; will soon be valuable.

April 1937

1 Dozen whales frolic in Ruby Beach swell.

1 Quinault salmon season opens.

6 Amos Berry and Thomas Boyles honored; Harbor's last two Civil War veterans.

6 250 Olympic Indians meet at Queets; praise IECW program.

8 Frank Hyasman, 94, Quinault Patriarch, dies.

13 Gale rakes Harbor region.

15 Cascara harvest opens at 10¢ per pound; highest since 1929.

20 Quinault Tribe to press Lake Quinault boundary case.

23 One hundred and two timber plants in Grays Harbor County.

May 1937

1 Clear day, first following wettest April on record.

6 Zeppelin, *Hindenburg*, bursts into flames and crashes.

6 First Atlantic to Pacific radio program.

10 Lone Mountain Lookout completed in 12 days. Horses pack in 19 tons of sand, gravel, concrete, and steel; IECW program. (*The tower was scheduled to be pulled down during a logging operation in June 1994, but the Quinault Nation Business Committee request a delay until its historic value could be determined.*)

28 President Roosevelt presses button in Washington, D.C. to open Golden Gate Bridge.

28 *Wonder Bread* comes to Harbor.

30 5,000 watch Indians perform at greatest water carnival in the region at Lake Quinault.

June 1937

4 Amelia Earhart leaves on World Flight.

5 Big fire on Quinault Reservation perils Spruce plantation.

5 2,000-5,000 Blueback caught each day.

9 Flames raze hotel at Moclips, two Aloha log bridges and 8,000 acres on reservation.

9 Queets-Taholah Road advances all the way to Raft River.

21 Three Russian airmen fly from Moscow over North Pole to Vancouver, Washington. They flew over Grays Harbor early in the morning on last leg of flight.

29 Elk trample Queets crops; arouse ranchers.

July 1937

4 Amelia short of fuel; down at sea is fear.

16 Three oil companies get oil leases on reservation.

22 Call for bids on 8.0 million feet of windfalls on reservation.

28 Heavy mist breaks dry month record.

August 1937

5 Quinault Reservation closed to all hikers and tourists from August 7 to September 15 to prevent forest fires.

14 Oakville logger high bidder on Milwaukee Trail Logging Unit.

16 Americans ordered to leave Shanghai.

27 *The Raymond Herald* prints its anniversary issue.

31 Al Becken to operate new fish cannery in Taholah.

September 1937

9 Quinaults returning from Eastern Washington hop fields.

16 Murphy Capoeman drowns on the Quinault River.

17 Tuna run proves windfall; warm water held as cause.

21 Chief William Mason, 73, dies.

22 Man bags three cougars before breakfast above Lake Quinault.

22 *The Aberdeen Daily World* has daily accounts about President Roosevelt's upcoming visit.

23 Raymond's population is 5,050.

25 Hitler and Mussolini join hands.

October 1937

1 President Roosevelt visits Lake Quinault and Grays Harbor.

7 Northern lights glow on Harbor.

16 Gale lashes Harbor.

21 40 year old photo of many large sturgeon in *The Aberdeen Daily World* recalls time when these fish were common on the Harbor.

28 Terrific gale rakes Harbor.

November 1937

1 WPA education help urged for young men on Quinault Reservation.

2 Rayonier Incorporated formed from the merger of Rainier, Grays Harbor and Olympic Forest Products mills. (*The name Rayonier dates from 1931 when Dupont backed Rainier Mill to produce a dissolving pulp of consistent quality. This new wood pulp was called "Rayonier" by combining the names of rayon and Mt. Rainier.*)

3 Big cranberry crop.

10 E.P. Pilsbury of Salt Lake City at Taholah to survey telephone and radio facilities.

11 Shanghai falls to Japanese.

13 Driftwood cuts Taholah fish catches.

15 Rains drench Harbor; South has blizzard.

17 *The Aberdeen Daily World* turns to new type and heads.

18 State forest nursery has first big crop of seedlings.

20 New bridge across Moclips River nears completion.

24 Taholah women weaving baskets.

30 Japanese grab Yankee boat near Shanghai.

31 Lake Quinault has only four rainless days this month. Near record rainfall for month.

December 1937

2 Taholah Federal school buildings transferred to public school district.

7 Harbor enjoys most brilliant sunrises and sunsets ever seen here.

9 Indian Service plans radio at Lake Quinault.

13 U.S. gunboat *Panay* sunk by Japanese in China.

23 Japan sets up new government for China.

24 Governor Martin dedicated the new Valley High School last week in Menlo.

25 First white Christmas in 15 years on the Harbor.

29 *Hume Street* now *State Street*. Pioneer name officially gone.

~ 1938 ~

January 1938

7 Universal Newsreel Picture's one reel film made by Chalmers Sinkey showing at Warner Brothers theater in Aberdeen. Shows canoe building, fishing, hunting and everyday life in Taholah.

8 Japan expects four years war in China.

22 Northern lights flash vividly in Harbor skies.

22 New telephone lines to replace old; 15 miles completed on Moclips-Olympic Highway.

February 1938

** Hearings continue on Wallgren Bill for the establishment of Mt. Olympus National Park. Most locals view the proposed park as tying up the natural resources.

24 Reece Woods, Taholah General Store Manager, applies for permission to build electric generator in Taholah.

28 Brilliant meteor hurtles across harbor sky.

March 1938

1 820,000 acre Peninsula Park ordered.

1 Stranded 48 foot Humpback whale south of Copalis is bonanza for Indians.

11 German troops march into Austria.

11 Hydroelectric generator brought to Quinault. Many houses on lake already wired for electricity.

11 Early blueback run produces good hauls at Taholah.

14 President urges great reforestation program.

14 Wet gale hits Northwest.

16 Roosevelt favors road improvement fund for Moclips-Taholah Road.

18 Coast drenched.

18 4 miles of road from Queets to Raft River surfaced.

19 Tribe demands that logs cut on Indian property be branded.

21 Snow blankets Harbor on first day of Spring.

28 Japanese install puppet governor in China.

29 Enchanted Valley road urged.

30 Mussolini predicts terrible air war.

30 Coldest day of the year; 25° F.

April 1938

4 Sun Oil is high bidder for oil leases near Queets.

7 New hearings on Olympic Park Bill granted after Governor Martin urges a park reduction.

9 15 Indian children between Bay Center and Kalalock hit by Trachoma.

16 Northern lights disrupt wires.

17 Taholah hosts 23 tribes at Easter Shaker Church meet.

22 $100,000 approved by Congress for improving the Toke-Point Channel on Willapa Harbor.

25 Shirley Temple; a star at age nine.

26 Hikers plead for road to Enchanted Valley; say would make good ski resort.

May 1938

19 First airmail to leave Harbor.

23 Continues hot and dry, but forest fires few.

24 Flames roar in Copalis Beach brush.

30 Clam diggers have best dig in 10 years.

31 Grand Coulee Dam reaches halfway mark.

31 Herb Capoeman wins Taholah to Quinault outboard canoe race in 2 hours 25 minutes 3 seconds. Queets captures lion's share of water events at 3rd annual Lake Quinault Trout Derby.

June 1938

6 Raging fires threaten Quinault timber region.

8 Japanese bomb U.S. University in Canton.

13 Cook Creek fires have devastated 8,000 acres.

14 150,000 or more perish in great China flood on Yellow River.

23 Civil Aeronautics Authority established, CAA. (*Later re-named the FAA.*)

29 President signs Peninsula Park Bill creating the Olympic National Park.

July 1938

9 Japan urges American gunboats out of the Yangtze.

9 58th day of no rain.

14 Howard Hughes completes record round the world flight in 3 days 19 hours.

17 Wrong-way-Corrigan flies to Dublin and claims he was headed for California.

20 92° F. Harbor drought and forest fire crisis; 200 fires in Northwest forests.

23 Northwest must manage its forests or face end in 50 years.

27 Joseph O'Neil, early Olympic explorer, dies in Portland at age 74.

** Nearly $500,000 allotted to Pacific County WPA for road construction and repair.

August 1938

1 Hoquiam pilchard industry gets under way.

5 Harbor drought falls far short of 1883, shows famous (Justin) Luark Diary.

13 Patrick Gray of the Spokane Indian Service, begins survey of selective logging on the Quinault Reservation to determine the results.

15 Hitler mobilizes Germany's army.

25 3-day Aberdeen Golden Jubilee opened by Governor Martin.

September 1938

1 Pat Logan and Joe Williams, Indians, arrested for fishing on Humptulips River.

5 Heavy rain ends Harbor drought on 114th day.

10 *Boeing Clipper* lifts record load of 77,500 pounds of ballast over sound.

11 Emil Yant, the "Flying Finn," sets record 47 mile hike from Elwa to Quinault Ranger Station in one day.

19 Underground peat fires menace several South Aberdeen streets.

21 Czechoslovakia-German crisis.

October 1938

1 45 miles of roads in western part of Grays Harbor County improved in last 18 months.

12 Wind and rain buffet Harbor.

14 Harbor scrap iron going to Japan.

25 Willie Bush, Grays Harbor Civil War Veteran, dies.

30 Orson Wells' radio broadcast of *War of the Worlds* sends much of the Eastern U.S. into panic.

31 Stone shelters and new trails to greet Olympic Park hikers.

November 1938

1 Heavy chum salmon run underway on Harbor.

3 Rain torrent pelts Harbor.

9 New Quinault power station on Ziegler Creek. It's only one of two hydro-power stations built with assistance of Rural Electrification Administration (REA).

10 Anti-Jewish rioting sweeps Germany.

12 "Typhoid Mary" dies at 70. She is most famous U.S. medical prisoner.

14 U.S. Ambassador to Germany recalled.

16 Harbor soaked in heavy rain.

17 The average motorist is 43 and owns an old car.

18 German ambassador to U.S. recalled.

21 John Carmody, REA Head, tours new Quinault hydro-power station.

24 The Olympic Stadium in Hoquiam dedicated by Don Abel, State Supervisor of the WPA; Thanksgiving Day Aberdeen-Hoquiam football game. (*Hoquiam purchased much of the land for the "playfield" on December 2, 1929, from the Electric land company. A CWA grant in 1932 cleared and filled part of the area. More land was purchased in 1937 from the same*

company. The official program cost ten cents.)

26 Fish ladder finished at Lake Aberdeen.

December 1938

2 Great storm lashes northwest coast.

8 Zelasko Park endorsed by Aberdeen.

12 Cold snap grips Harbor.

29 Wilderness urged by Secretary of Interior Harold Ickes for Olympics.

~ 1939 ~

January 1939

2 Gale damages Harbor.

5 Queets tribesmen seek Federal funds to repair village.

11 Huge Humptulips spruce defies fellers; saws too small.

14 Meandering Joe Creek tamed by WPA Pacific Beach project.

22 German Nazis tie army directly to party.

28 Selective logging may bring new era to Harbor forest.

February 1939

3 Deep snow blankets Harbor hills.

7 Taholah-Queets road sought.

11 400 acre cascara farm planned on Harbor.

15 Sheriff to enforce state's 50 mph law.

24 Northern lights glow over Harbor.

March 1939

11 Modern movie theater opens in Pacific Beach.

15 Adolph Hitler arrives in Prague, just eight hours after his troops take it.

22 Quinaults file suit to halt federal sustained yield regulations.

April 1939

1 New, big J.C. Penney store at Broadway and Heron in Aberdeen.

1 Northwest "peelers" going to Germany. (*High grade logs from which veneer is peeled.*)

1 12 miles of North Beach roads rebuilt under WPA.

5 Hitler conscripts all German youth.

8 British freighter on rocks at Quillayute.

17 82° F.

26 Lake begins to form behind Grand Coulee Dam.

30 President Roosevelt is first to appear on television from the New York World's Fair opening.

May 1939

5 Big Boeing Clipper flies low over Harbor.

13 92°F; fires peril Northwest forest.

17 First televised sporting event; The Princeton baseball team beats Columbia 2 to 1 in ten innings.

19 Moclips graduates 22.

20 Clipper inaugurates regular Atlantic service with load of mail.

21 Report shows 503 million acres in U.S. remain unchartered.

24 Quinault ranchers using electricity.

28 Sam Pickernell wins Taholah-Quinault derby race in 2 hours and 26 minutes.

June 1939

15 Congressional Bill would gobble up Quinault Reservation.

28 Pan-Am begins regular scheduled air passenger service to Europe.

29 Businessmen back Quinault tribe's fight on land sale.

July 1939

7 IECW work on Taholah-Moclips Road progresses with 45 men working on both ends.

19 Pilchard boats land 1,470 tons on first day. (*Pilchard are a small marine fish related to herring.*)

22 Air photos taken over the Quinault Indian Reservation for the first time. Completed on August 9th. (*An earlier flight was made of the coastline from Taholah south.*)

26 87° F.

August 1939

2 94° F; year's record.

9 Acute fire hazards, flames near Copalis.

14 Roosevelt wants to make Thanksgiving one week earlier. (*Move from 30th to 23rd this year.*)

18 *Wizard of OZ* has film premiere.

19 Governor orders State into ferry service.

19 George, Prince of Denmark, fishes Quinault River.

23 German-Russian Treaty.

24 16 tons tuna landed on Harbor.

25 Hitler takes war steps in Poland.

September 1939

1 German troops storm Poland.

3 Britain, France declare war on Germany.

5 America officially neutral in Europe's war.

11 Funeral of Alex Polson pioneer lumber man.

11 The first reference (*Time*) to the war in Europe, as "World War II".

18 The first reference (*Time*) to the first World War as "World War I".

15 Moclips-Taholah road being rebuilt.

15 Quinaults revive North Boundary land case.

23 Sigmund Freud dies at 83.

26 Quinault Shoreline Highway pushed.

October 1939

24 Nylon stockings sold for the first time.

26 Gale and rain lash Harbor.

November 1939

13 Two tremblers rock area; millions in damage in Seattle, but little on the Harbor.

17 Quinault homes at Lake get electricity.

30 Stiff gale lashes Harbor.

December 1939

2 Park tells settlers to move out in anticipation of extension of Olympic Nation Park.

8 Gale harries coast.

15 Terrific gale rakes Harbor.

15 Movie *Gone With the Wind* opens in Atlanta.

~ 1940 ~

January 1940

2 President adds 187,000 acres to Olympic National Park.

16 Grays Harbor PUD established.

25 Harbor snow.

29 60° F. on Harbor.

February 1940

13 Quinaults win first point in legal battle against selective logging.

March 1940

1 Fire destroys Aberdeen Plywood plant. One dies, 400 out of work.

25 Harbor views Northern Lights.

25 Harbor is 162nd of Nation's 3,070 counties in industrial ranking.

29 East county votes for Soil Conservation District.

April 1940

1 Indian fire fighters to install two-way transmitting system at Lake Quinault.

4 60" of precipitation so far this year at Wynooche Oxbow.

6 Old Indian pestle found at Moclips while clearing for a cabin.

9 Germans occupy Copenhagen; move on Oslo.

10 Harbor shipping beginning to feel effects of the war.

16 Moon Island has big possibilities as future aviation base.

17 WPA work resumes on Moclips-Taholah road.

29 Lands logged by Polson, Aloha, Hobi, and M.R. Smith on the Quinault Reservation to be closed due to extreme fire hazard.

May 1940

7 Half of Queets valley settlers have signed land options to sell their land to the Federal Government for inclusion in the Olympic National Park.

7 Pacific coast Indians meet for a two day conference at Lake Quinault to discuss fishing, hunting, trapping, timber claims, and law enforcement issues.

9 150 hummingbirds found dead in Clearwater cabin. Apparently the birds feeding on near-by field of flowers flew through open window and could not find their way out.

10 Churchill becomes British Prime Minister.

10 Scow *Nisqually* put to lumber use as ships have grown scarce.

11 $55,000 for Indian CCC. Most for use at Raft River Camp for construction of Queets-Taholah Road.

17 1,000 attend state PTA meeting at three day conference in Aberdeen.

18 Park Service to buy North Shore lands says Macy.

22 Polson charges Ickes logging ban on Queets cuts airplane spruce supply.

23 Three bomber "waves" roar over Harbor in eerie moonlight visit last night.

28 Holland and Belgium surrender to Nazis.

23 Humptulips-Copalis Highway approved.

June 1940

2 5,000 to 10,000 gather for fifth annual Lake Quinault Derby.

3 U.S. offers surplus arms to Britain.

4 New fill to be pumped into proposed Moon Island airport *(This fill set the stage to form a new habitat which migrating shore birds use today).*

5 Germans invade France.

10 Mussolini joins Hitler.

10 Indians celebrate anniversary of Raft River CCC Camp.

14 Campaign launched for Moon Island Airfield.

14 Nazis occupy Paris.

18 Harbor drought brings early hay crop and forest fire peril.

20 Polson's big Eureka Mill in Hoquiam razed by fire.

22 French and Germans sign armistice in Compiègne. *(Signing was held in the same rail car were Hitler felt Germany was humiliated by its defeat in 1918.)*

July 1940

1 Tacoma Narrow's Bridge dedicated.

2 Lake Washington pontoon bridge at Mercer Island dedicated.

3 U.S. Army's big McChord Airfield dedicated.

8 Forest fire crisis halts all logging.

15 Big tuna strike off Harbor starts fish fleet stampede.

16 Aloha mill men develop new low temperature dry kilns.

20 During past year, Indian CCC crew cleared and graveled 2½ miles from Raft River south.

23 42,000,000 men to be registered for U.S. Draft.

24 Quinault Indians to fight Federal ban on oil leases.

25 Hopes bright for Harbor Aviation Base.

26 Downpour ends 40 day dry spell on Harbor.

August 1940

1 Britain using coastal radar for advanced warnings of German air raiders.

2 Quinault Hatchery was having a fly problem, so the managers devised an electric screen by hooking electric wires to a copper screen and putting a light behind it. They electrocute nearly a gallon of flies a day which they feed to the fish, cutting down on their fish feed bills.

3 Northwest trees have a seedless year.

5 Troops mass for Northwest war games.

10 A new machine has been designed by the state to paint the yellow center line down the middle of highways.

15 2,000 attend three day American Legion Convention in Aberdeen.

16 Huge air battles over London continue.

23 The white line placed on drivers side of the yellow center highway line means "unsafe to pass."

27 First pole set for Copalis Beach power line.

September 1940

9 100 enrolled at Moclips High School.

11 Iron lung benefit show arranged in Hoquiam.

12 Peach harvest due at Queets Valley. Elk continue to invade ranch fields.

21 Figures show that 24 sections in T 21 N, R 8 W, is the heaviest timber stand in the nation and remains uncut. Section 30 alone has 78,000,000 feet. The east half of 30 and west half of 29 contains the heaviest concentration of timber anywhere. *(This is adjacent to the famous 21-9 timber tract. Today [1997], there is a stand of Douglas-Fir just east of Finley Creek in the Olympic National Park, on very steep ground, with comparable volumes.)*

27 Japan joins Axis Pact.

October 1940

1 Einstein is now a U. S. citizen.

14 Vanilla extract made from pulp mill waste liquor possible.

18 Harbor register tops 6,600 for Selective Service training.

22 The new American Plywood Plant has open house.

24 40 hour work week now covers Nation.

29 Nation arranges draft call list.

November 1940

2 Moon Island Airport gets WPA approval.

6 Roosevelt wins sweeping victory in third term triumph.

7 Tacoma Narrows Bridge collapses.

8 Four week old Harbor tug boat strike settled.

14 Axis-Moscow Accord reached.

December 1940

6 Harbor tug, *Tyee*, sinks.

6 Flu closes Harbor school.

10 "We'll conquer world," says Hitler.

13 23° F. cold snap still holds.

19 Park Service to authorize spruce logging for defense.

23 85 mph gale lashes Harbor.

24 Harbor barometer hits 28.70; all time low for this region.

26 Quinault CCC camp to have tallest flag pole.

28 7,500 Boeing men assemble to vote on Red purge issue.

29 Sea claims 82 year old North Cove lighthouse.

30 California's first freeway, The Arroyo Seco Parkway, officially opens. (*A year later, the parkway adopted the new word "freeway" and became the Pasadena Freeway.*)

~ 1941 ~

January 1941

3 New sea towing enterprise bulwark's log supply on Harbor.

15 Harbor's Public Power marks first year.

15 Indian Service will survey to salvage trees which blew down near Queets in the December storms.

16 New Aberdeen factory to cut airplane spruce.

25 Storm hits coast.

27 Harbor to launch anti-polio drive.

29 Twenty years after, dense new forest heals 1921 storm scars.

30 Hitler threatens American ships.

31 Big fill to give mile long runway for Harbor airport.

31 Quinault Indians replant logged land areas.

February 1941

4 United Service Organization, USO, formed.

13 Heavy salmon run enters Columbia River.

March 1941

7 Seattle douses its lights in first major city try out of air raid blackout.

10 2,100 diggers take 50 tons of clams at Copalis Beach on one dig.

11 FDR signs Lean-Lease Act.

15 Queets-Taholah Road half finished.

22 Grand Coulee Dam opens; goes to work producing electricity.

26 Great shark, 30 feet long, washes up at Copalis Beach.

31 Feds seize Danish ship on Harbor as part of nation wide seizure of Axis ships.

April 1941

1 Blueback season opens.

6 Quinault CCC has open house.

17 100,000 fire bombs rain on London in vast raid.

23 Queets Fir is largest, but Astoria scoffs.

23 205th Coast artillery battalion at Grayland, test fire their 3" anti-aircraft guns with live ammunition.

25 Humptulips site listed for war service objectors camp.

28 Nazis take Athens.

May 1941

1 Movie *Citizen Kane* premiers; New York City.

2 Iraqi-British War underway near great oil fields.

8 Harborites push private road to manganese ore site five miles from Neilton on Steven's Creek.

9 8,000 men quit in IWA strike; 900 on Harbor.

9 Queets Fir largest by far.

17 Quinaults petition Congress for the right to sell timber.

27 German warship, *Bismarck*, sunk.

27 Public barred from Electric Park Power Plant to forestall possible sabotage.

27 Moon Island Airport construction ahead of schedule.

June 1941

1 Quinault Derby draws about 4,000 people.

2 Puyallup farther and son drown on Quinault River in canoe accident.

4 Manganese mining shaping into a big Olympic industry.

11 90° F; fire peril mounts.

12 *Clemons Tree Farm* dedicated at Montesano by Governor Arthur B. Langlie.

16 U.S. stops sale of oil to Japan.

18 German attack on Russia.

28 Quinault boils as Blueback fight their way to the lake to spawn.

July 1941

** Enormous Blueback harvest nets 509, 140 this season. (*Largest single season catch ever recorded.*)

1 WNBT begins first commercial TV service at 2:29:10 PM. The first commercial is a 10 second time announcement by Bulova. The ad cost $9.

3 Olympic forest fire season orders issued.

6 Soviets slow main German drive.

9 Low Divide Trail, blocked by December storm to open in month.

9 Agency seeks delays in Indian Hearings.

14 97° F. Whole State roast.

15 Taholah tribesman, John Cliff, on visit to Hoquiam claims 111 years; awed by auto speeds.

17 Lighting sets 700 fires in state; 70 on Harbor.

22 Troops battle forest fire in Olympic Park.

22 Crews still fighting Quinault Reservation fires.

24 High winds fan Quinault fires; 3,500 acres burned.

30 Forest fires perils Taholah-Moclips.

31 Wind driven inferno rolls over Quinault lands.

August 1941

1 Flames near Reservation Tree Farm.

5 Wind and sunny skies renew Reservation fire menace.

6 Big Quinault fire scorches tree farm.

7 Grim fight to quell Quinault fire continues.

12 Quinault fire near control.

19 Hemlock bark to be tested for tannin content.

26 Quinault fire nearly quenched.

September 1941

6 Jews in Germany must wear Star of David.

Lake Quinault.

18 Myron Garfield dies.

22 Peninsula fire bans lifted. Quinault wildfire declared out.

October 1941

7   After two year study, geologist say Harbor ore of little value.

9   Whale cast up on beach at Kalalock.

13 Indians lose fight on timber rules on the Reservation.

30 Germany attacks American destroyers. Third this month.

November 1941

14 Moon Island Airport gets CAA approval.

22 Italians surrender to Ethiopian garrisons.

27 Oil well gives data on geological formation under Aberdeen.

December 1941

2   Harbor buffeted by 54 mph gale and rain.

7   Japan attacks Pearl Harbor.

8   Congress declares war on Japan.

10 Japan invades the Philippines.

11 U.S. declares war on Germany and Italy.

11 Weather prediction curbed.

~ 1942 ~

January 1942

** War news.

10 Queets-Taholah Road being pushed with 17 Indian CCC workers; six miles remain to be completed.

February 1942

9   All U.S. clocks turned ahead to Daylight Savings Time. (*They remain there for the duration of the War.*)

15 Japanese take Singapore.

20 Roosevelt authorizes the removal of Japanese-Americans (*Nisei*) to internment camps.

24 Voice of America (VOA) goes on the air.

March 1942

3   U.S. to intern 100,000 Japanese-Americans.

12 Japanese capture Philippines.

April 1942

13 Quinault Tribe to discuss stumpage prices with Polson.

16 Squall (tornado?) hits Harbor shipyard.

18 James Doolittle's bombers hit surprised Tokyo.

May 1942

1   Aloha crews go on 48 hour work week.

4   Battle of the Coral Sea. (*First naval battle in history where ships did not engage each other. All fighting done by airplanes.*)

5   Clams killing cat, dogs, and chickens. Don't eat clams until test done.

7   Clam poison only in entrails.

15 Women's Auxiliary Army Corps, WAAC, formed. (*Later shortened to Women's Army Corps, WAC.*)

21 Three year old, Leon Charles Strom, buys war bond.

June 1942

1   Grand Coulee Dam spillway gates open for first time.

1   Gas rationing starts.

3   Battle of Midway begins.

17 *Yank*, an Army sponsored newspaper, first published.

21 Oregon coast shelled by Japanese submarine.

26 Advertisement in *The Aberdeen Daily World*, "Lumber goes to War."

July 1942

1 104° F.

1 CCC dissolved.

13 Article in *The Aberdeen Daily World* about Airplane Spruce.

16 CCC camps close due to fire fears.

21 Belief is that the wing dams built by the CCC on the Upper Quinault River, peril farms of pioneers.

30 Scenes for the movie, *Lassie Come Home,* begins filming at Lake Quinault.

August 1942

7 Upper Hoh spruce goes to war for Uncle Sam.

7 U.S. Forces land at Guadalcanal.

14 95° F.

18 Quinault dams to be removed.

22 15 foot shark killed at Westport.

September 1942

22 Local trees dogged in war effort.

23 35 mph speed limit ordered.

October 1942

3 President orders cost of living stabilized.

3 First successful V-2 launch by Germany. (*Some feel this was the beginning of the Space Age.*)

9 State mine chief visits Cook Creek mine-to-market road.

17 Draft age lowered from 20 to 18.

20 Congress passes gigantic war time tax bill.

23 Douglas fir lumber selling frozen; U.S. to take output.

23 Lights must be dimmed further in civil defense efforts.

25 5,000 witness launching of Army ship, *Colonial Quackenbush,* at Aberdeen Shipyard; first big boat built here in 25 years.

26 Coffee rationing starts; one pound every five weeks.

30 First round of Solomon Battle over.

November 1942

3 Pacific County votes for Library District.

6 British in hot pursuit of Rommel.

6 Harbor gasoline rationing plans complete.

11 Nazis overrun France.

14 Eddie Rickenbacker rescued after three weeks on raft.

16 U.S. scores great victory in three day Solomon Island Battle. (*Guadalcanal.*)

21 Alaska Highway formally opens.

25 Quinault Tribal Court to get test of Judicial powers.

December 1942

1 Harbor traffic light, as national gas rationing starts.

2 Physicists at the University of Chicago achieve the first controlled nuclear chain reaction.

2 Two *P-47 Thunderbolts* hit 725 mph in dive on November 15th.

8 The U.S. Army *L.T. 1150,* a big war tug, launched from Grays Harbor Shipyard.

11 Million Yanks overseas, says FDR.

28 Flames lick-up big new cranberry plant at Markham.

~ 1943 ~

January 1943

13 Olympic National Park's Queets Corridor open to logging.

15 Work is completed on the Pentagon.

16 Happy youngsters frolic as Harbor gets mantle of snow.

18 14° F.

18 New Army transport ship slides into Hoquiam River.

20 Winter tightens grip on Harbor.

23 British banner flies over Tripoli; Italian Empire in Africa gone.

27 American aircraft make first bombing attacks on Germany.

February 1943

10 Forty-eight hour work week to be standard for everybody.

11 Eisenhower is supreme ETO commander.

March 1943

18 Fire destroys wartime magnesium factory in Port area.

22 Seashore cavalry guards the Washington coast.

24 Point values in meat rationing effective on the 29th. About 3½ pounds of hamburger per person per week.

29 National rationing of butter and cheese begins.

April 1943

5 Three perish in crash of Navy plane and six lost as ex-Aberdeen tug boat, *Maurine,* flounders in gale off the coast.

5 Blueback catch at Taholah is light.

13 Jefferson Memorial dedicated in Washington, D.C.

May 1943

1 U.S. takes over in mine strike.

8 National Park director, Newton Drury, on Harbor to see Park for possible selective logging for the war effort.

10 U.S. troops land on Attu in Aleutian Islands; held by Japanese since 1942.

21 Harbor lags in logging; "men have left the woods to work in the shipyards."

21 Coast Guard uses dogs on the beach to guard against sneak attack.

June 1943

3 20,600 acres added to the Olympic National Park brings Park total to 856,011 acres.

7 Pacific Beach runs out of water.

15 Boeing branch plant to open on the Harbor.

19 *Memphis Bell* is the first combat bomber to retire; flew 25 missions.

20 Bombers now strike Germany from Britain and land in North Africa.

July 1943

13 Biggest tank battle in history ends between Germans and Reds.

21 Television to be ready right after war, say scientist.

25 Mussolini deposed.

27 Ickes turns thumbs down on Olympic Park logging.

August 1943

2 Role of forest in war effort.

12 Indians play big war effort roles.

16 Hoquiam's Island airport leased to Army.

September 1943

2 Harbor forest fire losses for 1943 lowest in 20 years.

October 1943

1 Indian Agency employees set War Bonds mark; spend 43% of income on war bonds.

12 Censorship on weather news to be relaxed.

November 1943

1 All weather news restrictions lifted on West Coast.

3 Abolition of BIA due.

2 Labor-employer group organized for Aloha Lumber Company at Aloha.

23 Samuel Thompson appointed BIA supervisor of Indian Education at Taholah.

** Grays Harbor County Rural Library District established.

December 1943

3 Five inches of rain in last 24 hours reduces Harbor forest fire danger.

6 Churchill, Stalin, Roosevelt meet in Teheran, Iran to plot war strategy.

14 Penicillin in mass production.

22 Big 325 year old Douglas-fir, a landmark at the intersection of Quinault and DeKay Road, felled at noon. To go as airplane stock.

~ 1944 ~

January 1944

29 *USS Missouri* launched. Construction started on June 6, 1941. (*It was on this ship that Japan would officially surrender, September 2, 1945.*)

February 1944

17 Frank Briggs, Taholah Agency Forester, dies of an apparent heart attack.

18 The 1943 fire season on the Harbor is reported at a new low. Only 17 fires burned 262 acres with none on the Reservation.

22 Bids to wdFen highway and eliminate the steep grade of Adams Hill, to open on US 101 from Reservation's south boundary to the Quinault River.

March 1944

3 Series of articles on tree farming in *The Aberdeen Daily World* begins.

15 Quigg awarded contract to oil 1.25 miles of road from forest boundary to the Quinault river on Route 9 by September 1st.

April 1944

3 Two killed in Taholah shooting and a third injured in resisting arrest.

May 1944

3 All meat except beef steaks and roast made ration-free.

June 1944

2 Aleuts, who were evacuated from the Pribilof Islands two years ago, have been returned home.

6 D-Day; Allied troops land in Normandy.

July 1944

3 A 20 part series on the future of forests in Grays Harbor begins in *The Aberdeen Daily World*.

5 Grays Harbor County Rural Library opens at Pacific Beach, quickly followed by Moclips, Aloha, Carlisle, Copalis Crossing, Malone, Neilton, Newton, Porter, Quinault, Taholah, Vesta, and Upper Wishkah Valley. (*These collections numbered 50-100 volumes and were housed in store fronts, post 0®fices, and private residences.*)

18 The *S.S. Quinault*, one of two victory ships carrying munitions, blew up in San Francisco Bay and caused widespread damage and 350 deaths.

21 American forces land on Guam.

25 Stanley Charlie and Sam Pickernell saved the lives of five fishermen whose 80 foot fishing drag vessel (a converted 43 ton oil tanker) ran aground in fog 3/4 mile west of Taholah. They made three trips to the sinking ship in a dugout.

August 1944

23 Paris and Marseille liberated after four years of German rule.

28 BIA Superintendent George LaVatta is informed by the Secretary of the Interior that he can sell gas and mineral leases near Queets.

September 1944

11 Harbor loggers idle due to serious fire hazard.

October 1944

20 General Douglas McArthur returns in victory to Philippines.

November 1944

8 Roosevelt wins presidential election by landslide.

27 Superforts bomb Tokyo and Bangkok.

December 1944

17 Nazi army advances in France and Belgium. (*Battle of the Bulge.*)

18 *Quinault Victory* launched.

~ 1945 ~

January 1945

1 New Nazi attack.

8 Rivers run high in wake of storm.

24 Harbor seeks USFS set aside for Harbor mills.

31 Soviets 45 miles from Berlin.

February 1945

5 U.S. Court of Claims says 1892 Quinault survey (ordered in 1873) is in error. (*See October 22, 1946.*)

7 Roosevelt, Churchill, and Stalin meet in Yalta, Crimea to draft war end plans.

16 Nine hour raid on Tokyo with 1,500 American planes.

19 Americans land at Iwo Jima.

23 Old Glory hoisted atop Iwo volcano fortress. (*Produces one of the most famous war photos.*)

March 1945

2 Ninth American Army sweeps to the Rhine.

14 British 11-ton bomb biggest in world.

17 Iwo Jima taken.

April 1945

4 Tribe and PUD working on agreement for a power line from Moclips to Taholah. (*Completed in 1947.*)

12 President Roosevelt dies.

13 Truman sworn in as new President.

21 Soviets break into Berlin.

25 Delegates from 45 countries meet in San Francisco to organize U.N.

26 Americans-Russians link up on the Eibe.

May 1945

1 Nazis claim Hitler dead.

2   Red Army captures Berlin.

7   *The Aberdeen Daily World* headline: GERMANY QUITS. War in Europe lasted 2,076 days.

8   Truman proclaims V-E Day for victory in Europe.

22 "Japs have loosened balloon bombs on west coast over the past two years".

June 1945

5   Allies split Germany into four zones.

6   Charred remains of Hitler's body found.

6   First LORAN signal sent out from Point Grenville.

20 President Truman in Olympia for five days vacation.

21 Okinawa battle won says Nimitz.

22 Photo of famous Iwo Jima flag raising appears for the first time in *The Aberdeen Daily World* in an advertisement.

25 Cooperative agreement signed between the Grays Harbor and Pacific Counties Rural Library Districts.

July 1945

6   Record bomb raid in Japan.

7   Forest fire threat in Grays Harbor acute.

9   Fog hides spectacular sunrise eclipse. (*May have been seen on higher ridges in Grays Harbor.*)

12 *S.S. Grays Harbor* launched; a tanker claimed to be the world's fastest.

16 First atomic bomb explosion at Trinity site in New Mexico. (*No report until August 6th newspaper.*)

17 Truman-Churchill-Stalin begin parley at Potsdam.

18 Hoquiam police capture a bear cub and charge it with disturbing the peace. (*It turned out to be the mascot of Willapa Coast Guard.*)

19 Forest fires darken Harbor skies. The smoke pall recalls Black Day of 1902.

24 Continuous signals sent out from the Coast Guard's LORAN Station at Point Grenville. (*See December 31, 1979.*)

28 U.S. Senate ratifies U.N. Charter.

28 *B-25* crashes into Empire State Building.

29 Big tuna and pilchard season, with upward of 300 tons/ day coming in.

August 1945

** Most famous catchword "Kilroy was here" spreads.

2   Red July most destructive in Japanese history.

6   Earth-shattering force of atomic explosives loosed against Japan.

6   Earth's fate hangs on atom's control.

8   Russia declares war on Japan.

9   Nagasaki dies in Atom Blast.

14 Japan surrenders.

15 Gasoline removed from ration list.

15 The *Indianapolis,* the ship which delivered the atomic bomb, was sunk and many killed.

24 "Radio-activity" is taking a toll in Hiroshima.

25 Chalet in Low Divide is reported to have been destroyed by slides last winter.

30 McArthur takes up base in Japan.

September 1945

2   Japan signs surrender on *USS Missouri.*

28 Nationwide Labor Union strikes spread to Harbor mill industry, paralyzing it.

October 1945

1   IWA operations reopening on Harbor.

4   Seedling from Lone Tree planted in Montesano.

5   Walkout halts U.S. phone service.

13 Quinault Tribal Council sets up committee to work with Taholah Indian Agency to arrange timber cutting on north half of Reservation.

21 60 mile southwester rakes Peninsula.

24 United Nations charter takes effect.

29 Undeclared Civil War grips China.

November 1945

1   Mount Olympus' Blue Glacier shrunk 600 feet in last seven years.

21 Nuremburg war crimes trial begins.

26 50 mph southwester.

December 1945

5   Northwest lashed by terrific gale.

6   U.S.-Britain sign $4\frac{1}{2}$ billion dollar loan.

18 Moon stages celestial show for Harbor.

20 Tire rationing ends.

21 General Patton dies from auto accident 12 days ago.

~ 1946 ~

January 1946

1   1946 seen as big year for Harbor.

14 Strikes still plague nation.

26 Jet plane crosses U.S. in $4\frac{1}{4}$ hours.

February 1946

15 Northwest shaken by violent quake. The November 12, 1939 quake was felt stronger on the Harbor.

March 1946

11 Olympic tribes plan to fight Steelhead ban.

28 Seattle smallpox nears epidemic stage.

April 1946

1   2,500 vaccinated on Harbor over weekend for smallpox; 5,000 by week's end.

1   A five foot tidal wave races up the Quinault River.

May 1946

2   84° F; acute power famine hits nation due to coal strike.

10 Remade German V-2 rocket soars 75 miles at White Sands, New Mexico.

June 1946

22 Quinault sustained yield program series begins in *The Aberdeen Daily World.*

23 Severe earthquake shakes Northwest at 9:14 a.m.

29 Mrs. Francis Bowechop is first women elected to Tribal Council. (*Blanche Shale [McBride] said she was tribal secretary under her dad.*)

July 1946

1   First atomic bomb test at Bikini atoll.

8   Howard Hughes given 50/50 chance following air crash.

8   175 foot long dock built at LaPush.

12 Adolph Hague, Hoquiam Agency Forest Supervisor, to be replaced.

16 Restriction on loans to Indian Veterans to be eased.

20 96° F.

24 First underseas a- bomb mauls test fleet at Bikini Atoll.

30 U.S. joins UNESCO.

August 1946
12 20 tons of tuna brought into Harbor over weekend.

September 1946
4   Pacific Coast seamen begin strike.

6   Westport boat gets 14$^1/_2$ ton tuna haul.

19 Meat shortage here.

27 Seven Harbor firms begin logging on Olympic National Forest land.

30 Twenty-two Nazis found guilty of war crimes at Nuremburg. (*Nine would be hanged on October 16. Hermann Goering, Hitler's number two man, swallowed cyanide just before he was to be hanged.*)

October 1946
3   Atom War means return to "barbarism" says Eisenhower.

4   Truman urges all Jewish Nation; British opposed to idea.

8   William Pace carries 5,530,000 feet from Harbor; single largest load ever.

9   Fiery show of 200-300 meteor per minuet dazzles Harbor residents.

16 28° F.

22 U.S. Court of Claims opens to determine compensation owed Quinault Tribe because of erroneous 1892 survey which excluded 16,000 acres from the Reservation as determined by the Court in a February 5, 1945 ruling.

24 Six inches of rain in five days.

25 John Huelsdock, Iron Man of the Hoh, dies.

25 $25,000 is held true value of Indian timber error by the U.S. Court of Claims.

November 1946
1   Montesano enters into contract with the Grays Harbor Rural Library District.

2   Mervin Helander, new Taholah Agency head arrives.

12 Westcoast Airlines DC-3 arrives at Moon Island to preview air passenger services to begin on the 15th.

18 Heavy snow cripples Harbor.

22 Heavy rain soaks Harbor in wake of snow.

25 Mrs. Lillian Simmonds and her son Lawrence Klatush drown when their boat capsizes at mouth of the Quinault River, while fishing.

December 1946
4   Photo appears in *The Aberdeen Daily World* of the 15-year old Spruce Orchard plantation on the Quinault Reservation. Eight trees species planted here.

9   Big tide boosted by strong southwesterly laps at Harbor door step.

9   Members of Olympians Hiking Club escape death when bridge collapses over Falls Creek at Lake Quinault.

21 Big Japanese Quake kills 3,700.

21 Pacific Beach Naval Station purchase urged for a State park.

28 Super-highway for State visualized for Seattle to Portland.

~ 1947 ~

January 1947
14 20° F.

24 Kellogg Bill introduced to State Legislature for Moclips-Queets Road.

25 60 mph gale rakes Harbor.

31 Fifth day of snow and cold.

February 1947
1   Chinook ends cold snap.

** TV coverage reaches the Eastern Seaboard between Boston and Washington, D.C.

March 1947
15 78° F.

21 Kellogg Forest Bill passes by Senate to provide for survey of Olympic timber on State lands; vetoed by Governor.

21 Photo published of the earth from 100 miles up, taken by an automatic camera atop a V-2 rocket over the Southwest U.S.

April 1947
13 Moon Island airport (Hoquiam) transferred from War Assets Administration to county; 5,000 spectators view multitude of airplanes.

16 Texas City, Texas, destroyed in chain of explosions; 600 die.

May 1947
22 Blueback run best in five years.

23 Oil test well at Queets down 1,000'.

23 90° F.

June 1947
5   Marshall Plan proposed.

July 1947
2   Taholah Agency staff to be cut by 11.

5   Mystery discs reported over Raymond and Northwest.

24 "Flying saucer" phrase coined by Ken Arnold in his report of them at Mount Rainier.

31 321 tons of tuna brought in to date; may produce greatest run in Harbor history.

August 1947
7   The balsa wood raft *Kon-Tiki* crashes into a reef in Polynesia.

30 Settlement reached in 10 week Harbor boom strike.

September 1947
13 Kodak and NBC develop a film camera to record live TV; the Kinescope.

16 Hearings open on Olympic National Park boundaries.

30 First World Series game broadcast on TV; the New York Yankees and Brooklyn Dodgers. (*Of the 4 million viewers, 3.5 million were in taverns.*)

October 1947
14 Chuck Yeager in the *Bell X-1* rocket plane (*Glamorous Glennis*), breaks the sound barrier. (*Kept secret at the time.*)

17 56 mph winds lash Harbor.

24 I was born.

30 Oregon Governor Earl Snell found dead in plane missing for two days.

November 1947
2   Howard Hughes' mammoth flying boat, *Spruce Goose*, airborne briefly.

20 Rayonier acquires Polson Empire.

December 1947
4   Arab-Jewish strife mounts in Palestine.

13 65 mph gale lashes Harbor.

18 Southerly gale rakes Harbor.

19 Truman asks 17 billion dollars for Marshall Plan.

23 70 mph gale strikes Harbor.

27 *Howdy Doody* first appears on TV.

~ 1948 ~

January 1948

1 Gale lashes Harbor.

6 Quinault Road full of chuckholes from Hoquiam to Forks.

7 Harbor hit by electrical storm.

7 1,900 tons of tuna processed here in 1947.

27 Fire wipes out most of Moclips business district.

30 Mohandas Gandhi killed by assassin.

February 1948

1 Seattle weather bureau opens.

9 60 mile blow hits Harbor; storms continue for next six days.

March 1948

1 Diggers earn 14¢/lb for razor clams at season opening; up to 21¢/lb on the 5th.

21 Heavy damage in northwest gale.

31 U.S. Congress passes Marshall Aid Act.

April 1948

16 Blueback salmon run points to good season. Three official buyers pay $1.25/fish.

23 Commercial clam dig ends.

24 Sport clam dig opens; most get their 24 limit. Blueback catch curbed by high water.

26 Cold and snowy.

27 Japanese mine washes up at Bay City; exploded by Navy experts.

30 Jews launch battle for Jerusalem.

May 1948

1 Scores cross Quinault River to help construct three mile missing link in Taholah-Queets Road.

1 Arab states open Palestine Drive.

6 Heavy rains and flood smash dam at Aloha; mill shut down.

10 President Truman seizes railroad to head off strike.

14 Hebrews proclaim State of Israel.

15 Arabian armies attack Israel.

18 Five week old boom strike ends.

22 175 lb. sturgeon caught in Chehalis River. Largest since early days. A big one now is 60 lbs.

27 Time change has Harbor in big turmoil as cities shifting to DST on different days.

25 Freak hail storm bombards Harbor.

28 Harbor records wettest May.

28 Puyallup man to build big roller rink in Hoquiam.

June 1948

1 Northwest in flood horror.

3 Dedication of 200 inch telescope at Mt. Palomar.

7 89° F. heat wave boosts flow of present Columbia River torrent.

23 Columbia River floods may have affected the Harbor clam beaches.

26 Mystery foe girdling trees; bear suspect.

29 Berlin cries for UN action in blockade.

July 1948

1 High winds keep boats in Harbor.

8 Bonneville clearing wide swath for power line from Olympia to Cosmopolis.

14 Quinault timber in D.C. controversy. Timber policy delays contracts.

26 Mrs. Charles Clark first to die in most recent polio outbreak.

August 1948

** Berlin blockade crisis continues.

9 Rock removal from Porter Bluff completed. Will make way for State highway between Elma and Oakville.

14 Olympic games come to close. First held since 1936.

16 Babe Ruth dies in New York at age 53.

September 1948

15 Gale tangles Harbor power lines.

21 Milton Berle goes on television's *Texaco Star Theater.*

25 First news release that a U.S. rocket ship, the *X-1* has flown faster than the speed of sound and to nearly 900 mph.

October 1948

13 "Cold War" cartoon appears in *The Aberdeen Daily World.*

15 Fine new gravel highway from Hoquiam north to Y. (*Three Ways.*)

21 Construction begins on new Moclips-Aloha School.

24 Term "Cold War" used by Bernard Baruch.

25 Big sale of timber (108,000 acres) O.K.'d by the Interior Department on the Quinault Reservation.

30 200 pound sturgeon caught in the Chehalis River.

November 1948

3 Truman re-elected President, defeats Tom Dewey.

3 Rain, wind, and tide buffet harbor.

4 Aerial photograph of Pacific Beach appears in *The Aberdeen Daily World.* Caption says it was first settled in 1862 by Henry Blodget.

29 Winds lash Harbor for two weeks now.

December 1948

3 Rain storms change to snow.

23 Mid 20's and clear.

28 Moclips prospector says he found rich uranium deposits near Lake Quinault.

~ 1949 ~

January 1949

3 Heavy snow on Harbor.

9 Columbia introduces 33 rpm records. (*The standard was 78 rpm.*)

10 RCA introduces 45 rpm records.

13 Cold weather breaks Aberdeen's main water line and halts work at Harbor mills.

14 Largest Harbor railroad trestle, Bridge 15 on Clemons Logging Company line, razed.

21 Winter's worst snow hits Harbor.

26 Huge Quinault timber sale planned north of Quinault River. (*The 1929 sale of same the area was canceled after protest.*)

28 Contract for construction of UN building awarded.

31 Coldest January recorded in 56 years.

** TV coverage reaches from the Atlantic to the Mississippi.

February 1949

2 Heaviest snow of the year hits beaches; one foot at Pacific Beach.

4 New snow slows Harbor to a crawl.

7 36" of snow at Lake Quinault.

8 *XB-41* jet crosses U.S. in 3 hours 46 minutes.

10 Sudden thaw imperils Northwest.

12 Phone crews battle Taholah snow and hunger.

18 50 mph winds pummel Harbor.

18 One millionth ton flown into West Berlin since Russian blockade began. (*Flights began on April 24, 1948.*)

22 Heavy rains, on top of snow, flood country.

28 If built, the Taholah-Queets road would open a scenic wonderland.

March 1949

2 Boeing bomber circles globe non-stop.

15 Navy fighter plane crashes in ocean three miles north of Taholah.

16 Television from KRSO-TV Seattle regularly reached on Harbor now.

18 NATO organized.

April 1949

6 Downtown Aberdeen parking meters now in effect.

7 U.S. approved big Quinault timber sale of three big blocks north of the Quinault River on the Reservation.

7 Vapor trail appears in Harbor sky and sets hundreds of Harborites speculating.

13 Quake staggers northwest with major damage in Puget Sound region. Minor damage on the Harbor.

16 Plane-a-minute landing daily in Berlin.

May 1949

5 Heron Street Mercury vapor lights turned on.

11 At Quinault Council's request Rep. Henry Jackson asks a hold up on proposed sales north of the Quinault River.

12 Berlin Blockade ends.

15 2,500 see Moon Island air show.

20 President proposes putting all Columbia River power generation under one administration.

21 Blueback run strong.

25 Ocean City oil well down 4,923 feet.

26 Communist forces sweeping through China.

June 1949

1 Public hearings set for Federal Land (USFS) which would produce wood for Harbor mills.

6 Last in a series about pioneer logging in Grays Harbor appears in *The Aberdeen Daily World.*

9 Pacific County Historical Society organized.

14 Fire peril shuts off Harbor forest areas.

16 Spy uproar and anticommunist hysteria merely post war jitters says Truman.

22 Photo in *The Aberdeen Daily World* of four logs cut from single Douglas-fir on North Shore of Lake Quinault.

July 1949

3 Seven perish in Aberdeen La Fayette Hotel Fire.

9 Seattle-Tacoma Airport dedication.

26 Concrete work starts on Hoquiam airport building.

August 1949

1 Ocean at Point Grenville is a popular cooling off spot.

8 *Bell X-1* plane flies to 63,000 feet.

10 Harbor still see's *"Things"* race through the sky. First reports began 2 years ago.

12 250 tons of tuna landed by tuna fleet this season.

16 *Gone with The Wind* author, Margaret Mitchell, dies of injuries.

23 Freighter *Oregon Star of London*, loading lumber for Britain on Harbor.

24 Presto logs available on Harbor.

26 The 1949 Polio epidemic, worst in U.S. history.

September 1949

10 A beaver fells tree onto Bonneville highlines between Raymond and Cosmopolis to knock out Harbor power supply.

10 New techniques cut big hemlock log loss.

12 *Viking* maybe Spaceship forerunner.

16 Ocean City oil well, ready for production test.

18 Truman ordered huge A-bomb expansion.

20 The street car tracks on Heron Street are now concealed under new asphalt.

23 Russians have the Bomb.

24 Big timber sale is expected to ease Indian distress on Quinault.

** Sinatra popular with bobby-soxes.

October 1949

1 China establishes People's Republic.

5 Heron Street Bridge piers slip in Wishkah mud.

6 Lighting knocks out Harbor power.

7 Frost coats Harbor highways.

16 Harbor has good view of lunar eclipse.

17 Lumber slip, *Salina Cruz*, ablaze in ocean off Harbor.

24 Heavy Northwest fog virtually halts traffic.

26 Minimum U.S. wage raised from 40¢ to 75¢.

26 Wind and rains buffet Harbor.

November 1949

17 Blazes of first 1858 beach survey found.

27 Near-hurricane claims 28 Northwest lives.

December 1949

19 Weekend snow blankets Harbor.

27 Drenching rains ride with gale.

25 The number one Christmas gift in the Eastern U.S. is a TV set. A four month waiting list exist for some areas.

30 Heavy snow hits Harbor.

~ 1950 ~

January 1950

2 Snow, cold grip Pacific Northwest.

9 Record snowfall bogs Northwest.

13 Blizzard paralyzes Northwest.

19 Silver thaw glazes Harbor region.

23 Jerusalem becomes official capital of Israel.

24 Mercury cringes as polar blasts resume assault.

31 President orders production of Hydrogen bomb.

February 1950
1 Main Aberdeen water line breaks from cold.
2 Wishkah River freezes across.
4 Water emergency and mills close in Aberdeen.
7 U.S. recognizes one of the Viet Nams.
8 Aberdeen water emergency ends.
11 Ocean City oil well blows-out.
22 A rusty Japanese horn-type mine discovered 1/4 mile north of Moclips. First discovered on coast in several years.
23 The Moclips Mine was disarmed, moved 400 yards and detonated, failed to explode, but did split open. Tide should wash powder away.
27 Ocean City oil well produces 80 barrels.
28 24 days of rain this month.

March 1950
1 Commercial razor clam season opens; 35¢ this year compare to 16¢ last year.
3 Whooping cough outbreak in Hoquiam subsides.
4 Heavy rains the last two days.
11 *Chaunta*, an ocean going tug with a barge load of Columbia River logs, runs aground on the "Middle Grounds" across from Moon Island.
14 *Java Mail* arrives in Willapa Harbor with 9,242 cases of seed oysters for growers in the Twin Harbors area. The *Komatmotod* will be used to grow "Washington oysters." It is midway in size between the small Olympic and the big Willapa oyster.
20 The Harbor, once top Fir area, now imports it.
23 Gale winds sweep Northwest coast.

April 1950
30 The shift to Daylight Saving Time on the Harbor is not unanimous.

May 1950
4 Bonneville substation opens up new Harbor era. *The Aberdeen Daily World* presents a special power section.
5 14 sets of twins born on Harbor so far this year breaks total of any known previous years.
5 Dillon Myer appointed as the new BIA Commissioner. (*He develops Termination Policy to sell off Indian reservations, withdraw federal funds, and find jobs for Indians in urban centers. He was the war time director of the relocation of Japanese-Americans. Glenn Emmons, the Commissioner from 1953-61 would continue these termination policies.*)
15 Splash dams, relics of Logging's Golden Age, imperils Humptulips Valley.
26 First Whooping crane hatched in captivity.
28 Wilber Sampson of Queets, wins Taholah to Lake Quinault Canoe Race in 1 Hour 55 minutes and 30 seconds. He edged David Purdy (2nd) and James Jackson (3rd) by about one minute.

June 1950
5 Preliminary plans for Hospital at South Bend completed.
20 Slide endangers new Heron Bridge.
23 Hundreds flee Northwest floods.
24 Thousands see dedication of new Heron Street Bridge.
26 North Korean Reds invade South.
30 Truman orders troops to Korea in concert with the United Nations.
30 Taholah Logging Unit Timber Sale brightens Aloha-Quinault hopes. "It will keep us working for thirty years!"

July 1950
3 U.S. Forces see action for the first time in Korea.
7 U.S. orders draft of 600,000 men.
8 MacArthur named to head United Nation's force in Korea.
** Blueback harvest tops 91,000 this season

August 1950
17 It was reported that Robert Keys, 19, is the first Harborite killed in the Korean War.
14 Rain cuts down Harbor fire threat.
23 New Robert Grays School ready to open.
23 New Moclips North Beach School ready to open.

September 1950
21 84° F.
26 Seoul Liberated.
26 Storm blots out view of Total Lunar Eclipse last night.
30 35° F.

October 1950
6 World's longest pipeline, running 1,066 miles from U.S. owned oil fields on the Persian Gulf to the Mediterranean, goes into service.
7 U. S. Forces cross 38th parallel for the first time in Korea.
16 Two inches of rain and 40 mph winds buffet Harbor.
19 Red Korea capital falls.
27 Great gale lashes Pacific coast.
28 Pacific gale wane after four day siege.

Frost Covered Western hemlock.

November 1950
1 Truman assassination try fails.
2 U. S. population tops 150,000,000 this year.
7 The jet saw its first combat when a U.S. *F-86* downed a *MIG-15* in Korea.
9 Chinese Reds enter the Korean War.
26 Chinese and North Korean halt U.N. offensive.
29 Aloha opens new span across the Quinault River near Mounts Creek.

December 1950

1 2,200 drive-in theaters in the U.S.

6 Quinault rainfall nudges 12 feet.

16 National emergency proclaimed in wake of Korea set back.

30 State to buy Puget Sound Ferries and their routes.

~ 1951 ~

January 1951

2 High winds, rain bombard Harbor.

2 Arabian American Oil Co. agrees to share profits with Saudi Arabian Government.

10 Sinclair Lewis dies.

13 Storm holds up in-bound Harbor ships.

15 U.N. forces halt Red drive in Korea.

27 Diesel engine now pulls passenger train on Seattle to Grays Harbor run.

29 Fire sweeps Aberdeen's Washington Fish Plant on icy winds.

30 Twenty one die in Hoquiam rest home fire.

February 1951

9 Rain sloshes Harbor. Moclips flooded.

10 Flood and logs break Wishkah dam.

13 Freeze checks floods, but adds new hardships.

21 Relentless rain bogs down Korea War.

26 Aloha issued permit for $600,000 addition.

26 XXII Amendment added to U.S. Constitution (*Limits President to two terms*).

26 AFL mill strike idles 500 on Harbor.

March 1951

5 Near-blizzard snarls Traffic on Harbor.

7 Swirling snow smothers Harbor for fifth day.

15 Iran nationalizes oil.

15 Seoul retaken without a shot.

30 Rosenburgs found guilty of wartime espionage.

April 1951

5 Rosenbergs, convicted atomic spies, sentenced to death.

27 Showers bring cheer to region.

11 Truman fires MacArthur in Korea.

28 Plans unveiled for super highway from Vancouver, WA to Canadian border.

May 1951

12 Hydrogen bombs being tested by the U.S.

18 Costly roads opening vast Olympic forest.

25 Allies drive to destroy Red Army in Korea.

28 High Court clears way for color TV.

June 1951

7 Super-accurate clock to keep time for U.S.

9 Quinault Tribe protest Agency shift to Everett.

19 Truman signs new draft law lowering age to 18$^1/_2$.

20 Agency FM radio tower near completion at Lake Quinault. "Will provide better fire control."

22 Tree Farm marks ten years.

23 Television changing U.S. social scene.

25 Korea War begins second year today.

28 Bark-stripping bear declared predators on Harbor.

28 90° F. Drought continues.

July 1951

3 Bridge over the Quinault River, redecked.

4 Logging returns to normal operations.

5 Aphids affect spruce is report.

10 Quinault Tribe lays claim on 1855 Treaty against government allotting land to other tribes.

17 400 to 500 barrels of oil wash ashore at Taholah from Army barge. Loggers pay $2.50 to $3.00 each for them.

21 Tillamook burn rages through re-planted forest. (*See August, 24, 1933.*)

25 Camps again curtailed by dry weather.

30 Forest Service's Quinault area sets cutting mark.

** Driest July since 1944.

August 1951

6 Humptulips fire out of control.

6 Taholah Agency money handling goes to Everett.

8 Scores of fires burn in Northwest woods.

9 Taholah Agency records moved despite protest.

13 Tribe will fight Agency removal.

September 1951

4 President Truman makes first live coast-to-coast TV broadcast.

5 Bear study launched in tree stripping here.

10 Harbor to get $5 million *Voice of America* station.

14 Mounting fire danger closes woods again.

20 Forks residents flee forest fire.

22 Forks fire.

27 Harbor round-logs exported to Japan.

October 1951

2 Rain soaks Harbor area.

6 U.N. troops retake Heartbreak Ridge in Korea.

8 Forest fires ten times those of 1950. September worse fire month records show. 1,600 acres burn on the Harbor and 35,422 State wide.

9 Summer in fall hits Northwest.

10 Bears kill off more trees then fires say foresters.

17 Biologist study clam conditions.

25 Indian Agency shift appealed to Interior Secretary.

November 1951

10 Direct-dial coast-to-coast telephone service begins.

10 Rayonier ask to buy burned timber at Forks.

15 28° F.

18 Edward R. Murrow premiers on CBS with *See It Now.*

19 Lone Tree Monument to Gray, doomed.

21 New Rayonier span opens big timber stand above Queets on Clearwater.

26 Blowy weather rakes Harbor.

27 FCC predicts U.S. will have 1,200 to 1,500 TV stations within five years.

28 Truce draws neutral zone along the 38th parallel in Korea.

29 Harbor rides out storm.

30 65 MPH gale rakes Harbor.

December 1951

3 High winds lash coast for third day.

7 Storm and tides topple historic Lone Tree marker.

13 Tree planting scheduled on 4,000 acres of USFS lands in the Northwest this season.

21 U.S. records millionth traffic death.

~ 1952 ~

January 1952

3 Snow covers Harbor.
5 Olympic gets bulk of U.S. seedlings.
14 NBC *Today* show premiers.
21 Heavy snow covers area.
22 Winter grip tightens on Harbor.

February 1952

27 Rayonier acquires big block of Forks timber.
26 Churchill says Britain has developed an atomic bomb.

March 1952

21 27° F.
29 U.S. program freeing tribes to make Indians independent of government.

April 1952

1 First Quinault Salmon arrive.
2 Crane Creek timber on the QIR put up for sale.
15 Olympic beauty rated with America's best in May issue of *Holiday Magazine.*
15 Truman signs the Japanese peace treaty officially ending World War II in the Pacific.
17 Revival shown in Grays Harbor bottom fishing industry.
18 Forty Western Washington tribes mull ending U.S. trusteeship.
26 U.S. destroyer, *Hobson,* sinks after colliding with the aircraft carrier *Wasp.*
30 Near gale lashes Harbor.

May 1952

3 Science aiding Harbor in timber production.
8 Allies make biggest air strike in Korea.

June 1952

14 *Nautilus,* world's first atomic submarine, dedicated by President Truman.
18 Tribesmen oppose timber sales in big units.
18 Huge block of timber on QIR goes to Rayonier.
23 Indians to ask voiding of big timber sale.
23 Three tribes protest big timber sale.

July 1952

8 Hoot-owl shift goes on.
9 96° F.
29 UFO stories in D.C. and all over U.S.

August 1952

14 *The Aberdeen Daily World* feature, "Early day Quinault travel difficult."
15 Indians get first payment from Rayonier; big timber sale.
26 Geodetic crew re-mapping Harbor.

September 1952

6 Slash and forest fire smoke from Queets shrouds Lake Quinault.
22 Logging banned as heat mounts.

October 1952

3 British explode their first atomic weapon.
6 Finest Fall on Harbor in 14 years.
6 Safeway opens spacious new store at South L and west Heron in Aberdeen.
7 *Taisumiya Maru,* first Jap ship here since 1941. (*The ship was sunk two times in shallow water during World War II*).

14 Fire erupts in old Forks burn.

November 1952

5 The UNIVAC Computer receives much public attention on TV in its prediction of the electoral outcome. Ike victory huge in record vote.
8 U.S. allegedly sets off H-bomb.
13 Navy *P4Y2 Privateer*, believed to have crashed in the Olympics with eleven aboard.
14 Electric storm, wind, and hailstones bombard Grays Harbor region.
18 Increasing imports of Japanese tuna are damaging the American salmon industry.
29 100,000 salmon taken on Harbor this season.

December 1952

4 Harbor gets drenched.
5 Aberdeen-Quinault highway carries more logging traffic than any highway in state.
5 The Aberdeen to Olympia highway among most heavily traveled 900 miles of road in the state.
8 Storm drives Calmar freighter *Yorkmar* aground at Point Brown.
12 5.73" rainfall at Lake Quinault in last 24 hours.
18 Sand-bound *Yorkmar* pulled free.
22 25-barrel flow from the Ocean City #3 Oil Well yesterday.
30 50 mph gale hits Harbor.

~ 1953 ~

January 1953

2 Heavy rains.
2 Twenty-one highway fatalities on Harbor in '52.
6 47,753 acres added to Olympic National Park.
7 Truman confirms U.S. has H-bomb.
9 Storm forces school closures as winds and rain batter Harbor for third straight day.
10 PUD power line damage worst in 25 years.
17 Baby foods and TV included in new cost of living index.
17 Pussy willows out in Grayland area.
20 Ike takes oath as 34th President.
22 Torrential rains.
24 Flu epidemic reaching world-wide proportions.
27 Perilous road causes Taholah "revolt." School board pulls school bus run to Moclips as road is unsafe.
31 January rain fall beats 1914 record.
31 Indian fishermen at Taholah want State to stop interfering with their traditional fishery.

February 1953

1 20th Century Fox converting its entire movie making operations to Cinemascope.
2 Photo to Taholah-Moclips road appears in *The Aberdeen Daily World.*
4 Flash storm rakes Harbor, cuts power.
13 Rain gauge dry for the first time in 50 days.
20 Indians push Queets Unit Timber Sale.

March 1953

2 Snow, small blizzard hit Harbor area.
5 Joseph Stalin succumbs to stroke.
6 Malenkov succeeds Stalin as Premier.

6 Harbor cut pilings support New York Freeway.

6 Aloha firm completes Quinault River Span (Chow Chow).

9 Stalin enshrined in Lenin's Tomb.

17 The Office of Price Stabilization ends its controls on all prices.

19 Academy Awards televised for the first time.

26 Salk polio vaccine is used successfully.

April 1953

1 Department of Health, Education, and Welfare (HEW), established.

3 *TV Guide* begins publication with ten editions.

11 Harbor bank deposits exceed $38 million.

11 Reds ask for full-scale Korean Armistice talks.

18 3-D movies in fashion.

21 Sixty-four Yanks freed in Korean POW exchange.

23 *C-46* vanishes over Cascades.

23 U.S. Weather bureau's rain-maker, sure Harbor won't suffer from experiments.

25 Vapor trail marks Harbor sky.

25 H-bomb can wipe out race, AEC Chief warns.

May 1953

1 Moon Island Airport renamed Bowerman Field.

2 25 foot spray of oil reported at Hogan Well in Ocean City.

18 First U.S. Triple Ace, Capt. Joe McConnell gets 16th Mig.

22 New phone cable laid under the Chehalis River at Aberdeen.

22 The Submerged Land Act allows state jurisdiction over submerged coastal lands.

25 World's first atomic artillery fired successfully at Nevada test site.

31 Quinault Derby draws record entries and crowd.

June 1953

1 Fire fighters mop up the first forest fire of the year near Moclips.

1 35,000 holiday visitors jam resorts on beaches and Lake Quinault over week-end.

2 Elizabeth crowned Queen of Britain.

4 ACE sets off biggest atomic blast.

5 Peace fever runs high in U.S., Korea.

11 Bowerman airfield linked in radio beacon network.

12 Planetary air wave, not A-bomb test, causing this Spring's wet U.S. weather.

17 3-D movie, *House of Wax,* opens at the Aberdeen Theater.

18 129 GI's die in *C-124* crash near Tokyo; history's worst air horror.

20 Rosenbergs go to chair for betrayal of U.S. atomic secrets.

21 Soviet tanks crush East Berlin uprising.

30 Harbor company packing whale meat for pet food; first whale products on the Harbor in almost 30 years.

July 1953

10 Big firemen's program in Aberdeen.

11 150 visiting firemen's wives stuck near Graves Creek in pleasant weather.

24 Enchanted Valley Chalet open as a public shelter.

27 Korean Truce signed; fighting ends. 28th in Korea.

** Blueback harvest proves a poor 15,600.

August 1953

11 Biologist warn clam diggers.

11 Soaring heat may ban logging.

14 Soviets say they have hydrogen bomb.

19 First concrete poured for Chehalis River Bridge.

September 1953

1 There are 25,233,000 TVs in the U.S.. There were 44,000 in 1947; 600,000 in 1948; 2,150,000 in 1949; 7,535,000 in 1950; and 13,000,000 in 1951.

4 Heat and wind, lighting starts 63 fires in state.

11 Second payment made to Taholah Unit allottees.

12 Dark day Holocaust hit area 51 years (1902) ago. Also one in 1847. (*Forest fires.*)

19 Forest Service to burn 1,100 acres.

21 New wing to Moclips school completed.

22 Moving Humptulips bridge.

24 Bridge construction across Joe Creek near Pacific Beach underway.

28 Gale lashes Harbor. Quinault rainfall tops 100" for the year.

October 1953

1 Quinaults ask more time to study legislation; Bill would terminate federal supervision over tribes in Western Washington.

6 3¢ letter and 2¢ postcard rates.

23 *Indian Legends of the Pacific Northwest* by E. Clark published.

November 1953

4 Harbor rain to be studied by scientists.

20 Chuck Yeager flies at twice the speed of sound.

22 *Colgate Comedy Hour* is the first TV show to broadcast in color.

27 Scientist indicts DDT as root of many ills.

December 1953

10 Heavy rain and 55 mph gale.

21 Heavy rain and 60 mph gale; lumber washes ashore from *Barbara Olson* which lost the deck load off the Columbia River; rudder had jammed during the storm on the 10th.

28 $160,780 gym construction begins at Moclips.

~ 1954 ~

January 1954

5 Gale whips Harbor for 4th day.

6 It started out as one to six inches of snow, depending on where you were in the County. Then nine more inches fell by the 18th, and another foot by the 21st. Rains and melting snow on the 22nd caused flooding. By the 25th, it was cold again, and 10-20 inches of new snow fell, creating the worst utilities snarl in the history of the County. It wasn't over yet. Still more snow fell on the 27th, 28th, and 29th. The total in Aberdeen was 27 inches, but there was as much as five feet in some parts of the County. All logging was shut down.

February 1954

13 Second storm in last two days has 60 mph winds and

heavy rain.

15 Eisenhower's reservation termination begins.

23 Cleve Jackson, Quinault Tribal Chairman, in Washington, D.C. to attend hearings on Indian Affairs.

March 1954

9 Edward R. Murrow denounces Senator Joseph McCarthy's communist witch hunt on *See It Now*. (*Chet Huntley, then in San Francisco, denounced the Senator ten days earlier.*)

12 Some type of explosive device washes ashore just south of Taholah.

23 Largest ship to enter Grays Harbor, now loading lumber.

April 1954

1 First photos and reports of H-Bomb test conducted in the fall of 1952 released. Stories about continuing testing through rest of the month (*Prompts bizarre hysteria in Northwest*).

16 Mass hysteria strikes Seattle when inexplicable "pitting" of car windshields appear overnight. Tiny holes are blamed on the H-Bomb test. The pits first appeared in Seattle and the "Pox" or "Plague" spread to Aberdeen and Portland. (*In recalling the event, some locals recount that when most people examined their car's windshields to see if they had been afflicted, no unexplained pits were present. Yet, each seemed to recall "hearing from someone" whose car was badly damaged. At this time, the "Cold War" was heating up and Chinese troops were fighting American troops in Korea.*)

26 Nationwide polio vaccine test begun.

28 Senator Joe "I have 100 names of communists in the State Department" McCarthy dominates newspapers and TV. (*He added to the confusion of the country thus the fuel of the "cold war" in his infamous "witch hunt". Television was available to over 26 million homes and McCarthy took full advantage of it.*)

May 1954

4 State changes road centerline from yellow to white.

7 82° F.

18 Bears damaging trees.

20 Forty-eight foot sperm whale washes ashore at North Cove.

26 A fire on the *USS Bennington* kills 103 men.

28 Forty foot whale washes into Westport.

30 Sixth Annual Quinault Derby Day.

31 Dying forty foot whale beaches at Kalaloch.

June 1954

16 Waterspout off Westport, violent electrical storm. Brilliant white lunar rainbow appears at 10 p.m. near Westport.

July 1954

19 $40,000 street paving project begins in Taholah. It is the forerunner to the $114,000 paving of the road between Taholah and Moclips.

19 Boeing's *Dash Eighty*, a prototype of a model *707*, debuts.

August 1954

3 Sixth week of the timber strike.

17 Apparent oxygen starvation kills tons of crabs and clams along Grays Harbor beaches.

31 4.41" of rain in Aberdeen. It is second wettest August on record (*5.16" in 1937*). Only five days without rain.

September 1954

1 Old North Church Steeple in Boston falls during recent flurry of hurricanes.

27 Senate Committee Hearings recommend the censure of Senator Joseph McCarthy.

** September the most "summery" month of the year.

October 1954

4 *USS Nautilus* becomes first atomic submarine to join U.S. Navy.

7 Heavy rain and gale.

27 *Disneyland* premieres on NBC.

November 1954

11 Statue of Iwo Jima flag raising dedicated.

18 Harbor storm causes severe damage. Washes out Dry Creek bridge on U.S. 101 and marks 17th day of consecutive rainfall.

December 1954

1 $46,500 Prairie Creek Bridge on U.S. 101 opens recently.

11 Aircraft carrier, The *USS Forrestal*, is launched. Considered the "mightiest" ship afloat.

25 An unusual white Christmas this year.

~ 1955 ~

January 1955

3 Soviets barred from travel in the U.S. in reaction to travel ban in USSR.

7 Taholah School construction to start soon.

17 *Nautilus*, the first nuclear sub, pulls away from the dock under nuclear propulsion.

17 Photo of the earth from 100 miles up over the U.S. Southwest appears in *The Aberdeen Daily World*.

19 Presidential news conference filmed for TV for the first time.

February 1955

18 24° F. Coldest of the year.

22 Eisenhower submitted $101 billion interstate highway program to Congress.

28 Howling storm with 70 mph gusts batters the Northwest.

March 1955

1 *USS Missouri* decommissioned at Bremerton.

4 22°F, coldest in five years.

7 Continuing series of articles and stories about the numerous A-bomb testing and the effects of fallout if used in a war.

21 Wind and rain.

28 New $450,000 school opens to students in Amanda Park.

April 1955

5 Churchill resigns as Prime Minister.

13 War on Polio begins.

May 1955

2 Civil war explodes anew in Viet Nam.

9 Rayonier Promised Land Recreation Area dedicated.

16 Polio shots underway in Aberdeen.

June 1955

9 Weyerhaeuser announces plans to build $20,000,000

pulp plant in Cosmopolis.

9   94° F.

20 Let atom serve in "Glorious Life" says Ike.

21 Forty acres purchased for proposed Grays Harbor College.

24 Neuberger raps poor prices for Quinault timber.

July 1955

8   Bert Thomas first to swim across Strait of Juan de Fuca; 11 hours, 10 minutes from Pt. Angeles to Victoria.

11 U.S. Air Force Academy dedicated.

15 Big lightning display.

17 Disneyland opens.

21 *Seawolf,* 2nd atomic submarine launched.

August 1955

5   Hiroshima's resigned to "A-bomb Disease." Many doctors say it's psychosomatic.

8   Physicist vision of limitless power harnessed from Hydrogen bomb in 20 years.

26 Photo of three giant spruce logs taken from the Quinault Indian Reservation's Taholah Logging Unit appear in *The Aberdeen Daily World.*

27 Construction starts on bridge across Humptulips River, road 9-C (*109*).

Chehalis River at Satsop.

September 1955

5   88° F. and acute fire danger.

18 Geneva Conference underway to ease Cold War.

21 36°F low.

24 President Eisenhower has a heart attack.

October 1955

1   Forest areas opened again after being closed most of summer.

8   Fall's first gale romps along coast.

13 Pan American announces it will buy 45 jet liners and begin first commercial jet service.

20 Quinault Lake School dedicated.

29 Heavy rain lasts six days.

November 1955

4   Gale and high tide continued to batter Harbor. Lake Quinault 20 feet above normal.

5   LaPush spit washed away overnight beaching boats.

12 17° F. 30-40 mph winds.

14 11° F.

17 33° F. First day above freezing; five inch snow fall.

20 Soviets announce it exploded most powerful H-bomb yet. Atomic rainfall in Japan.

28 Joint Senate House Committee meet in Aberdeen in Quinault Timber probe.

December 1955

17 USFS marks half century.

18 Harbor digs out of deep snow.

20 County may take over the Quinault Indian Reservation.

22 Stiff winds and rain slam Harbor.

** 146.94" at Lake Quinault in 1955.

~ 1956 ~

** Washington Library Services Act of 1956 helps develop reciprocal service between Aberdeen, Hoquiam, and the Grays Harbor County Library.

January 1956

7   Chehalis reaches flood stage.

9   Ike proposes soil bank (land retirement).

15 Winds and rain blast Harbor.

19 Aberdeen's G and H Streets to be one-way at midnight.

21 Six foot prehistoric "tusk" found near Wigwam Inn. (*North of Hoquiam, west side U.S. 101, where Mayr Logging is today [1997].*)

27 23° F.

27 Five million dollar Chehalis River Bridge in Aberdeen dedicated by Governor Arthur Langley.

30 22° F.

30 First failure of Chehalis Bridge; drawbridge stuck in up position.

February 1956

6   Near riot at University of Alabama when Black enrolls.

14 20° F. Two inch snowfall in Aberdeen.

22 Europe remains in worst freezing in 200 years, 800 perish.

22 U.S. to spend $1,770,000 on Pacific Beach Naval Station.

24 Wet snow.

28 54 mph gale hits Harbor. End one of coldest Februaries.

29 Sixty-three glass balls found by man at Copalis Beach.

March 1956

3   Thunderbolts, rain, snow, 65 mph gust belt Harbor.

6   25° F.

16 Moon and Venus romance has Harbor agape at sunset.

23 Harbor slashed by wind.

** March rain two times normal.

April 1956

2   Big airliner crash lands in Puget Sound.

2   First ever commercial shrimp load brought into harbor (test fishery).

6   Indian Agency may return to Hoquiam Office; has been in Everett since 1951.

14 Quinault General Council.

17 *F-104,* a 1,400 mph jet, unveiled by the USAF.

23 *Squire vs Capoeman;* U.S. Supreme Court says the federal government could not tax a Quinault allottee's

profits for the logging of their allotments.

** Driest April in 65 years.

May 1956

1 Strike closes Aloha operations.

2 *GMC Parade of Progress* at Aberdeen.

4 Press allowed to view H-bomb test at Bikini Atoll.

17 90° F.

21 First H-bomb air drop at Bikini Atoll.

30 Senate votes 37 billion dollars for roads and 40,000 miles of (*Interstate*) construction.

June 1956

3 700 fishermen at annual Lake Quinault Derby. Ralph Capoeman wins canoe feature.

8 *The Aberdeen Daily World* installs AP photofax unit; "Harbor readers now see today's photos today." One of first is of ambulance at White House as President Eisenhower is hospitalized with an intestinal attack.

12 Chief Joseph Dam dedicated.

26 Congress votes 33 billion for Nation's (*Interstate*) roads.

27 Harry Shale, Taholah Leader, dies at 84.

29 Eisenhower signs approval of legislation establishing the Interstate Highway System. (*Meanwhile, nurtured by the Marshall Plan, Europe was developing their rail transit system.*)

30 Worst commercial air disaster; 128 killed when two planes crash over Grand Canyon.

July 1956

4 Soggy Fourth-of-July.

19 98° F.

26 *Andrea Doria* sinks after collision in fog off Massachusetts.

31 *The Aberdeen Daily World* has an article about the Kalaloch Lodge.

** 112,600 fish caught in this year's Blueback harvest.

August 1956

1 $41,126,176 allocated for Washington in new roads program.

4 Pacific Beach saved from erratic Joe Creek waters.

24 Helicopter flies across U.S. (*the first to do so*) in 37 hours.

22 Cinerama makes first appearance in Seattle.

September 1956

4 Fire danger explosive in woods.

6 Liberian Freighter *Seagate* aground on the Sonora Reef one mile northwest of Point Grenville.

9 Elvis Presley appears for the first time on the Ed Sullivan Show.

10 *Seagate* breaks free of reef and drifts aground near beach ¼ mile south of Taholah.

10 Two million dollar Pacific Beach Navy job to begin soon.

11 Four tugs fail to free *Seagate.*

21 USFS burns 706 acres in Quinault District this week.

22 *Seagate* breaks in half.

24 First transatlantic telephone cable laid.

28 William E. Boeing dies.

October 1956

8 Claude Cooper, 17 of Moclips, drowns on return visit from *Seagate* when the boat he is in turns over.

15 Failor Lake Dam complete and lake begin to fill.

18 State refusal to take over Moclips-Taholah Road; delays improvements.

20 Storm drenches Harbor with 2" rainfall.

November 1956

3 Henry Cultee and others seek return of right to fish in Humptulips River as guaranteed by the treaty.

8 Two men balloon to 76,000 feet over South Dakota and drop rapidly in emergency decent.

29 *Seagate* sold for salvage.

30 Videotape first used on television.

30 An unusually dry and warm month.

December 1956

5 Arctic storm sweeps Northwest.

10 Gale winds, heavy rain sweeps area; 15.43" of rain in two days at Lake Quinault.

20 Work begins on 4-lane highway between Olympia and Aberdeen.

21 Segregation ends on Montgomery buses.

~ 1957~

January 1957

2 Mrs. Helen Abel Moore, who died in an automobile accident on December 28th, bequeaths in her will $70,000 "to be used by the governing officials of the city of Montesano as they determine proper for a memorial to my deceased father William H. Abel." (*In October, it was decided to give the money for a county library in Montesano. See September 9, 1960.*)

7 Heavy rains and snow pelt Harbor.

20 Eisenhower takes second term of office oath.

21 BIA to pave the Moclips-Taholah Road for $85,000; it then plans to turn the road over to the state.

28 Thirteenth day of cold snap.

February 1957

9 Argonne National Lab in Chicago, first Atomic-electrical plant, starts generating on experimental basis.

25 Fierce storm batters Harbor.

March 1957

13 Weyerhaeuser's pulp mill in Cosmopolis begins operation.

28 Mickey Mouse Club hottest show on television.

29 Pacific Beach Navy Base ground breaking ceremony for new "oceanographic research station."

30 Second atomic submarine, *Seawolf*, commissioned.

April 1957

20 *Mayflower II* set sail from England.

26 Paving of Taholah-Moclips road should be done this summer.

29 Arend-Roland Comet in Harbor skies, brightest since Halley in 1910.

29 First nuclear power reactor dedicated at Fort Belvoir, Virginia.

30 Biggest electrical storm in 50 years shatters Harbor sleep.

May 1957

16 *U.S.S. Skate*, third atomic sub, launched.

28 Indian canoe racing; *The Aberdeen Daily World.*

June 1957

12 *Mayflower II* lands at Provincetown, Mass.

18 #3 locomotive placed at Promised Land Roadside Park.

July 1957

4 First Annual Taholah Days; Carol Simmons, Princess.

10 First supersonic bomber, *B-58 Hustler*, unveiled.

17 Oil strike at Ocean City; oil fever brings leasing rush.

August 1957

1 Ocean City oil fever brings leasing rush to Grays Harbor.

3 Pacific Beach undergoing face lift with construction of Naval Facility.

5 *American Bandstand* debuts with Dick Clark.

21 Governor Albert Rosellini opens oil valve before 500 spectators at Ocean City.

27 BIA announces sale of timberlands on reservations; 65 tracts will be sold on the Quinault on September 24.

27 Military bullet from plane hits new Taholah School.

28 New phone building to be built in Pacific Beach.

September 1957

11 Grass Creek and Chenois Creek bridges completed on highway 9-C. (*109.*)

14 September heat wave continues; fire hazard high.

24 First transatlantic telephone cable goes into operation.

October 1957

1 Taholah-Queets "Missing Link" Highway endorsed by Washington State Good Roads Association.

3 Paving completed on Moclips-Taholah road. New Wreck Creek bridge to be built.

4 Russia launches *Sputnik*, first satellite. World listens to beep-beeps from space.

30 Dedication to transfer Moclips-Taholah road to State Highways.

November 1957

1 Russia blasts dog into space (*America suffers cold war punch*).

25 President Eisenhower has cerebral attack (*stroke*). Vice-President Richard Nixon takes up duties.

December 1957

1 First American satellite launch attempt fails; many see it on live TV.

19 Storms continue to hit area.

23 Raymond Harbor Veneer mill burns

26 Storms continue to lash Harbor.

31 Lester McKeever retires from Hoquiam Indian Service.

~ 1958 ~

January 1958

3 U.S. forms two missile squadrons with ICBM's.

10 Glass ball harvest big on beaches.

21 Blue Glacier on Mt. Olympus, is believed wettest part of U.S.

23 60-mile gale and rain.

29 Storm hit Harbor at 71 mph.

31 U.S. Army launches *Explorer I*, first U.S. satellite.

February 1958

7 1,116 Harbor aliens register.

11 Fiery Aurora glows in Grays Harbor sky.

16 Indians forming Quinault Reservation Policy Committee with BIA.

24 Sudden blow blacks out Harbor.

March 1958

5 Pacific Beach Elementary School dedicated.

17 U.S. Navy's *Vanguard* hurls "moon" into space; second successful U.S. satellite.

23 Lightning display over Harbor.

24 Elvis Presley inducted into Army.

26 The Army's Jupiter rocket flings third successful satellite, *Explorer III* into space.

27 Nikita Khrushchev, Communist Party Head, becomes Soviet Premier.

27 U.S. orders rocket attempts at moon.

April 1958

2 Wrecker from Vashon plans to salvage wrecked freighter *Seagate*.

4 Heavy surf lashes Harbor beaches; highest ever seen.

5 World's largest non-nuclear blast; 1,375 tons of high explosives used to destroy Ripple Rock, a peril to shipping in the inside passage between Vancouver Island and the mainland.

5 Fidel Castro begins "total war" against Batista's government in Cuba.

7 Smoking-cancer link confirmed.

16 Moclips family collects 223 glass floats in one day.

24 Grays Harbor College dedicated.

25 QIR Policy Committee, formed in February, votes for State law and order jurisdiction on Reservation.

25 Taholah's new school dedicated. Gladys Philips, Aberdeen Attorney, is principle speaker.

May 1958

1 Satellites record radiation in space; space travel may not be possible.

5 Record number of tourists hit Harbor beaches.

15 Russia launches 1½ ton satellite.

16 Dry weather closes logging on Harbor.

19 Spectacular lightning storm over Harbor.

23 Greedy clam diggers pass 24 limit.

June 1958

15 Dolly Papp chosen Indian Princess; to reign at Taholah Days.

17 Loggers go on hoot owl.

28 Mackinaw Bridge dedicated.

July 1958

3 *The Aberdeen Daily World* features history of trolley era on Harbor.

5 Dolly Papp is Taholah Days Princess and Stanley Capoeman wins Chow Chow canoe race.

7 President Eisenhower signs bill to make Alaska a state.

10 Navy homes O.K.'d for Pacific Beach.

12 Camp Olallie, at Lake Quinault, featured in *The Aberdeen Daily World.*

12 Hoquiam's fifty-acre sewage lagoon 75% complete.

15 5,000 Marines land in Lebanon.

16 Harborites crane necks to view *Sputnik.*

29 National Aeronautic Space Administration (NASA) created.

** Driest July since 1922.

August 1958

1 U.S. explodes A-bomb 100 miles up.

5 The nuclear sub *Nautilus* is first to make undersea crossing of the North Pole.

September 1958

10 55 mph wind and rain.

11 U.S. heads toward lowest polio year.

15 *Seagate* salvagers plagued by trouble.

** Hula Hoop fad.

** Jack Kiby of Texas Instruments makes first working integrated circuit.

29 Third Annual Washington State Indian conference opens in Olympia.

October 1958

3 78° F.

3 New Grays Harbor PUD building has open house.

4 British inaugurate Atlantic jet service.

6 Quake jolts and Monsoon-like rains break Harbors' Indian summer.

6 The nuclear sub, *Seawolf,* sets 60 day underwater record.

11 *Pioneer* reaches 79,193 miles above earth for new record.

15 *X-15* unveiled.

28 Harbor shrouded with thick fog.

November 1958

4 Hurricane-force storm slams Harbor.

22 Jesse Curtright new president of Taholah-Queets Highway Association.

25 Aloha Lumber strike in third week.

26 26° F.

29 U.S. fires *ICBM* 6,325 miles.

December 1958

2 Steady storm lashes Harbor.

10 National Airlines inaugurates jet passenger service.

18 Giant satellite launch by NASA opens new U.S. rocketeer era.

25 Heavy winds and rain mark Harbor yule.

~ 1959 ~

January 1959

1 Batista flees Cuba.

2 Winter's first snow hit Harbor.

2 Russia launches rocket toward moon.

3 11° F. Two year low.

3 Alaska becomes 49th State.

8 Fidel Castro enters Havana to tumultuous welcome.

9 Pacific Beach-Moclips will soon have cable TV now that master antenna is up.

12 *Boeing 707* makes maiden flight.

15 Mrs. Florence Strom, Taholah, says the people of Taholah have turned from the old ways to embrace Christianity.

19 Ike allows $117 million for BIA.

21 Taholah-Queets road "missing link" conference in Olympia.

23 High winds, heavy rains drench area.

25 American Airlines begins first coast to coast service with *Boeing 707.*

30 IWA pickets idle 840 loggers on the Harbor.

31 Ocean Beaches' division of the Hoquiam Chambers of Commerce oppose clam license.

February 1959

3 Buddy Holly dies in plane crash.

5 Bridge for Taholah requested by Russell Mark.

6 Titanic *ICBM* fired the first time.

7 Twenty-two mercury vapor lights on East Market Street in Aberdeen, turned on.

16 Castro becomes Cuban Premier.

17 U.S. orbits *Weather eye* satellite.

March 1959

3 *U.S. Pioneer IV* satellite launched for orbit of sun.

10 *X-15* taken on first flight by it's mother-ship. Called a "captured" flight.

18 Ike signs bill to make Hawaii a state.

31 Heaviest rain in two years.

April 1959

3 Radiation from "dirty" Russian A-test falling on U.S.

9 U.S. names seven pilots for spaceman project.

14 U.S. launches *Discovery II,* a recoverable satellite into polar orbit.

16 Four gunmen capture a Cuban airliner and land in Miami. (*One of first air hijacks.*)

18 At 11:01 p.m., Aberdeen and Hoquiam cut over to telephone dial system.

25 "Don't worry about Communists," Castro says. "It's impossible for them to infiltrate. They are not in my government... we are a democracy."

25 St. Lawrence Seaway opens.

30 Rain of last four days exceeds five inches.

May 1959

1 Pacific Beach women operates tiny library.

2 Cement bridge over Little Hoquiam now in use.

20 Dealers protest gas war.

20 U.S. Japanese-Americans regain citizenship lost in World War II.

22 Indian remains found at Oyehut when road grader cuts into bank.

23 Fire danger critical.

25 John Dulles dies.

28 Two monkeys survive U.S. space journey.

June 1959

9 *George Washington*, first nuclear submarine with ballistic missiles, launched.

16 TV Superman, George Reeves, takes own life.

26 Surf caster at Iron Springs takes 95 pound yellow fin tuna.

26 Louise Chenois named princess for Taholah Days.

26 President and Britain's Queen dedicate St. Lawrence Seaway.

July 1959

2 Fire protection on Quinault Reservation is contracted to State.

4 49 star Old Glory, raised for first time.

5 Norman Capoeman and Ted Simmons Jr. tie in thrilling Chow-Chow canoe race.

6 Dog rides Russian rocket into Space.

6 Pay 'n Save store grand opening in downtown Aberdeen.

30 94° F.

** 25,300 Blueback harvested this year.

August 1959

3 Aloha strike ends and men back to work.

18 Mighty earthquake rocks Yellowstone.

20 Quinaults may get 15.3 acres at Queets.

** Large razor clam die-off on beaches.

21 Hawaii becomes fiftieth State.

September 1959

9 U.S. fires and recovers space capsule.

14 Russian rocket hits the moon.

15 Khrushchev arrives for U.S. visit.

17 *X-15* flies under its own power.

22 First telephone cable linking U.S. Europe inaugurated.

25 Khrushchev and Ike in Camp David talks.

28 First U.S. satellite takes TV picture of U.S. from space.

October 1959

14 North Shore residents at Lake Quinault, fight Government buy out (*for Park*).

14 Harbor loss of 3,600 acres of oyster beds in past 5 years due to South Jetty.

15 Errol Flynn, 50, dies.

20 Scandal rocks TV quiz shows.

24 CBS debates use of "canned" applause on shows.

24 Big Freighter, *Lipari*, grounded at Grayland.

27 Soviets publish photo of far side of moon.

November 1959

9 Northwest cranberries embargoed; weed killer blamed in FDA warning.

10 State orders cranberries withdrawn from market.

13 24 lane Aberdeen Bowl opens.

19 State Supreme Court rules that Federal Courts alone have exclusive jurisdiction in major crimes on Indian reservations.

21 Torrential rains flood rivers.

23 Local cranberries OK'd for sale.

December 1959

1 International agreement makes Antarctic preserve for scientific research.

3 New Grays Harbor Community Hospital opens.

15 Near record deluge causes slides and flood on Harbor.

24 "Satellites imperil Nick on his visits to chimneys of the world."

29 U.S. to end nuclear test moratorium.

** 150.13" rain at Lake Quinault in 1959.

~ 1960 ~

January 1960

11 Highways hazardous with snow on Harbor.

21 U.S. monkey rehearses man's space trip.

23 U.S. Bathyscaphe *Trieste* dives seven miles under ocean.

29 Fish boat, *Barbara Lee,* and two lives lost on Grays Harbor Bar, while trying to aid U.S. Coast Guard vessel, during storm.

February 1960

2 Heavy Harbor gale.

6 Charlie Choker, a wooden statue erected at entrance to Grays Harbor College. (*See September 28.*)

11 Rep. Magnuson introduces bill in Congress to transfer Federal property on the Quinault Reservation to Washington State DNR to facilitate fire fighting work. The State DNR took over fire fighting responsibilities on the Reservation last year under agreement with the BIA.

12 Jack Parr quiets TV show in anger.

13 France explodes its first A-Bomb in Sahara.

29 Eighteen razor clam limit goes into effect at midnight.

March 1960

3 Belated snowstorm gives Harbor traffic bad time.

9 Ball of fire touches down in Strait of Juan de Fuca.

11 U.S. fires *Pioneer V* into Solar orbit.

18 Gas drops to 22.9¢ a gallon in gas war.

22 New *Aberdeen Daily World* press rolls for first time.

29 Wind belts Harbor.

April 1960

2 U.S. fires *Tiro I* "Weather Eye" satellite into orbit.

4 Oyehut land acquired for state park.

14 Savage spring storm batters coast.

16 Sand dune removed near Oyehut, so drivers have clear view of road ahead.

18 Chehalis Indians claims granted official status.

May 1960

1 Ocean breeze "saves Harbor" in mock nuclear attack.

3 Russians shoot down unarmed U.S. weather plane.

7 Taholah students fly to Seattle to see zoo.

9 U.S. admits shot down *U-2*, is spy plane.

10 U.S. sub., *Triton*, circumnavigates globe under water.

14 Sharp curve at Oyehut cleared.

17 Big 4 Summit breaks up over U-2 incident.

22 Chilean quake sends tidal wave alert on Harbor's coast.

23 Hawaii hit by tidal wave; series of two foot tidal waves at Tokeland.

24 Gigantic tidal waves batter Japan.

27 Indians fight TV portrayals.

June 1960

1 Ocean Shores sales near one million dollar mark.

7 Jack Turner, Indy 500 driver, presents Championship Highway Safety program at Pacific Beach Naval Base.

21 Officials of the Association of American Affairs visit Harbor.

July 1960

1 Photo story of Quinault fishing at Taholah in *The Aberdeen Daily World*.

4 Fifty star "Old glory" makes official debut.

5 95° F.

8 Gary Powers, *U-2* pilot, indicted by Soviets as spy.

13 Ocean Shores Estates transform peninsula.

19 Twin Harbors goes on Hoot owl.

31 Harbor rainfall totals .06" for July.

August 1960

5 Harbor TV installing microwave.

8 91° F. Logging closure idles 1,600 Harbor workers.

12 *X-15* rockets pilot to record 25 miles high.

12 *Echo I*, giant balloon, launched into orbit.

15 Heavy rainfall ends dry spell.

17 Gary Powers pleads guilty to espionage.

22 Hugh O'Brien, TV's Wyatt Earp, and other Hollywood stars on weekend Harbor visit.

24 Oral Polio Vaccine "suitable" for use.

September 1960

9 88° F.

9 The new library building in Montesano is dedicated to William H. Abel. An open house is held on the 10th. (*See January 2, 1957.*)

15 Rayonier railroad bridge over Quinault River modernized for diesels.

23 Ocean Shores reports sales at three million dollars.

24 Last *Howdy Doody Show.*

28 Charlie Choker installed at entrance to Grays Harbor College.

26 Kennedy and Nixon meet in first presidential TV debate.

October 1960

4 U.S. launches first active telecommunications satellite, *Courier I-B.*

7 MGM blows-up trestle and train on the Wynooche for the movie *Ring of Fire.*

12 Khrushchev bangs desk with shoe at U.N. session.

13 Work progresses well for the new span over the Quinault River at Amanda Park.

14 Castro confiscates Cuban industry.

17 72° F.

November 1960

8 Nation cast record breaking vote. Kennedy victorious by narrow margin.

16 Clark Gable dies.

17 High wind, heavy rain lash Harbor.

21 Freak November snow cuts area phone and power lines.

22 North Beach bus begins operations.

23 *Tiros* weather satellite in nearly perfect orbit.

24 Heavy showers drench Harbor.

December 1960

3 New log-loading rig invented by Harborites.

6 U.S. releases photos of 1945 A-bombs.

16 Two airlines collide over New York in snowstorm.

16 Bridge over the Quinault River at Amanda Park is 50% complete.

19 Heavy rain, wind, and tides hit Harbor.

27 France triggers Sahara atom blast.

~ 1961 ~

January 1961

2 Deep-laden freighter, *Texmar*, buckles on Grays Harbor mud flat.

6 Americans begin exodus from Cuba.

9 $9,582,000 for Grays Harbor roads.

16 Torrential rains bring floods to Harbor.

31 A chimpanzee named Ham, launched into space and returned safely by U.S.

February 1961

1 First U.S. solid fuel rocket, *Minuteman,* launched.

20 Rain-soaked Harborites find February too long.

21 Tropical sea-turtle found near Westport.

** Record February rainfall.

March 1961

1 President Kennedy announces formation of the U.S. Peace Corps.

4 17" tall urn found on beach near Ocean City.

4 Queets-Taholah Road backers, travel route.

6 Aberdeen's Doughboy statue moved and rededicated.

8 Rare lancet fish caught at South Jetty.

27 Quinaults close Lake Quinault to whites. Ban hunting, too.

30 *X-15* reaches 31.25 miles and 2,650 mph for new record.

31 Quinaults ban Indians from Lake Quinault fishing, too. Part of conservation move.

April 1961

11 Quinaults say they closed Lake Quinault to fishing to conserve fish.

11 Adolf Eichmann goes on trial for World War II war crimes.

12 Yuri Gagarin, a Soviet Major, is first man in space.

13 Forty-foot whale washes up at Copalis.

** There are more than 60 million TVs in American homes, 600,000 of which are color.

28 *Bay of Pigs* fiasco.

May 1961

1 Castro makes Cuba Socialist.

5 Alan Shepard's suborbital flight, makes him first U.S. man in space.

9 New Bridge spans Quinault River on U.S. 101.

11 Sen. Henry Jackson helps to return 85 acres to Quinault Tribe at Cape Elizabeth. The U.S. acquired it in 1915 for $581.12 to use for light housing, but never did use it.

12 Quinault Indians rule out bridge at Taholah.

13 Gary Cooper dies.

13 The movie *Ring of Fire*, filmed in part on the Harbor, has its premier in Olympia.

24 State and Quinault Tribe agree to tentative agreement for highway across the Reservation.

25 TV Microwave service begins for part of the Harbor.

25 Kennedy ask for money to send man to the Moon.

June 1961

4 Soviet-American Summit.

8 A 1906 Baldwin Pacific Steam locomotive (#45) is new Hoquiam park center piece.

13 Fire races through wreckage of the *Texmar* near Grays Harbor City.

13 Quinaults block Rayonier on Quinault Reservation.

27 Kuwait to fight Iraqi grab.

30 Highway 101 bridge across the Quinault River is now open.

July 1961

11 96° F. scorcher hits Harbor.

12 Metlakatla impresses Quinault Tribal heads.

21 Gus Grisson becomes second American in space. Upon splash down the capsule sinks and he nearly drowns.

27 Indian problems prove complex.

August 1961

8 Most logging on Hoot-owl.

8 Humble drills new oil well near Aloha.

12 96° F.

23 Huge fire erupts in Queets area of the Olympic National Park.

29 First Peace Corps contingent leaves (for Ghana).

31 Berlin is cut in two by communist wall.

September 1961

1 Wynooche riverbed dry for three days.

6 Quinault Tribal Council license rules made broader business licenses.

19 Fishing slow on Quinault due to low water.

25 Indian canoe builder carries on at Taholah.

October 1961

5 Olympic oyster making comeback.

10 Quinaults sue over fish law.

13 Forty-nine geographic features in Olympic National Park get official designation.

14 84° F.

26 Taholah-Queets Road location under survey.

28 American and Soviet tanks face each other in Berlin.

30 Soviets explode a record-size 50-megaton H-bomb.

November 1961

2 Rep. Julia Butler Hansen praised tribal planning of Quinaults.

4 Quinault bridge at Taholah slated for.

10 Gust hit 80 mph. Storm, rain plaster Harbor with leaves.

13 Sport catch tops 100,000 salmon here.

27 Harbor Douglas-fir ready for trans-continental trip to White House.

December 1961

1 Indians truck fish for sale.

4 50 mph gale lashes bar.

7 Representatives meet from five "Timber-land" counties at the Washington State Library to discuss a library demonstration project.

8 Harbor's tree at National Capital.

13 Quinaults oppose new fish commission.

18 Storm howls

22 Quinaults buy truck to haul fish for sale.

~ 1962 ~

January 1962

13 The Mountain beaver is a forestry problem.

13 Steelhead threatened: non-treaty Indian face arrest.

19 26° F.

22 Quinaults invite state legislators.

February 1962

5 Quinault explain policy on shakes.

20 Glenn rockets three times around Earth. First American in orbit.

28 7" snowfall.

March 1962

2 Biggs asserts Indian fishery.

5 Quinaults propose fishing program; ask that tribes be allowed to enforce conservation.

9 Permanent jetty asked for Harbor.

23 50 mph wind gust.

25 The Space Needle in Seattle is completed.

29 Quinaults file Steelhead transportation case (*See September 30, 1964*).

April 1962

1 Rayonier steam locomotives give way to diesel.

2 Tribe ok's opening of Lake Quinault to fishing.

7 Restrictions put on Lake fishing by Quinaults.

21 *Century 21*; Seattle World's Fair opens.

28 Quinault's tell fisheries problems.

30 Lake Quinault Fete.

Bald Eagle.

May 1962

12 *The Aberdeen Daily World* feature's "Gray; 175 years ago."

31 Israel hangs Eichmann for death camp act in WW II.

June 1962

25 Supreme Court bans prayer in schools.

July 1962

9 Inky Charlie wins Chow Chow canoe race.

10 *Telstar* communications satellite launched.

11 *Telstar* transmits first live world wide TV show.

14 Quinaults sign Taholah-Queets Road permit.

19 *The Aberdeen Daily World* features photos of coast and proposed road on the Reservation.

25 Razor clams, crabs, and bottom fish wash up in mass at the mouth of Raft River.

** Cold, but dry overcast month.

** Blueback harvest dips to less than 19,000; worst since 1953.

August 1962

5 Marilyn Monroe found dead.

16 Eleven foot white shark caught at Tokland.

27 Queets' Douglas-fir listed as one of seven champs in Olympics. Others champs include, Pacific silver fir, Sitka spruce, Western redcedar, Western Hemlock, Alaska yellow cedar, and red alder.

September 1962

3 *The Aberdeen Daily World* prints *Seagate* photo.

5 Kennedy warns Cuba on Soviet arms.

21 Quinaults request hatchery aid on Cook Creek.

27 Wynooche Dam authorization.

28 A tornado sweeps across part of Seattle and Lake Washington.

October 1962

11 Seven mile section of the Elma-McCleary Freeway dedicated.

12 Massive storm rakes Pacific coast. Near-hurricane does

heavy damage on the Harbor.

17 Authorized $40 million Wynooche Dam would be in magnificent setting.

22 U.S. reveals missile sites in Cuba. Kennedy declares blockade of Cuba, Soviet warned on missiles.

24 Cuba-bound Soviet ships turned back.

29 Blockade stays till missiles go.

November 1962

2 Soviet dismantle bases in Cuba.

17 Grays Harbor City is growing community on wind swept hills.

25 Walloping storm sideswipes Harbor.

27 *Boeing 727 Trijet* flies for the first time.

December 1962

5 Heavy smog in London kills 55.

14 *Mariner 2* beams report from Venus.

~ 1963 ~

January 1963

7 Postal rates rise today: First class letter, 5¢; airmail letter 8¢; postcard, 4¢; and postcard air, 6¢.

7 First of a three part series appears in *The Aberdeen Daily World*; "Salmon rejuvenation planned by the Quinaults."

11 Barometer sets all time high on Harbor; 30.86". Mercury drops to 18° F. as massive Arctic front sweeps nation.

12 New Aberdeen Lumber Company stud mill destroyed in spectacular blaze.

14 $4.5 million sought for Harbor roads.

14 Slippery ice-glaze covers Harbor area.

19 Busy mountain, Capital Peak, relays TV to Harbor homes.

24 Garbage dumping problem attacked.

25 Quinault Hatchery study fund okayed.

29 Robert Frost succumbs.

29 Late-hour telephoning at low rates proposed.

31 The State Supreme Court rule Quinaults and other Indians are ruled under State law for certain matters.

February 1963

1 Harbor weather returns to normal after third driest January.

1 Clearing nearly done for Taholah bridge.

9 Quinaults warn non-Indians of crack down on illegal hunting and fishing on the Reservation.

9 Boeing conducts initial flight of *727* aircraft.

21 New Aberdeen Post Office opens.

26 *Mariner II* reports Venus' surface temperature at 800° F.

28 Quinault tackle stream clearance on the Moclips River.

March 1963

9 Soviet charge poison gas used in Viet Nam; U.S. Army says it is just weed killer.

12 The Norwegian freighter, *Bjorgheim*, carries largest Port of Grays Harbor timber load ever; five million feet. Sails for Japan.

13 Governor Roselini signs bill with misgivings which puts State in jurisdictional control of Indians on certain matters.

15 Quinaults take the lead in test of new State law.

18 Pacific Beach incorporation hearing inconclusive.

31 Quinault General Council meets.

April 1963

3 Quinaults Indians plan legal fight on jurisdiction.

6 Harbor swept by Sou'wester.

9 JFK makes Winston Churchill a U.S. Citizen.

11 All hands feared lost on the nuclear sub *Thresher.*

13 Dedication of the new Aberdeen Post Office.

13 Largest A-plant to bloom in state's sage brush wilderness. (*Hanford.*)

18 *Wynooche Dam* gets "Go."

29 Weekenders jam Harbor highways.

May 1963

1 Jim Whittaker is first American to reach the top of Everest.

2 January weather intruding on May on the Harbor.

7 U.S. rockets *Telstar II* into orbit.

15 Cooper launched into space for 22 orbits of the Earth.

18 Kennedy sends troops to reestablish order in racially troubled areas of Alabama.

18 Photo of Point Grenville on the front cover of *The Aberdeen Daily World.*

18 Bridge piers raising at Taholah.

20 96° F. All time high for Aberdeen in May.

27 Beach traffic jams Harbor highways; near 20,000 cars in Aberdeen bottle neck.

30 A 20 vessel Soviet whaling fleet is 300 miles off the Washington coast.

30 Pepper, a house cat, traveled for ten months from Seattle to former North River home.

30 Taholah Canoe Club readies for big race. *The Aberdeen Daily World* has feature on canoes and history of the club.

June 1963

1 False work for Quinault River span at Taholah nearly across.

5 Hemlock looper poses tough control problem.

11 President Kennedy forces Governor Wallace to allow enrollment of Negro students at the University of Alabama.

14 Saginaw Mill in South Aberdeen ready to switch to electricity; has been steam powered since April 1920.

14 Rayonier's rail engine *No. 90* removed from active service last year has been sold to Oregon Memorial Steam Train Association in Rockaway, Oregon.

17 Court bans required reading of *Bible* in public schools.

19 Soviets put first woman in space.

22 Fred's Hum-Dinger has grand opening in Hoquiam.

25 Food stamps planned for here September 1.

26 Kennedy at the Berlin Wall.

29 The new quarters of the Quinault Ranger District are ready to be occupied. It is located on the old Quinault fish hatchery grounds.

July 1963

1 Zip code use starts today.

2 Marilyn Mowitch Taholah Princess.

2 Work trestle spans river at Taholah.

7 Roger Hoiland is first to swim the Grays Harbor entrance from Ocean Shores to Westport in 2¹/₂ hours.

9 The new Ocean Crest dinning room opened recently in

conjunction with the motel.

19 *X-15* flies to 67 mile altitude.

20 Total eclipse over Canada. The particle eclipse on Harbor almost eclipsed by clouds.

23 52,500 silver salmon fingerlings from Quilcene Federal Hatchery planted in Moclips River.

26 JFK calls atomic test ban treaty "a victory for mankind."

31 Great Fire once swept from the Columbia to Lake Ozette 500 years ago.

31 *The Aberdeen Daily World* has special Aberdeen Diamond Jubilee Edition; Aberdeen history.

August 1963

5 Charlie Brown comic strip appears in *The Aberdeen Daily World* for the first time.

5 Aberdeen celebrates its 75th Jubilee.

8 85° F.

28 Martin Luther King Jr. gives his "I have a dream" speech in Washington D.C.

30 Raft River wilderness to lose isolation with construction of new road.

30 "Hot-line" between Washington D.C. and Moscow goes into operation.

September 1963

9 Spectacular lighting on Harbor in evening.

18 Story on the Taholah-Queets Road appears in *The Aberdeen Daily World*.

27 While in Tacoma, President Kennedy said "Recreation is a necessity, not a luxury in modern life."

October 1963

8 $5 million for Ocean Shores canals, air field, and golf course.

22 Storm with 73 mph winds.

24 80 mph storm hits Harbor.

November 1963

4 Large squid caught off Westport.

7 Elk thrive on logged off areas.

11 Tribal leaders express disappointment at State's view of tribal relations during the Eighth Annual State-Indian Conference.

14 Weyerhaeuser ships first logs to Korea.

22 President Kennedy assassinated.

24 Jack Ruby shoots Lee Harvey Oswald.

25 President Kennedy's funeral. (*Television distinguishes itself with the coverage of the events over the last four days.*)

December 1963

3 Senate passes and sends to House a bill that would remove 53 restrictions on timber logging in Indian reservations.

19 State Supreme Court ruled that State can restrict Indian fishing to protect resource.

20 New portable spars make appearance in Harbor woods.

21 New BIA Community Services office opens in Hoquiam.

~ 1964 ~

January 1964

11 First Federal Health Reports on the hazards of smoking.

19 75 mph winds.

20 State Department of Fisheries urge 15 clam limit next year.

25 *Echo-2*, a thirteen story tall balloon launched into orbit.

27 Julia Butler Hansen meets with Jim Jackson and John Shale during NCAI in Washington, D.C.

29 *Saturn* rocket lifts largest load (37,700 lbs.) into space.

February 1964

3 *Ranger 6's* camera failed to work when it crashed to moon.

14 Quinault, Queets, Makah, Quileute, and Hoh tribes meet in Forks to confer on fisheries rehabilitation and conservation.

26 Quinaults ask Governor to lift State legal jurisdiction from Reservation.

March 1964

2 Marlon Brando arrested as he fishes with Puyallups to dramatize the Indian fisheries claim.

5 More arrests as Nisqually fish off Reservation to bring attention to Indian treaty fishing rights.

11 Barge filled with 2.0 million gallons of gas and oil beached at Moclips.

17 Barge on Moclips beach freed. Nearly half of its cargo leaked or was pumped out damaging clam beds and beach life for ten miles up and down the coast.

18 Clam digging closed north of Copalis.

20 *Jeopardy* premiers on TV.

27 The Good Friday Alaska earthquake strikes. North Beach hit by first tidal wave at 11:30 p.m. destroying Joe Creek and Copalis Beach Bridge. (*Great damage from waves at Crescent City and elsewhere along Oregon coast where people, camping on beaches, were drowned.*)

April 1964

3 BIA calls for bids on four bridges located two and 16 miles northeast of Moclips.

11 General Douglas McArthur buried.

14 Rachel Carson, author of the 1962 book *Silent Spring*, dies. (*The book sparked a national debate on the effects of pesticides.*)

22 Opening day of New York World's Fair.

May 1964

18 Radio-equipped bears roam Harbor hills.

20 End of salmon predicted if there is "Indian War."

27 Nehru, Indian Prime Minister, dies.

28 *Apollo* program begins with orbiting of first unmanned *Apollo* Moonship.

29 War games on the upper Wynoooche.

30 Fiery crash halts Indy 500 for the first time.

June 1964

3 Series appears in *The Aberdeen Daily World* about rash of self-inflicted shootings in Taholah.

5 Tribe plants Moclips River with silvers from Quilcene Hatchery.

July 1964

1 Electricity for Queets may be made possible with $182,000 federal grant.

2 President Johnson signs Civil Rights measure.

25 Department of Interior recommends that the Quinault Tribe receive a settlement for land in the 1855 treaty.

31 Unmanned *Ranger-7* televised the first close-up photos of the moon before crashing into it.

31 NCAI urges a survey of fishing rights and supports the Quinaults in its effort to return jurisdiction to the Tribe, taken away by the state in 1958.

August 1964

19 Four day NIYC begins at Neah Bay.

20 Supreme Court Justice William O. Douglas with 159 conservationists, hikes 15 miles of beach at Toleak Point to protest proposal to build a highway along the coast in the Olympic National Park wilderness.

September 1964

15 Natural gas piped into Aberdeen and Hoquiam begins to flow to first customers.

23 A portion of Chow Chow Bridge gave way when a truck was on it; support cable broken by electrolysis.

24 U.S. Government seeks $200,000 for the Quinault Tribe in a suit (filed against Rayonier and Aloha Logging companies) in the Federal District Court at Tacoma,. The Government says they received "unauthorized allowances" for interest on certain advance payments and "excessive allowances for profit and risk of this interest."

27 Warren Commission Report issued.

30 Quinaults win court action which excluded them from 1961 State ruling that halted Steelhead sale and transportation.

October 1964

5 Point Grenville surf draws surfing enthusiasts.

7 Enrollment pressures spreads Grays Harbor College into six new structures.

12 Russia orbit a 3-man spacecraft; first time for more then one man.

15 Khrushchev ousted as Russian Premier. Alexei Kosygin and Leonid Brezhnev fill top spots.

15 Cole Porter dies.

16 China explodes its first atomic bomb.

20 Ex-president Herbert Hoover dies.

November 1964

3 Nation cast record vote; LBJ over Goldwater.

6 Record high salmon run on the Columbia River.

6 Following her recent visit to the Quinault Reservation, Congress woman Julia Butler Hanson says she envisions a richer future for the Quinaults.

12 West Coast pulp and paper strike halts work at Harbor Mills.

14 The new Malinowski Dam (*on the site of the old splash dam*) in the Wishkah headwaters nearly completed; to provide for Aberdeen water supply.

18 Evans Products buys Aloha Company.

23 A & M buys Blagen's Mill and timber; most of the timberland is on the Quinault Reservation in the Raft River area.

23 50 mph gale and rain pelt Harbor.

24 West Coast pulp, paper strike ends.

26 200th home built at Ocean Shores.

27 Snow and a rat plague PUD with power outages on the Harbor.

December 1964

5 Quillayutes sue to halt State ban on fishing.

5 Taholah students plant trees on the Reservation.

7 Federal Judge, George Boldt, said his court has no jurisdiction in a case involving State laws on the Quinault Indian Reservation.

14 *Quinault Indian Tribe vs Washington;* Judge Wright of Thurston County Superior Court (*the Court is in Olympia and many suits against the State are heard there*) rules that Quinaults have a right to catch, sell, and transport fish from the Reservation's waters.

16 Arctic wind keeps state in icy grip; 15° F.

19 Snow blankets Harbor.

21 Two tugs sink on Hoquiam River overnight. (*Floating dock sticks and pulls tugs down when tide came in.*)

28 Viet Cong control most of Viet Nam.

30 Harbor digs out of new snowfall; up to 16" on hills.

~ 1965 ~

January 1965

1 70 mph gale breaks winter's grip. *USS Catala* "sunk" at Ocean Shores.

4 12" snowfall at Lake Quinault .

18 Agreement reached with county to house law violators until a jail can be built on the Reservation.

20 Jim Jackson meets with Representative Julia Butler Hansen to discuss plans to improve living standards.

25 Winston Churchill dies.

27 Representative Julia Butler Hansen introduces a bill that requires consent of the Quinault Tribal Council before State law and order.

30 Heavy rain the last four days.

February 1965

11 USFS breeding super trees at Quinault.

11 Air strikes on North Vietnam. Situation heats up since the first conflict between U.S. and North Vietnam troops on August 5, 1964.

21 Malcolm X killed by assassins.

March 1965

12 74° F. and the 10th day of sunny warm weather.

18 Russian floats in space. (*First space walk.*)

20 Quinault granted $70,000 for law agency.

23 Grissom and Young on the first two-man *Gemini* flight.

24 First live TV broadcast into American living rooms from the unmanned spacecraft, *Ranger 9*, as it approaches, then crashes into the moon.

25 Civil rights marchers, led by Martin L. King, arrive in Selma, Alabama.

31 Giant fireball meteors light up the skies over the Northwest.

April 1965

1 *Early Bird (Intelsat I)* becomes first commercial communications satellite.

11 Palm Sunday Tornadoes level Midwest.

27 Rayonier to build new log camp at Crane Creek.

29 Strong earthquake rocks Western Washington at 8:24 a.m. Over 7.0 on the Richter scale.

May 1965

8 U.S. stages biggest North Viet Nam raid.

14 Red China explodes second A-bomb.

20 Old Aberdeen library building being demolished.

26 Swanson Grand Opening.

June 1965

3 First American walks in space.

23 Washington State attempts to take over jurisdiction of Quinault Reservation.

26 Moclips River Bridge completed.

29 U.S. troops in first Viet Nam offensive.

July 1965

3 Tidal wave alert causes thousands to flee beaches, but no tidal wave develops.

11 Spectacular dock-ship fire at Weyerhaeuser's South Aberdeen mill.

15 *Mariner 4* takes 21 photos of Mars from as close as 7,000 miles.

16 Clam digging ban on Tribal beach continues until fish biologists make inspection.

24 Photo in *The Aberdeen Daily World* of a 12-15 foot great white shark attacking a seal in Grays Harbor last week.

28 U.S. to increase Viet Nam force from 75,000 to 125,000.

29 Logging halted because of fire danger.

** 21,600 Blueback harvested this year.

August 1965

5 Tribe fights development of Moclips Resort development at Santiago.

11 Watts Riots, 11th-16th.

16 Soviets release photo of back side of moon.

September 1965

4 Albert Schweitzer dies.

17 *The Aberdeen Daily World* features Hoquiam's 75th anniversary.

25 A weeks worth of activities celebrating Hoquiam's Diamond Jubilee culminates with the 75th Anniversary parade and logging show. The logging show held at Emerson Field cost 50¢. (*The following year, this would be called the first Logger's Playday.*)

21 The new Aberdeen Library is under construction.

24 Rivers flow at low levels.

October 1965

7 U.S. boosts Viet force to 140,000.

9 Forty Indians battle State Game men in Nisqually.

14 Hearing set for Coastal Canal.

15 Student marchers protest Viet Nam War throughout country.

28 Keystone tops St. Louis Arch.

November 1965

6 Tree Farm stamp sought.

9 Massive blackout in Northeastern U.S.

19 65 mph winds rake Grays Harbor.

December 1965

4 Timberman's National Bank Grand Opening in Pacific Beach.

15 *Gemini 6* and *7* make first rendezvous in space.

27 100 mph wind gusts hit Harbor with driving rain.

~ 1966 ~

January 1966

2 Three drown at mouth of Raft River; 75 mph winds.

19 Four H-bombs fell from B-52 in Spain. (*One fell into the Mediterranean and recovered on April 7.*)

27 First of a 6-part series on pioneer family Higley appears in *Daily World.*

February 1966

24 "Tide of battle, turned in Viet Nam War": Vice-President Humphrey.

26 *Saturn 1B* launched; most powerful U.S. rocket.

26 Rayonier dedicates modern living complex at Crane Creek; "another demonstration of our permanent operation in this area."

28 Second weather camera put into orbit.

March 1966

16 First successful docking in space (Gemini VIII) cut short when maneuvering rocket failed.

24 UFO sightings in Michigan; spread to rest of U.S. including Harbor; proved to be Michigan swamp gas.

31 $170,000 approved for Cook Creek Hatchery.

April 1966

2 Mattie Howeattle celebrates 105th birthday in Taholah.

2 Spearheaded by Tribal Chairman James Jackson, Taholah and Queets Indians instigate self-help program; first of its kind in State.

12 B-52 bombers used for first time over North Vietnam.

May 1966

6 No action yet to reopen beach to surfers; was closed two weeks ago by Tribal Council to curb littering and disorderly behavior.

21 Four year old Freda Capoeman and her father, Stanley Capoeman, drowned on Quinault River while tending fishing nets.

June 1966

2 *Surveyor* soft-lands on moon; sends back television pictures.

13 Contract awarded for clearing and filling proposed Cook Creek Hatchery site.

24 Mysterious ship influx jams Harbor facilities.

July 1966

5 U.S. orbits 29 ton satellite.

10 Martin Luther King, Jr. at rally in Chicago.

13 Closing of hydrants in Chicago heat wave produce riots.

29 Traffic begins to move across new Astoria-Megler Bridge on Columbia River at 6 a.m.

August 1966

16 Anti-Viet Nam War probe opens in uproar.

23 First photo of earth sent back from moon orbit by *Lunar Orbiter I.*

29 Astoria-Megler Bridge dedicated by Governors of Washington and Oregon.

31 Representative Julia Hansen asks for one year moratorium on "Development of Quinault Beaches."

September 1966

7 Quinaults object to 18½ acre Point Grenville housing development.

10 First year the logging show is officially called "Loggers Playday". Established the first week-end after Labor Day. (*See September 25, 1965.*)

11 A white tornado sweeps north of SeaTac Airport, but does not touch ground.

14 *Gemini XI* 850 mile orbit is new altitude record for manned flight.
21 U.S. Court of Appeals on State Law and Quinault Reservation.

October 1966
14 U.S. extends exclusive U.S. fishing zone to 12 miles.
20 Rain deluge soaks Harbor.
26 LBJ makes secret visit to Viet Nam.
28 70 ton crane erected at the Port of Grays Harbor.
29 Small clam set phenomenal.

November 1966
11 *Gemini XII*; last to be launched in series.
14 Gale warnings remain.
17 Record size Sitka spruce found 21 miles south of Forks.
28 The Japanese ship *Kodo Maru* is first to dock at the Port of Grays Harbor's newest terminal.

December 1966
1 Rain soaks Harbor.
10 NASA released photo of earth from 23,000 miles away; shows nearly entire disk.
12 Storm whips Harbor.
15 Walt Disney dies in Los Angeles.
21 47th straight day of rain.
31 Boeing wins Government contracts to build *SST.*

~ 1967 ~

January 1967
3 Jack Ruby dies.
10 U.S.-Viet troops in biggest assault of war.
27 Three astronauts killed in *Apollo 1* launch pad fire during training exercise.
28 Dedication of new Port terminal.

February 1967
12 Popular singer Pat Boone kicks off '67 sales campaign in Ocean Shores.

March 1967
25 Quinault Coastal Wilderness Zone established.
29 Radio and TV strike.

April 1967
4 500th plane lost in Vietnam.
8 Hoquiam police spot UFO.
14 Official Seal of Washington State approved.
15 More than 100,000 rally against Vietnam War in each New York and San Francisco.
19 *Surveyor* soft lands on the moon and takes a soil sample.
24 Soviet cosmonaut perishes in spacecraft landing crash.
25 A Hoquiam resident's UFO turns out to be a loud owl.
27 Cook Creek Hatchery construction progresses well.

May 1967
2 Elvis Presley marries, Priscilla Beaulieo.
11 100 millionth telephone installed in U.S.
19 First air strike on Hanoi.
31 James Jackson, President Quinault Business Committee, asks all Taholah Unit Allottees to contact members of Business Committee immediately.

June 1967
5 Arab-Israeli War flames.
8 Israel claims Suez.

9 Nasser resigns.
28 Loans to build 20 rental homes in Taholah obtained.

July 1967
1 Inferno sweeps East Aberdeen. (*Near site of current main entrance into Wishkah Mall [1997].*)
3 Hoquiam airport jammed with planes bringing in fire-fighters for Sams River Wildfire.
7 Iroquois John Big Tree dies; one of three who posed for Indian head nickel in 1912.
13 Raft River Forest Fire starts. (*Would burn 5,200 acres by 19th.*)
14 500 men battle raging Quinault fire.
22 Carl Sandburg dies at 89.
24 Detroit riots.
** 37,600 Blueback caught this year.

August 1967
3 635 planes lost to date in Vietnam War.
14 Fire threat halts logging.
20 First Sunday sale of alcohol since 1930's.
22 Contract to build $16 million Wynooche Dam signed.

September 1967
16 Aberdeen City Hall dedicated.

October 1967
2 Thurgood Marshall, first "Negro" on Supreme Court.
5 100,000 Americans killed or wounded in Vietnam to date.
17 Draft protest in 30 cities.
18 Russian space package lands on Venus.
21 25,000 march on Pentagon.

November 1967
7 President Johnson signs bill establishing the Corporation for Public Broadcasting.
9 Wind and rain whip Harbor.
9 In preparation for *Apollo* Program, U.S. launches *Saturn 5*, largest rocket ever launched.
10 LBJ calls for U.S. unity in Vietnam.
20 Official U.S. population count reaches 200,000,000 at 11 a.m. EST.

December 1967
3 First heart transplant. (*Capetown, South Africa.*)
4 Years highest tides plague harbor in wake of storms.
9 *Queen Mary* arrives at Long Beach, California on last voyage.
13 Elma-Montesano freeway link opens.
22 LBJ "secretly" visits Thailand base.

~ 1968 ~

January 1968
7 First class postage goes from 6¢ to 7¢.
7 First U.S. heart transplant.
9 Harbor buffeted by 55 MPH storm.
9 *Surveyor 7* lands on moon; is 28th and last unmanned lunar spacecraft.
19 High wind and record rainfall on Harbor.
22 *Rowan and Martin's Laugh-In* premiers on NBC-TV.
24 North Korea seizes the *U.S. Pueblo.*
24 Evergreen State College gets its official name.
25 Four H-bombs missing in crash of *B-52* in Greenland.

29 Snow whitens Harbor.

30 Viet Cong begins Tet offensive; biggest of war.

31 826 sea otter pelts sold in Seattle for $140,982.

February 1968

** Newspapers question segregation status of school in Taholah.

13 10,500 men rushed to Vietnam for added insurance; 525,000 total there by mid-summer says Pentagon.

15 State suspends commercial clam dig except on detached spits of Willapa Bay.

16 Harbor flu epidemic on wane.

16 The nation's first 911 system inaugurated.

28 70° F.

Bonaparte's gulls at Point Grenville.

March 1968

1 Rising waters behind Aswan Dam covers old civilizations.

2 President unveils *C-5A Galaxy*, largest U.S. plane.

6 President Johnson delivers a precedent-establishing message to Congress enunciating a new completely different policy for treatment of Indian people and their trust properties. "...programs of self-help, self-development, and self-determination."

11 Half of Americans feel Vietnam war is mistake.

14 World gold panic.

15 Allies open biggest thrust of war.

31 LBJ's shocks U.S. with "I shall not seek and I will not accept..." another term as President.

April 1968

4 Martin Luther King, Jr. assassinated.

6 Violence wracks ghettos in wake of King's death.

13 Lunar eclipse seen in all its beauty over Harbor.

16 Lake begins to form behind John Day Dam, probably the last to be built on the Columbia River.

23 United Methodist Church formed by huge merger.

** Rayonier merges with International Telephone and Telegraph Corporation.

May 1968

2 "Poor Peoples March" begins in Washington, D.C.; to run through June.

13 U.S.-North Vietnam Peace Conference begins in Paris.

16 Grays Harbor beaches evacuated in Tidal Wave Alert.

21 Olympic North Beach Chamber of Commerce meets with State on Taholah-Queets Road.

23 Santiago Beach property nearly 75% sold.

28 U.S. nuclear submarine *Scorpion* missing and feared lost.

28 Pacific Beach has had six women postmasters in 58 years. Zany Zebra Zip-in at Pacific Beach nears completion.

29 National crisis plunges France towards bankruptcy.

30 Electricity comes to Queets Village.

June 1968

5 Senator Robert Kennedy killed by assassin in California.

14 Taholah housing project set; first 20 of 60 homes now being built.

17 Bees swarm on downtown Aberdeen traffic light.

22 Today, at six years, six months, and one day, Vietnam War becomes longest in U.S. history.

25 180 foot weather tower mounted atop Cobb Sea-mound nearly 300 miles west of Grays Harbor.

27 University of Washington says old Ozette Indian house found at landslide site.

28 History of the Low Divide Chalet in *The Aberdeen Daily World*.

July 1968

3 U.S. aircraft stage heaviest raid of Vietnam war.

3 Aberdeen library dedicates new bronze owl.

5 London Bridge being shipped to U.S.

9 Queets-Kalaloch electrical hookup nearly done.

9 Quinault Tribe enters tax suit of Aloha Corporation and Rayonier, Inc.

12 Cobb Seamount weather station shattered.

19 Big oil find in Alaska arctic.

24 Cleveland race violence spreads to other U.S. cities including Seattle.

August 1968

1 92° F.

16 Navy fires new multi-headed missile.

21 Soviet troops invade Czechoslovakia.

27 Violence breaks out at the Democratic convention in Chicago.

September 1968

15 Towering seas flip 50 foot pleasure craft off Grays Harbor bar. Three perish.

27 1,500 pound shark caught in Grays Harbor gillnet.

October 1968

2 The North Cascade and Redwood National Parks created.

11 *Saturn* rocket puts three men into orbit aboard *Apollo* 7.

12 Military takes control in Panama.

14 *Apollo* 7 sends first live TV from space.

20 Jacqueline Kennedy marries Aristotle Onassis.

26 Grays Harbor supermarket clerks go on strike.

November 1968

1 All bombing of North Vietnam stops.

5 Voters approve the Timberland Regional Library System.

5 Nixon wins close presidential race over Hubert Humphrey. George Wallace's third party played a substantial role in outcome.

8 Grays Harbor grocery strike ends.

11 Hoquiam High School dedicated.

30 Pacific Beach Post Office dedicated.

December 1968

3 Heavy gale pummels Harbor region.

20 First in a series of eight articles about frontier life on the Queets River in late 1800's by Mrs. Clara K. Dooley.

21 *Apollo 8* astronauts Borman, Lovell, and Anders become first humans to escape grip of earth's gravity.

23 *Pueblo* crew released.

23 Rain washes away four inches of snowfall.

24 *Apollo 8* orbits moon ten times. Transmits dramatic live TV picture of moon and earth and crew reads aloud from *Genesis.*

28 Snow and ice on Harbor.

29 Harbor gripped by cold; 13° F.

~ 1969 ~

January 1969

9 Grisdale's 1968 rainfall of 190" is highest in U.S.

10 *The Aberdeen Daily World* features Indian canoe races.

13 Taholah-Queets Highway tops highway list.

15 Lightning crackles on Harbor along with snow.

16 President scratches Boeing's *SST* funds from budget.

17 Heaviest snowfall in years.

20 Nixon becomes 37th President.

21 Bids called for Wynooche Dam.

25 NASA unveils Moon Landing Craft.

27 Snowstorm buries Harbor.

28 Santa Barbara oil well blowout.

31 31" of snow this month in Aberdeen.

February 1969

3 Yasir Arafat acknowledged leader of PLO.

7 Santa Barbara oil slick reaches 800 square miles before the well was capped.

9 *Boeing's 747* flies for the first time.

11 Ribbon is cut near Montesano at 11 a.m. to open the last segment of *Ocean Freeway.*

21 Jim Jackson is *The Aberdeen Daily World's* (first) Man of the Year.

24 *Mariner 6* begins trip to Mars.

March 1969

1 *The Aberdeen Daily World* becomes *The Daily World* with the first Sunday edition. Includes special 116 page historical section and first color comics.

2 *Concord* flies for first time.

17 Washington Coast Busline to take the Grays Harbor-Olympia run.

17 60 mph wind and rain storm buffets Harbor.

17 Golda Meir sworn in as Israel's Premier.

22 Seattleites dash Hoquiam's State Basketball Title 39-38. Grizzlies settle for second in State.

28 Death takes Eisenhower.

April 1969

3 Strike closes Weyerhaeuser.

3 33,641 U.S. deaths in Viet Nam pass Korea toll.

4 *Smothers Brothers TV Show* canceled as too controversial.

22 Fluoride to go into water supply say Hoquiam councilmen.

23 Nixon launches *War on Crime.*

23 Sirhan convicted of killing Robert Kennedy.

May 1969

7 Aloha Shake Mill destroyed by fire (during remodeling).

8 Quinault Nation adopts building code.

13 Nixon asks lottery system for draft.

16 Soviets land unmanned craft on Venus.

18 First live color pictures of earth as *Apollo 10* heads to moon.

22 The *Apollo 10* lunar landing craft flew to within 50,000 feet of the moon.

June 1969

20 Joe Namath at Pat Boone Golf Tournament at Ocean Shores.

22 Judy Garland found dead.

July 1969

19 Kennedy auto crash kills rider.

20 *Apollo 11* lands on the moon. Neil Armstrong and Edwin Aldrin first humans to walk on the moon as 700 million people on earth watch by TV. "One small step for [a] man, one giant leap for mankind."

31 Sea otters released at Pt. Grenville.

August 1969

12 4,000 lb white shark caught in gillnet off Westport.

17 Woodstock.

24 Wynooche Dam ground breaking.

24 Quinaults Indians close Reservation beaches to public.

** *Star Trek* goes off air, after 3 years.

September 1969

1 WSU dig underway near Ocean Shores at Oyehut.

4 Ho Chi Minh dies.

17 Hoquiam voters oust fluoridation.

19 Congresswoman Hansen praises Quinaults for closing beaches.

27 Jim Jackson wins the Indian Council Fire Achievement Award.

October 1969

2 U.S. reassumes jurisdiction over Quinault Reservation from the State.

10 Nuclear power plant proposed near Pacific Beach.

November 1969

10 *Sesame Street* debuts on PBS

11 Historians believe that the Wobblies were not the aggressors in the Veterans Day Incident at Centralia 50 years ago today.

19 *Apollo 12* becomes second U.S. manned moon landing.

December 1969

1   U.S. Government holds first draft lottery since 1942.

5   My Lai probe.

12 70 mph winds buffet Harbor.

12 A tornado plays hit and run in south King County.

23 A 235 foot barge loaded with three cranes and a grader breaks loose from its tug and goes aground near Taholah.

~ 1970 ~

January 1970

1   National Environmental Policy Act.

13 Weyerhaeuser ask state for probe of frequent Harbor ship groundings.

22 First Boeing *747* commercial flight; New York to London.

26 17th straight day of rain.

27 Fire destroys luxury Tyee Motel in Tumwater.

29 Gas 27.9¢ in wake of gas war.

February 1970

1   Cornerstone laid for Harbor Fish Protein Plant in Aberdeen.

9   Shell oil begins exploratory test drilling in Harbor.

15 Monsoon floods low areas.

28 Fire sweeps South Aberdeen's Saginaw Mill.

March 1970

** The Quinault Indian Nation establishes the Quinault Resources Development Project, QRDP, to rehabilitate the natural resources on the Reservation.

1   *The Daily World* Progress edition; "Moving forward into the seventies."

10 Army accuses five in My Lai case.

11 Series of articles begin in *The Daily World* on the Harbor's environment.

17 Grays Harbor County adopts sales tax.

20 FBI probes gambling in Aberdeen.

28 Tug *H.H. Hubble* sinks in Chehalis River when air tank explodes.

31 Olympic cedar facing threat of depletion.

April 1970

1   ITT Rayonier adds air pollution units.

2   PUD employees on strike.

3   260 idled in Evans Aloha strike because of the new requirement requiring a physical.

9   40 mph storm lashes coast.

10 *Age of Aquarius* spawns hair problems at Hoquiam High School.

10 Beatles break-up.

13 *Apollo-13* moon landing aborted on voyage to moon when fuel cell explodes.

15 Astronauts plight perilous.

17 Odyssey ends; Astronauts safe.

22 First Earth Day.

May 1970

1   Log Scalers' strike halts logging on Harbor.

1   8,000 U.S. troops push into Cambodia.

4   Kent State.

6   Campus unrest continues.

17 Quinault Reservation beaches to stay closed.

June 1970

2   95° F.

15 ITT Rayonier installing river pollution control.

17 Sasquatch prowls Harbor roads.

27 Wynooche Dam concrete work to start soon.

28 Quinaults debate clamming management plans.

July 1970

8   President proposes legislation to give Indians more power.

10 Denny's Restaurant planned for Aberdeen.

11 Thirty more sea otters from Alaska, released at La Push.

15 Logging shut down in wake of dry weather.

19 Quinaults ask State to enforce authority on JDs.

21 Aswan Dam completed.

27 Ozette 'long house' artifacts uncovered.

** Less than 6,000 Blueback caught this year; all time low.

August 1970

23 Fog envelops Harbor, keeping boats at sea.

September 1970

7   Lost Army surveillance plane debris found in Grays Harbor's North Bay.

15 County wide bus system eyed.

18 Jimi Hendrix dies of drug related causes.

21 The *Chunetsusan Marie*, one of largest ships to visit Weyerhaeuser Harbor docks, is loading chips for Japan.

October 1970

*   Taholah school now has seventh grade class.

2   Trees are Washington's number one crop; remain key to economy.

7   Gas war flares on Harbor; down to 29.9¢.

13 Harbor tabbed for fifth Northwest N-plant.

18 Olympic yellow cedar is largest of species.

21 Harbor reported as wettest spot in nation.

22 Train derails in Central Park.

24 Taholah's three ton totem pole nears completion.

November 1970

4   Voters legalize abortion.

4   Ocean Shores residences vote to incorporate.

7   Foresters discuss slash disposal problems.

10 Charles DeGaulle dead at 79.

12 Scenic Moclips motel being built.

22 Winter grips Harbor.

December 1970

2   Harbor roads treacherous with ice, snow.

6   Airport at Elma is officially open.

7   Winds, rain lash Harbor.

15 FDA recalls more then one million cans of tuna fish because of mercury contamination.

15 Quinaults have legal right to close beaches.

15 Wet 'n windy storm.

16 Near record down-pour drenches Harbor.

19 Seattleites buy Allman-Hubble Tug Company.

22 Quinaults win battle with State and leave a $3.5 million road to nowhere.

22 New Hoquiam bridge officially called "Riverside."

29 Dark rain storm soaks Harbor.

~ 1971 ~

January 1971

1 President signs Clean Air Bill.

1 Quinaults get $98,000 fisheries grant.

4 Explosion blasts North Beach Realty office.

4 Frigid weather grips Harbor.

11 Snowfall slows Twin Harbor activities.

15 100 mph gusts lash coast.

18 Russia to support Egypt.

26 Slides and floods hit area.

30 Forgotten generator at Lake Quinault hums to life again.

February 1971

1 Evens proclaims Grays Harbor County flood disaster area.

5 *Apollo 14* on moon.

9 Powerful shake hits L.A.

10 58 mph gale lashes Harbor.

12 Ocean City oil well capped.

12 J. C. Penney dies at 95.

26 Snow returns to Harbor.

March 1971

1 22° F.

6 Ho Chi Minh Trail cut.

12 50 mph wind and rain lash soaked Harbor.

14 Quinaults try fish ranching at Lake Quinault.

18 Bert Cole says log exporting saves Harbor economy.

24 Senate votes to halt financing of Boeing *SST*.

27 Wind storm kills two.

31 Westport oil spill.

31 Mylai Trial ends, longest war crimes trial in U.S. history.

April 1971

12 Troop levels drop below 300,000 in Vietnam.

12 Camping clubs mushroom in Harbor area.

17 Dedication of Aberdeen Fish Protein Concentrate Plant.

19 Ping-pong initiates China-U.S. contact.

27 Fire sweeps part of downtown Raymond.

28 Jury rules Estavillo innocent of bombings (*See January 4, 1971*).

29 Long Beach oil spill.

May 1971

1 *Amtrak*, the new government backed rail-system, goes into service. Final run for the *Wabash Cannon Ball*.

3 3,000 Vietnam protesters arrested in Washington, D.C.

16 First class mail rates go from 6¢ to 8¢. Airmail, 10¢ to 11¢.

16 52 mph winds, rain lash coast.

20 Weyerhaeuser strike spreads.

June 1971

22 The 60-year old Hoquiam Eighth Street Bridge is closed.

30 Dedication of Hoquiam's new Riverside Bridge.

30 Three cosmonauts die on return to Earth.

30 Supreme Court upholds *The New York Times* and *The Washington Post* printing of the *Pentagon Papers* (*secret Pentagon study of the Vietnam War*).

July 1971

2 Shoalwater Tribe blocks Tokeland road in right-of-way dispute.

6 Reforestation funds added to USFS.

7 Photo of 43 pound salmon caught on the Hoh River in *The Daily World*.

8 Makah barbecues salmon on Mall in Washington D.C.

17 Beatrice Black, 80, goes to Washington D.C. to the Festival of American Folklife and featured in the *Washington Evening Star*.

25 Sports fishermen simmer over Sockeye controversy.

29 Weyerhaeuser to halt logging because of dock strike.

30 Shoalwater Indians enter the cigarette business.

31 Clearcutting defended.

30 A warm July after a wet June. Coastal fog.

30 *Apollo 15* lands on the moon.

31 *Apollo 15* astronauts take first "car" ride on the moon.

August 1971

12 Tribal Arts and crafts opens. New industry aim of Taholah effort.

14 Two trees planted for every person in state.

19 Quinault rain dance brings drizzle to launch first Rain Fair in Aberdeen.

26 Slash burning is an effective forestry technique.

28 *The Daily World* features forestry practices in the Clearwater.

September 1971

7 Ken Grover wins fourth State checker crown.

11 Quinaults shut down all logging on the Reservation to protest logging practices and stumpage payments. (*Chow Chow.*)

11 Nikita Khrushchev dies in obscurity.

14 ITT Rayonier plans court action to lift logging ban.

17 Quinaults continue to halt logging, defying court order.

19 Fire danger high in Northwest forest.

25 Tribe allows ITT to resume work.

25 Clearcutting held best in Western Washington.

October 1971

1 Aloha crews back to logging on the Reservation.

1 Disney World opens in Florida.

2 BIA halts work.

2 *The Daily World* features "Whistles vital for communications in logging's early days."

5 Quinaults file law suit asking for new Taholah Logging Unit contract.

9 Quinaults enlist Sierra Club support.

10 The Washington Environmental Council supports Quinaults.

10 The London Bridge opens in Arizona.

13 Cranberry harvest in full swing.

19 50 mph gale rakes coast.

22 New dam creates Wynooche Lake.

28 Local firm dumps berries.

November 1971

6 BIA to probe Quinault dispute.

10 45 mph winds.

13 *Mariner 9* placed into orbit around Mars.

15 People's Republic of China enters the United Nations.

12 Harbor Indians to receive job funds.

24 D.B. Cooper parachuted from *727* with $200,000 in ransom.

28 *The Daily World*; "Pictures perpetuate history of the Harbor."

** Mitchell vs U.S. (*The Quinault Allottees Association, their president, Helen Mitchell, and the QIN initiated this law suite against the BIA for mismanagement of the regeneration of the Quinault Reservation's forest. In 1986 the U.S. Claims Court ruled the allottees and the tribe could sue, but only for the six years immediately prior to the filing of the lawsuit. Final judgement awards funds for regeneration and repairing fisheries damage.*)

December 1971

9 52 mph winds and rain follow snow.

11 *The Daily World* features Chehalis Tribal history.

16 13.45 feet of rainfall so far this year at Lake Quinault.

29 Snow blankets Harbor.

~ 1972 ~

January 1972

11 Snow covers the county and melts by the next day.

19 The Olympic Beach Chamber of Commerce and others seek fast completion of the road from Taholah to Queets now blocked in a dispute between the state and the Quinaults.

20 Storm lashes Harbor.

22 Harbor flood danger subsides.

22 Britain, Ireland, Denmark and Norway join the Common Market.

23 Razor clams reported at 20 year low.

25 Ten inch snow staggers Harbor area.

26 Gospel singer, Mahalia Jackson, dies.

28 14° F.

31 Taholah school board condemns the film *Lament of the Reservation.*

February 1972

1 Snow and cold continue.

7 Thaw forces load limits.

22 Nixon meets with Mao Tse-tung in Peking.

25 Quinaults charge timber firms with manipulating timber prices.

28 50 mph wind whips coast.

29 Quinaults warn logging operators.

29 Winds batter coast.

March 1972

2 *Pioneer 10* launched for Jupiter.

3 Harbor jobs at stake in wilderness issue.

6 Heavy rains over weekend.

10 Quinaults ask BIA to improve logging.

April 1972

2 Hanoi takes half of Quangtri province.

5 High winds lash coast.

8 Weyerhaeuser plants ten millionth tree.

10 *The Daily World*; photo of "Squaw Rock" near Point Grenville.

21 *Apollo 16* lands on the moon.

May 1972

2 J. Edgar Hoover, 48 year head of the FBI, dies.

4 Indian off-reservation fishing rights in court.

15 Governor George Wallace shot.

22 Nixon becomes first president to meet with Soviet leader (*Brezhnev*) in Moscow.

31 Demolition of St. Joseph Hospital 1919 brick building begins. Two new wings to be added to the newer hospital built in 1952.

June 1972

14 Near total ban ordered on DDT.

17 Five burglars caught in offices of the Democratic National Committee in the Watergate complex.

19 U.S. pilots halt overseas flights to protest need for better protection from hijacking.

30 Today has 86,401 seconds making it the longest day.

July 1972

3 Forest fire across the river from Taholah. Many wet their roofs to keep burning embers from setting fires.

13 Five inches of rain in last two days, Lake Quinault rose four feet.

17 The bridge over the Hoquiam River (*dedicated June 30, 1971*) wins an award of merit for design and functionalism.

17 90° F.

August 1972

1 EDA funds Quinault Tribal seafood plant.

12 *B-52's* stage biggest bombing raids on North Vietnam.

31 Millions of anchovies die in Copalis River when so many entered river that the oxygen ran out.

September 1972

3 96° F.

4 Mark Spitz wins seventh gold medal at the Munich Olympics.

5 Arabs massacre eleven Israeli Olympians.

30 Quinault Tribe and ITT Rayonier unveil two hatcheries.

October 1972

4 Big coastal cranberry crop harvest now in full swing.

8 *The Daily World* recalls Columbus Day Storm of ten years ago.

16 Beautiful fall weather continues.

16 Two forest blazes near Grisdale.

17 This year's leaves most beautiful in last twenty years.

17 Pool begins to fill behind Wynooche Dam.

November 1972

5 Indians continue to occupy BIA office in Washington D.C.

7 U.S. *B-52's* set one-day bombing record in Vietnam.

8 Nixon in stunning win.

8 Home Box Office, HBO, goes on the air.

14 Archway dedicated at Taholah health clinic.

16 Harbor has a 50/50 shot for N-plant.

December 1972

5 First snow of winter grips Harbor.

11 *Apollo 17* settles down safely on the moon. (*Last manned mission to the moon. In all, twelve men spent about 159 man hours exploring the surface of the moon.*)

12 Warming trend brings new snow.

12 Wynooche Dam declared operational.

18 Standard oil gas station closed when oil spills into the Quinault River at Amanda Park.

18 Harsh winds lash Harbor.

19 *Apollo 17* returns safely to earth.

22 Coastal storm lashes Harbor.

26 Storm buffets Harbor.

31 EPA's ban on DDT takes effect.

~ 1973 ~

January 1973

2 Rainy Quinault records 174.28" in 1972.

8 Wind adds to 19° F. chill.

18 Drinking age at 18 proposed in executive State bill.

19 Storm and tides damage North Jetty.

20 Nixon takes oath, predicts era of peace.

22 Ex-president Lyndon B. Johnson (L.B.J.) dies.

22 U.S. Supreme Court; *Roe vs Wade* decision.

24 Coastal storm brings wind and rain.

26 Ground breaking for Grays Harbor Community College's *Bishop Center.*

27 Agreements signed to end fighting, and for U.S. troop withdrawal from Vietnam.

February 1973

6 Ocean Shores bans sand dune driving.

12 142 U.S. POW's arrive at Clark.

15 U.S. and Cuba sign pact to curb hijacking.

16 Harbor solons (legislators) pledge to fight beach driving ban bill.

28 Militant Indians seize Wounded Knee and hostages.

March 1973

1 Indian keep control of Wounded Knee.

19 Longest held POW in U.S. history heads home.

27 900 workers idled by Rayonier pickets.

25 Marlon Brando refuses Oscar; to join Wounded Knee Indians.

29 U.S. Vietnam involvement finally ends; last troops leave Saigon.

April 1973

2 *The Daily World* now printed on new Goss Urbanite off-set press with today's issue; cost $340,000. New format used today.

5 Meat sales drop 70% across U.S. because of price.

9 Pablo Picasso dead at 91.

10 Satsop top site for nuclear plant.

14 Japan to voluntarily cut back on U.S. log imports.

17 "**Dramatic**" Watergate decision predicted.

18 Nixon orders new probe of Watergate bug affair.

19 Plans for Aberdeen south side shopping mall announced by Steinmans.

19 Quinaults to rebuild river salmon run.

30 Four Nixon aids quit over Watergate.

May 1973

2 Nixon begins White House shake-up in wake of Watergate.

8 Indians end occupation of Wounded Knee.

14 *Skylab* zooms into space.

14 90° F.

17 Senate panel begins Watergate hearings.

25 Astronauts chase crippled *Skylab.*

26 The 61 foot *Amigo*, built in the Little Hoquiam Shipyard, is largest fiberglass boat ever built on the Harbor.

June 1973

3 Soviet *SST* crashes at Paris air show.

4 Soviet vessels reported fishing off the Harbor area.

12 Harbor gas prices spiral; 45.9¢ per gallon.

12 Heavy rain soaks Harbor.

12 *The Daily World* unveils modern new $1 million plant.

16 Fifteen saved just as the 50' charter boat, *Susan,* sinks south of Harbor.

18 Nixon welcomes Brezhnev.

19 4½ million feet of timber have been loaded onto the 590' *Maria Rubicon*; one of the largest log ships to visit here.

30 The total eclipse in Africa, is the second longest one in history..

July 1973

5 Howie Hudson won *Chow Chow Race* in the *Halfbreed.*

11 Movie crew on the North Beach shooting footage for the John Wayne film *McQ.*

12 Aberdeen to allow light gambling.

19 Indian court jurisdiction challenged.

30 It is reported that nearly all of Nixon's official discussions in Oval office are on tape.

31 Beef crisis hits Harbor.

August 1973

26 Wynooche Dam dedicated.

27 Treaty Indian fishing rights open in court with Judge Boldt.

September 1973

2 J.R.R. Tolkein dies.

10 80° F. weekend.

October 1973

11 Agnew resigns as U.S. Vice President.

13 Gerald Ford to become new Vice President.

November 1973

10 State highway board reduces speed limits to 50 mph.

16 Nixon signs bill to build 789 mile long Alaska Pipeline.

26 President Nixon's secretary, Rose Mary Woods, says she accidently erased 18 minutes in one of the Watergate tapes.

December 1973

3 Lighting, rain, and 55 mph winds.

3 *Pioneer 10* takes first close-up picture of Jupiter.

6 Gerald Ford sworn in as 40th Vice-President.

12 59 mph winds and heavy rain and high tides.

~ 1974 ~

January 1974

2 55 mile speed limit law signed by President.

3 Gasoline passes 50¢/gallon.

6 Daylight Savings Time begins; first since World War II.

16 Strong winds and heavy rains for past three days.

February 1974

1 Elton Bennett, famous for his silk screen prints, killed in crash of *707* in Pago Pago.

13 Soviets oust Solzhenitsyn.

12 *United States vs Washington;* Tribal fishing rights affirmed in Judge Boldt's ruling.

18 Military revolt in Ethiopia.

March 1974

6 Bishop Center opens with Milton Katims directing the Seattle Symphony Orchestra.

9 Quinault outline stand on off-reservation fishing.

10 Logs from U.S. Public forest lands banned from export.

16 Quinault Tribal Government Office Building dedicated.

April 1974

10 Ken Grover appears in *The Daily World* with story about his checkers championship and program in Taholah for the youngsters.

30 Joe DeLaCruz and Tribe battle all month long with non-Indian landowners about zoning along coast. *(This is a battle that remains on simmer. In spite of several Federal court decrees, some fee owners refuse to recognize the Tribe as having any jurisdiction over Reservation lands.)*

May 1974

4 Nixon opens "Expo '74" World's Fair in Spokane.

5 First photo map of United States published; made from 595 images from *ERTS (later renamed LANDSAT).*

June 1974

** Quinault Dancers perform at Expo '74 in Spokane.

30 11.1 million seedlings planted on the Capital Forest between 1937 and today.

July 1974

9 Guy McMinds considered by *Time* magazine in their list of 200 men and women destined to provide the U.S. with a new generation of leadership.

23 Interior Department includes Quinault Tribe in FY75 for a $400,000 forestry program and $320,000 in other programs.

24 Supreme Court says President must surrender tapes.

August 1974

8 Nixon resigns as president.

9 Ford becomes 38th president.

9 Northwest Indian Fish Commission begins operations.

26 Charles Lindbergh dies.

September 1974

7 ESPN makes cable TV debut.

8 Evel Knieval makes failed attempt to leap Snake River Canyon.

9 Ford grants pardon to Nixon.

24 88° F.

30 The last two months have been clear, warm and dry.

October 1974

1 Clam season opens on public beaches.

8 County Planning Commission meets to discuss zoning on the Quinault Reservation.

13 Geodetic survey now on Harbor as part of their 320 mile route on the Olympic Peninsula to determine change of elevation since 1931-32 survey.

14 Watergate trial opens.

14 Ed Sullivan dead at 73.

18 Can this be fall? Bless you Mr. Weatherman.

** The Quinault Nation assumes the tree planting program from BIA.

November 1974

3 Spokane Worlds Fair closes.

8 Harbor gillnetters sue state.

15 Fiery meteor gouges crater near Chehalis.

20 First *747* crash. (*Nairobi, Kenya.*)

20 Weather back to normal with buckets of rain.

23 Mayr Steelhead pond dedication.

23 Ford-Brezhnev summit begins.

26 Taholah-Queets link approved.

December 1974

3 *Pioneer II* sweeps past Jupiter.

12 Grays Harbor unemployment 14.7%.

17 Image from NASA's *Earth Resources Technological Satellite* (ERTS) of southwest Washington appears on front page of *The Daily World.* (*The satellite would later be renamed LANDSAT.*)

17 Winds whip Harbor.

19 Indians attack state tax plan.

21 Howling storm hits Harbor.

21 Jack Benny dies at age 80.

27 First snow hits Harbor.

31 Private U.S. citizens allowed to buy and own gold for the first time in 40 years.

~ 1975 ~

January 1975

4 Public Law 93-638 enacted; Indian Self-determination and Educational Assistance Act. (*Would have a profound effect on the Quinault and other Indian reservations in the U.S.*)

8 Wicked storm hits the Harbor with 72 mph winds.

15 Two nuclear power plants at Satsop will cost one billion each.

28 Thick wet snow on the Harbor.

February 1975

20 50 mph gale followed by snow.

March 1975

21 *C-141* crashes in the Olympic Mountains.

25 King Faisal assassinated.

29 Quinault Constitution adopted.

30 Clarence Esses is *The Daily World* "Man of the Year."

April 1975

10 Two women murdered in Moclips.

29 Ford orders final evacuation from Vietnam.

30 VC take Saigon.

May 1975

26 Plane falls into ocean at Moclips.

June 1975

1 80° F.

12 Two flamingos feed in Grays Harbor basin for several weeks.

July 1975

8 Electric storm hits Harbor.

17 Americans and Russians dock in orbit.

28 70 acres wildfire in Queets Unit contained.

** 73,600 Blueback netted this season; best since 1956.

Sandpipers.

August 1975

1 Hoffa is missing.

22 Pulp tank collapses at Rayonier Mill causing nearly million dollar damage.

September 1975

7 Photo and article about Quinault Billy Charley, the world champion birler (*water log rolling*) of 1909.

11 84° F. hottest day of the year.

18 Quinault postpone opening of Chehalis fisheries because of lack of fish.

25 800 acre blaze in upper Wynooche out of control.

25 200 mile fish zone approved by Federal Government.

October 1975

6 Series of articles about cedar county thefts in *The Daily World*.

12 State completes paving many one-lane log roads in Hoh-Clearwater drainage.

November 1975

14 Queets Douglas-fir largest at 14'5" diameter, 221 feet tall with broken top.

17 50 mph wind and rain leave its calling card.

20 Work on North Jetty completed.

16 50 mph winds and rain leave their calling cards.

29 President Ford leaves for China.

29 National Park Service proposes trading North Shore of Lake Quinault for Quinault Reservation ocean shoreline.

December 1975

1 High tides, wind, and rain combine to cause flooding.

5 Flood threats mounting as rain continues.

12 A little tornado hits Ocean Shores Marina.

16 40 mph winds, but portions of coast hit by much stronger freak winds causing extensive damage.

25 Heavy rain.

~ 1976 ~

January 1976

12 The Quinault Resource Development Project (QRDP) becomes the Quinault Department of Natural Resources and Economic Development (QDNR-ED).

12 Sportsman irate over Boldt Decision.

15 Heavy rains lead to flood threat.

19 Twelve new HUD houses in Taholah.

20 Steelheaders protest Boldt Decision.

February 1976

18 60 mph winds hit Harbor.

24 Former President Nixon in China.

29 Old Yew wood Indian paddle found on beach.

March 1976

3 Oil spill of unknown origin kills thousands of coast birds.

12 Wildcat strike at Crane Creek Reload.

13 Flu rampage continues.

24 Winds gust to 58 mph.

25 Winds gust to 53 mph.

27 The Kingdome opens.

April 1976

6   Howard Hughes dies.

11 *The Daily World* runs series of articles on Joe DeLaCruz' crusade for Indian Rights.

14 President Ford signs 200-mile fish limit.

29 Robert Crick killed while felling trees across river from Taholah. (*He is last to die in harvest of Taholah Unit Timber Contract which ended in 1978. Nearly one thousand men died, and thousands more were injured while logging in the Grays Harbor woods since the 1880's.*)

May 1976

4   Tribe gets go ahead to plant fish in Humptulips River.

June 1976

5   New Teton Dam fails in Idaho, sending mountain of water downstream; 150 killed.

9   Taholah Golden Age Club holds Playday on beach; filmed by BBC-TV for its *Americans Series*.

July 1976

4   Special Bicentennial edition of *The Daily World*.

20 *Viking* lands on Mars and transmits first photo.

28 Nearly 750,000 die in an earthquake in Tangsha, China.

August 1976

11 Albertson's is first store to open at Wishkah Mall. (*Current building Price Plus occupies [1997].*)

14 Indian Museum opens in Tokeland on Shoalwater Reservation.

26 Governor Evans okays Satsop nuclear plant for $2.9 billion.

September 1976

5   Grant for Humptulips hatchery made.

9   Mao Tse-Tung dead at 82.

12 Pelicans appear on beach and at mouth of Quinault River for first time in anyone's memory. (*David Douglas reported them in his journal south of Point Grenville in July 1825.*)

21 Space shuttle *Enterprise* brought out for public view.

26 Two freak 15' waves hit Harbor beaches causing damage.

October 1976

3   Quinaults close Grays Harbor fisheries due to small Chinook and Coho returns.

3   Swine flu vaccine program begins.

13 Tribal zoning clash looms.

15 Slash burning featured in *The Daily World*.

20 Photo of 15' diameter Redcedar cut in Crane Creek Unit appears in *The Daily World*.

November 1976

2   Jimmy Carter elected President and Dixie Lee Ray wins stunning victory for the Governor's seat.

4   Ernst and Pay'n Save stores open at Wishkah Mall.

8   Original Smokey Bear dies at age 26.

*   Quinaults and Gillnetters battle all month on fisheries issues.

17 Visitor abuse grandeur of Olympic Park.

December 1976

3   Checkers big in Taholah.

7   First plug hemlock seedlings planted on the Quinault Indian Reservation.

17 WTCG-TV begins using satellite transmission. (*It later changes its call letters to WTBS.*)

~ 1977 ~

January 1977

20 Jimmy Carter becomes 39th President.

23 *Roots* debuts with 12 hours over eight consecutive nights. On January 30, eighty million people tune-in for the final two hours.

February 1977

23 Gray Whale washes up on beach at North Cove.

23 First National Indian Timber Symposium opens in Seattle.

March 1977

1   200 mile fish zone in effect.

6   *The Daily World* rejoins AP.

6   Heaviest rain in one year breaks drought.

8   Storm slaps Northwest.

20 Nearly 600 die in Canary Islands in worst air disaster.

15 Legal battle looms over Indian control of Reservation lands.

20 USCG improve navigation unit at Point Grenville.

30 Uranus found to have Saturn-like rings.

April 1977

5   Oil slick discovered off coast.

10 *The Daily World* runs feature on the Quinault Tribal Fisheries program.

11 Clearing begins at Satsop Nuke Site.

19 Joe DeLaCruz receives Thomas Jefferson Award for achievements in Leadership and Public Service.

25 Meetings begin at Taholah on new elementary school.

May 1977

21 Lights being turned off in Northwest to save electricity.

25 Quinaults plan to levy taxes on businesses.

June 1977

10 Fish war rages anew.

18 Strike closes three local mills.

20 Oil begins flowing through Alaska pipeline.

23 Senate debates neutron bomb.

30 Quinaults sue BIA to protect Bald Eagles.

July 1977

3   Special history section in *The Daily World*.

16 700 protest Satsop Nuke at Elma.

31 First tanker loads oil at Valdez.

August 1977

*   Treaty fish wars in news all month.

1   Quinault Tribe begins B&O Tax.

4   Department of Energy created by President Carter.

9   Wishkah Mall Grand Opening.

16 Elvis Presley dies at 42.

19 Groucho Marx dead at 86.

24 Mastodon recently unearthed near Sequim.

September 1977

5   *Voyager I* launched.

24 Polson Museum dedicated.

30 President Carter gets approval to produce neutron bomb.

30 Quinault Hatchery gets grant for back-up water supply system.

October 1977

3 Laetrile goes on sale.

25 Storm pummels Harbor.

November 1977

2 Howling winds hit Harbor.

13 Doonesbury strip begins run in *The Daily World*.

20 Sadat visits Israel between 19th and 21st.

27 Heavy rains bring flood threat.

29 Quinaults push for County lands on Reservation.

December 1977

12 Area again hit by flooding.

17 Timberland Library Service Center opens at Airdustrial Park in Olympia. It was built with an EDA grant.

25 Begin visits Sadat in Egypt.

25 Charlie Chaplin dies.

29 President Carter off on nine day, six nation visit.

~ 1978 ~

January 1978

1 Treaty Tribes cut catch of Steelhead.

13 Federal Regional Fisheries Task Force proposes "Fish War" peace plan.

14 Hubert H. Humphrey dies.

24 Soviet nuclear satellite crashes near Great Slave Lake in Canada.

February 1978

3 Baby clams washed out to sea during recent series of storms.

3 Bottom fish industry gets boost.

8 Floods hit Harbor again.

12 Bald Eagle listed as threatened in Washington State.

14 Panama Canal Treaty hot topic everywhere.

16 Ted Bundy recaptured in Florida.

27 Indian Rights issue goes to Supreme Court.

March 1978

17 Supertanker *Amoco Cadiz* breaks up off France.

18 Bald Eagle near Taholah pictured on front of *The Daily World*.

22 The Bank of Grays Harbor to open this year if State approves application.

26 Quinaults say logging a threat to wildlife.

April 1978

1 *Portrait of Our Land* published; a Quinault Tribal Forestry perspective.

6 Feds want to enforce Boldt's fishing decision.

10 Quinault Tribe gets million dollar loan from FHA for land purchases.

14 *The Daily World* features "Quinault Rejuvenating Reservation Forest Land."

18 U.S. to relinquish the canal to Panama by the year 2000.

May 1978

10 Northwest Fish War shifting to bargaining table.

11 Feds want Boldt extended to trout and sturgeon.

15 Asbestos: "A time bomb."

22 Evergreen State College dedicated.

26 Gambling begins at Atlantic City.

June 1978

7 All state beaches close to clam digging because of greed and heavy wastage.

22 Pluto has a moon.

25 Satsop nuclear plant protest at Elma.

25 Governor Ray urges new treaties be negotiated with Indians.

July 1978

9 *The Daily World* features Chehalis Indian Hazel Pete and her basket weaving.

11 J.D. Rockerfeller dies in car crash.

16 *King Tut* exhibit opens in Seattle.

18 A & M sawmill closes after 86 years in Aberdeen.

21 Paper strike hits Harbor.

21 Threats of fire suspends forest work on the Quinault Reservation.

** 21,000 Blueback caught his year.

August 1978

8 1.6 billion federal guarantee loan to help New York City fight off bankruptcy.

8 92° F.

September 1978

6 Satsop nuclear plant costs jump to 40 million.

17 Private non-Indian landowners on the Quinault Reservation argue rights of Indians on the Reservation.

17 Camp David Accords.

17 Pulp and paper strike closes Crane Creek Reload.

** Rip rap replaces the old sea wall facing the ocean at Taholah.

25 Sec. of Interior, Cecil Andrus says he'll help Quinaults during his visit to the Quinault Reservation.

29 Industry backs Colonel Bob Wilderness.

October 1978

13 Grand Opening of Capital Mall in Olympia.

17 Supreme Court to review Boldt Decision.

20 Wall Street ends its worst week in its history.

November 1978

3 Rain and wind storm.

9 Illustrator Norman Rockwell dies at 84.

18 915 religious sect members are killed or commit suicide at Jonestown in Guyana.

20 Snowfall.

December 1978

8 Golda Meir dies at 90.

16 Cleveland, Ohio becomes the first city to default since the depression.

30 19° F.

~ 1979 ~

January 1979

1 Aloha Mill burns down.

1 U.S. and China formally resume relations.

3 Ocean Shores marina frozen.

10 Above ground construction underway at Satsop nuclear site.

10 All time high log exports at Grays Harbor Port docks.

11 No doubt that smoking causes lung cancer.

15 Westport fire destroys crab plant.

16 Shah leaves Iran.

February 1979

1 Millions greet Ayatollah Khomeini on his arrival in Iran.
5 Deng Hsiaoping, Chinese Deputy Premier, leaves from Seattle after nine day U.S. visit.
8 Judge Boldt bows out of fishing case.
13 Storm slams coast with 70 mpg wind. No power on beach for nearly four days. Hood Canal Bridge sinks.
14 Iranians storm U.S. Embassy.
26 Total solar eclipse sweeps across Northwest. Overcast skies on Harbor.
28 Supreme Court hears Boldt Case.

March 1979

1 Mystery slick near Ocean City kills seabirds.
5 *Voyager I* approaches close to Jupiter.
5 Storm slams Harbor.
8 Quinaults seek *$50* million for land loan.
8 President Carter in Cairo.
13 Active volcanoes discovered on Jovian moon.
14 *The Daily World* features Quinault Cook Creek Hatchery.
20 *The Daily World* features Julia Butler Hansen.
22 Natural herbicide ban "hampers" Harbor forest.
26 Egypt and Israel sign peace treaty.
28 Three Mile Island; worst nuclear accident in U.S. history.
31 Long Grays Harbor paper strike ends.

April 1979

6 *USS Ohio* the first Trident-class submarine christened.
22 Historic Indian cemetery discovered near Ocean City.
26 Gasoline cost spurs rising U.S. inflation.

May 1979

3 Margaret Thatcher becomes British Prime Minister.
14 Gas lines form on Harbor, but no crisis yet.
25 99.9¢ gas is here.

June 1979

1 Sonics win their first NBA Championship.
6 Makah Indians open new museum.
11 John Wayne dies.
13 Quinaults close Lake Quinault to conserve low sockeye salmon run.
18 Brezhnev, Carter sign SALT II pact.

July 1979

2 High Court backs Boldt fish case.
5 More rain than gas on Independence Day.
11 *Skylab* debris falls on Australia.
13 Gas pump prices given in ¹/₂ gal amounts as pumps can't read over 99.9¢.
17 97° F. is hottest in years.
17 Scrap yard is last port for *Catala*.
22 *The Daily World* runs feature on Colonel Bob.

August 1979

1 Trollers protest at State Capital.
3 WPPSS probe confirms a buried vibrator at Satsop.
4 *The Daily World*'s first Saturday *morning* issue.
5 Quickly built roads plaguing Ocean Shores.
8 Northwest volcanoes seethe beneath quiet surfaces.
13 Fire danger closes peninsula to logging.
19 Grandma Black featured in *The Daily World*.
20 Rains return with a bang.

September 1979

1 *Pioneer II* makes close pass of Saturn.
6 Beautiful red lunar eclipse seen on Harbor.
10 Most spectacular electric storm for these parts.
18 *Hoegh Minerva* is largest ship in history to visit Harbor. 660 feet long, 101 feet wide and carries 44,000 tons. Average ship 510 feet long and carries 16,000 - 22,000 tons. This is first port of call on its Maiden Voyage.
28 Gold hits historic $400/oz level.

October 1979

1 Pope begins U.S. tour.
2 Developers now committed to South Shore Mall.
2 First "modern" prescribed burn on the Quinault Reservation.
7 Technology and change are the silent revolutions.
17 Mother Teresa wins Nobel.
22 Shah of Iran, brought to New York hospital.
30 Mel Ingram, 76, the Harbors greatest athlete, dies.

November 1979

1 Log ship *Asian Assurance* first to dock at Port of Grays Harbor's new Terminal 2 complex.
4 Students seize U.S. Embassy in Iran; hold hostages.
15 Tentacles of timber industry slump reach Harbor.

December 1979

14 Storm hits Forks hard. Bogachiel Bridge approach washes out.
18 Flood danger high on Harbor.
19 *M.S. Sierra*, breaks moorings, drifts away, and sinks against Union Pacific railway bridge, clogging Harbor ship traffic. Freed on the 21st and moved to a watery grave.
26 Soviets fly 5,000 troops into Afghanistan.
31 The Coast Guard ends its Point Grenville LORAN operations at midnight. (*LORAN is an acronym for Long range navigation. See July 24, 1945.*)

~ 1980 ~

January 1980

2 Indian Tribes study relations with Washington State.
8 Snow blankets Harbor.
20 Justice William Douglas dies.
28 Cold snap has Harbor shivering.
28 Poll shows majority favor abandoning Satsop nuclear plant.

February 1980

26 Soggy weather reigns over Harbor as rivers rise.

March 1980

13 Deal closed for SouthShore Mall property.
20 Earthquakes under Mt. St. Helens.
28 Crater appears at top of St. Helens.
31 St. Helens activity remains brisk.

April 1980

7 Volcano 'perking' away.
10 Sears to build at SouthShore Mall.
15 Supreme Court: Quinaults lose $100 million suit under General Allotment Act of 1887. (*A different course of action would lead to settlement in 1989.*)
17 Policeman, Don Burke, killed in shootout.

28 Hostage rescue attempt in Iran is Fiasco.

29 Alfred Hitchcock dies.

May 1980

7 Log ship, *Lupinus*, is first at Roderick Dock.

8 World Health Organization announces worldwide eradication of smallpox.

18 Major eruption and landslide on Mt. St. Helens.

20 Apocalypse under the cone.

22 Volcano awes President Carter.

25 Volcano's wrath reaches Grays Harbor; Ash Sunday.

28 Spar gutted by fire.

June 1980

1 Grays "Harbor seals" featured in *The Daily World*.

3 A. C. Nielsen, inventor of Nielsen ratings, is dead.

3 Harbor shows true grit as it battles the ash from Mt St. Helens.

3 New Quinault forestry plan (*Taholah Unit Agreement*) proves controversial.

12 Volcano spews ash, then cools.

18 First set of graves moved from mouth of the Quinault River to a new cemetery.

July 1980

1 Twenty-seven tribal workers fired or laid off; shocks Taholah.

18 India becomes sixth nation to put satellite into orbit.

19 Soviets Olympics; boycotted by many nations.

21 82° F.

25 100 men mop up fire near Taholah.

27 Deposed Shah of Iran dies in Egyptian exile.

31 "Wonder Drug," DMSO, sold by smoke shops.

August 1980

7 Fight brews to save Cape Elizabeth Old Growth Preserve.

8 Wild and crazy storm hits Harbor.

17 *The Daily World*, features "Baby Volcanoes at Taholah."

September 1980

1 Candy and pop banned in school vending machines.

9 Thresher shark caught at the mouth of Grays Harbor.

10 Rayonier to build deep water dock in Hoquiam.

11 Water problems in Taholah.

22 Toxic Shock linked to tampons.

30 Iran-Iraq War erupts.

30 Judge rules Indians entitled to hatchery bred fish.

October 1980

2 Paving begins for new SouthShore Mall.

6 Summery temperatures set record across the State.

18 St. Helens keeps puffing. New lava dome forms.

26 DeLaCruz gets vote of confidence.

26 *The Daily World* runs a feature on Weldon Rau and the search for gas and oil here.

November 1980

1 First Satsop tower shell, topped off.

2 Aberdeen's Ice Palace being torn down.

4 Heavy rains.

5 It's Reagan in an avalanche over Carter.

7 Steve McQueen dies of cancer at 50.

11 *Voyager I* entering strange kingdom ruled by Saturn.

21 Storm rips into Harbor.

22 Las Vegas fire toll could reach 100.

30 *The Daily World* features, "Chehalis; The Tribe and the River."

December 1980

4 Freeze due in the wake of slushy snow.

8 John Lennon shot to death.

8 Volcano puffing again.

12 *The Daily World* features the Indian Shaker Church.

20 Weyerhaeuser's big Raymond saw mill closes.

27 Rain and wind keep coming.

~ 1981 ~

January 1981

5 Huge lava dome now forming in Mt. St. Helen crater.

16 State moves to halt Indian fishing on Quinault River.

22 Official refuses to halt Quinault Steelhead fishing.

31 Iran releases hostages as Reagan sworn in as new U. S. President.

February 1981

14 Earthquake, east of Centralia, rattles Harbor.

16 Rivers under close watch in wake of heavy rains.

19 Lighting-spiked storm K0's power.

March 1981

4 Quinaults close tribal beach to clam digging for at least one year.

12 Aberdeen to get old Armory.

15 Rip rap replaces old wooden sea wall facing the river at Taholah.

29 Gray whale watching gains popularity off Harbor.

30 President Reagan shot in assassination attempt.

30 DeWitt Wallace, founder of *Readers Digest*, dies at 91.

31 Quinaults attempt to rescue bankrupted business (QUINCO).

April 1981

7 Logs to stay under Ocean Shores roads.

11 Northwest Indian Youth Conference at Ocean Shores.

12 *The Daily World* features, "Quinaults have a Challenging Future."

12 *Columbia* launched as first space shuttle flight

22 Cuts closing priceless Ozette archeological site.

27 Ancient fossil found near Moclips.

29 Bowerman Basin attracts bird watchers.

May 1981

3 *The Daily World* features the Olympic mud minnow.

13 *Vibrasels* trucks search for oil on Harbor.

13 Assassin wounds Pope at St. Peter's.

17 Reactor and steam generators move up Chehalis River to Satsop.

24 *The Daily World* features the old Cook Creek Lookout.

June 1981

5 AIDS first mentioned in *Medical Science*.

7 Israeli planes destroy Iraqi nuclear reactor.

** *Raiders of the Lost Ark*, premiers this month.

10 YMCA top bidder for the old Hoquiam High School building.

18 N-plant moratorium approved (includes Satsop plant).

24 Israelis have capacity to make A-bomb.

July 1981

3 Sheriff raids Indian Fireworks near Oakville.

12 *The Daily World* features the Willapa Bay oyster beds.

15 Mysterious spotted owl could be high buck bird.

17 Shoalwater dedicate new center.

18 Hikers stream toward Paradise Ice Caves *(within a few years, they would become non-existent)*.

20 Rainy weather for the second year is limiting slash burning.

22 Hoquiam high of 58° F. is coldest in nation.

24 The *Green Echo* is the first ship at the new ITT Rayonier dock in Hoquiam.

29 Millions watch fairy-tale wedding of Prince Charles and Lady Diana; Harborites give the royal wedding a collective yawn

August 1981
5 The SouthShore Mall opens.

6 Reagan fires striking air controllers.

9 Difficult, important decisions will face foresters.

10 105° F.; all time Harbor high.

18 Fire destroys historic A & M sawmill.

23 Christopher Boyce, most wanted spy, captured in Port Angles.

24 Storm snuffs out power on Harbor.

26 Olympic Loop turns 50 today.

28 AP's "Earth station Aberdeen" signs on at *The Daily World*.

** IBM enters the Personal Computer (PC) field.

September 1981
1 Unique Ozette project fights for support.

2 Article about Christopher Boyce at Moclips, featured in *The Daily World*.

8 Fire fighters battle windblown blaze on the Quinault Reservation.

12 Stuntman killed in Playday fall.

16 93° F.; hottest September record for Harbor.

17 Forest blaze in heart of the Olympics.

18 Clam digging season delayed till 1982 because of clam scarcity.

28 Storm drenches Harbor.

October 1981
1 Scientists making interesting finds off Northwest coast; hot water vents.

2 Movie theaters open at SouthShore Mall.

5 Storm dumps 6" of rain on Harbor.

6 Anwar Sadat Assassinated.

11 Man grows 2½ pound potatoes in Aberdeen.

15 USFS to protect volcanic devastation area at Mt. St. Helens in new interpretative area.

16 Rare whale washes ashore near Grayland and dies.

19 Blaze destroys old Aloha Mill.

27 End of tower job, puts WNP-5 *(at Satsop)* on ice.

November 1981
1 First class stamp goes from 18¢ to 20¢.

4 Voters back 394; anti-WPPSS initiative.

8 Feature in *The Daily World* about the *Mamala*, the survey boat on Grays Harbor.

11 Lusty Vets Day storm howls in.

12 *Columbia* is first craft to make return trip to space.

14 Olympic National Park is "World Heritage Park."

15 Mean storm roars through Harbor.

16 Worst storm since '34.

December 1981
5 Gusty winds, drenching rain blast Harbor.

6 Arrest sparks court battle on Chinook fishing rights on Chehalis River.

10 Red China big customers for Harbor logs.

11 Hail, high water and ice strike Harbor.

14 A Quinault Indian perspective on the Steelhead in *The Daily World*.

15 First of a six part series in *The Daily World*; "Forest wood waste: A resource or refuse?"

16 Driftwood players close deal on new playhouse.

29 16.3% unemployment on Harbor.

~ 1982 ~

January 1982
2 Snow (*10" at Lake Quinault*) persists; roads dangerous.

4 Snow should ease up tonight.

10 Tribes offer compromise fishing plan.

11 BIA planning to combine its local offices.

16 WPPS considers termination of two nuclear plants.

19 "Blobs" of oil washing ashore near Moclips.

23 Storm douses Harbor.

25 High court rules Tribes can collect taxes on resources.

February 1982
1 Pacific Beach among risk areas for nuclear attack.

3 Weyerhaeuser to develop subdivision in Central Park.

18 Stormy weather keeps coming.

14 Massive landslide across State road 12 near Porter, sweeps highway worker to death.

21 Hoquiam police station nears completion.

24 D & R Theater may be dead at 58.

28 1981 crab season a disaster.

March 1982
1 State unemployment hits record 12.4%.

5 Observation tower going up in Westport.

5 John Belushi dead at 33.

7 *The Daily World* features conflicting land ownership at Lake Quinault.

17 County's new Juvenile Center dedicated.

19 Mt. St. Helens blows its top again.

27 The 700' long German flagship, *Emma Johanna*, is largest ship ever to visit Harbor.

April 1982
5 St. Helens rumbles after two eruptions during night.

19 *The Daily World* begins running the comic strip, *Garfield*.

23 The Olympia oyster making a come back.

25 Ed Van Syckle named Citizen of the year in *The Daily World's* Perspective '82 issue.

30 Satsop nuclear plant survives termination.

May 1982
21 British launch attack on Falklands Islands.

25 PUD bills to increase 50% on June 1.

28 Rayonier's Crane Creek crews best in the NW for safety.

28 *The Daily World* features Quinault fisherman Mike Curley in "Fishing for a way of life."

29 Heavy slash burning season in store for Harbor.

Mount St. Helens.

June 1982

5 Parents warned of aspirin link in lethal disease.
5 Quinaults dedicate new hatchery.
6 Restoration of Enchanted Valley Chalet.
7 Courts will decide if Quinaults can sue Uncle Sam.
11 The film *E.T.* opens in Aberdeen.
15 Brits victorious in Falklands.
18 100° F. hits ten year high for June.
26 County Pavilion dedicated at the fair grounds.

July 1982

2 Man soars to 16,000' in balloon-lifted lawn chair in California.
4 Timberland Libraries going electronic with CALS.
4 Loggers say State rules complicate logging.
5 New firework laws cause headaches around the State.
15 46 Timber firms default on Washington State timber sales.
18 *The Daily World* features salmon at Wynooche Dam.
20 Willapa's channel buoys will stay.
27 Fire chars remains of *M.S. Sierra.*
31 Noisome dead sperm whale on beach at Ocean Shores.

August 1982

7 Hoquiam Police Station dedicated.
8 State can not find buyers for some big timber sales.
12 First Trident submarine, *USS Ohio,* arrives at its home base at Bangor.
12 Henry Fonda, 77, dies.
16 Cherokee woman manages Taholah School.
20 Officials hope to rebuild elk herds by closing some logging roads.
22 ITT Rayonier pulp mill testing generation of electricity from wood waste.
25 Circus Vargas comes to Aberdeen.
27 President Reagan signs bill creating Mount St. Helens National Volcanic Monument.
29 A *Daily World* feature; slash burning.

September 1982

5 A *Daily World* feature; "Rafting the Queets."
9 Bottom fishing growing industry for coast.
16 Clam digging won't open before February, maybe later.
17 Driftwood Players christen new theater.
18 *The Daily World* does a feature on the Electric Park; demolition to soon begin. (*See January 17, 1985.*)
19 Italpu Dam in Brazil, the world's largest hydro-electrical dam, nears completion.
26 A *Daily World* feature; picking tree cones.
26 The permanent dome lifted into place on Satsop's reactor containment vessel.

October 1982

1 Disney opens giant Epcot Center in Florida.
2 Cyanide-laced Tylenal claims seventh victim in Chicago.
6 Storm brings first taste of winter to Harbor.
9 *The Daily World* review of *Mountain in the Clouds* by Bruce Brown. (*Salmon on the Olympic Peninsula.*)
12 Historic E.C. Miller Cedar Lumber Company Mill, put on the auction block.
13 Aberdeen hottest spot in the State at 75° F.
15 First WordPerfect (2.20) ad campaign begins.
22 Big storm hits Harbor with 55 mph winds.
23 Rebuilt Hood Canal Bridge opens. It was ripped apart by storm 3^1/$_2$ years ago.
28 Aberdeen welcoming sign goes up on Wishkah Bridge.

November 1982

1 DeLaCruz asks Hoquiam City Council to rescind anti-Boldt vote.
7 Faulty underground line keeps PUD busy in Queets-Clearwater area.
11 Soviet leader, Brezhnev, dies.
12 Andropov takes over in the Soviet Union.
15 Lottery tickets are hit on the Harbor.

December 1982

2 Quinaults make good on threat to boycott Hoquiam businesses.
3 Storm and high tides.
4 Ocean Shores dedicates its new convention center.
10 Harbor born dare devil gives up vigil on wire above Hoover Dam in protest of Reagan economic policies.
14 Hoquiam's $24 million sewer project 99.9% done.
16 Howling storm KO's power.
16 County roads and bridges crumbling.
16 Air Force gets its first cruise missiles.
22 Savage storm.

~ 1983 ~

January 1983

2 WPPSS top State story in 1982.
5 Baby it's wet outside, even for here.
5 Ma Bell's break-up has little effect here; yet.
7 State's first Lottery ends at midnight tonight.
9 A *Daily World* feature; "Hundred Autos Eaten by Treacherous Creek." (*Copalis*.)
16 Illegal garbage dumping is big problem.
17 Gas prices under $1.00 at some places.
18 The flu bug stalking Twin Harbors.
19 "Reservations are shameful example of 'failures of socialism'," says Watt.
28 Moclips hardest hit by high tides.

February 1983

4 Phantom fireball streaks over Hoquiam.
6 Quinault Blowdown.
14 G.M. and Toyota to begin joint venture.
28 Queen Elizabeth in California on U.S. tour.
28 Final *M-A-S-H* episode.

March 1983

8 Reagan says Soviet Union is Evil Empire.
9 Taholah accepts school settlement over construction problems at school.
11 Chehalis, Shoalwater tribes sue for fishing rights.
21 Warm sunny weather ushers in Spring.
22 A-train rolls through Elma.
23 Reagan proposes Star War defense plan.
30 Construction of new K-Mart store underway in Aberdeen.

April 1983

4 Much delayed *Challenger* roars off on Space mission.
18 23 arrested in big undercover drug bust on Harbor.
21 The Tacoma Dome opens.
30 PUD rates go up tomorrow.

May 1983

6 Hitler diaries called "obvious fakes."
7 Harbor jobless rate steady at 16.3%.
8 Goldie Todd: champion of Indian mothers rights.
9 Salmon market reportedly the worst since World War II.
11 *The Daily World* feature: Stalking wild Steelhead redds.
14 GM tries Japanese Techniques.
14 Emil Yuni, "the flying Finn" dead at 83.
15 *The Daily World* feature on the Olympic Candy Company.

27 Construction halted at the last Satsop nuclear plant.

June 1983

1 Some mad, some sad; all out of work at Satsop.
4 Aberdeen twins give birth in the same day.
5 Game biologist band birds on Harbor's islands. Tern colony largest of its kind in the State.
11 Indian fishing: some say one step ahead of poverty and some, they say, make millions.
13 *Pioneer 10* becomes first man-made object to sour out of solar system.
12 Aberdeen-Hoquiam lose 800 residents in the last year.
13 Boldt decision also divided the Indian fisherman.
14 *El Nino* could be bad news for fish.
15 Quinault Indians keep clam beach closed. Beach already closed for two years.
18 Sally Ride becomes first U.S. woman in space.
21 Ephrata, Washington becomes first U.S. city to use geothermal well.
26 Safeway in Aberdeen now has express lanes.
26 Olympians, Park Service restoring Chalet in Enchanted Valley.
27 Quinaults can sue over timberland management, Supreme Court says.
27 Quinaults post Quinault River Steelhead victory.
28 Boy Scouts find spy buoy on beaches.

July 1983

1 New state drunk driving law in effect today.
2 Oregon is first state with wood stove law.
4 Aberdeen revives 4th of July Splash.
6 Neutron bomb production equipment approved.
8 Court says Quinaults may tax non-Indians.
12 *Newport* dredge on maiden voyage to Harbor to preform maintenance work.
14 Lung cancer state's number one killer of women.
22 Montesano centennial celebration begins.
26 2,700 year old Indian sculpture found on coast at the mouth of the Hoko River.
** July rain fall short of July 1916 record by $^1/_4$".
** Blueback season nets only 679 fish; pooest season ever.

August 1983

1 AIDS called top health emergency.
4 Horton Capoeman, 74, "Granddaddy" of the Quinault Tribe dies.
15 56,330 attendance at five day Grays Harbor County Fair shatters all attendance records.
24 Quinault Tribal Hatchery ranks second highest in release among 16 treaty tribes in Washington.
28 El Nino hits Northwest coast hard.

September 1983

1 U.S. says S. Korean *747* shot down by Soviets.
1 Sen. Henry "Scoop" Jackson dies.
4 Times and even the trees changing in timber biz.
14 Aberdeen man dies in Crane Creek Logging Unit when tower topples. (*Last logger to die in era of giant old growth logging units on the Quinault Reservation.*)
16 State delays clam season indefinitely due to serious drop in clam population.
17 Grays Harbor estuary plan hotly debated.
20 The landmark E. C. Miller Cedar Mill in South

Aberdeen, lost in fire.

23 600 line up for K-Mart jobs.

29 Salmon catches down all along the West coast.

October 1983

1 Steelheaders and Quinaults seeking common ground to improve fishery.

5 Canada's coins are a problem on the Harbor.

9 Fungi fanciers find a forest full.

9 History of the Enchanted Valley Chalet featured in *The Daily World*.

11 "Satsop: Billions in limbo" featured in *The Daily World*.

12 China passes Japan as top log customer.

17 Economic disaster status sought on Grays Harbor in wake of El Nino.

23 206 U.S. Marines killed in Beirut truck bombing.

25 U.S. invades Grenada.

27 $7 million plan unveiled to modernize Community hospital.

31 ITT Rayonier sawmill running after 18 months shut down.

November 1983

1 IBM unveils its PC.

3 K-Mart opens in Aberdeen.

4 Harbor escapes worst of Washington weather woes.

10 The Corps' newest dredge, *Essayons,* working on the harbor this week, testing its equipment.

10 Storm zaps power.

13 Storm causes outages, road closures.

19 High winds whistle up lots of damage.20 *The Day After* becomes the most watched made-for-TV movie in history.

24 Holiday storm hits Harbor with 80 mph gusts.

30 Quinaults hope for self-sufficiency; commission five economic development studies.

30 Weyerhaeuser log truck dumps load in southbound lane of Chehalis River Bridge.

** Soggy November; rain first 27 days.

December 1983

3 Oregon hopes to regain "big tree" title from Queets fir.

7 LeMay ordered to control leachate from land fill.

10 Clam catastrophe prompts call for governor to declare disaster. A yet unnamed micro-organism is wiping out clam populations.

10 Pizza Hut opens in Aberdeen.

24 Cold weather continues with today's 10° F.

25 Holiday storm slams Harbor with 50 mph winds.

28 Load restrictions in place as result of rapid thaw; trucking grinds to halt.

28 '83 better, but no boom year for forest products. Port sets record year for exports with 668 million feet.

~ 1984 ~

January 1984

1 WPPSS Project 3 halt, default, tops 1983 Grays Harbor news stories.

3 High tides and heavy rain.

9 Quinault Tribal tax get Justice Department. review.

13 State Parks and Recreation Commission propose a five

acre park at mouth of the Copalis River.

14 Queets villagers upset; no water since December 21.

17 State wildlife agents uncover large G.H. poaching ring.

18 UW task force sorts through El Nino's wake.

21 Loggers glum as insurance rates soar.

25 Torrential rain.

25 American's TV watching tops 7 hours/day.

27 Queets finally has water again.

27 Firing prompts strike at Mayr Bros.

30 Bowerman's birds come first, agencies say.

February 1984

6 Police chief and Sheriff hope this was the last fog-A-thong in Ocean Shores.

7 First ship at the new Weyerhaeuser dock in Bay City.

7 Taholah voters want high school.

9 Andropov, Soviet leader, dead.

12 Electric Park falling to wreckers.

13 Chernenko now heads Soviet Union.

16 Quinault tribal steelheading restricted.

17 Quinaults second in fish production of tribal hatcheries in state.

26 Boldt ruling standing firm at ten year mark.

March 1984

1 Razor clam count declines 20%.

2 *Sea-Tac* name reinstated to airport; was *Jackson International Airport* for less than six months.

4 Willapa National Wildlife Refuge land swap with Weyerhaeuser will preserve 119 acres of ancient redcedar grove.

12 New hope for the "Road to Nowhere."

18 Judge George Boldt, judge in landmark fishing decision, dies.

20 The oil tanker which ran aground in the Columbia River near St. Helens, continues to leak.

28 Globs of oil wash ashore on G.H. beaches.

30 Big Port of Grays Harbor crane being dismantled following sale.

April 1984

7 Acid rain damage to European forest affect markets.

10 Quinaults mull hunting appeal in park.

12 *The Daily World* uses new nameplate today; only third one in 94 year history.

23 A year after opening, the Tacoma Dome is gold mine.

27 Violet Stanley of South Bend wins one million in state lottery game.

28 Old foes forge steel(head) partnership.

29 Russ Ellison, champion log roller, dies.

30 Huge crowds greet President Reagan in Shanghai, China.

May 1984

7 250 out of work along coast as result of timber closures.

8 Soviets to boycott Summer Olympics.

12 10,000 tons of reinforcing steel from Satsop WPPSS site, bought by China, sits at Grays Harbor Terminal 4.

14 The *USS Missouri,* "Mighty Moe," moves out of mothballs.

16 Betsy Carroll is first woman to fly Boeing *747* jumbo jet across Atlantic.

18 *Le Ping Ling* is first Chinese log ship on Grays Harbor.

19 Head of U.S. Forest Service says there is too much wilderness.

29 Business tax imposed by Quinaults upheld by Supreme Court.

31 Fire destroys the Moclips Trade Winds Lodge.

June 1984

1 *San Juan Airlines* begins service on Harbor.

3 The Enchanted Valley Chalet gets final restoration touches.

21 Summer arrives after near record wet Spring.

30 Ferry service begins between Hoquiam and Westport.

July 1984

1 Strange "red tide" hurts oyster men.

3 President Reagan signs Wilderness Bill. It includes 93,000 acres in five new wildernesses in the Olympic National Forest, including 12,120 acres in the Mt. Colonel Bob Wilderness near Lake Quinault.

3 U.S. Sen. Slade Gorton dedicates new barge terminal at the Port of Grays Harbor.

6 Controversial spraying to begin on Grays Harbor and Willapa Harbors oyster beds.

7 Amoco has drilled 1,740 feet in search of oil and natural gas in Wynooche Valley.

13 Hoquiam's Don Bell Logging quits business.

19 Shellfish closure ordered because of bacteria in ITT Rayonier's pulp mill waste discharge.

28 Olympics open in Los Angeles.

** Harbor records one of the driest Julys in history.

August 1984

9 Logging auction draws 2,000 to Mayr Bros logging yard. Sale nets $6.5 million of Mayr and Don Bell logging equipment.

27 Fire danger high despite rain.

28 Mayr Bros Logging files for bankruptcy.

31 Log truck and train collide near Elma.

September 1984

8 Twentieth Loggers Playday.

9 Uncle Sam promotes Colonel Bob Wilderness.

20 Suicide bomber kills 23 at U.S. Embassy annex in East Beirut.

22 First WPPSS N-plant dedicated at Hanford.

26 Baby clams show well, but are infected with the mysterious disease.

28 Biologist, fisherman differ on seal-salmon impact.

28 President Reagan signs Shoalwater settlement.

October 1984

1 Rivers seem to be jumping with salmon.

6 Quinaults debate "The Road to Nowhere" and show support by narrow margin.

8 DeLaCruz says Tribe wants respect on road plan.

9 Weyerhaeuser mill closure jolts Raymond and Willapa Harbor.

13 Hail and thunder hammers Harbor.

19 Aberdeen's Boise Cascade Mill closes permanently.

26 Quinaults give go-ahead to coast highway.

27 "Missing Link" (Quinault section of the coast highway) now hinges on federal funding.

31 *Timber in Trouble,"* first in a series of articles, begins in *The Daily World.*

November 1984

1 Wild autumn storm.

6 Reagan elected for four more years. Booth Gardner elected as Washington Governor.

7 Part of skull found by beachcomber near Pacific Beach on October 24, belongs to Indian of long ago.

8 Last segment of *The Daily World* series *"Timber in Trouble."*

11 ITT Rayonier's steam engine No. 38 removed from the Crane Creek Reload (*last week*) after sale to the Great Western Railroad Museum in California.

20 Joint project between Indians and State to boost stock of salmon.

26 Harbor escapes worst of storm.

December 1984

3 A gas leak claims nearly 2,000 in India.

5 Crab catch dismal.

5 Aberdeen to abandon parking meters.

9 Cabbage Patch doll fever on Harbor.

10 Free parking in Aberdeen and parking meters removal begins.

12 WPPSS Plant 2 begins commercial operation.

16 U.S. and Canada reach agreement on salmon.

21 The *Ogden Dynachem* is largest ship (by dead weight) to visit Port of Grays Harbor. Picking up 11 tons of lignin liquor.

~ 1985 ~

January 1985

1 Timber collapse heads area list of top '84 stories.

3 Ice wreaks havoc on roadways.

5 Farmers and foresters object to proposed eagle's nest rules.

10 1984 is second biggest year for log exports; 638 million feet (1983 record year).

16 Quinaults to leave on trade mission to China.

16 Queets has been without water for a week as a result of a burned out pump.

16 Battle over Bowerman Basin resumes in hearing.

17 PUD's 1907 Electric Park Power Plant little more than pile of rubble (*See September 18, 1982*).

18 Historic rail line from Hoquiam to Moclips, now history as last rails and ties removed for scrap.

19 The 525' Japanese log ship, *Southern Accord,* nearly capsizes at Port of Grays Harbor terminal.

21 Reagan takes second inaugural oath in record freeze.

22 Fire destroys Grass Creek Shake Mill.

23 "Mac" Polson of pioneer logging clan, dies.

28 States "Gravel Gertie" part of salmon stream clean-up project.

30 Ivar Haglund, zany restaurateur, dead at 79.

31 ITT Rayonier lumber mill in Hoquiam goes on indefinite closure.

** January may have been the driest January ever on the Harbor.

February 1985

4 Weyerhaeuser start-up of Aberdeen mill to fill recent Japanese orders.

8 Duffy's opens restaurant in Hoquiam; it's third in the area.
11 Howling storm with gust to 51 mph.
15 Copalis and Quinaults at odds over fish.
17 Postage stamps go from 20¢ to 22¢.

March 1985
6 "Missing Link" route pushed by officials.
6 60 protesters at fish meeting about Copalis River.
8 Canada-U.S. Salmon Treaty hailed as boon for Harbor.
9 "Timber: An Industry in Transition" First of a nine part series in *The Daily World.*
18 President signs Salmon Treaty.
27 Slow down building over the "Missing Link" highway.
28 750° F. water found 200 miles west of Grays Harbor.
30 Old growth is crucial study says.
30 Quinaults debate "Missing Link." Vote to keep options open.

April 1985
1 Last three months of rainfall the lowest ever.
** Month long debate on the coast highway's "Missing Link."

May 1985
8 Governor signs Quinault Highway bill.
9 Joint effort rescues Mayr Brothers fish ponds.
17 Harbor hot spot, 89° F. in Aberdeen.
22 Consultants warn of new efforts to abrogate treaties.
27 Bangladesh toll may surpass 40,000 in typhoon.
** CD-ROM first displayed on the cover of *Byte Magazine.*

June 1985
6 Record low rainfall in Northwest.
18 88° F.
19 Queets Douglas fir still number one.
28 Clam parasite gaining ground again.
28 1,200 fewer live in county now.

July 1985
2 First six months driest in 50 years.
10 Fall razor clam season still in question.
10 Log exports at red-hot pace.
11 Largest fire fighting force ever on lines in Western U.S.
20 Foresters praying for rain.
22 Quinaults surprised by excellent salmon run.
24 Dry weather curtails logging.
25 Harbor forest almost into "Blow-up condition."
31 Steelhead success story unfolds; Mayr and Quinault Tribe.

August 1985
1 Huge hollow spruce on Burrows Road falls victim to fire.
11 National debt nears $2,000,000,000,000.
13 90° F.
14 Deadly clam parasite strong on North Beach.
16 Mount Rainier ice caves are no more.
16 Alcohol most costly to health of Indians.
29 Forest fire is now biggest in history of Olympic National Park.
29 Fire danger extremely high State wide.
30 Pacific Beach-Moclips water officials put emergency restrictions into effect.
31 Forest fires burn hole in budget.

September 1985
1 Water trucks feed Pacific Beach-Moclips.
3 Fire fighters contain $2 million park blaze.
6 Timber firms reopen Twin Harbor forest lands; still quite dry.
15 Phase I development of Morrison Park in Aberdeen dedicated. (*Land for the park was donated in 1977. The park would not be completed until 1996 at a total cost of 3.5 million dollars.*)
19 Two large earthquakes kill 8,000 in Mexico City.
27 BIA dedicates new Hoquiam office.
29 Bombers drop loads on Quinault fire; slash burns out of control as dry east winds come up.
29 *The Daily World* features two special sections on Camp Grisdale.
29 Photo of pelicans at Taholah in *The Daily World.*

October 1985
1 Putting ITT Rayonier locomotive back on tracks, after it is sold to California company.
2 Firefighters gain on the Quinault fire in the Humptulips.
3 ITT Rayonier creates timber partnerships.
9 1985 could be record year for log exports.
10 Four log ships in Harbor on Maiden voyages.
15 Clam season open for first time in two years.
22 Greedy clam diggers cause cut backs.
27 Eight inches of rain and more predicted.

November 1985
13 Harbor log exports pace 15% ahead of 1984.
18 Tribes given rights to hatchery fish.
19 25,000 die in Columbian earthquake (Nevado del Ruiz Volcano).
20 First snow of the year.
27 Snow in Puget Sound while Harbor remains in "Snow shadow."

December 1985
2 Ice storm hits Harbor.
11 Halley's Comet appears only as a faint fuss ball over the Harbor. (*Despite its poor appearance from earth, spacecraft gives it our best view yet. See May 1910.*)
26 1985 may be driest year of the century.
26 Oil spill near Port Angles is largest in Puget Sound history.
** Twenty days of dry and cold (20's) longest dry spell for December.

~ 1986 ~

January 1986
5 Howling storm hits Harbor with gust to 60 mph.
16 Angry storm in evening with gust to 90 mph.
19 Heavy rain and strong winds. 100 year storm for Seattle.
20 Swollen Chehalis could flood east county.
27 Court won't review Tribal fishing quota.
27 Space shuttle *Challenger* explodes shortly after lift-off.

February 1986
4 Everyone in garbage together, county says.
7 Harbor one day closer to the Orient with the completion of fuel area at the Port.
18 Fireball streaks across Northwest sky.

25 Marcos calls it quits and flees the Philippines.

March 1986

2 Redcedar keeps secrets of the ages on Willapa's Long Island.

6 Deeper draft plan expensive, but vital.

24 Falling pump prices in Harbor may have hit bottom; 75¢/gal for regular.

April 1986

6 Terrorists bomb nightclub in Germany.

15 U.S. air raid against Libya.

26 Chernobyl nuclear accident.

30 Quinault Tribe and USFS to give State million Steelhead to replace its hatchery loss.

May 1986

1 Long Live the Kings project launched.

2 Expo 86 opens in Vancouver, Canada.

7 Tsunami fails to appear.

22 Reagan approves tariff on Canadian shakes.

25 Hands Across America.

29 Washington State Centennial license plates unveiled.

June 1986

1 *San Juan Airlines* ends flights at Hoquiam.

9 George Lamb dies.

23 Ozone hole discovered above South Pole.

July 1986

3 Statue of Liberty begins four day birthday party.

4 Rudy Vallee dies while watching the relighting of the Statue of Liberty.

6 100 skydivers link together at 6,000 feet.

7 World population reaches five billion.

30 45-day strike at Weyerhaeuser mills ends.

August 1986

18 Boeing rolls out 5,000th jetliner.

24 Work begins on Kings project.

25 2,000 dead from volcanic gas in Cameroon.

26 46 rainless days.

September 1986

10 Parasite ravages fall clam season.

22 Peace Corps observes 25th anniversary.

October 1986

5 Missile-carrying Soviet submarine on fire near Bermuda; later sinks.

9 Hubbard Glacier blocking Alaska's Russell Fiord, bursts.

13 Vancouver's Expo 86 closes after drawing 22 million.

23 Dome-building eruption underway at St. Helens.

November 1986

8 State files new suit in Indian fishing dispute.

12 Iran story begins to break.

15 Last movie shown at Aberdeen Theater.

16 Boundary changes add 15,000 acres to Olympic National Park.

17 Dramatic population decline on Harbor during past year.

24 Heavy rains swell rivers. Quinault and Queets hit hardest since 1935.

26 Iran-Contra scandal spreads.

29 Cary Grant dies.

December 1986

1 Study shows that lower tire pressure could cut logging road repairs.

11 Aberdeen revives Tall Ship Project after defeat in November election.

12 Pacific Beach residences can drink from tap after 457 day "no drink" order.

14 *The Daily World* begins nine part series on the health of the Harbor's water.

16 Grocery strike begins on Harbor.

23 *Voyager* lands safely after first non-stop, unrefueled flight around the world.

Tree planter.

~ 1987 ~

January 1987

3 $700,000 earmarked for deeper draft in Harbor.

14 Harbor spared as snow hits State.

14 Pesticide ban in oyster beds.

19 Ground breaking for fish farm at Westport.

20 Remains of mystery ship exposed at Copalis Beach last Thanksgiving is talk of county.

24 Harbor grocery strikers march to show solidarity.

31 Terry Waite's whereabouts remain mystery. May be hostage.

31 Howling storm and heavy rain.

February 1987

3 Rumors that the Pacific Beach Naval Facility to close.

3 The Grays Harbor Soil Survey is released to the public by the SCD.

8 Timber firms, Tribes, and Environmentalists negotiate Timber, Fish and Wildlife (TFW) tradeoffs.

21 First Gray whales spotted off coast; on annual migration.

23 TFW asks for State funding.

March 1987

1 World War II *U.S. Enterprise* scrapped.

3 Blustery storm.

7 Quinaults say BIA timber cutbacks false economy.

10 Alder pollen begins week and half early.

22 100 millionth U.S. housing unit.

24 Durbo Bay Oil produces five billionth barrel of oil. It took Texas 57 years to reach this, Alaska 10.

24 County opts for middle ground in gravel harvest from rivers.

28 *Golden Hinde* replica docks in Aberdeen.

28 Harbor grocery strike ends.

April 1987

1 80° F. on Harbor, no fooling!

8 Have Soviet subs entered Puget Sound?

29 Many glass floats wash ashore this month.

May 1987

** First week in 80°'s. Gray whale washes up at Wreck Creek.

15 Iran-Contra ("Irangate") funds used in attempt to purchase land on the Quinault Indian Reservation.

17 *U.S. Stark* attacked in Persian Gulf.

23 USFS has open house in newly rebuilt Quinault Ranger Station.

28 West German teenager lands *Cessna* in Red Square in Moscow.

** Garbage barge from Islip, New York can find no place to dump.

June 1987

4 Cost of reforestation likely to rise in wake of new immigration law.

7 Money for attempted Quinault land purchase by General Secord came from Iran arms profits. (*Iran-gate forest.*)

7 Quinaults top list in hatchery production.

13 Cryptumanuds turn Harbor Rivers Red.

30 County Officials tour Quinault Reservation.

July 1987

** Oliver North testifies in Iran-Contra hearings.

** There are 197 million television sets in the U.S.; 716 million world wide.

** Blueback season nets 24,400.

August 1987

6 Joe DeLaCruz elected as President of the Affiliated Tribes of the Northwest.

6 Quinault Reservation forests closed due to drought.

6 Russian defects to U.S. while his ship was in port in Aberdeen.

28 Pacific Veneer dedicated in South Aberdeen.

September 1987

1 96° F. Most woods closed.

2 Quinaults hope to regain lost timberland.

13 Keel of *Lady Washington* replica in Aberdeen is laid.

29 85° F.

29 Quinault and Quillayute Tribes fell redcedar for huge canoes as part of a Washington State Centennial project. (*See January 29, 1994.*)

October 1987

1 Pacific Beach Naval Facility "closes."

7 Mercury skyrockets as summer lingers.

10 3,000 year old Makah basket found.

16 Jessica McClure rescued from an abandoned well in Texas before live TV audience.

19 Stock market record loss of 22.6% in one day.

** State closes all lands due to fire hazard.

November 1987

4 First natural forest fire in Olympic National Park allowed to burn near Kimta is now out.

6 An iceberg twice the size of Rhode Island breaks away from Antarctica.

6 The Northwest drought uncovers ancient Chinook village on the Columbia River.

12 KFC open in China.

18 Iran-Contra report released.

24 Quinault Tribe warns of law suit if it is kept out of Hoquiam's watershed for fish management purposes.

December 1987

1 Blustery storm hits Harbor.

8 In Washington D.C., Soviet leader Gorbachev and President Reagan sign treaty to eliminate intermediate range nuclear missiles.

14 Quinault public hearings on Taholah-Queets Road.

14 Quinault Sitka spruce named co-champ with one in Oregon as world's largest.

~ 1988 ~

January 1988

2 Diesel oil spill in Philadelphia affects one million people in seven states.

10 55 Bald eagles sighted about Lake Quinault in annual count.

13 Taholah High School assured.

13 Harbor log export record in 1987.

14 New woodstove law begins today in Washington. Woodstove smoke is growing into most serious air pollution problem.

15 Washington's Wildlife Commission lists the Spotted owl as endangered.

15 84 mph wind causes havoc on beach.

24 Quinault spruce (at Lake) shares national title as largest.

26 Hoquiam watershed contracts with Quinaults remain in effect.

27 Aspirin can reduce heart trouble.

30 Boeing *747* sets 'round the world record: Seattle to Seattle in 36 hours.

February 1988

4 Congressional investigation into BIA shaping up.

March 1988

16 Governor signs limited summer driving ban on Washington beaches.

18 *Alaskan Solitude* launched from Little Hoquiam shipyard.

21 Aberdeen celebrates 100th birthday as photographers record "A day in the Life." Will be book for December 1988 publication.

26 Fifth blustery storm this week.

April 1988

8 Chow Chow Bridge collapses.

13 Wenatchee artifacts could be oldest yet found: more than 10,000 years old.

15 Taholah garbage truck destroyed by fire.

15 Quinaults close Federal Land Bank deal for 9,400 acres.

17 U.S. engages Iranian forces in Persian Gulf.

May 1988

3 Julia Butler Hansen dies.

4 Quinault, Curt Stanley, wins UW Vice-president Award.

9 New book on Reagan says Nancy used astrology to set presidential schedule.

22 *The Daily World* features Pt. Grenville tide pools and the UW early *Outreach Program.*

24 U.S. Government brochures on AIDS arrives in mail.

31 President Reagan in Moscow.

June 1988

16 Nuu-chah-nulth completes four-day workshop on the Quinault Indian Reservation.

21 PBS show *Indian Country* features the Quinault Tribe and Joe DeLaCruz.

28 Gorbachev asks for sweeping Soviet reforms.

28 Shale Creek Imprinting Facility dedicated.

30 Much of U.S. undergoing severe drought; Mississippi River at lowest level in 110 years.

July 1988

3 U.S. accidentally shoots down Iranian passenger jet.

19 98° F.

23 Poll shows Olympic Peninsula, most preferred travel destination in State.

25 Quinault crews leave to fight Yellowstone Fires.

** 44 Japanese students and instructors spend 3 weeks studying on Harbor.

August 1988

5 Sub makes first dive to bottom of Crater Lake.

9 Port of Grays Harbor dedicates viewing tower.

11 President signs biggest drought relief bill in history.

17 Soviet and U.S. scientists conduct nuclear test together.

22 President signs Bowerman Basin Bill.

24 92° F.

25 Spotted owl controversy grows.

September 1988

1 Forest closed due to dry weather.

2 95° F.

4 Three day black out of 50 blocks of downtown Seattle.

7 WPPSS fraud trial opens.

12 Quinaults testify before Senate Indian Affairs Committee about North Boundary.

13 EPA puts out a radon gas warning.

14 St. Joseph Hospital closes.

18 Cosmopolis Treaty "Centennial Mural" dedicated.

19 Israel launches satellite, *Horizon - 1.*

26 Computer virus' may threaten computer world.

29 *Discovery* launched. First shuttle since *Challenger* explosion 2½ years ago.

October 1988

8 Senate passes Quinault Land Bill.

11 Grays Harbor County per capita income of $9,320 ranked 22nd out of 39. King County is first with $13,192.

18 Site of new N.B. High School may be site of Indian burial ground.

18 Three Gray Whales trapped by ice near Barrow Alaska.

31 Coyote runs into Wishkah Mall.

November 1988

6 Ground breaking for Taholah Community Center.

8 First week marked by blustery storms.

8 President Reagan signs Quinault North Boundary Bill.

17 President signs Bill setting aside 872,000 acres of the Olympic National Park as wilderness.

22 Super-secret Stealth Bomber rolled out.

December 1988

7 Armenia earthquake.

10 Quinaults celebrate North Boundary return with dinner.

14 First transatlantic fiber optic cable goes into operation.

15 Quinaults sign letter of intent for Weyerhaeuser land purchase.

23 Oil spill off the mouth of Grays Harbor when tug rams the 300' barge *U.S. Nesfucca.*

28 $100 million West Hoquiam By-pass dedicated.

29 First full-blown monsoon of winter.

30 Large number of oiled sea birds begin to appear at Point Grenville (*See December 23*).

~ 1989 ~

January 1989

1 John Marcus McCrory is first Grays Harbor baby of Washington State's Centennial year.

2 Oil spill of December 23rd, now ranks among State's worst

** Oil spill and clean up of coast and birds dominate local headlines all month.

6 Emperor Hirohito dies.

24 Ted Bundy executed.

** Spotted Owl debate continues and intensifies.

27 U.S. Army Corps Engineers say Mount Rainier 14,411.1 feet tall.

February 1989

** First week with snow and cold near record lows.

5 Report shows temperatures the warmest of decade in 1988. '88, '87, '86, '83, '81, and '80, six of the warmest years of the 20th century.

24 *727* Jumbo jet rips open over Hawaii; points to growing problem with aging jet fleet.

March 1989

2 Two types of flu circulating at once are taking big toll.

2 Harbor only dusted while snow storm buries Puget Sound.

6 Poaching in state has become high-tech with Asian links.

7 *Lady Washington* launched in Aberdeen as Centennial event. Particle solar eclipse, too.

7 Quake jolts Forks; third in western Washington in last three days.

7 Massive solar flare disrupts communications around the world.

14 Grocers remove Chilean fruit from shelves due to cyanide scare.

24 Scientists skeptical of claim that a cheap experiment produced nuclear fusion.

24 Tanker *Exxon Valdez* spills 11.3 million gallons of oil near Valdez; worst ever in U.S. history.

April 1989

4 Gas prices begin to sky rocket in wake of Alaskan oil Spill.

7 Log ship, *Norman Queen*, runs aground in Harbor.

8 Soviet nuclear sub sinks off Norway.

18 First fiberoptic cable across the Pacific, goes into service.

19 Fire and explosion kill 47 on the U.S. Battleship *Iowa.*

22 Bowerman Basin Wildlife ceremony.
23 Quinault timber venture provides a solid land base for the tribe.
26 Lucille Ball dies at 77.
29 Second warmest April on record.

May 1989
4 *Magellan* probe launched from Space Shuttle *Atlantis*.
8 *Lady Washington* departs for sea trials.
12 U.S. troops deployed to Panama.
17 TV crews scramble for satanic clues in Grays Harbor.
19 Students demonstrate all month for democracy in China.
20 Warren "Maggie" Magnuson dies.
27 AP articles series begins on future of old growth and the timber industry in the Northwest.

June 1989
4 At least 500 die as troops crush protest in Beijing student demonstrations for democracy.
4 Ayatollah Khomeini dead at 86.
4 Seven mile section of I-90 opens in Seattle. It's the most expensive section of freeway in the world.
6 Scouts clear old USFS Campbell Tree Grove Campground.
29 U.S. Supreme Court limits tribal power over land use in Yakama Case.

July 1989
3 U.S. Supreme Court cuts abortion rights.
12 Los Angeles bans cedar shakes for roofing.
17 Maiden flight of *Stealth Bomber*.
21 Northwest Indian canoes "Paddle to Seattle" Centennial event.
29 136 page issue of *The Daily World*, largest ever.

August 1989
4 State and Tribes sign Centennial Accord.
5 Harbor Aviation Day draws 10,000 to Bowerman Field.
14 Black and Chehalis Rivers hit by fish kill.
24 *Voyager* makes closest approach to Neptune.

September 1989
22 Irving Berlin, 101, dies.
23 Clam NIX may be at all-time high.
23 91° F. on beaches for first day of fall.

October 1989
9 Collegians ignorant of history, poll says.
13 Friday the 13th stock market drop is second largest in history.
17 San Francisco battered by killer earthquake.

November 1989
9 East Germany said it would permanently lift travel restrictions on its citizens; the end of the Berlin Wall.
11 Washington States celebrates its 100th birthday.
17 Senate investigators recommend self-governance for Indian tribes.
18 Researchers report biggest structure in the Universe; a great wall of galaxies 500 million light years long.
18 Last expendable NASA rocket launched.

December 1989
14 Rainfall totals 8.35" at Lake Quinault over the weekend.
11 Wave of Asian property investors hitting Seattle.
15 Wood smoke ban over entire state remains in effect; first ever state wide ban.

18 Fire levels Taholah Merc.
18 Congressional report concludes significant amount of radioactivity was released from Handford between 1945-51.
20 U.S. attacks Panama to oust Noriega.
31 *The Daily World* looks at the decade on the Harbor and world.

~ 1990 ~

January 1990
1 Minimum wage goes from $3.85/hour to $4.25/hour.
7 Winds and rain bring flooding. I-5 closed at Centralia due to flood.
10 More blacks moving south; 100 year trend is reversed.
16 Special Grays Harbor PUD history section in *The Daily World*.
21 Charter boat capsizes at La Push claiming seven lives.
27 Maureen Finnerly took charge of Olympic National Park this week; highest ranking woman in National Park Service history.
30 McDonalds' opens in Moscow near Red Square.
31 This January wettest in last 26 years.

February 1990
7 16" snow at Lake Quinault.
12 Harbor receives 7" precipitation over wild weekend.
13 Quinault Indian Nation closes deal to purchase 3,200 acres of Weyerhaeuser land on the Reservation.
24 500-year "up datable" Centennial time capsule sealed in Olympia.
24 Ground breaking for the new North Beach High School at Oyehut.

March 1990
7 *SM-71 Blackbird*, sets coast to coast record of 68 minutes on its retirement flight.
24 Puyallup Indians sign $162 million settlement.

April 1990
4 *Pegasus* rocket launched from *B-52* and carries a 450 lb. satellite into orbit.
5 Spotted owl plan "impact clearly severe."
5 IBM writes its initials with atoms.
15 Beach driving ban begins on 40% of the beach.
17 Aberdeen listed in top 10 small cities.
24 Shuttle *Discovery* carries *Hubble Space Telescope* into orbit.
28 1,500 loggers block bridge in Hoquiam to protest logging cut backs.

May 1990
9 Log export restrictions gain momentum.
12 Once pristine Columbia River laced with significant levels of Dioxin.
16 Dead whale stuck fast in pilings at Port of Grays Harbor Terminal 4.
16 Sammy Davis Jr. dead at 64 of cancer.
16 Jim Henson, creator of Muppets dies at 53.
17 *Yortown Clipper,* a 257' luxury cruiser carrying 94 passengers, docks in Aberdeen.
18 Rayonier Point, a Hoquiam waterfront park is dedicated.
21 Photos taken for *A Day in the Life of Hoquiam.*

25 *The Daily World* 24 page centennial salute to Hoquiam.

June 1990

19 *The Excalibur*, the worlds largest hotel opens in Las Vegas with 4,032 rooms.

22 Spotted Owl listed as threatened.

22 Check Point Charlie is removed from site of Berlin Wall.

24 Japan out-invests U.S. for the first time.

28 Focusing flaw cripples the *Hubble Space Telescope.*

** Nan-Sea Stables, near Oyehut, opens for business.

July 1990

1 Scientists now call Steelhead a salmon.

1 Two German states unite economies.

2 Aberdeen takes control of Wynooche Dam.

4 Taholah police kill man in melee.

7 Farmers market moves to F Street in Aberdeen.

12 Taholah protest over killing.

19 Gardner backs plan to clean up Washington's dirty air by 2010.

** Less than 9,000 Blueback caught this year.

20 Ex-Hoquiam mayor, Jack McGire, dead at age 69.

20 Goodwill Games open in Seattle.

27 Quinaults named as one of six tribes to manage own funds and to take over former BIA programs. (*Self-Governance.*)

August 1990

1 Ocean Shores station fills last gas tank as last full service station between Taholah and Hoquiam.

2 Iraq invades Kuwait.

4 Kuwait invasion boosts gas prices.

8 Dry weather prompts logging restrictions.

10 Mayr Bros eye a new niche of smaller logs.

11 *Magellan* orbiter arrives at Venus.

14 McChord forces deployed to Middle East.

16 Seaport launches passenger trips on the *Lady Washington.*

20 Bush demands that Iraq release all foreigners.

22 Bush calls up Reserves.

22 State proposes ambitious forest land experiment north of the Quinault Indian Reservation.

27 Strike idles 270 workers at Hoquiam pulp mill.

September 1990

6 Group seeks to protect Yew tree.

22 Experts tell Ocean Shores to brace for growth.

29 The book *Land of the Quinault*, published by the Quinault Indian Nation, is released for public sale.

30 Last stone laid in the Washington National Cathedral, completing 83 years of work.

30 Air tanker crash near Wynooche Lake.

** One of driest September's ever.

October 1990

1 Quinault Indian Nation begins three year project of self-governance. (*This project would become a permanent program in October 1993. QIN would sign an annual funding agreement with the Indian Health Service on June 27, 1994 and assumed responsibility for that program on October 1, 1994.*)

2 Prices for barrel of oil $40. Almost double since Iraq's invasion of Kuwait.

3 Germany unification.

9 Kennedy Assassination tops 50 years of TV most memorable programs. Next were: #2, *Apollo 11* Moon walk; #3, *Roots*; #4, *Challenger* disaster; #5, *See It Now*; #6, *The Day After*; and #7, the final episode of *M.A.S.H.*

9 Snow cover on the northern half of the Earth dwindled in the '80's.

15 Leonard Bernstein dies.

24 Spartina, also known as cordgrass, was introduced 100 years ago into Willapa Bay with east coast oysters; is now spreading extremely fast.

November 1990

9 *Pineapple Express* storm slams into State.

10 Lamb dedicates futuristic Tech center in Hoquiam.

11 Lake Quinault at highest level in 20 years after weekend of nearly 14" rain.

11 Historian, Murray Morgan's review of *Land of the Quinault* appears in *The Tacoma Tribune.*

12 Beatrice "Grandma" Black, celebrates her 100th birthday.

17 New rail link moves Port closer to Orient.

20 The 696' *Hual Transporter*, is the largest ship to visit the Harbor.

21 Coast Guard chopper makes emergency landing at Point Grenville after rescue of two from *Natashias Faith* near there.

23 70 mph gust and heavy rain on Harbor.

25 Old I-90 floating bridge sinks.

December 1990

1 Last week, the Quinault Indian Nation and ITT Rayonier agreed on option to buy land on Reservation in four options.

1 British, French meet for the first time in tunnel under the Channel (*See May 6, 1994*).

3 Wind and rain slam Harbor.

7 John Hughes' review of *Land of the Quinault* appears in *The Daily World.*

19 Arctic storm plasters state, but Harbor gets off easy.

21 11° F.

** This year's 173.30" rainfall at Lake Quinault is 3" short of 1983 record.

~ 1991 ~

January 1991

15 U.N. deadline for Iraq to withdraw from Kuwait.

17 U.S. and coalition begin bombing of Iraq in *Operation Desert Storm.*

17 Iraq attacks Israel with *Scud* missiles.

17 Classes begin at the new North Beach High School at Oyehut.

** Most "live TV" war coverage in history.

19 Eastern Airlines shuts down after 62 year history.

23 Five month strike at Rayonier is over.

23 More then 12,000 missions flown in first week of war.

25 U.S. AIDS deaths hit 100,000 mark over decade; expect 215,000 Americans to die in next three years.

26 Iraq dumps huge quantities of oil into gulf from Kuwait.

February 1991

3 First class letter goes from 25¢ to 29¢.

4 Strong winds and rain over weekend with gust to 65 mph.

6 *The Daily World* features Taholah seafood expanding market.

** Gulf War dominates news.

19 Heavy rain.

21 Seattle-Tacoma 14th largest U.S. metro area.

23 Ground battle begins (*24th in Kuwait*). Allied forces strike Iraqi troops in Kuwait and Iraq.

27 Kuwait all but liberated.

27 Sunny and 68° F. Seventh day of sunshine.

27 100 hour war with Iraq comes to an end.

March 1991

9 Cooperative project breeds life into Steelhead survival.

9 Makah Tribe closes access road to wilderness beach.

12 *Aberdeen Review Club* celebrates 100 years.

12 Grays Harbor County roads due for new names.

26 Fire fighters "kill" first spewing Kuwaiti oil well fire.

27 Guy Capoeman featured for his art in *The Daily World*.

April 1991

2 Idaho's Snake River Sockeye proposed as endangered species.

5 It has rained almost non-stop since April first.

5 Forces may be gathering for huge coastal quake.

5 Ozone layer weakening fast 20° north and south of equator.

6 DeLaCruz re-elected. Nearly 700 members and guests attend the Quinault General Council meeting.

7 Once threatened cormorant now threatens some salmon.

11 U.N. Security Council officially ends Persian Gulf War.

18 Taholah police chief exonerated by Grand Jury in July 4th (1990) man's death.

19 12,500 teachers picket at Olympia.

25 Federal timber program "a disaster" officials say; Forest Service paints bleakest picture yet.

May 1991

2 Ground breaking for the new Amanda Park Library.

3 Seattle traffic rated fourth worst in U.S.

6 *The Daily World* features bridge tenders on the Harbor.

11 The last Boeing *707* rolls off the assembly line.

23 Judge halts timber sales in Northwest National Forest.

23 Timber rally at State capital draws 3,500.

31 Shooting stuns Taholah.

June 1991

* Nike athletic shoes washing up on the beaches from Oregon to Canada. 40,000 pairs washed from the decks of ship bound from South Korea.

2 A special section in *The Daily World* marks the 50th anniversary of the Clemons Tree Farm.

3 Rededication of the Clemons Tree Farm.

5 Washington residents treated to light snow. Unusually bright Aurora Borealis.

9 Cosmopolis celebrates centennial.

11 Savings & Loan bailout costs are soaring.

14 Historic Hoquiam Library building reopens after new addition and renovation.

19 Series begins in *The Daily World* on the Wynooche Dam dilemma.

22 Mill pollutants cause closure of Grays Harbor oyster harvest.

23 The Quinault Indian Nation's book, *Land of the Quinault,* wins NFPW national award for best historical book.

26 $20 million voted for forestry projects to employ Northwest loggers.

27 Forest manufactures must diversify in order to survive.

29 Big Taholah Potlatch.

30 The 2,800 foot peak which appears southeast of Lake Quinault has been renamed Bell Mountain, for its nearly perfect bell curved silhouette.

July 1991

1 The Quinault Indian Nation has open house for self-governance.

1 The Clearwater and Olympic Correction Centers combined into the Olympic Correction Center. (*The Honor Camp system begun in California was followed by Oregon, then Washington. The first Honor Camp in Washington was at Yacolt in 1955. The Clearwater Honor Camp, built in 67-68, served as an adult correction center until 1972. From 72-76 it was used as a State DNR Youth Conservation Corp Camp until it resumed as a corrections center. The Olympic Correction Center was established adjacent to the Clearwater Camp in 1980.*)

3 The Taholah boxing program featured in *The Daily World*.

5 World wide financial scandal erupts as regulators of eight countries shut down the Bank of Credit and Commerce International (BCCI).

11 Weyerhaeuser Pulp Mill in Cosmopolis ranked the nations's 5th top polluter in nation in 1989.

22 Large private timberland owners in western Washington drew down their softwood supply 20% between 1979-1989.

22 A 610' Chinese vessel, *Tou Hai*, and a 365' Japanese factory vessel, the *Tenyo Maru*, collide off coast this morning, sinking the Japanese ship.

23 Temperatures reach the century mark in east county.

31 Fingers crossed that the oil from the sunken Japanese ship off Cape Flattery will drift by.

August 1991

3 Dan's Service station closes. Only three full-service stations remain in Aberdeen-Hoquiam.

8 Jim Irwin, former moon-walker, dies at 61.

10 *The Daily World* features JB's (*Francis McCrory*) reunion with his first daughter.

13 Largest proposed bank merger in U.S. history to affect two Aberdeen banks.

15 Part of State 109 from Hogan's Corner to Taholah resurfaced with a gravely texture in areas prone to ice.

18 Soviet Union Coup ousts Gorbachev.

19 Ten years ago IBM introduced PC.

21 Gorbachev poised to return as coup crumbles.

24 Gorbachev resigns from Communist Party and urges Party to disband.

29 Fierce summer storm zaps region.

September 1991

3 Classes begin at the new Taholah High School.

13 *The Daily World* computers crash on Friday the thirteenth.

17 Harbor night-owls see Shuttle's meteoric streak across Harbor sky.

18 Kamp Kiwanis meeting draws 130 at Hoquiam. (*The Olympic National Park staff had burned the camp building on the north shore of Lake Quinault.*)

20 Ocean refuge sought along Olympic coast.

20 Group of thirteen Soviet professionals tour Harbor and recall horrible hours of coup.

24 Four and one half foot "alligator" (caiman) found at Ocean Shores.

24 Author "Dr. Seuss" dies at 87.

26 Biosphereians embark. Sealed in 3.15 acre self-sustaining environment.

27 President Bush said he is eliminating all U.S. battlefield nuclear weapons.

** One of driest Septembers on record.

October 1991

5 Dam failure floods Chehalis.

8 Federal Auditors dismiss most Quinault Landowners Association claims.

11 Senate panel hears Anita Hill's graphic sexual accusations about Supreme Court nominee Judge Thomas.

12 State pants for rain; fire danger high. Seattle 41 straight days without rain.

12 Taholah High School dedication.

17 *Lady Washington* skirts disaster at Pasco as railroad bridge lowers onto ship.

23 Oakland, California fire one of costliest in U.S. history.

23 Reggie Ward, Sr., poised for some *Northern Exposure.*

29 Mid-East Peace Conference begins.

November 1991

2 New Amanda Park Library dedicated.

7 Magic Johnson revels he is infected with HIV, the virus that causes AIDS.

8 Aurora fills the night sky across Canada and northern U.S.

9 Quinault defeats Taholah 20-10 in first Quinault River Bowl Game in downpour. Many players burned when lime mistakenly used as line marker.

14 Snake River Sockeye listed as endangered; will affect Columbia River water usage.

16 Storm winds fall huge Hoquiam crane.

19 Wet blustery day.

24 Tree-eating Asian gypsy moth has been found in Washington State for the first time. Has the potential to be the most serious exotic insect ever to enter the U.S. The Asian moth can feed on coniferous trees and fly for miles.

24 Entire coast is closed to harvest of shellfish as the marine toxin domoic acid has been found in razor clams near Ocean Shores.

December 1991

4 Terry Anderson, the longest held Western Hostage in Lebanon, and last American, released.

4 Pan-Am, the pioneer of commercial aviation, stops flying.

8 Eagle tree falls at Wreck Creek.

22 Soviet Union passes into history.

25 Gorbachev becomes last Premier of the Soviet Union.

31 Mid-week holidays put work places in a end-of year twilight zone.

~ 1992 ~

January 1992

3 Weyerhaeuser to post first loss in its history.

4 *Nirvana,* band founded in Aberdeen, hits big time.

4 Washington 1991 traffic deaths (682) lowest in 18 years.

12 Mammoth or Mastodon ivory found at big slide on the Quinault River.

12 Flu epidemic spreads across the U.S.

31 Winds with 92 mph gusts on coast KO power; fifth straight day of deluge; 8" for week.

February 1992

10 Alex Haley, author of *Roots* dies at 70 in Seattle.

10 U.S. begins airlift to Russia.

16 In wake of Spotted owl and Snake River Sockeye salmon, Eastern Washington farmers send 25 tons of potatoes to Grays Harbor food banks for out of work loggers. In turn the loggers send sea food, cranberries and mill ends for firewood.

17 Enhanced 911 becomes operational on Grays Harbor.

18 *Pestova*, a Russian ship, takes on 65 tons of donated food and supplies here.

16 George Streater, claimed to be first white man born on Queets River (*April 15, 1895*), dies.

26 73° F; ties 100 year high record for February.

March 1992

9 Winter is warmest on record so far.

9 Kamp Kiwanis gets new 10 year lease.

14 Asian gypsy moth a Northwest emergency.

19 Navy jet *EA-6B Prowler* crashes near Kalaloch.

20 Lumber prices soar; industry blames owl, urges more logging.

27 Congressman seeks experimental forest on State lands north of the Quinault Reservation (*Clearwater*).

30 Montesano moves into new high school.

** March one of driest on record.

April 1992

3 Fungi in Michigan that covers 38 acres is believed to be largest living thing in the world.

6 Elvis stamp voting begins.

6 Author, Isaac Asimov, dies at 72.

13 *U.S.S. Missouri* returns to Bemerton.

18 Record heroin bust in East County.

21 Gypsy moth spraying begins in Washington (Tacoma).

24 NASA's *CBE* spacecraft finds ripples at the edge of the universe.

30 Riots in LA begin in wake of Rodiny King beating case; worse race riots of the century.

May 1992

3 78° F. on beaches, 86° F. in Aberdeen.

7 200th anniversary of Robert Gray entry into "Gray's Harbor."

13 Boeing delivers its final *707*. In all, 1,011 built since 1954.

14 NWIFC meets at Ocean Shores for annual meeting.

18 An *Armillaria ostoyae* fungus near Mt. Adams covers 1,500 acres, making it the world's largest living thing.

18 Fictional character, Murphy Brown on the popular *Murphy Brown* TV show, gives birth out of wedlock and sets off controversy from Vice-president down.

20 563 foot cruise ship *Sun King* arrives on Harbor.

22 Johnny Carson's last show.

22 Smoking reported at lowest level in last 37 years.

31 Army starts to build genetic files of service personnel.

Redcedar and spotted owl.

June 1992

1 SAC comes to an end today.

3 U.N. Conference on Environment and Development in Rio de Janeiro is largest summit meeting in history.

13 Taholah fetes its West Point grad, Greg Law.

14 Japan offers $7 billion for earth goals at Earth Summit in Rio de Janeiro.

17 *Yamato 1,* first ship powered by electromagnets on Kobe Bay.

24 Rayonier pulp mill complex up for sale.

24 Native blackberries are nearly a month early and bigger and more abundant than ever.

24 Harbor air-conditioned as rest of state broils.

26 Port drives piles made of plastic that won't pollute at Terminal 2.

28 Earliest and largest peach harvest in state history underway.

26 New Queets bridge on U.S. 101 opens to traffic.

28 Double earthquake, strongest in 40 years strikes Southern California.

July 1992

1 New Queets bridge on U.S. 101 dedicated.

4 Snake River flow hits record low; it has now been below normal for 34 consecutive months.

6 *Sentimental Journey,* a *B-17,* lands at Bowerman air field for a four day visit.

8 Kamp Kiwanis, on Lake Quinault, back from the ashes.

9 Work starts on boring new hole under Chehalis River for phone lines earlier this week. Waterline also approved in wake of deeper draft project.

9 El Nino turns ocean green off Oregon Coast.

19 Extreme fire danger in Western forests.

23 First ever shipment of Russian lumber arrives on Harbor.

26 Quinaults honor Congressman Norm Dicks at Point Grenville Potlatch. More than 500 attend.

August 1992

** Espresso Bars appearing all over county.

26 Hurricane Andrew having caused the greatest natural disaster in U. S. history when it crossed Florida on Monday, slams Louisiana coast.

29 Washington's wildlife "perilously" close to disaster.

September 1992

1 Aberdeen leads way as recycling begins. The whole county should be on line in next 12-16 months.

18 Ban set for all State-land log export.

19 Joe DeLaCruz, president of the Quinault Indian Nation, survives recall bid.

20 Walt Failor, three time Aberdeen mayor and store owner, dies at 81.

20 "Indian" Pete Pickernell, noted Taholah boxer, dies at 90.

21 Last horse race at Longacres. It is being closed to make way for new Boeing headquarters.

22 TV's *Murphy Brown*, takes on Vice-president in fall premier of weekly show.

30 One of strongest red tides on coast, postpones clam season.

October 1992

3 Toxic clean-up of home waste at SouthShore Mall bigger than expected.

9 Scientists say they have created first birth control shot.

13 Billy Frank, Jr., awarded the Albert Schweitzer Prize for Humanitarianism.

14 *The Daily World* relates story of kayaks navigating the Queets Canyon last summer.

16 New highway with view of Mount St. Helens volcano, opens. Second largest project in U.S. history built with Federal emergency funds; $165 million.

21 Voter rolls swell on Twin Harbors.

25 Montesano city council recently unveiled new rest stop proposal on Highway 12.

29 ITT pulp mill closes for what may be the last time.

November 1992

3 Clinton wins in a landslide.

7 Washington, which grows about half of the nation's apples, has a good but mushy crop this year; 66 million

42 pound boxes.

11 Quinault Veterans Memorial dedicated.

12 Asian gypsy moth not a threat to this years Northwest forest.

15 Specialty coffees streaming across the country from Seattle spawning craze.

22 *The Daily World* begins series "A Global Drama on Willapa Bay."

24 *Marshal Krylov* recovers Russian space capsule (launched November 22) 80 miles off Grays Harbor.

December 1992

2 Groups eye orderly growth for Lake Quinault area.

9 Value-added timber products cutting wider swath on Olympic Peninsula.

10 Westport crosses fingers as storm and seas batter seawall.

13 *Ocean of Air* (about the Olympic Peninsula) premiers on the Discovery TV channel.

17 First snow in nearly two years whitens Harbor country.

17 KAYO-AM knocked off air when a cold weasel looking for a warm place crawled into the transmitter area and bit through some wires. Pop! went the weasel.

30 Traffic deaths will hit 30 year low in U.S.; about 39,500.

~ 1993 ~

January 1993

4 "Omar" Youmans, former Hoquiam mayor and county commissioner, dead at 72.

5 Westly Dodd executed by hanging in Washington. First hanging in U.S. since 1965.

6 Harbor jobless rate 14.2%; State level 7.7%.

6 Cigarettes about to be lumped with asbestos as human carcinogen.

6 Dizzy Gillespie, jazz trumpet master, dies at 75.

8 3-7" of snow blanket Twin Harbors.

8 Harbor gives Elvis stamp, stamp of approval.

9 Pacific County Courthouse at South Bend sports new glistening copper dome.

13 Moclips-Cook Creek Road remains covered with ice in cold snap.

13 U.S. lead forces in bombing Iraq.

13 Gov. Booth Gardner's farewell address was an epiphany gleaned from Grays Harbor.

15 Iced-up TV tower on Capitol Peak knocks out Seattle channels on the Harbor.

16 Couple starts Audubon chapter on the Harbor.

17 The 562' tall ASARCO smokestack at Ruston (Tacoma) leveled by explosive as part of environmental clean-up effort.

19 Westport crew snags World War II plane.

20 Clinton becomes 42nd President on a beautiful Washington, D.C. day.

20 Inaugural Day Wind Storm claims five in Washington State.

22 First ever shipment of cars from Harbor, loaded aboard *FESCO Pravdinsk*, bound for Vladivostok Russia.

25 Officials monitoring rivers in wake of heavy rains.

February 1993

8 Espresso like liquid gold for the Harbor.

8 Whitman County highest among State's poor; Harbor in the middle.

16 Out-of-season forest fire near Forks.

24 Wrong turn for smelt sends unexpected bonanza into Quinault and other Harbor rivers.

** One of driest February's on record.

March 1993

4 March rain already tops February as blustery storm blows off the Pacific.

6 State lawmakers urged to avoid coastal Appalachia.

13 State Fisheries and Wildlife to share new digs in Montesano.

13 Quinault Tribal chairman arrested for crossing Police line (*See June 18, 1993*).

17 'Shock and outrage' in wake of railroad's decision on bridge and UP's considering ending rail service to Grays Harbor.

18 Navy to abandon practice bombing runs over Copalis Wildlife Refuge.

23 Gray whales now off endangered list; start early migration off the Grays Harbor coast.

25 Taholah torn by new dispute.

26 Quinaults asserting rights to dig clams off-reservation.

27 Quinault General Council retains police chief.

28 Secretary of Agriculture, Mike Espy, arrives on the Harbor. Governor here, too. Tours Harbor and meets with eleven tribes at Lake Quinault.

29 Espy vows forest ecosystem approach.

April 1993

1 Hundreds duped by radio station in *April Fool* hoax that had space shuttle landing in San Diego.

2 President Clinton convenes Northwest Forestry Conference in Portland.

3 Clinton-Yeltson summit in Vancouver, B.C.

4 Newest calendar from Quinaults, focuses on "Transformations."

7 Charles Clemons, long time judge and historian, dies.

19 Waco stand-off comes to a fiery end.

24 *The Daily World's* "Perspective 1993" issue.

30 Society of American Foresters tour bus rolls off forest road near Porter killing one.

May 1993

5 Ban on State log exports is ruled unconstitutional.

10 Eleven cows stuck on railroad trestle near Central Park.

13 Many small landowners cashing in on high demand for timber.

15 A single old growth Sitka spruce near Forks sells for $22,276.00.

19 The 642-foot *Regent Star*, is largest passenger ship to visit Harbor.

20 The 1,015 passenger ship *Nordic Prince* visits Harbor.

21 Asian immigrants find resentment in competition for wild mushrooms.

22 TV executives chagrined over sweeps; vow less violence.

24 Pollen season packs extra punch this year.

26 Olympic tribes set out on 1,150 mile canoe journey

from LaPush to Qatrwas, B.C.

26 Pat Gallagher, Aberdeen police chief for 20 years, dies at 90.

29 Washington Fisheries and Wildlife Departments to merge.

June 1993

2 ITT Rayonier celebrates planting of 75th million tree. The first one was planted in 1948.

2 Taholah police chief cleared of allegations.

4 East Aberdeen rail project well underway.

5 Pacific Crest Trail completion celebrated along with first National Trails Day.

8 Oakhurst convalescent center in Elma closes.

9 Taholah school heavily damaged by vandals.

10 Aberdeen Police Department's month old bike beat proves successful.

14 Governor Lowry's Hoquiam town meeting, long and lively.

18 DeLaCruz family cleared by jury in stand-off case (*See March 13, 1993*).

19 700,000 old tires being used to repave U.S. 101 from Cosmopolis to Hoquiam from now until end of August.

July 1993

1 Clinton plan whacks logging; Harborites "discouraged" over out come of the forestry conference from last April.

10 U.S.-Japan trade pact caps summit in Tokyo.

18 More rain in Midwest as Mississippi River continues its month and a half flood.

19 County Commissioners sign MOU (making some changes) with QIN.

25 Reforestation work rife with illegal aliens, other conflicting problems.

27 Quinault information center opens at Amanda Park.

31 The Coast Guard's Morse code emergency distress system (in Boston) ends service.

** One of coldest and wettest July's on record across Washington.

** The 32,100 Blueback caught this year is best since 1975, but no where near the half million caught in 1941.

August 1993

3 95° F.

10 Cougar enticed to Kalaloch campground had to be shot after it threatened pets and ate one.

12 Crab crunch divides Harbor-area fishermen.

12 Report laments loss of biological diversity in U.S. National Forest.

17 News report of a 30 million year old whale skeleton found near Pysht.

17 A delegation of twenty Chinese, in timber interest, visit the Quinault Reservation.

18 A.J. West Elementary school begins "year-round school."

18 Former top-secret sub spotting system (*the Pacific Beach facility is one of the relay stations*) finds deep-sea volcano 270 miles west of Astoria. It erupted June 22nd.

28 The *Daily World* features the information center at Amanda Park.

29 Cottonwood plantations raise interest of Harbor area farmers.

31 Quigg group buys the Grays Harbor Paper Mill (closed last November 12, 1992).

31 First seed crop collected from the Quinault Nation Seed Orchard.

31 Senator Pat Murray visits the Quinault Reservation for a Town Meeting.

September 1993

1 Xabaria invasion of Yeltin (Grays Harbor war games) continues.

1 Washington ranks high in book censorship.

8 Weyerhaeuser cuts first crop of taxol.

8 Survey shows 47% of Americans adults possess only rudimentary literacy skills.

9 Austin G. Cooley, who help develop first Fax machine, dead at 93.

11 Boeing rolls out 1,000th *747* jet.

12 Lake Washington span is the symbolic last I-90 link; Seattle to Boston and end to era of Interstate highway building.

12 Raymond "Perry Mason" Burr, dies at 76.

13 Israel and PLO sign historic peace pact.

20 $5.5 million settlement in Weyerhaeuser South Aberdeen Ponds case.

20 Wynooche Dam officially turned over to Aberdeen. First time U.S. Government relinquished control and ownership of a federally built dam.

22 President Clinton outlines health plan.

27 James Doolittle dies at 76.

28 Kathleen Coady becomes Aberdeen's first female beat cop.

29 National accident rate hits lowest level since 1922.

October 1993

2 Hoquiam's Grays Harbor Paper reopening ceremony draws hundreds.

6 Foreign plants, animals do damage in the billions around the country.

13 Diversified cargos are likely to out-pace log exports for the first time in decades at the Port of Grays Harbor.

22 Record El Nino longest on record and may be strengthening.

22 Deeper Draft in deep trouble as Army Corps of Engineers announce it will not proceed until funding questions answered.

28 Coastal tribes air concern over treaty rights concerning the proposed federal marine sanctuary.

November 1993

11 Five crewmen killed and hundreds of cars derailed in train collision near Kelso.

12 Community Hospital buys ultra X-ray machine.

13 Domoic acid in clams causes premature season closure.

17 House passes North America Free Trade Agreement (NAFTA).

18 President Clinton arrives in Seattle for Asian Pacific Economic Cooperation Conference (APEC).

22 Arctic blast blows into state.

23 Nine out of ten major salmon species at risk of extinction, environmentalists say.

30 Dedication of the Quinault Indian Nation's Bernard "Buzz" Bumgarner Memorial Forestry Fire Cache.

December 1993

6 Taholah teens improve math scores.

7 NOAA-42, a *P-3 Orion "Hurricane Hunter"*, spending several weeks off NW coast studying winter storms.

7 Governor Lowery at ground breaking for state's new $35.8 million history museum in Tacoma.

10 Overnight rain and wind hammers Grays Harbor.

11 Savage storm carves new channel at Westport jetty.

13 Astronauts return in triumph after repairs to *Hubble Space Telescope.*

15 General Agreement on Tariffs and Trade (GATT) approved at Geneva.

21 *Washingtonian Print,* second oldest business on Harbor, to close.

24 The last vials of smallpox scheduled to be destroyed, are given a reprieve.

~ 1994 ~

January 1994

3 Dixy Ray, 79, first woman Governor of Washington dies.

6 Barriers going up on Highway 12, coming into Aberdeen, closing two lanes for the next four months of work while crews cut back bluff to widen highway.

17 4:31 a.m., 6.6 earthquake rocks Los Angles.

18 Postal Service pulling back and destroying stamp of Bill Pickett in case of mistaken identity; first in 147 year history of stamp production in the U.S.

23 Ten foot headrig at Weyerhaeuser sawmill in Aberdeen, one of last in Northwest, giving way to a smaller more efficient one.

29 Quinaults steam cedar canoe log in ancient tradition and ceremony at Taholah (*See September 29, 1987 and April 9, 1994*).

31 Woman and 13 children missing overnight on the North Fork of the Quinault River found.

February 1994

8 Port of Grays Harbor grants lease for cottonwood plantation.

11 Old Lokie #3 bids adieu to Harbor and heads for Elbe, Washington.

18 The $3¹/₂ million Lighthouse Suites Inn opens in Ocean Shores.

20 Common bacteria evolving stronger than ever.

23 100 million watch women's figure skating from Olympics on TV.

25 FDA considers calling nicotine a drug.

March 1994

12 Wynooche Dam's new generator humming.

14 Lady bug population exploding on the Harbor and Western Washington.

15 Controversial Quinault Indian Nation police chief told to resign.

17 A marketing manager escapade jolts Port of Grays Harbor. He charged nearly $17,000 in topless table dancing and liquor in New Orleans last summer.

21 75 mph gusts blast the coast.

26 Pearl Baller is first woman elected to head Quinault Indian Nation.

April 1994

5 19th Annual Northwest Indian Youth Conference attended by 700 youths begins four day program in Ocean Shores.

8 Kurt Cobain, Aberdeen-bred rock star of *Nirvana,* commits suicide in Seattle home.

8 Ocean salmon season closed for summer to all commercial and sport fishery.

9 Boeing rolls out its *777.*

9 Quinaults launch ocean canoe with ceremony and a potlatch.

19 Taholah police chief cleared of assault complaint by BIA.

22 Nixon succumbs to a stroke.

23 *The Daily World* "Perspective Issue." One of the features is the Quinault Indian Nation's natural resources program.

26 First black vote begins in South Africa under democratic rule.

27 Five presidents gather to say good-by to Nixon.

29 Pearl Baller, QIN President, and former QIN President, Joe DeLaCruz, attend historic meeting at White House with other representatives of the 547 federally recognized tribes. Clinton issues orders to government agencies to improve relations.

29 $15 million sought for fishing communities in wake of Pacific Northwest salmon crisis.

May 1994

2 Government being strangled by special interest.

5 U.S. teen suffers four lashes in Singapore.

5 Smallest smelt run ever on the Cowlitz River.

6 Queen/Mitterand cut ribbon to open England to France *Chunnel (See December 1, 1990).*

10 Mandela sworn in as South Africa's first black president.

13 Grays Harbor County declared in an emergency status over salmon closure.

13 WPPSS board vote to stop paying $10.5 million per year in preservation cost for two moth balled nuclear plants in an agreement with BPA (takes effect January 13, 1995).

13 The *Cypress Point,* a 56 foot pleasure yacht, launched by Shaw Boat in Aberdeen.

17 Aberdeen's new Wal-Mart has Grand Opening (*it had a "soft opening" on the 14th).*

** KING-TV begins using its own Doppler radar (at SeaTac) to show where precipitation is falling in Western Washington.

June 1994

1 Highland Golf Course opens nine new holes making it an 18 hole course.

9 Canada imposes first-ever fee on U.S. fishing vessels in wake of failure of negotiations of new salmon treaty.

11 New library dedicated in Elma.

13 *777* in nearly perfect first flight.

14 Henry Mancini dies at 70.

15 Sperm whale washes up on South Beach.

16 Nearly half of county kids live in poverty.

16 Gray whale taken off federal endangered species list.

17 Dramatic manhunt ends. O.J. Simpson arrested for murdering his ex-wife and her friend.

18 Mystery bottle washes up on the 13th, uncorks Japanese message.

25 Aberdeen Rotary Log Pavilion dedication.

July 1994

6 *Mighty Morphan Power Rangers* top kids show. O.J. case dominates news.

14 *The Daily World* features the new Olympic Coast National Marine Sanctuary.

14 Ground breaking for the new Quinault Indian Nation Administrative office complex.

16 Dedication of the Olympic Coast National Marine Sanctuary.

16 First of 21 fragments from Comet Shoemaker-Levy 9 explodes into Jupiter.

21 *The Daily World* printed on the *Centralia Chronicle* press due to malfunctioning press.

25 World's oceans fished to the limit.

30 Huge gathering in Taholah to honor Joe DeLaCruz following his retirement for 27 years of service.

August 1994

1 One of the most volatile fire seasons in history in the Western U.S.

8 Geologist adore the Aberdeen exposure.

13 Air Force bombs rattle North Beach residents.

16 First in a series of pros and cons of having a proposed prison near Aberdeen.

17 British Columbia creates huge wilderness tract, containing the world's largest coastal temperate rain forest, 400 miles north of Victoria.

20 Cougar attacks boy on the Olympic Peninsula's Dungeness River.

21 Forest companies pay for surveys of marbled murrelet.

24 Lumber output from Western lumber mills at lowest level in 12 years. Sixth straight year production has decreased, yet wholesale value rose 15%.

26 Filming begins near Point Grenville for the movie Katie. (*Later retitled* Born to be Wild.)

29 Four babies boost world population each second.

September 1994

3 Quinaults flourish with less federal bureaucracy.

7 Three large new steel pipes now mark southern boundary of the Quinault Reservation on the beach at Moclips.

13 World Series called-off in wake of baseball strike. First time there will be no World Series since 1904.

21 After months of intense debate, Harbor voters favor locating a prison along the south side of Grays Harbor.

October 1994

4 Undersea earthquake off Japan sets off Tsunami warning here.

12 Ivan the Gorilla leaves Tacoma for Atlanta.

16 Antibiotics losing the fight against infection.

18 Bodies of two crewmen found in tuna boat which sank dock side in Westport on Friday (14th).

20 Burt Lancaster dies.

22 Northwest split from nation in forest views.

25 Reports of massive oil spill in Russia.

26 Wind and rain batter area, but damage slight. Ship breaks loose and drifts into bridge at Astoria.

28 State and federal prison population surpasses one million this year.

31 Halloween morning storm no treat.

November 1994

5 Former President Reagan discloses he has Alzheimer's disease.

7 Largest U.S. harvest ever of corn and soybeans nears completion.

8 Republican tidal wave now dominates both House and Senate for the first time since Eisenhower.

17 *Lady Washington* has staring role in the release of the feature film *Star Trek 7- Generations.*

17 All day shooting at Preachers Slough on the Chehalis River for a scene in the Imax movie *The Great American West.*

19 Youngster discovers bell believed to be hung in Hoquiam's first church from 1890-1904 (First Presbyterian Church).

30 Soggy storm slams coast. Seven inches of rain at Lake Quinault in past two days.

December 1994

1 Moclips Bridge on State 109 is open after nearly two day closure due to high water. Rock added to seawall at Taholah as ocean waves sweep over the spit at the mouth of the river.

3 Homeless families could number 200 here.

3 Shoalwaters want pollution study done.

14 Power outage hits eight states; 28,000 on Harbor.

17 Series begins in *The Daily World* on timber industry's future.

20 Historic ruling on Indian shellfish rights.

21 Rising rivers, raging surf disrupt lives on the Harbor.

~ 1995 ~

January 1995

1 Postage rates go from 29¢ to 32¢.

9 U.S. (Washington) apples make their debut in Japan.

15 206 area code becomes 360 for Harbor.

17 Devastating earthquake hits Kobe, Japan.

24 Harbor picked for state prison.

24 Nation, world watches first day of O.J. Simpson's trial.

25 Saving Northwest salmon pegged at $160 million per year.

25 El Nino two times as strong as in 92-93.

28 5.0 earthquake rattles Puget Sound.

** Warmest January on record for Seattle area.

** *The Tree People,* a novel set at Quinault by Naomi Stokes, published this month..

February 1995

3 A report from a special panel of the National Marine Fisheries Service (NMFS) says that wild Steelhead are not endangered on the Olympic Peninsula.

10 U.S. Weather Service commissions a Doppler radar system on Camano Island.

12 Cold and snow interrupt spring-like weather.

18 Shortages to change American diet by 2050 due to population growth.

19 World's 6,000 languages are quickly dying off. Only 600 may survive to 2100. (There were once nearly 13,000).

20 Harbor soaked, but only minor flooding.

23 71% over the age of 25 are overweight in the U.S.

28 Weyco here to stay, but Cosi dicey.

March 1995

5 Pearl Capoeman-Baller, QIN President, featured in the *Daily World's* newest regular Sunday feature, "Profiles."

9 Storm KO's power, but no injuries.

14 Norman Thagard, first American launched on a Russian rocket.

16 Thagard arrives aboard the *Mir Space Station.*

25 Quinaults vote to study casino gambling at their annual General Council Meeting.

April 1995

2 Baseball strike ends without lasting peace.

7 Union Pacific closes Chehalis River railroad bridge at Aberdeen.

9 Long awaited Dike Project, begins in South Aberdeen.

12 Rail service to Aberdeen in jeopardy as Port seeks federal funds.

14 Folk singer, Burl Ives, dies.

15 Farmers Market has grand opening in Hoquiam.

19 Bombing of Federal Building in Oklahoma City most devastating terrorist attack ever inside the U.S.

20 New Area Codes creating "black holes" in the U.S.

26 Scientists using giant crane to study old growth forest canopy at Wind River.(*Vocal opposition from residents prevented the crane from being located on USFS land near Lake Quinault.*)

May 1995

8 A young Gray whale appears in the Chehalis River near Cosi.

9 Hoquiam couple win $4 million Lottery.

19 Gulls a big hit despite 4-3 loss as pro-baseball returns to the Harbor.

20 World War II mine caught in fish net near Coos Bay, OR.

27 Ford joins others in largest recall in history because of defective seat belts.

28 Eight billion cigarettes recalled

June 1995

4 Hoh Rain Forest Campground closed as a mother elk chased people into their RV's and a cougar appears in the campground.

6 Oklahoma City bomb plans, allegedly stolen in an Aberdeen warehouse burglary seven years ago.

10 *Lucky Eagle Casino* opens near Oakville on the Chehalis Indian Reservation.

20 GH County expects to spend $53.5 million on roads and bridges in next six years.

28 *Carson & Barnes'* 5 ring circus appears in Aberdeen.

29 The American shuttle *Atlantis* and the Russian *Mir* complex dock in space.

29 The Supreme Court rules that Government regulators can ban destruction of the natural homes of endangered or threatened species on private property.

29 Last two days the hottest of the year. 93°F in Hoquiam yesterday.

July 1995

2 Wolfman Jack, popular disc jockey, dies at 57.

3 U.S. 101 realignment on Cosi Hill nears completion.

5 Dr. David Lush opens the 18,000 sq. ft. Riverview Medical Clinic in Raymond.

8 A more affordable link to the Internet is now available on the Harbor.

15 Ribbon-cutting for the new Olympic Natural Resources Center in Forks. (*To manage the Clearwater Experimental Forest.*)

18 95°F in Aberdeen.

22 *The Daily World* begins looking at methamphetamine; the biggest drug problem on the Harbor today.

** A mere 207 Blueback netted this season; all time low. (*22,000 fish did make it to escapement.*)

August 1995

6 One day August rainfall shattered: 1.79" in Hoquiam, 4.16" in Forks, and 3.71" in Ocean Shores.

11 Shilo is Ocean Shores newest and biggest hotel.

12 Three slain at McCleary; teen and friend in custody.

13 Mickey Mantle dies.

18 Ron Mullins, candidate for mayor of Elma, accused of illegally dumping untreated septic sludge on the QIR.

20 360 area code becomes mandatory.

21 Federal budget cuts put crimp in USFS timber research.

21 Pope and Talbott announces it will close mill in Port Gamble this October after 142 years of operation.

22 *Gulls* play final season home game before 5,156.

23 Tribal leaders decry Senate's proposed cuts.

24 *Windows 95* introduced in Microsoft media blitz.

29 Western Cedar Recycle business set to open in Hoquiam.

September 1995

2 Ceremonies mark 50th anniversary of the signing of Japan's surrender. Today, the U.S. and Japan is the world's odd-couple partnership.

3 Lighting fills the night sky along the Washington Coast.

6 Cal Ripken plays 2,131 consecutive baseball games, breaking Lou Gehrig's 56 year old record.

7 Thirty-nine Harbor built homes heading for Indians near Nome, Alaska.

13 Rayonior says new building affirms Hoquiam commitment at open house at ribbon cutting celebration.

21 Indian leaders call delays and cuts to forestry programs "senseless."

21 Crane flies and late tomato blight bugging area residents.

22 Quinaults dedicate their new Administrative Complex with ribbon cutting and open house.

28 New $100 bill introduced.

29 Federal program gives more Quinaults homes of their own.

30 PTI takes over phone systems in parts of Grays Harbor and Pacific Counties.

October 1995

2 Mariners win Western Baseball Championship in special play-off game.

3 O. J. Simpson acquitted.

4 Hoquiam recycle pick-up begins.

8 M's win in one of the greatest post season series in baseball history.

16 Million Man March; Black men rally in Washington, D.C.

The young and old forest of Grays Harbor.

31 Its now unlawful to feed birds in Aberdeen parks.

** UW reports that evidence from an account of a Tsunami in Japan and in deposits found along the Northwest coast, suggest that a magnitude 9 earthquake off the coast of Washington/Oregon resulted in a 30 foot Tsunami on January 26, 1700.

November 1995

4 Assassin kills Israeli leader, Yitzhak Rabin.

4 North Shore Road at Lake Quinault reopens after five year closure (the South Shore Road would wash out four days later).

11 Werner Mayr, pioneer logger, dies.

14 Federal government workers sent home in wake of stalemate over budget (they return to work on the 20th).

14 U.N. Report says 30,000 species face extinction.

17 Stiff winds knock out power to many in G.H. County.

27 Aberdeen gets nearly 4" of rain.

30 This November one of the wettest in 30 years.

December 1995

2 Quinaults seeking artifacts returned.

3 Large numbers of Fulmars, a gull-like bird of the open sea, found dead on North Beaches. 83 were counted in one mile at Pacific Beach.

4 Tribes crack crab market.

7 *Galileo's* probe parachutes into Jupiter's atmosphere and the spacecraft itself goes into successful orbit.

9 National 55 mph speed limit ends.

12 Harbor spared worst of violent storm. Peak gust of 97 mph at Westport.

14 Crowd of 250 split on Quinault Casino plan at State Gaming Commission information meeting in Ocean Shores.

20 Historic Humptulips Grade School burns down.

~ 1996 ~

January 1996

1 Leaded gasoline now banned.

5 Researchers report 1995 as the warmest year ever.

7 Keiko, the killer whale from the *Free Willy* movie, moved from Mexico City to Newport, Oregon.

30 Bassett Murder trial and violent dogs dominate this month's local news.

30 15°F. - frigid weather to remain.

31 Clinton names Guy McMinds as one of three commissioners on the North Pacific Anadromous Fish Commission.

February 1996

2 McDonald "guilty" in two of the Bassett murders.

2 Harbor newsman, Ade Fredericksen, dies.

2 Gene Kelly dies.

9 East county bears the brunt of flood waters raging across the Northwest; I-5 closed at Chehalis due to flooding.

15 60-70° and sunny this week.

17 Rear wall pulled down on the 1906 Weir Theater in Aberdeen, after the roof collapsed the night before.

25 Francis McCrory featured in *The Daily World's* Profiles.

March 1996

2 SeaTac Airport records soggiest four month period since record keeping began in the mid-40's.

3 Smoke Shop in Aberdeen closes after 80 years.

6 Dismantling the Union Pacific railroad bridge over the Chehalis River at Aberdeen has begun.

9 George Burns dies just weeks after turning 100.

22 Bassett "guilty" on all counts.

April 1996

1 Bassett gets three consecutive life sentences.

2 Photograph appears in *The Daily World* of Hyakutake's comet which recently shone in the Harbor's northern night sky.

2 Freon number two smuggling problem behind illegal drugs.

11 Mayr Bros. may have sawn its last log.

14 Quads born to Hoquiam couple.

23 Twin Harbors spared the worst of storm.

27 Bill Jones, photographer/historian, named citizen of the year in *The Daily World's Perspectives* issue.

27 Quinault Hereditary chief Oliver Mason dies.

29 McDonald's opens in Raymond.

May 1996

18 Pacific Paradise Family Fun Center now open in Ocean Shores.

18 Driest spring in 100 years in Oklahoma.

31 Timothy Leary drops out of life at age 75.

June 1996

1 State Gambling Commission approves the Quinault Nation's plans to build a casino at the Sampson Johns Allotment near Ocean Shores.

15 Marbled murrelet ruling limiting logging upheld in court.

16 Ralph Flowers, bear expert, featured in *The Daily World's* Sunday Profile.

19 Northwest honey bee populations declining due to parasitic mites.

21 Emerald Downs opens after four year absence of thoroughbred horse racing.

25 *Metallica* frenzy as the heavy metal band hits Aberdeen.

July 1996

9 Governor Lowry signs compact with Quinaults for casino at beach.

14 104° in Montesano. Aberdeen's 92° nears July record.

14 Grays Harbor Port legend, John Stevens, dead at 85.

17 747 with 228 people explodes off Long Island.

19 The 26th Summer Olympics open in Atlanta as the Centennial Games.

28 Ancient skeleton found in Kennewick (*See September 8*).

30 Olympic Peninsula Steelhead not on "endangered list."

August 1996

7 Quinaults buying the Marina at Ocean Shores.

7 Quinault sturgeon catch may complicate allocation.

7 NASA scientists say a rock from Mars provides evidence of possible ancient microbial life there.

8 South side/Cosi dike 80% done and coming in on budget.

10 New Washington State Historical Museum opens in Tacoma.

19 John Kendrick's descendant, visits Aberdeen. (*See October 1787 - December 1794.*)

19 Jail and prison population in U.S. soaring.

21 Spectacular fire guts Aberdeen landmark. Fire destroys the Smoke Shop Building, the old Roxy Theater, and spreads to the Finch Building.

21 Bremerton to lose the battleship *Missouri "Mighty Mo"* to Pearl Harbor.

23 President Clinton declares tobacco an addictive drug.

23 Scientists announce they have decoded the genes of the microbe *Methanococcus jannaschii,* found in near-boiling water on the ocean floor, and say it is a member of a third major branch of life.

September 1996

3 The Puyallup's $32 million Chief Leschi School near Tacoma opens.

5 Last winter's severe flooding has brought a rebirth of salmon habitat in many (Oregon) streams.

8 9,000 year old skeleton sparks controversy. (*See July 28, 1996.*)

10 Grays Harbor will produce 15 million tons of corn this year.

10 Bronze logging sculpture erected in Morrison Park. (*See November 23.*)

13 REI opens its new flagship store in Seattle.

13 Washington farmers harvested a record 182.7 million bushels of wheat.

16 North Beach High School begins the school year, after delays to repair the building.

18 Anatoly Shimansky, the Roaming Russian, passing through the Grays Harbor region with his "buggy" and Belgian draft horse. He is on a transcontinental quest to discover America.

18 Thousands of tons of logs removed in reconstruction of Point Brown Road in Ocean Shores.

19 Quinault Pearl Capoeman-Baller confers with President Clinton during his bus caravan from Tacoma to Portland.

24 Harbor ranks high in '90-94 pollution study.

26 Astronaut Shannon Lucid returns to earth after 188 days and 5 hours in space; sets record for woman longest in space.

26 Beautiful copper colored lunar eclipse rises out of the early evening haze over the Harbor.

27 Port of Grays Harbor learning center taking shape.

28 Fire destroys Major Line Cabinet Mill in Hoquiam.

30 Bill Gates richest U.S. man at $18.5 billion.

October 1996

3 Promising experiment fertilizes ocean with iron in the equatorial Pacific.

4 Women crew of the Washington Conservation Corps building new board walk at the Bowerman National Wildlife Refuge.

5 Rockslide on the Aberdeen Bluff blocks part of highway.

6 Seymour Cray, developer of the use of transistors in computers, dies.

7 Frank Pickernell wins series championship of the Coast Canoe Club season.

9 Douglas Osheroff, an Aberdeen native, wins Nobel Prize for physics.

9 Scientists begin erosion study along the Washington coast.

12 Third cranberry Festival at Grayland.

13 Fire destroys historic Aloha Mill Shop.

15 The Quinault's proposed casino is approved by the Secretary of Interior.

17 Lake Quinault Community Action Forum attempts to unify communities near the lake.

19 Rock bumpers only band-aid to arrest erosion at Ocean Shores.

20 Speed limit to increasing from 55 to 60 mph between Montesano and Olympia.

24 Clarence Esses, logger, dies.

25 Violations of athletic code prompts Hoquiam High School to cancel remaining football games.

31 Reggi Ward, promoter of coastal tribal culture, dies.

November 1996

5 Clinton reelected president and Gary Locke, the nation's first Chinese-American chief-executive, elected Governor.

10 Helen Sanders featured in *The Daily World* Sunday Profiles.

11 Crab conflict growing as Indian crab fishermen move closer to claiming their 50% share.

11 Swiss needle cast, *Phaeocryptopus gaeumanni,* attacking millions of Douglas fir along the Oregon coast.

11 Washington DNR land sustainable harvest rate set at 655 million bd. ft.

15 Hundreds of anglers line Humptulips and other county rivers for a chance at hooking salmon.

19 Early snow whitens most of the Harbor.

21 Methane hydrates discovered off the Oregon coast could become energy source.

23 "Tribute to Logging," a bronze sculpture, unveiled at Morrison Park.

December 1996

2 Scientists find evidence of ice at the moon's south pole.

1-5 A *Seattle Times* special HUD report: *Tribal Housing.* The last article in the series features Quinault Housing. (*This series goes on to win a Pulitzer-prize in March 1997.*)

15 Boeing in proposed mega-merger with MacDonnell Douglas.

17 Green meteor-like flash over Western Washington.

20 Noted astronomer Carl Sagan dies.

26 Ice storm causes East county havoc.

29 Puget Sound buried under snow.

29 Bluff, on Hwy. 12 entrance to Aberdeen, collapses sending 10,000 cubic yards of mud and rock across all four lanes.

~ 1997 ~

January 1997

1 '96 blasts out, '97 comes in with gusto.

3 TV stations begin to use new TV rating system.

25 Technological Industry now employees more than natural resources in Washington State.

February 1997

1 *World Gone By* series featuring history from *The Daily World* begins its run in *The Daily World.*

12 Three Coast Guard men die in rescue attempt near La Push.

17 Scottish Scientists disclose they have cloned a sheep from adult cells.

28 Anyone under 27 must show ID to get cigarettes.

March 1997

3 Quinaults clear major land-use hurdle for casino.

10 BIA is now fully operational in their new office in Aberdeen near Community Hospital.

19 More than 20" of rain has fallen in the last two days at Wynooche Dam, melting much of the snow. Montesano isolated as 100 year flood waters from the Wynooche and Satsop rivers cover Highway 12.

20 *Asphalt Nation* by Jane Holtz Kay published.

23 A lunar eclipse, Hale-Bopp comet, and Mars provide an astronomical triple delight over the Harbor.

30 Wicked Easter windstorm rips coast.

April 1997

1 The failure of the old Makinowski log dam during the rain storm of March 18-19 has kept Aberdeen under a boil-water advisory since March 22nd. Hoquiam is offering free water to Aberdeen residence at a spigot outside Olympic Stadium.

5 Pearl Capoeman-Baller re-elected QIN Chairman at the Annual General Council Meeting.

6 Predator European green crab creeps northward along coast; turns up in Coos Bay.

13 *A History of Lake Quinault Lodge* by R. H. Jones is now available.

16 Cigarette makers negotiating $300 billion settlement.

23 BIA opens new Aberdeen office with celebration.

26 *The Daily World* Perspectives issue *"Changing Tides"* is one of largest in the newspapers history.

May 1997

11 After 17 years of publishing on a main frame computer system, *The Daily World* has installed a half million dollar Apple Macintosh-based system.

11 90° in Aberdeen is hottest May 11th in 31 years.

17 Johnston Ridge Observatory opens at Mt. St. Helens.

18 Quinault exhibit opens at the Polson Museum.

19 The South Aberdeen-Cosmopolis Dike dedicated.

29 Evidence shows that millions of house-size "snowballs" strike the Earth's atmosphere every year.

June 1997

2 Timothy McVeigh convicted of murder and conspiracy in the April 19, 1995 bombing of the federal building in Oklahoma City. (*He would later be sentenced to death.*)

5 New agreement gives tribal plans to protect fish and wildlife on Indian lands priority over government enforcement of the Endangered Species Act.

12 Baseball Interleague games make history.

20 Landmark tobacco deal will limit ads and sales. "The most historic public health achievement in history."

20 Dr. Doug Osheroff, Nobel Prize winner, gives commencement address at GHC.

20 Gov. Locke and his family move out of the Governor's mansion until it is rid of bats.

22 Studies discover that Pacific salmon are getting smaller.

25 Jacques Cousteau, famed sea explorer and film maker, dead at 87.

29 Blacktail deer in Western Washington beset by

mysterious disease which manifests itself with large bald patches, bluish skin, and white blotches on the remaining fur.

28 Mike Tyson disqualified after he bites ears of Evander Holyfield during heavy weight boxing match.

30 The *Mir* space station back under control after collision with cargo ship four days earlier.

30 Hong Kong rejoins China at midnight after 156-year-old British rule.

** *The Listening Ones,* a novel set on the Quinault Reservation by Naomi Stokes published.

July 1997

2 Common murrers, (*sea birds*), are starving along the Oregon coast, north to Point Grenville in Washington; could signal ominous changes.

2 Actor James Stewart, dies at 89.

3 The tug boat *Marie M* sinks off Westport at the mouth of Grays Harbor in calm water. One crew member still missing.

4 *Pathfinder* lands on Mars and broadcasts live public TV pictures.

5 Canoes roar at Taholah Days.

21 *Malaspina*, an Alaskan ferry, blockaded at Prince Rupert by Canadian fishing boats in U.S./Canada salmon fishing dispute.

23 Ocean Spray Cranberries Inc. plans to close its bottling line at Markham this mid-fall.

25 Ammonia leak at Ocean spray send eleven to hospital.

29 Pollution cancels Clean Water Oyster Feed at Elk River.

30 Puget Sound & Pacific Railway Company has signed an agreement to acquire the routes between Grays Harbor and Centralia, and between Shelton and Elma from Burlington Northern and Santa Fe Railway Company. (*They begin operations at 12:01 a.m. on August 30.*)

** Just over 2,500 Blueback caught this season.

August 1997

1 Washington's welfare system begins tracking how long people stay on welfare with a five-year lifetime limit for public assistance.

4 McDonnell Douglas merges with Boeing.

4 Ground Breaking for the Quinault Indian Nation's new Department of Natural Resources Building.

6 Microsoft Corp. and Apple Computer, Inc., unveil alliance.

7 Secretary of the Interior, Bruce Babbitt, visits the Quinault Indian Reservation.

11 BIA denies federal recognition to the Chinook tribe.

12 Grays Harbor County, the Port, and PUD vote to pursue the formation of a new agency to be charged with marketing and operations of the terminated Satsop nuclear site.

19 The two week old UPS strike comes to an end.

22 25 million pounds of beef, possibly tainted with E. Coli bacteria, recalled.

26 El Nino of the century may be looming.

26 A mini-twister near Elma picks up a car and driver and puts them back down. Summer storm plagues Western Washington.

31 Britain's Princess Diana killed in Paris car crash.

31 25th Kelper's Parade in Moclips/Pacific Beach. (*Began in 1973 when some clam digging tourist held an impromptu parade on the Labor Day Weekend.*)

September 1997

2 Gulls win first-ever playoff; 11-7 over Reno at Olympic Stadium.

3 A 104 pound Marlin caught off Westport; likely sign of El Nino.

3 Quinault President, Pearl Capoeman-Baller, along with 200 other tribal leaders in Washington, D. C. to combat Congressional proposals that would take away sovereign immunity.

4 Mosquitoes driving Harborites to itchy distraction.

5 Big Rock Point, the nation's oldest and smallest nuke plant near Charlevoix, Michigan, closes.

5 Mother Teresa, who dedicated her life to helping the poor and outcast, dies at age 87.

9 Bowerman Field airport available for sale if Nucor Steel decides to locate here.

12 Harborite, Rita McMahon, dies in helicopter crash on a search and rescue operation near Mount Baldy.

14 $6.8 luxury yacht launched from the Westport Shipyard.

17 Comedian Red Skelton dies at 84.

18 Late summer rain has left its mark; nearly $7^1/_2''$ on the coast in five days.

21 *The Daily World* begins a six part series on an overview of Nucor Steel.

October 1997

6 The Quinault Indian Nation files a complaint in U.S. District Court in Tacoma against the BIA and the Department of Interior for their refusal to make public all records and evidence in the Cowlitz and Chinook petitions seeking federal recognition.

8 A half million dollars damage from vandalism done to heavy machinery on the Stafford Creek Prison construction site.

9 Harbor weathers blustery storm.

11 Governor Locke visits Jilong, China, his ancestral home, while on a week long trade mission to China.

12 Singer John Denver killed in experimental airplane crash.

13 Andy Green unofficially speeds to 764 mph, breaking the sound barrier in a British rocket powered car. (*He officially breaks it the following day.*)

14 One out of every fourteen Washington drivers, has no drivers license.

15 The *Cassini* spacecraft is launched on trek to Saturn.

16 Author James Michener dies.

16 Pacific decadal oscillation, or PDO, is a phenomena where it takes 20 to 30 years to shift ocean temperatures, spreading climatic fluctuations and effect salmon populations, say UW scientist.

17 Rep. Jack Metcalf and animal protection advocates file a lawsuit against the U.S. to block the Makahs from whaling off the Olympic coast.

17 Parrotfeather, an aquatic plant native to the Amazon

River, is blossoming in the Chehalis River and may lead to environmental problems.

18 The Women in Military Services for America Memorial dedicated in Washington, D.C.

18 Benny Charley Field dedicated at Taholah.

18 Americans set a record by consuming more than 336 million gallons of gasoline a day for the first eight months of this year. Consumption peaked at 356 million gallons per day in July.

20 *The Daily World,* introduces a new name plate and layout design.

24 The book *Land of Trees* published.

**

**

**

November 1997

December 1997

January 1998

February 1998

March 1998

April 1998

May 1998

June 1998

July 1998

August 1998

September 1998

October 1998

November 1998

December 1998

January 1999

February 1999

March 1999

April 1999

May 1999

June 1999

July 1999

August 1999

September 1999

October 1999

November 1999

December 1998

January 2000

February 2000

March 2000

April 2000

May 2000

June 2000

July 2000

August 2000

September 2000

October 2000

November 2000

December 2000

CONSUMER PRICE INDEX
Based on Urban Wage Earners and Clerical Workers
Bureau of Labor Statistics Data
Base Period: 1967=100

Year	Index		Year	Index
1850	25.0		1980	247.0
1900	28.0		1885	318.5
1910	29.7		1990	384.4
1915	30.4		1995	446.1
1920	60.0		1996	459.1
1925	52.5		1997 *(first six months)*	467.7
1930	50.0			
1935	41.1			
1940	42.0			
1945	53.9			
1950	72.1			
1955	80.2			
1960	88.7			
1965	94.5			
1970	116.3			
1975	161.2			

This chart allows you to find the relative value of the dollar in any given year compared to today's dollar.

Divide the current year index (1997) by the earlier year and multiple by the dollar figure. For example, an ox sold for $11.00 in 1850.

$467.7 \div 25.0 = 18.708 \times \$11.00 = \$205.79.$

Using the same arithmetic, you would find that $5.00 in 1997 would have been worth $24.71 in 1965, $32.39 in 1950, $56.82 in 1935, $78.64 in 1910, or $93.42 in 1850.

CENSUS

Year	Aberdeen	Hoquiam	Montesano	Elma	Grays Harbor	Washington
1880	<200	<200	<200	---	921	75,116
1890	1,638	1,302	1,632	345	6,238	357,232
1900	3,747	2,608	1,194	894	15,124	518,103
1910	13,660	8,171	2,488	1,532	35,590	1,141,990
1920	15,337	10,058	2,158	1,253	44,745	1,356,621
1930	21,723	12,766	2,460	1,545	59,982	1,563,369
1940	18,846	10,835	2,224	1,370	53,166	1,736,191
1950	19,653	11,123	2,328	1,543	53,644	2,378,963
1960	18,741	10,762	2,486	1,811	54,465	2,853,214
1970	18,489	10,466	2,847	2,227	59,553	3,413,244
1980	18,739	9,719	3,247	2,720	66,314	4,132,156
1990	16,565	8,972	3,060	3,011	64,314	4,866,663
2000						

BIBLIOGRAPHY

The majority of this work is from the micro film file of *The Daily World* at the Aberdeen Timberland Library. Original copies and micro film of the Montesano *Vidette* at the Montesano Timberland Library also provide an important source of information, particularly from 1884 to 1904. The *Weekly Puget Sound Courier, Olympic Transcript,* and the *Washington Standard,* all of Olympia, also provided some information as did *The North Coast News* of Ocean Shores.

The following publications provided additional information:

Bagley, Clarence B. *In the Beginning.* (First published in March 1905). Everett, WA: The Historical Society of Seattle and King County, 1980.

Bancroft, Hubert Howe. *History of the Northwest Coast.* 2 volumes. New York, New York: The Bancroft Company, 1880.

Brown, Bruce. *Mountains in the Clouds; A Search for the Wild Salmon.* New York, NY: Simon and Schuster, 1982.

Capoeman, Pauline K., editor. *Land of the Quinault.* Taholah, WA: Quinault Indian Nation, 1990.

Carey, Charles H. LLD. *A General History of Oregon.* 2 volumes. Portland, OR: Metropolitan Press. 1935.

Cook, Warren L. *Flood Tide of Empire.* New Haven, CT: Yale University Press. 1973.

Cotton, Anne. *Historical Sites in Grays Harbor County, Washington.* Aberdeen, WA: Grays Harbor Regional Planning Commission, January 1973.

Crose, Michael A. *Timberland: A History of Library Development in Washington.* Olympia, WA: Master of Public Administration Theses, Evergeen State College. 1985.

Daniel, Clifton, editor. *Chronicle of the 20th Century.* Mount Kisco, NY: Chronicle Publications, 1987.

Davies, John. *Douglas of the Forests: The North American Journals of David Douglas.* Seattle, WA: University of Washington Press. 1980.

Davis, Mary B., editor. *Native America in the Twentieth Century: An Encyclopedia.* New York, NY: Garland Publishing, Inc. 1994.

Deegan, W. Dr. Harry. *History of Mason County.* Shelton, WA: ? , 1971

Denny, Arthur A. *Pioneer Days on Puget Sound.* Fairfield, WA: Ye Galleon Press, 1965.

Felt, Margaret Elley. *Capitol Forest; the Forest that Came Back.* Olympia, WA: Washington State Department of Natural Resources, July, 1975.

Felt, Margaret Elley. *Rivers to Reckon With.* Forks, WA: Olympic Graphic Arts, Inc., 1985.

Ford, Sidney, et al. *Reports from the Quinaielt Indian Agency 1857-1902.* Copies on file at the Quinault Historical Foundation, Taholah, WA.

Greenhow, Robert. *The History of Oregon and California and the Other Territories of the North-West Coast of North America.* Original, Boston: Charles C. Little and James Brown, 1844; Facsimile, Los Angeles, CA: Sherwin & Freutel Publishers, 1970.

Harris, Stephen. *Fire and Ice; The Cascade Volcanoes.* Seattle, WA: The Mountaineers, April 1976.

Howay, F.W. *A List of Trading Vessels in the Maritime Fur Trade, 1785-1825.* (Edited by Richard A. Pierce). Kingston, Ontario: The Limestone Press, 1973.

Howell, Erle. *Methodism in the Northwest*. Nashville, TN: The Parthenon Press Printers, 1966.

James, Karen and Martino, Victor. *Grays Harbor and Native Americans*. Seattle, WA: U.S. Army Corps of Engineers, Seattle District, October 1986.

Jensen, Malcolm C. *America in Time; America's history year by year through text and pictures*. Boston, Mass: Houghton Miffin Company, 1977.

Kay, Jane Holtz. *Asphalt Nation*. New York, NY: Crown Publishers, Inc., 1997.

Lucia, Ellis. *Tillamook Burn Country* Caldwell, ID: The Caxton Printers, Ltd, 1983..

Marston, Elizabeth. *Rain Forest*. Boston, MA: Branden Press Publisher, New edition 1974.

Martin, Paul. *Port Angeles, Washington: A History*. Port Angeles, WA: Peninsula Publishing, Inc., 1983

Meany Edmond S. *Vancouver's Discovery of Puget Sound*. London: The Macmillan Company, 1915.

Mears, John. *Voyages Made in the Years 1788 and 1789, From China to the North West Coast of America*. London: Logographic Press, 1790.

Morishima, Gary and Workman, Larry. *Portrait of Our Land*. Taholah, WA: Quinault Indian Nation, 1978.

Morris, Richard B., editor. *Encyclopedia of American History*. New York, NY: Harpor & Row, Publishers, 1970.

Morgan, Murray. *Puget's Sound*. Seattle, WA: University of Washington Press, 1979.

Mourelle, Don Francisco Antonio. *Voyage of the Sonora in the Second Bucareli Expedition; A Journal kept in 1775 on the Sonora*. Translated by Daines Barrington and published in London in 1781. San Francisco, California: Thomas C. Russel, 1920.

Murray, Keith A. *The Pig War*. Pacific Northwest Historical Pamphlet No. 6. Tacoma, WA: Washington State Historical Society, April 1968.

Newell, Gorden. *History of Olympia and Thurston County, Washington*. Olympia, WA: Warren's Printing and Graphic Arts Co., 1950.

Newell, Gordon. *Rogues, Buffoons, and Statesmen*. Seattle, WA: Superior Publishing Company, 1975 .

Olsen, Mrs. Nels, editor. *The Willapa County: History Report*. Part 3 of the Community Betterment Study. Raymond, WA: Raymond Herald and Advertiser, 1965. (*Be careful of information in some sections of this report.*)

Owens, Kenneth N. and Donnelly, Alton S. *The Wreck of the Sv. Nikolai*. Portland, OR: Western Imprints, The Oregon Historical Society, 1985.

Quinn, Daniel. *Ishmael*. New York, NY: A Bantam/Turner Booh, February 1992.

Randall, J.G. and Donald, Dave. *The Civil War and Reconstruction*. Boston, Mass: D.C. Heath and Company, 1961.

Roe, Joann. *Seattle Uncovered*. Seattle, WA: Seaside Press, 1996.

Rue, Walter. *Weather of the Pacific Coast*. Mercer Island, WA: The Writing Works, Inc. 1978.

Schlesinger, Arthur M. Jr. *The Almanac of American History*. New York, NY: Barnes and Noble Book, 1993.

Schlesinger, Arthur M. Jr., editor. *The Almanac of American History*. New York, NY: G. P. Putnam's Sons, A Bison Book, 1983.

Schoenberg, Wilfred P. *A History of the Catholic Church in the Pacific Northwest: 1743-1983*. Washington, DC: The Pastoral Press, 1987.

Smith, Alleck *Survey of the Quinaielt Indian Reservation 1861*.

Spencer, James. *Rayonier: Northwest Loggers, Volume 1*. Burbank, CA: Darwin Publications. 1982

Stokes, Naomi M. *The Tree People*. New York, NY: Forge, St Martin Press, January 1995.

Ullman, Bud; Lane, Barbara; and Smith, Hazel. *Handbook on Legislation and Litigation Affecting the Quinault Reservation*. Taholah, WA: Quinault Indian Nation, March 2, 1977.

Van Syckle, Edwin. *Brief Historical Sketch of Grays Harbor Washington*. Aberdeen, WA: Rayonier, Incorp., January 1942.

VanSyckle, Edwin. *The River Pioneers; Early Days on Grays Harbor*. Seattle, WA: Pacific Search Press, 1982.

Vaughn, Wade. *Puget Sound Invasion*. Seattle, WA: Leschi Improvement Council, 1975.

Weiner, Ed, entail all. *The TV Guide, TV Book*. New York, NY: Harper Perennial. 1992.

Wood Robert, L. *Across the Olympic Mountains; The Press Expedition 1889-90*. Seattle, WA: The Mountaineers, 1967.

Wood, Robert L. *Men, Mules and Mountains; Lieutenant O'Neil's Olympic Expeditions*. Seattle, WA: The Mountaineers, 1976.

About Larry J. Workman

Larry was born in Franklin, Indiana on October 24, 1947, to Jack and Martha "Schroer" Workman. He attended school in Edinburg, Indiana. He enrolled at Purdue University, first in the forestry program, but switched into conservation to get a wider perspective of the environmental sciences.

From 1970-1973 he volunteered to a Peace Corps reforestation assignment in Northern Ethiopia and developed an ardent interest in human-land relationships.

He started working for the Quinault Indian Nation (QIN) in 1974, helping to lay the foundations for the forestry program. His interest in assisting people gain a greater understanding of natural sciences, surfaced in the QIN publication *Portrait of Our Land* (1978). Since 1979, Larry has helped produced the annual QIN calendar, a newsletter which grew into a magazine called *Quinault Natural Resources*, and other publications such as the nationally acclaimed book, *Land of the Quinault* (1990).

From these publications came a growing store of knowledge of this area's history and its consequences to the health of the land, the people, and the culture. It was from these observations that this book, *Land of Trees*, was born.

Larry is married with two children.

INDEX

The Quinault River upstream of Lake Quinault.

INDEX

This index does not use page numbers as is found in most books, but instead uses dates (month and year) and bullets to help you to look for and find information.

Bullets:

▲ Local (Grays Harbor, Northern Pacific, Western Jefferson, and Southwest Clallam Counties).

▼ Regional (Washington, Oregon, Idaho, Northern California, Southeastern Alaska, and Southern British Columbia).

▶ National (United States).

◀ International (Outside of current United States borders).

Dates:

Bold type - Eighteenth Century (1774-1800)

Italic type - Nineteenth Century (1801-1900)

Regular type - Twentieth Century (1901-2000)

For example (▲Land of Trees: **5-92, 10-92;** *7-41, 6-67;* 9-14, 2-95.) would read as a local item found in May 1792, October 1792, July 1841, June 1867, September 1914, and February 1995.

Setting the chokers, May 1982

Unloading a log truck at the Crane Creek Reload, August 1976.

many, 9-18; India, 12-84; Viet Nam, 3-63.

▸Poke: *12-48.*

Polio: ▲1-41, ▲7-48, ▸8-49, ▸3-53, ▸4-54, ◂4-55, ▲5-55, ▸8-60.

▲Pollen: 5-93.

▲Polson: Alex, *7-85, 9-86, 11-87, 2-88;* 9-07, 9-39; "Mac", 1-85; Robert, 2-36; Experimental planting, 3-27; Museum, 9-77, 5-97.

▲Polson Bros. Logging Company: Bunkhouse, 11-01; Camp 7, 8-28; Camp 14, 8-35; Camp telephone, *2-99;* Carlisle stand, 8-26; Eureka Mill, 6-40; Incorporates, 5-03; Locomotive, 1-33; Logging engine, 8-03; Queets logging ban, 5-40; Quinault Reservation, 11-12, 10-22, 11-22, 5-34, 8-34, 9-34, 5-35, 2-36, 4-36, 8-36, 9-36, 4-42; Railroad, 5-34; Sold, 11-47; Trains, 1-11; Washington Logging Company, 12-03: Weyco., 8-02.

◂Polynesia: 8-47.

▸Pony Express: *4-60.*

▲Poor Farm: *3-91, 4-92.*

▸Poor Peoples March: 5-68.

▾Pope and Talbott: 8-95.

◂Pope, John Paul: ▸10-79, 5-81.

▲Pope: Robert, 3-33.

Population: ▲Grays Harbor, 11-86; ▸U.S., 11-50, 11-67; World, 7-86, 8-94.

▲Porgies: *4-88.*

Porpoise: ▸ *8-38,* ▸*9-40,* ▾*4-41,* ▾*5-41.*

▾Port Angeles: Boom, 12-12; Founder, *4-62, 7-65;* Land purchase, *4-62;* Military set-aside, *6-62;* Name, **5-91;** Official name, *6-62;* Survey, *52.*

▾Port Discovery: *5-41.*

Porter: ▲Bluff, 8-48; ▲Creek, *10-87*; ▸Cole, 10-64; ▲Ford's Prairie, *6-57;* ▲Home, *9-55;* ▲Railroad, *7-00.*

▾Port Gamble: 8-95.

▾Portland: 7-97.

▾Portland, Oregon: *8-53;* Lewis and Clark Centennial Exposition, 6-05; O'Neil, *10-90.*

▲Port of Grays Harbor: Dedication, 9-22; District, 12-11, 10-29; Cottonwood, 2-94; Crane, 10-66, 3-84; Cruise ships, 5-90, 5-92, 5-93; District, 12-11; Dredging, 1-31; Escapade, 3-94; (*See*) Export; Fuel area, 2-86; Deep draft, (*See Grays Harbor, body of water*);Learning Center, 9-96; Pilings, 6-92; Rail link, 11-90; Satsop steel, 5-84;

Size, 10-29; Terminal, 11-66, 1-67, 11-79, 7-84; Tidelands, 9-30; Viewing Tower, 8-88.

▾Port San Juan (Poverty Cove): **9-92.**

◂Portsmouth, NH: Japan/Russian Treaty, 7-05, 9-05.

▾Port Townsend: Fort, *5-57, 10-59*; Expedition, *7-85;* Shipwreck, 4-21; Town site created, *10-51;* Vancouver names "Townshend" Bay, **5-92.**

▲*Portrait of Our Land:* 1-78.

▾Portuguese: **7-92.**

▸Postage: Rates, 10-53, 1-63, 1-68, 5-71, 11-81, 2-85, 2-91, 1-95; Stamps, *7-47, 1-56;* 4-92, ▲1-93, 1-94.

▸Post office: ◂*12-67;* Zip Code, 7-63.

▸Post, Wiley: 7-31, 8-35.

▲Potatoes: *8-65, 8-79, 3-83, 8-92, 8-00;* 7-08, 8-13, 10-81, 2-92.

◂Potlatch: Moclips, 9-11; Site (Hoquiam): *55;* Taholah, 6-91.

◂Potsdam: 7-45.

▲Powder River Company: 8-20.

▸Powers, Gary: ◂7-60, 8-60.

▲Prairie Creek Bridge: 12-54.

▸Prayer in school: 6-62.

▲Preachers Slough: 11-94.

▲Precipitation (*See Rain, Snow*)

▾Presbyterian: *36, 9-36;* 5-08, ▲11-94.

▸Presidential term limit: 2-51.

▸Presley, Elvis: 9-56, 3-58, 5-67, 8-77, 4-92.

▾Press Party: *12-89,* ▲*5-90, 7-90.*

▲Presto logs: 8-49.

▾Pribilof Islands: 6-44.

▲Price, Dr. *6-83, 4-84, 4-85.*

◂Prince Charles: ◂7-81.

▾*Prince of Wales:* **7-87.**

▾*Princesa:* **5-89.**

◂Princess Diana: 8-97.

▾*Princess Real:* **4-90, 5-90.**

▾*Princess Royal:* **7-87, 6-89, 7-89.**

Prison: ▲Clearwater 7-91; ▲Grays Harbor, 8-94, 9-94, 1-95, 10-97, (*Also see Stafford Creek*); ▲Olympic, 7-91; Population, ▾10-94, ▸8-96.

▾*Privateer, P4Y2:* 11-52.

Prohibition: Amendment, ▾1-19, ▸1-19; ▸Education, 10-30; Ends, ▲4-33, ▲12-33; ▲Grays Harbor, 11-14, 1-30; ▸In effect, 1-20; ▲Raids, 1-17, 12-30;

▲Promised Land: Locomotive, 6-57; Name, *89;* Recreation area, 5-55.

▲Prospecting: *8-91, 7-97, 3-88, 9-13.*

▾*Prowler, EA-6B:* ▲3-92.

▸Public land: *5-62.*

▲Public land grabber: *1-86.*

▸Public Law 93-638: 1-75.

▲Public Utilities District, PUD: Building, 10-58; (*See*) Electric Park; History, 1-90; Power line damage, 1-53, 11-82; Rat, 11-64; Rates, 5-82, 4-83; Strike, 4-70.

▲Public Works Administration: 11-33.

▸*Pueblo, USS:* ◂1-68, 12-68.

▾Puerto de Nuestra de Señora de Los Angelos: *5-91.*

▾Puerto Nuñea Gaona (Neah Bay): **8-90, 5-92.**

▸*Puerto Rico: 12-98.*

▾Puget Sound: Agricultural Company, *5-33;* Body of water, **5-92, 6-92;** *5-33, 5-41, 10-45, 47, 10-49, 11-51, 3-53, 5-53, 11-82;* Logging camps, 6-03; Milling Company, *8-47.*

▾Pugets Sound: **5-92, 6-92.**

Pugilist (*See Boxing*).

▸Pulitzer, Joseph: 10-11.

▲Puncheon road: Hoquiam-Humptulips, *9-93, 1-95;* Humptulips, *9-96;* Humptulips-Joe Creek, 5-03; Point Grenville, 1-05;

▲Purdy, David: 5-50.

▸Pure Food and Drug Act: 6-06.

▲Pussy Willows: 1-53.

▾Chief Leschi School: 9-96.

▾Puyallup: Fair, 10-11; Indian Agency, *4-88;* Indian fisheries, 3-64; Indian Settlement, 3-90.

197

200

202

Mount Olympus and the Olympic foothills as viewed from a clearcut in the Taholah Logging Unit, February 1976.

Young even age tree stands now dominate the forests of Quinault Country and Grays Harbor, September 1993.